THE SOURCES OF INTERNAT

WITHDRÁWN

The Sources
of International Law

Second Edition

HUGH THIRLWAY

OXFORD
UNIVERSITY PRESS

OXFORD

UNIVERSITY PRESS

Great Clarendon Street, Oxford, OX2 6DP,
United Kingdom

Oxford University Press is a department of the University of Oxford.
It furthers the University's objective of excellence in research, scholarship,
and education by publishing worldwide. Oxford is a registered trade mark of
Oxford University Press in the UK and in certain other countries

First Edition published in 2014
Second Edition published in 2019

Impression: 1

Published in the United States of America by Oxford University Press
198 Madison Avenue, New York, NY 10016, United States of America

British Library Cataloguing in Publication Data
Data available

Library of Congress Control Number: 2018967692

ISBN 978–0–19–884182–1 (pbk.)
ISBN 978–0–19–884181–4 (hbk.)

Printed and bound by
CPI Group (UK) Ltd, Croydon, CR0 4YY

Preface

For a new edition of a work of this kind to be called for only five years after the original was published is an indication of the extent to which its subject-matter is still in continuous development. This is not to say that new sources are being discovered or devised: one of the contentions advanced in this book is that in this respect international law is fully developed, that what may appear to be a new source of law will turn out, on inspection, to be a variant, or a derivation, of one of those classically recognized. But that does not mean that the law itself deriving from those sources is static; it is continually called upon to apply to new questions, or to mould itself to new requirements, and these may be revelatory of particular aspects of sources-theory.

It is one recognized source in particular that goes on requiring or attracting the attention of international scholars and judges: customary international law, to use the form of reference preferred by the International Law Commission; also referred to in the past simply as 'custom'. Despite a very visible presence in international relations of major multilateral treaties and other documentary material (some in effect codificatory, e.g., ILC reports and conclusions), custom continues to attract the most attention, and this for two reasons. First, being a more flexible concept and process than treaty law, it is continually being revised and re-examined in practice and, significantly, in judicial decisions; and secondly, it is the most fertile field for the enunciation of new theories of how it operates, or how it ought to operate. These, or some of them at least, whether one agrees with them or not, demand to be noticed, if not necessarily discussed, if a study of sources is to make a claim to completeness.

In this context, a development since the first publication of this work that required to be taken into account was the completion, by the International Law Commission, of its study of the Identification of Customary International Law, with the adoption of a restatement in the form of sixteen conclusions, with detailed annotations (see Chapter III). However, in addition, new treaties have been adopted, and new judicial and arbitral decisions given, and the nature of the sources of law is such that they have been in background of most of these, avowedly or not. The work of preparation of this new edition has not lacked material.

As in the case of its predecessor, many of the ideas presented in this edition have benefitted from discussion with my good friend and former colleague

Dr Cristina Hoss, Legal Officer, ICJ. Once again also, I owe a great debt of gratitude to the Library of the International Court of Justice, now directed by Mr Cyril Emery, Librarian (the successor to Juliana Rangel, whose assistance I acknowledged in the previous edition), for help and support in my researches. I wish particularly to thank Mr Artur Brodowicz, Deputy Librarian; not only was he able to find everything I asked for, with great promptitude, but in other respects he went out of his way to be helpful. The staff of the Oxford University Press have guided the text from draft to publication with their usual courtesy and efficiency.

The Hague, 27 January 2019
Hugh Thirlway

Table of Contents

Glossary of Latin Phrases

a fortiori	Indicates that if A is so, then B will be so too, as the same reasons apply even more strongly to B
contra legem	(Of equity) contrary to law
erga omnes	(Of an obligation) owed to all other subjects of law
et hoc genus omne	And this whole category
exceptio non adimpleti contractus	The objection that the other party has not performed his side of the litigated contract
inadimplementit non est adimplendum	One side of a contract does not have to be complied with if the other side has not been complied with
infra legem	(Of equity) within the law
in statu nascendi	Coming to birth, not yet in existence
jure gestionis	The opposite of *jure imperii* (defining the class of acts that a State performs in another State's territory not as a State, but as e.g. a commercial activity)
jure imperii	By right of sovereignty (defining the class of acts that a State performs in another State's territory as a State, and not as e.g. a commercial activity)
jus cogens	Peremptory norms
jus dispositivum	Non-peremptory norms, which can be departed from by agreement
jus naturale	Natural Law
lex ferenda	Law to be created, desirable law
lex lata	The law that exists
non liquet	A judicial finding that no decision can be given because there is no law on the point
obiter dictum	A statement of law in a judicial decision that is not necessary to the determination of the case (and is thus, in Anglo-American law, not regarded as authoritative)

opinio juris sive necessitatis	The view that something is required by considerations of law or of necessity
pacta sunt servanda	What has been agreed to must be respected
pacta tertiis nec nocet nec prodest	No benefit is derived, and no injury suffered, from something agreed between third parties
par in parem non habet imperium	Between equals, neither has dominion over the other
praeter legem	(Of equity) alongside the law
quod est absurdum	Which is absurd (as conclusion, demonstrating that the argument was unsound)
ratio decidendi	The legal considerations on which a judgment is based; to be distinguished from an *obiter dictum* (q.v.)
res inter alios acta	Something done or agreed between other parties (from which therefore no benefit or burden arises: cf. *pacta tertiis nec nocet nec prodest*)
res judicata [pro veritate habetur]	What has been judicially determined [counts as truth]
ubi judex, ibi jus	The law is found in judicial decisions (literally, 'Where there is a judge, there is law')
usque ad coelum	Vertically upwards to the sky (in full, *ab inferos usque ad coelum*: from the underworld up to the heavens: classical description of the extent of sovereignty)
usus	Usage: an alternative term for the practice required to support the existence of a custom

Table of Cases

INTERNATIONAL COURT OF JUSTICE

PERMANENT COURT OF INTERNATIONAL JUSTICE

HUMAN RIGHTS COURTS

European Court of Human Rights

Inter-American Court of Human Rights

INTERNATIONAL CRIMINAL TRIBUNALS

International Criminal Court

Table of Legislation

RECOMMENDATORY
INSTRUMENTS

NATIONAL

France

United States

I

The Nature of International Law and the Concept of Sources

1. Introduction

The concept of the 'sources of law' is frequently to be encountered in legal writing in the field of international law, and in the decisions of international tribunals. Most treatises of a general nature on international law find it necessary to include a survey of the concept of 'sources'.[1] While at the level of the application of this system, that is to say in the direct relations and negotiations between States, the notion of sources is less visible, it nevertheless underlies any claim to a legal entitlement, and any complaint of a breach of international law.

This is one way in which, considered from the standpoint of the systems of law in force in the various countries and regions of the world, international law is different. While it is no longer possible, as historically it once was to suggest that as a system it does not deserve the name of 'law',[2] the lawyer versed in one or more systems of domestic law may well be confused by the absence of certain familiar landmarks, and the presence of unusual features. The concept of 'sources of international law' is one of these, as is the very fact that international law, in its everyday application, appears to require such a concept, which does not normally need to be invoked in domestic (national) systems, though it is of course present there also.[3]

---

[1] A rare exception is J. Trachtman, *The Future of International Law: Global Government* (Cambridge 2013).

[2] Cf. H. L. A. Hart, *The Concept of Law*, 2nd edn. (Oxford: Clarendon, 1994), 213ff.

[3] Cf. Hart., *Concept of Law*, 95 ff. Neither the term 'sources' nor the concept is a familiar part of the everyday lexicon of English or American lawyers. In French legal terminology, the term *source* 'se rapporte aux procédés de creation de régles juridiques' for purposes of domestic law, but has a wider meaning for international law, covering 'à la fois les modes de production normatifs (des régles generales, du droit objectif) et les modes de création de droits et obligations particuliers (du droit subjectif)' (M. Kohen, 'La pratique et la théorie des sources du droit international', in *Société française pour le droit international, Colloque de Genéve* (2004), 81 at 82). Another way of expressing the point is to observe that in domestic law, contracts create obligations but do not make law, while

Even a definition of 'law' in the international context may not be an entirely simple matter; but let us offer a simple working definition for immediate purposes: it is, shall we say, a system of precepts governing relations between a defined group of persons or entities (the 'subjects' of law), such that an act of compliance or non-compliance with those precepts involves certain consequences, which are independent of the will of the actor; this in the sense that the actor may choose to comply, or to refuse, in the knowledge and possibly with the intention that the appropriate consequence will follow, but is not free to choose whether or not the act will have those predetermined consequences.[4]

From where does international law derive its content and its authority? At the level of domestic law, questions of this kind rarely need to be posed, because the answer in most cases is evident. A fundamental element of a legal and social structure is a legislature, whatever particular form it may take. If the legislator has spoken, the result is (unless otherwise stipulated) binding law, to be observed by all persons present on the territory. The primary 'source' of law is thus the legislature. In some legal systems, there may exist also a body of law established over the years by decisions of the courts, not in application of legislation but of a body of 'common law' or 'customary law', and this too may be regarded as a 'source'.

Also absent from the international scene is any system of public courts, including a court of last resort, not only open to all members of the international community, but having compulsory and binding jurisdiction over each of them. The jurisdiction of the International Court of Justice (hereafter 'the ICJ') remains voluntary, even for members of the United Nations, who are as such parties to its Statute. There exists, however, a large and continually growing number of treaties, bilateral and multilateral, providing for each of the parties to bring a dispute with another party before the ICJ, or before another instance having powers of binding settlement. The details of international judicial and arbitral settlement of disputes are not our concern here: but the existence of dispute settlement mechanisms is in itself significant. All law has ultimately to be put to the test of 'How would a court decide?' (*ubi judex, ibi jus*), even when, as in the case of disputes between many members of the international community, there exists no mechanism

---

in international law, treaties are a source not merely of obligations but of law. See further Ch. II sect. 1.

[4] It is in this sense that law is said to be 'binding', another slippery concept to define (Hart, *Concept of Law*, 216). Another way of looking at this aspect is with the idea of 'authority': see B. D. Lepard, *Customary International Law: A New Theory with Practical Applications* (Cambridge: Cambridge University Press, 2010), 47 ff. See also the idea of 'sanction' in H. Kelsen, *Allgemeines Staatslehre*, French trans.: *Théorie générale du droit et de l'État* (Paris: LGDJ; Brussels: Bruylant, 1997), 11.

for judicial examination and settlement unless and until the parties so agree. In the courtroom the question has to be 'What is the law?' and not 'What ought the law to be?'[5]

At the international level, broadly speaking such a legislator and such a supreme court are thus absent; but law exists and is created or changed, and one way of expressing this phenomenon is through recognition of certain 'sources'. The term itself has, however, become indissolubly associated with the theory of international law known as 'positivism',[6] and with a special status attached to a particular international text: Article 38 of the Statute (the international convention) that created the Permanent Court of International Justice (PCIJ) in 1920, a text that was re-enacted in almost identical terms in the 1946 Statute of that body's successor, the ICJ. This text forms a convenient starting-point for study of the concept of sources; but that is not to say that the present work is necessarily imbued solely with a positivist spirit. Any theory of international law has to answer the same question: how do we know what is, and what is not, law, and how did this or that rule come to have that status? We shall examine at a later stage how some modern philosophies deal with the problem, and whether or to what extent this involves the notion of 'sources'. Nor has Article 38 of the PCIJ and ICJ Statutes, in the years since 1920 and 1946, been universally regarded as the final and only definition of the sources of international law: indeed, we shall have to examine a number of contentions or proposals for a widening or even abandonment of the sources listed, or even of the concept of 'sources' itself. But these are best understood when confronted with the structure of legal thinking that underlay Article 38, or has developed around its terms.

Some reference should be made to a more recently developed concept which bears some relation to that of sources: that of 'meta-law'. The idea is seen principally in the context of custom as a source:

Meta-law on custom (or 'meta-custom') can be defined as the law relating to the formation and identification of custom or, in other words, to 'norms which regulate the

---

[5] Similarly, when the ICJ was engaged in determining a territorial frontier, between El Salvador and Honduras, it rejected arguments based on El Salvador's greater need for territory, due to demographic pressures, and 'the superior natural resources . . . said to be enjoyed by Honduras'; the Court observed that 'the question is not whether the colonial province [that became El Salvador] needed wide boundaries, but where those boundaries actually were': [1992] ICJ Rep 396, para. 58. See also *Continental Shelf (Tunisia/Libyan Arab Jamahiriya)*, excluding economic considerations from affecting the position of the boundary between two continental shelves: [1982] ICJ Rep 77–8, paras. 106–7.

[6] For explanation, see sect. 4.

making of "simple", first-order norms, the meta-rules on the making of customary law (i.e. State practice and *opinion juris*)'[7]

It seems that the concept is not confined to custom: that there may well be a meta-law relating to the other sources, either individually or as a group along with custom: a meta-principle, though the same author tells us that 'the existence of such meta-meta-law is considered doubtful'.[8] For present purposes, the concept, whatever its philosophical value, does not appear to be of assistance, being simply a name for what international lawyers have long been doing in identifying the sources of their discipline, and will not be further referred to.

Establishing the existence of a rule of law means establishing that it has a binding quality: that is the *raison d'être* of the attribution of the rule to a recognized source.[9] If a feature, or a concept, of international law (to use neutral terms) is recognized not to have that binding quality, this may be for a number of reasons. First, the concept may belong to an area of law where there are regular practices, but it is established by general recognition that these are not matters of obligation: the standard example is that of the courtesies of diplomatic relations. Secondly, it may be that there is a standard practice, creating an expectation of consistent continuation, so that a *potential* custom is discernible, but either the practice is insufficiently general or not clearly enough established, or there is no clear evidence of the existence of *opinio juris*, so that (as will be explained in Chapter III) no legal rule has come into existence. Thirdly, the matter may be one that, of its nature, or in its present stage of development, is not binding, in the sense that it does not involve enforceable rights and duties at all.[10] An example—perhaps currently the most clear example—is the idea of sustainable development. This is an

---

[7] M. Fitzmaurice, 'History of Article 38 of the Statute of the ICJ' in Besson and d'Aspremont (eds.) *The Oxford Handbook of the Sources of International Law* (Oxford: Oxford University Press, 2017), 188, citing J. Kammerhofer, *Uncertainty in International Law: A Kelsenian Perspective* (Routledge, 2011,-).

[8] Fitzmaurice, previous note. 188.

[9] D'Aspremont seeks to distinguish between 'ruleness and bindingness' 'The Idea of "Rules" in the Sources of International Law', 84 BYIL (2013) 103, at 105; this for the purpose of establishing that something that is binding need not necessarily be a 'rule', but may belong, for example, to a 'set of communitarian constraints' (*ibid.*). Whether this is a real distinction or a change of appellation must be left to the reader of this article himself to decide. See also the same author, *International Law as Belief System* (Cambridge, 2018), 37–9.

[10] Cf. the observation of the International Court in the *Kosovo* case, that 'it is entirely possible for an act not to be in violation of international law without necessarily constituting the exercise of a right conferred by it' [2010] ICJ Rep 425–6, para. 56, quoted more fully at text preceding n. 51 below. Cf. also Judge Simma: 'The neutrality of international law on a certain point simply suggests that there are areas where international law has not yet come to regulate, or indeed, will never come to regulate'. (Declaration, [2010] ICJ Rep, 481, para. 9.)

idea that is much bandied about in legal discourse and even in the context of potential conventions contexts; but it does not seem that this necessarily, or in fact, involves an assertion that there can be said to be a *right* of sustainable development, or an *obligation* to refrain from non-sustainable development, such that a custom to this effect could be said to exist *in esse* or *in posse*.[11]

In the *Kosovo* case,[12] already referred to, Judge Simma also suggested that international legal rules might not be limited to classifying conduct as 'forbidden', 'permitted', or 'neutral', [13] but that there might be 'degrees of non-prohibition, ranging from "tolerated" to "permissible" to "desirable" '.[14] This does not seem to be borne out by international practice; and indeed, it is difficult to see how the distinction could be manifested in practice (except possibly in the case of *jus cogens*[15]).

Much of the discussion that follows will be in terms of the rights and duties of States in relation to each other; but this is merely for simplicity and clarity; it is backed by recognition that the *dramatis personae* of the international legal scene include other entities, referred to in the literature as, for example, 'non-State actors', and 'multi-stakeholders'. It is at the least a practical working hypothesis that the law governing relationships with and between these entities, insofar as it varies from that governing inter-State relations, is nevertheless attributable to the same classic sources:[16] see further section 5 of this chapter.

Lastly by way of introduction, it should perhaps be explained that we are concerned with sources as establishing rules. Any of those rules may come to be inapplicable, or to apply in a modified form, in a particular case, through the application of one or other of such factors as waiver, acquiescence, or

---

[11] In this sense, e.g., V. Lowe, 'Sustainable Development and Unsustainable Arguments' in Boyle and Freestone (eds.), *International Law and Sustainable Development: Past Achievements and Future Challenges*, (OUP, 1999); F. Francioni expressly excludes the idea as 'a norm of international law capable of bringing about specific obligations for States', 'Revisiting Sustainable Development in Light of General Principles of Environmental Law' in M. Cremona et al. (eds.), *Reflection on the Constitutionalisation of International Economic Eaw: Liber Amicorum for Ernst-Ulrich Petersmann*, (Leiden: Brill-Nijhoff, 2014), 491. For a fully argued contrary view, see V. Barral, *Le développement durable en droit international: essai sur les incidences juridiques d'une norme évolutive*, (Larcier-Bruylant, 2016), Ch. II.

[12] Advisory Opinion, *Accordance with International Law of the Declaration of Independence in respect of Kosovo* [2010 = II] ICJ Rep 403.

[13] These terms must be understood as not necessarily absolute: depending on the context, 'prohibited' (for example) may mean 'a breach of the rights of a specific other State or States', not necessarily those of international society.

[14] [2010-II] ICJ Rep 480, para. 8.   [15] See Chapter VII.

[16] Note for example the reliance on customary international law by the WTO Appellate Body in the *Hormones* case (WTO Report of the Appellate Body: Australia—Measures Affecting Importation of Salmon, 6 November 1998, WT/DS18/AB/R. para. 123); discussed in D. Pulkowski, 'Universal International Law's Grammar', in Fastenrath et al. (eds.), *From Bilateralism to Community Interest: Essays in Honour of Judge Bruno Simma*, (OUP, 2011)144–5.

prescription (or even the common-law concept of estoppel). These factors will not be studied: they are independent of sources doctrine, in the sense that they take the rule as a 'given' before proceeding to bend or exclude it, and do not, in principle, take account of which source produced the rule.[17]

2. Formal and material sources

The 'source' of a given precept is at once the historical basis; the manner in which that precept came into existence; and—more importantly—the answer to the question, Why is this a binding precept, which I must respect? For these three meanings two terms are generally used: the 'formal source' of a rule and its 'material source', but unfortunately they are not used entirely consistently by different writers. The important distinction for our purposes is between the place, normally a written document, where the terms of the rule can be found conveniently stated: this is the *material* source; and the legal element that gives to the rule its quality as law: this is the *formal* source.

It is noticeable that the term 'sources' is sometimes used too indiscriminately:

Sometimes the word 'source' is used to indicate the basis of international law; sometimes it is confused with the social origin and other 'causes' of the law; at others it is indicative of the formal law-making agency, and at others again it is used instead of the term evidence of the law ...[18]

The distinction formal/material is directed to avoiding this confusion. It has been most clearly expressed perhaps in Oppenheim's *International Law*, where the distinction is that the formal source is 'the source from which the legal rule derives its legal validity', while the material source 'denotes the provenance of the substantive content of the rule.... [T]reaties are one formal source, and custom is another: thus, for example, the formal source of a particular rule may be custom, although its material source may be found in a bilateral treaty concluded many years previously, or in some state's unilateral declaration'.[19] It is also possible for a scholarly statement of a rule which has

---

[17] A different view is taken by A. Orakhelashvili: book review of the first edition of the present work, 84 BYIL (2014), 355, 356.

[18] D. P. O'Connell, *International Law*, 2nd edn. (London: Stevens & Sons, 1970), 7.

[19] 9th edn. by R. Jennings and J. Watts, *Oppenheim's International Law* (Oxford: Oxford University Press, 1992), 23 §8. The distinction may perhaps be different for French writers: cf. N. Q. Dinh, P. Daillier, and A. Pellet, *Droit international public*, 5th edn. (Paris: LGDJ, 1994), 111 §59, using the term 'sources formelles' to mean 'les fondements sociologiques des normes internationales, leur base politique, morale ou économique plus ou moins explicitées par la doctrine ou les sujets du droit.'; H. Thierry, 'L'évolution du droit international', 222 *Recueil des cours* (1990-III), 30.

come to exist in State practice, but in an ill-defined manner, to constitute the material source, as being the best available enunciation or definition thereof; or of course, a rule may be advanced as one that would be desirable or useful, and subsequent State practice may conform to it. In either case, the formal source of the rule is custom, as explained in section 3.

The distinction is, as mentioned already, traditional; but the terms have been borrowed for the purposes of more contemporary views of the international lawmaking process. Thus, for example, one writer suggests a distinction on the basis that the term material sources refers 'to all the moral or social processes by which the content of international law is developed (e.g. power play, cultural conflicts, ideological tensions), as opposed to the formal processes by which that content is then identified and usually modified to become law (e.g. legislative enactment).'[20] Usages of this kind are, it is suggested, to be deprecated, since whether or not the traditional doctrine of sources still has validity, its terminology has an established meaning, and it is the doctrine, not the terminology, that may be the target of re-thinking or redefinition.[21] Less objectionable from this viewpoint, as not involving a redefinition of established terminology, is the distinction made by some writers in the context of sources between the *negotium* and the *instrumentum*. This distinction is normally (perhaps solely) relevant in the context of a written instrument as a source, for example, a treaty: the norm, the obligation considered as an abstract entity, is the *negotium*; the written document in which it is set out is the *instrumentum*. The latter is the 'container'; the former the content.[22] This relationship is complicated by the fact that even the most clearly drafted text does not speak for itself: it has to be read and interpreted in order to be applied; and particularly with the passage of time the interpretative meaning and the (presumed) legislative intent may come to diverge; but this is an aspect which need not be explored here.[23]

[20] S Besson, 'Theorizing the Sources of International Law', in S. Besson and J. Tasioulas (eds.), *The Philosophy of International Law* (Oxford: Oxford University Press, 2010), 163–85 at 170.

[21] Note that this usage also does not reflect the possibility that the material source and the formal source may be unrelated, in the sense that, for example, a rule developed in customary law may be defined in the terms found in a treaty. The formal source is not necessarily the legislative culmination of the process referred to by the material source.

[22] See J. d'Aspremont, *Formalism and the Sources of International Law* (Oxford: Oxford University Press, 2011), 174–5, who emphasizes that '*both the content and the container can potentially serve as a formal signpost that indicates whether the norm in question is an international legal rule*' (emphasis original). See further Ch. VI sect. 2, in connection with the distinction in relation to soft law.

[23] Reference may be made to the very wide-ranging and authoritative study of I. Venzke, *How Interpretation Makes International Law: On Semantic Change and Normative Twists* (Oxford, 2012), of which the striking opening phrase is 'Texts cannot talk—they are talked about'.

Are the sources of law in a particular system simply those that happen to have arisen in that system; or is there any underlying principle as to what such sources *should* be? Probably all that can be said in this respect is that there is a broad resemblance between the sources of law recognized in different legal systems, that *ubi societas, ibi jus*, that is, that the nature of society itself implies certain legal principles or concepts, seen as 'normatively appealing' which may undergo adaptation to the nature of the society examined.[24]

3. Enumeration of the recognized formal sources

Reference is here made to the 'recognized' formal sources as, for the purposes of the application of international law, there is in effect a principle, or a fundamental rule, that only those recognized sources may be referred to, or relied on, as creative of rules of international law.[25] In this connection reference is inevitably made to Article 38 of the PCIJ and ICJ Statute, which reads as follows:

1. The Court[, whose function is to decide in accordance with international law such disputes as are submitted to it,] shall apply:
   (a) international conventions, whether general or particular, establishing rules expressly recognized by the contesting states;
   (b) international custom, as evidence of a general practice accepted as law;
   (c) the general principles of law recognized by civilized nations;
   (d) subject to the provisions of Article 59,[26] judicial decisions and the teachings of the most highly qualified publicists of the various nations, as subsidiary means for the determination of rules of law.

---

[24] 'In an ideal world, a source of law ... would be both descriptively accurate (i.e. it would reflect what actually happens and thus be both descriptively and predictively accurate) and normatively appealing (i.e. it would reflect notions of what should happen based on some external normative principles such as principles of procedural or substantive morality). In practice there is often tension between these two values'. A. Roberts and S. Sivakumaran, in *Evans, International Law* 5th edn. (OUP, 2018) Ch. 4, 109–10.

[25] It has recently been argued by Professor d'Aspremont that in taking this view international lawyers are deceiving themselves, and that a rule-based system of this kind is open to the fatal objection that a 'rule' is needed to explain the authority of these initial rules, and then a further rule to explain the authority of the higher rule, and so ad infinitum (infinite regression): 'The Idea of "Rules" in the Sources of International Law', 84 BYIL (2013) 103: to the same effect, *International Law as a Belief System* (Cambridge, 2018), 57. This, it is suggested, is a trivial objection: at some point all regulatory systems have to build their structure on some agreed and convenient starting-point, even the system based on 'communitarian constraints (=rules)' offered by d'Aspremont as the more correct analysis. See also what has been said above as to 'meta-rules'.

[26] Article 59 provides that 'The decision of the Court has no binding force except between the parties and in respect of that particular case.'

2. This provision shall not prejudice the power of the Court to decide a case *ex aequo et bono*, if the parties agree thereto.

Although in form this is merely a directive to a particular international body as to what rules it is to apply, the opening phrase stating that the Court's function is 'to decide in accordance with international law' (which was in fact added to the Statute of the PCIJ when it was readopted as the ICJ Statute[27]) confirms that the application of sub-paragraphs (*a*) to (*d*) will result in international law being applied; that is, that no international law is to be found elsewhere, and that everything pointed to as being such by those sub-paragraphs is indeed international law.[28] This is qualified by the indication that judicial decisions and teachings are no more than 'subsidiary' sources; what this means will be examined at the end of this section.

A different view has been advanced by Judge Shahabuddeen in his book *Precedent in the World Court*, that

subparagraphs (*a*) to (*d*) of Article 38, paragraph 1, are not exhaustive of 'international law' as more generally referred to in Article 36, paragraph 2 (*b*). Since the Court's function is 'to decide in accordance with international law', if a principle can be shown to form part of international law the Court must decide in accordance with that principle where relevant, whether or not it falls under subparagraphs (*a*) to (*d*) of Article 38, paragraph 1 ... On that view, it is at least arguable that the Court is not prevented from discovering international law by other means if it can.[29]

The context makes clear that the 'other means' that Judge Shahabuddeen has in mind are the ICJ's own earlier decisions, which, in his view, are not always and necessarily limited to the role of 'subsidiary means' for the determination of rules of law. This theory will be considered in Chapter V, section 2(a); at this point we need only note that the more widely accepted view is that paragraph 1 of Article 38 lists exhaustively, if not the only existing sources of international law, at least the only sources available to the ICJ for purposes of decision, and that these two categories are, for all practical purposes, the same

---

[27] Added at the San Francisco Conference on the proposal of Chile, in order to give a clearer picture of the Court's mission as an international judicial organ. This text has been invoked in support of the holding that the existence of a dispute is 'the primary condition for the Court to exercise its judicial function': *Nuclear Tests* [1974] ICJ Rep 271, para. 57.

[28] Article 38 is often referred to as having this significance; see e.g. the reference in UNCLOS (the United Nations Convention on the Law of the Sea): see n. 21. Some authors nevertheless take the view that 'There is no *numerus clausus* of legal sources': see Fastenrach, 'A political theory of law: escaping the aporia on the validity of legal arguments in international law', in Fastenrath et al. (eds), *From Bilateralism to Community Interest: Essays in Honour of Judge Bruno Simma*, (OUP, 2011), 58, 63, who points out that even the ICJ has treated, for example, unilateral declarations as a source of law. On these, see Ch. II, sect. 4.

[29] *Precedent in the World Court* (Cambridge: Cambridge University Press, 2007), 81.

To avoid misunderstanding, it should be emphasized that the drafting of Article 38 of the PCIJ Statute was not an act of creation, but of recording: Article 38 in itself is not the 'source of sources'. International law as it had developed, and as it then stood, derived from the relations built up among States (including, but not limited to, what could be classified as 'State practice' for purposes of custom), and Article 38 reflected what was, in the view of those who drafted it, already there. This point might be thought to need no emphasis, were it not for the appearance of the view (if only as a target for refutation) that the recognized sources are 'derived from' Article 38, in recent writings of Professor d'Aspremont; but examination of this will be reserved for a later chapter.[30] Each of these sources will require a chapter to itself, but some outline at this point of the nature of each, and how it operates, will be useful, as well as some reflections on the relations between them (discussed more fully in Ch. VI). Since the ICJ, and by implication each State as a subject of law, is thus provided with more than one source, more than one place to look for the law to be applied, the question also arises of the relation between them: the problem known as the 'hierarchy of sources'. Are the sources to be consulted in any particular order, and if an adequate rule is found in the first source consulted, does the quest for the applicable law stop there? Is there any order of rank: does a rule found in one source prevail over a rule found in another? And does the adoption by the international community, or simply by two or more States, for example, by treaty, have an impact on any more general rule that then existed? These questions also will be examined more closely in Chapter VI.

Without prejudicing that question of hierarchy, then, let us briefly consider the sources in the order in which Article 38 states them.

Treaties and conventions are of course a major feature of international relations; their defining function is to impose agreed duties on the parties to them, though of course not every provision of every treaty plays this role.[31] Such duties may be active—duties to take certain steps in certain situations—or restrictive—duties not to do certain things that they may otherwise be

---

[30] Ch. IX, sect. 1 (5)(ii), discussing d'Aspremont, *International Law as a Belief System* (Cambridge, 2018). Note also S. Yee on the rationale of treating custom as a source: 'Article 38 of the Statute and Applicable Law', Journal of International Dispute Settlement (2016), 472.

[31] It has been argued, in particular by Sir Gerald Fitzmaurice, that treaties should be regarded, not as sources of law, but as merely the source of rights and obligations, since they cannot (as can custom) produce norms of general validity and universal application: 'Some Problems Regarding the Formal Sources of International Law', *Symbolae Verzijl* 1958). While this is correct as an observation, it is no longer regarded as justifying any hierarchical down-grading of treaties: cf. M. Prost, 'Source Preferences and Scales of Values' in Besson and d'Aspremont (eds.)_ *The Oxford Handbook of the Sources of International Law* (Oxford: Oxford University Press, 2017) 640 at 651–2.

fully entitled to do. In this treaties resemble the contracts of private law, which similarly impose obligations; those obligations are not normally considered to be 'law' for the parties,[32] but this linguistic difference relates to the essentially socially imposed, centrally determined nature of municipal law. The binding force of treaties rests on a principle usually expressed as *pacta sunt servanda*—what has been agreed to is to be respected.[33] At this point we need not concern ourselves with the question where that principle itself fits into general international law: sufficient to note that if an agreement, as to what is to be done or not done in the future, could freely be departed from, there would be no point in making it.

International custom is described in Article 38 as being 'evidence of a general practice accepted as law'. This definition has been challenged, questioned, ridiculed, supported, and generally argued over ever since the PCIJ Statute was adopted; its adequacy will be considered in Chapter III. The idea is straightforward enough, and corresponds to a regular feature of national legal systems. At least in some fields, a practice of dealing with a particular matter or problem, affecting the interests of more than one subject of law, grows up because it presents advantages, or at least convenience, for both sides. At some subsequent moment there is recognition (not necessarily unanimous among those concerned, but at least widespread), that this has become *the* way to deal with that particular problem, so that, at least, the onus is on any participant in the matter to show why in this or that case some other solution should be adopted. Finally, it becomes recognized that the practice is binding, in the sense that any participant who wishes to depart from it can do so only with the agreement of any other actor or actors concerned. Thus the formula, according to one view, should rather be that the general practice is evidence that the rule it embodies is accepted as law.

The general principles of law were included as a precaution. During the discussions of the Advisory Commission of Jurists that produced the original draft of the PCIJ Statute, the question arose whether international treaties and international custom would supply an answer to every legal question that might arise before the planned international tribunal; and if not, what was to be done about it. There was general agreement that one scenario that should be avoided if at all possible was that in which the new court would have to

---

[32] But cf. Art. 1134 of the French *Code civil*, providing that agreements 'tiennent lieu de loi à ceux qui les ont faites'.

[33] Even in a positivist approach, it does not, however, follow, as has been suggested, that the phrase implies that States are *only* 'bound by the laws they have consented to' (e.g. Besson, 'Theorizing the Sources of International Law', 165). The whole importance of the theory of custom is in establishing commitment without specific acceptance, while leaving room for specific rejection (the 'persistent objector': see Ch. III sect. 5).

refuse to resolve a dispute brought before it on the ground that the applicable law provided no answer—what is technically known as a *non liquet* decision. Exactly what general principles may be invoked is controversial; what was originally envisaged seems to have been that a principle developed in national systems of law might be relied upon in an inter-State dispute which was in some way parallel to the circumstances of the national case; but we shall have to consider wider views that have been advanced.[34] The jurisprudence of the two Courts has produced very little in the way of example, either of indication of such principles[35], or of a *non-liquet* (a finding that there is no law on the point).

The judicial decisions and teachings of publicists are specifically stated to be invoked merely 'as subsidiary means for the determination of rules of law'. This last phrase goes to the question of hierarchy of sources mentioned earlier: it is clear that the opinion of even the most highly qualified publicist cannot prevail over a rule clearly laid down in a treaty or established in customary law. They are also 'subsidiary' in another sense: they do not normally purport to be ultimate sources, but rather intermediaries. Neither a judge nor a scholar says 'This is the law, because I say so'; they both lay down what they regard as established by one of the other sources, or (in the case of the scholar) what might be considered as *lex ferenda*—law that ought to exist. The paradox is, of course, that the ICJ will probably only be turning to the judge or the scholar because the Court has not succeeded in finding authority in one of the other sources. The point will be considered further in Chapter V.

Each of these sources will be studied more closely in a separate chapter; but the brief outline here given will serve as basis for examination of some wider questions.

4. Nature and operation of the sources

It will be convenient to adopt two general assumptions, which may have to be re-examined later. First, that the existence and content of all international law is best understood in terms of the system by which the various principles and rules have established themselves, that is, a system of sources.[36] Some other recent theories will be considered in a later chapter; this is not to discount

---

[34] Ch. IV sect. 1.   [35] Except in the realm of procedural law: see Ch. IV.

[36] This was the starting-point for the United Nations Charter, the preamble to which declares the determination of the peoples of the United Nations 'to establish conditions under which justice and respect for the obligations *arising from treaties and other sources of international law* can be maintained' (emphasis added).

their possible importance, but the primary aim of this book is to convey an understanding of the traditional approach. Secondly, it is assumed here that the available sources are the same for all branches of international law, even though the extent to which each specific source (treaty, custom, general principle) has in fact operated in, or affected, that branch will vary, sometimes quite markedly. For much of the history of international law, these starting-points would have been widely accepted. More recently, however, attention has been called to the multiplicity of fields in which international law has branched out, or divided itself, and it is argued by some scholars that this 'fragmentation'[37] of international law means, among other things, that the traditional doctrine of sources is no longer adequate. Fuller examination of this contention must be reserved for a later stage (Ch. IX).

It is perhaps when changes and developments are needed in a legal system that the concept of sources proves its utility. Law established by treaty can of course be modified by a further or supplemental treaty; in bilateral relations this will not normally cause problems, but the renegotiation of a multilateral convention is more complex, and a new or amending convention may have to await successive ratifications to become effective. Customary law is in this respect usually more flexible and responsive.

A legal claim is made by a subject of law (a State, in the context with which we are concerned) that has not been made before. How are other States to react? And when they have reacted, what is the significance of their reaction for purposes of assessing the validity of that claim, and of similar claims that may subsequently be made? That this may be a problem, even in a system that has reached such a comparatively advanced stage of development as has modern international law, is demonstrated by the rapid changes in the law of the sea that have occurred since the middle of the last century. Up to, say, the end of the Second World War, the nature and extent of the claims that

---

[37] See in particular J. Pauwelyn, *Conflict of Norms in Public International Law* (Cambridge: Cambridge University Press, 2001); A. do Amiral Júnior, 'El "dialogo" de las fuentes: fragmentación y coherencia en el derecho internacional contemporaneo', Revista Española de Derecho Internacional, 62/1 (2010), 61; M.Andenas & E Bjorge, *A Farewell to Fragmentation (CUP, Cambridge,2015)*. Note also the Report of the ILC Study Group on the question, A/CN. 4/L682 (see Ch. III, text and n. 49). It has been very well observed by Condorelli that much (if not all) of the fragmentation of international law emphasized by some scholars may in reality be attributable to 'the fragmentation of the observing eye': the 'relentless expansion and diversification of international law are increasingly leading to specialization: international law practitioners tend to shut themselves up in the various sectors in which they work and to ignore all or nearly all of the others': 'Customary International Law: The Yesterday, Today and Tomorrow of General International Law', in A. Cassese (ed.), *Realizing Utopia: The Future of International Law* (Oxford: Oxford University Press, 2012). For a cynical view of the responsibility of scholars for this phenomenon, see J. d'Aspremont, 'Softness in International Law: A Self-Serving Quest for New Legal Materials', 5 EJIL (2008), 1075.

a State with a coastline could make over or in relation to the waters off its coasts were fairly clearly defined. As the technical possibilities of exploitation of the seabed advanced, and also under the influence of increased competition for fishery resources, increasingly extensive claims began to be made by coastal States. There was sufficient similarity or uniformity in the nature of such claims for a consistent practice to give rise to a development of customary law, which was reflected in the four Conventions on the law of the sea adopted at Geneva in 1958;[38] further developments were similarly reflected, or extended, in the detailed provisions of the United Nations Convention on the Law of the Sea adopted at Montego Bay in 1982. The point of collision of State interests, both literally and figuratively, fell where the claims of one coastal State confronted or overlapped with those of another: where was the line to be drawn? It is significant that the negotiations leading up to the 1982 Law of the Sea Convention, which had successfully reconciled States' interests to the degree that made possible detailed provisions on the territorial sea and the continental shelf (as well as such tricky questions as the position of archipelagic States), failed completely to resolve this crux. All that could be done was to include a provision on delimitation drafted in such vague terms as to be almost a pious redundancy.[39]

As already observed, the concept of sources is primarily associated with *legal positivism*, of which the central tenet is that international law derives from the consent of the States that are its subjects.[40] This consent has to be looked for either in treaties, where the consent of those who will be subject to the rule is direct and immediate, or in international custom, which reveals or embodies what the general community of States has consented to regard as required of each individual subject of law. Thus treaties and international custom are the two main sources of law; customary law may be found stated

---

[38] On the Continental Shelf, the High Seas, Fishing and the Conservation of the Living Resources of the High Seas, and the Territorial Sea and the Contiguous Zone.

[39] UNCLOS, Article 83(1): 'The delimitation of the continental shelf between States with opposite or adjacent coasts shall be effected by agreement on the basis of international law, as referred to in Article 38 of the Statute of the International Court of Justice, in order to achieve an equitable solution.'

[40] A particularly clear account of this approach is given by J. Salmon, 'Le droit international à l'épreuve au tournant du XXIème siècle', Cursos Euromediterráneos Bancaja de Derecho Internacional 35 (2002). An extreme version of this approach was the Soviet theory of international law, of which little is heard nowadays. 'The fundamental principle of this theory is that in an international system consisting primarily of sovereign and equal states there is no other means of creating rules of law binding upon these states except by the coordination of the wills of states regarding the contents of the rules and their recognition as legally binding': G. Tunkin, *Festschrift für Stephan Verosta* (Berlin: Duncker & Humblot, 1980), 67–77 at 69. The author recognizes that this theory is in effect taken from the pre-existing bourgeois theory, but is at pains to differentiate the two. See also this chapter, text and n. 107.

in opinions of scholars, or in decisions of international (or indeed national) tribunals, but these are not themselves sources.

Another way of looking at the positivist or voluntarist approach is to see it as holding that the identification of a norm or binding rule of law within a given system—in this case, international law—is effected by reference to the origin of the rule, the way in which it came into existence.[41] This is a familiar, if invisible, intellectual process in the context of national systems of law (what international lawyers refer to as 'municipal' legal systems): if national legislation, an act of a national parliament, lays down a rule of law, then that is an authoritative norm for the purposes of the national system. Whether it is a sound rule, a good or a just rule, is for this purpose irrelevant; presumably the legislature thought it appropriate to legislate to this effect *because* it was considered a sound rule, but its legal force does not depend directly on such intrinsic qualities. For those citizens (if there are such) who think it an unjust or inappropriate rule it carries exactly the same legal force and weight as for those who approve its enactment; and if circumstances change so that it becomes less appropriate, it nevertheless remains law until repealed.[42]

The underlying reason for this is less evident at the national, municipal-law level than it is in the context of international law. It is, however, at least one possible interpretation of national legal systems (though one that is less widely adopted today than in the past[43]) to say that the structure of government, including in particular the process by which laws are made, is established by a social contract, by the agreement of the governed. On that basis, a democratic national system of law may be deemed voluntaristic. Similarly, according to the positivist view of international law, it is the collective will of States, the members of the community regulated by international law, that underlies the law by which they are bound.[44]

---

[41] As one recent writer puts it, 'legal positivism' is the label affixed to 'the view that a norm's status as law, its membership in a legal order or system, is solely a matter of its social source *without regard for its merit*': D. Lefkowitz, 'Law as Necessarily Posited and the Challenge of Customary Law Creation', in Besson and d'Aspremont (eds.) *The Oxford Handbook of the Sources of International Law* (Oxford: Oxford University Press, 2017), 323 at 325 (italics added). The last phrase might be reworded on the lines of 'and not on the basis of its ethical cogency'. The whole section entitled 'Why positivism' in this context is recommended as a valuable summing up of arguments for and against that approach.

[42] Subject to any provision in the relevant municipal system for expiry through obsolescence, such as the 'sunset clause' included in e.g. the USA Patriot Act, and similar provisions in legislation in a number of other countries.

[43] For a severe criticism of 'the rigidity and narrow-mindedness of nineteenth-century positivism' in an international law context, see O'Connell, *International Law*, i. 20.

[44] It has been objected that 'the very idea of self-imposed obligation contradicts the implication of obligation that it is an imposition': A. Carty, 'Critical International Law: Recent Trends in the Theory of International Law', 1 EJIL (1991) 1, at 6, commenting on Kennedy, *International Legal Structures*. It is, however, evident that actors in a legal system (human beings) can and do accept

The classic judicial statement to that effect is to be found in the judgment of the PCIJ in the case of the *SS Lotus*:

International law governs relations between independent States. The rules of law binding upon States therefore emanate from their own free will as expressed in conventions or by usages generally accepted as expressing principles of law and established in order to regulate the relations between these co-existing independent communities or with a view to the achievement of common aims. Restrictions upon the independence of States cannot therefore be presumed.[45]

The point is of course clearest in the context of conventions and treaties, one of the recognized sources of international law, according to the classical conception of international lawmaking. If two States conclude a treaty obliging them to follow, in relation to each other, a particular course of conduct in defined circumstances, their subsequent legal obligation was created by the meeting of their wills: what is involved is a self-imposed limitation on the freedom of action of each.[46] The same is equally true if the treaty in question is a multilateral one, with a great number of parties: the obligations imposed on United Nations member States by the Charter are treaty obligations, freely accepted by each Member by the act of ratifying the Charter.[47] The same principle also operates even if the parties to an instrument have deliberately left themselves freedom to manoeuvre, either by committing themselves in vague terms (such as undertaking 'to use their best endeavours' toward a particular end), or by employing a legal form less automatically binding than a treaty; these are varieties of what is known as 'soft law', to be discussed in more detail in Chapter VII section 2.

The second major generally recognized source of international law, international custom, is also derivable from, or attributable to, a voluntarist view. International customary law, as we shall see, comes into existence from a combination of two factors: State practice and a psychological element referred to

---

obligations, i.e. commit themselves to behaviour that they would, but for the acceptance, have been free to leave undone.

[45] PCIJ (ser. A), no. 10 (1927), 18. For the relationship between this principle and the concept of *non liquet*, see Ch. IV sect. 3. The passage has also been given an alternative interpretation as being less far-reaching than it might appear, and also as an *obiter dictum* not essential to the Court's argument in the case: H. Lauterpacht, *The Development of International Law by the International Court* (Cambridge: Cambridge University Press, 1996), 359–61; A. Pellet, '*Lotus*: Que de sottises on profère en ton nom? Remarques sur le concept de souveraineté dans la jurisprudence de la Cour mondiale', *Mélanges en l'honneur de Jean-Pierre Puissochet* (Paris: Pedone, 2008), 215–30.

[46] For this reason, it has been argued that treaties are less a source of *law* than a source of *obligations*: see Ch. II, text and n. 7.

[47] Many of the more general obligations are also matters of customary law, but that is because they were so prior to the adoption of the Charter, or have developed as such alongside—and partly under the influence of—the Charter, not *because* they are in the Charter.

as the *opinio juris sive necessitatis*, a Latin expression difficult to translate literally, but which signifies something like 'a view that something is required by considerations of law or of necessity'.[48] States choose to regulate their affairs in relation to other States in accordance with certain practices, or customs, which become—gradually or perhaps sometimes quite quickly—the established or recognized way of doing things, so that eventually it is tacitly agreed that departures from these practices are not automatically authorized, but require the assent of the other State or States concerned. At that point, a customary rule of law has become established, not just by repetition, but because repetition, and general or widespread participation, are taken to indicate the consent of those subject to the rule that it should be so.

This aspect is accentuated by the recognition of international lawyers that it may happen that one State (or a small group of States) with special interests or subject to special circumstances may make it clear from the outset that it or they do *not* consent to the growth of the customary rule; and in that event a State in that position will or may be exempted from the application of the new rule as what is referred to as a 'persistent objector'.[49] The recognition of this possibility emphasizes the consensual nature of custom.

The function of sources in the international legal structure is to supply the rules of law that make up that system; if no source can credibly be cited for a rule that is claimed to exist, then the conclusion follows that the alleged rule does not exist. It is therefore important in each case to settle the question: what sort of rules are to be looked for—enabling or prohibitory? If the actions of a State are challenged as being contrary to international law, must the challenger show, by reference to the established sources, that there is a rule of international law with which those actions are inconsistent; or must the challenged State show, on a similar basis, the existence of a rule positively authorizing those actions? Or does the answer to this question depend on the area of law, or the type of rule, concerned? The classic approach to the matter invokes the decision of the PCIJ in the case of the *SS Lotus*, just cited. This approach, which was controversial even at the time, and in the context, of that decision, is that since '[r]estrictions on the independence of States cannot … be presumed', in case of dispute it is the party arguing for such a restriction to establish that it results from a rule deriving from one of the recognized sources.[50]

[48] The precise role of considerations of necessity is difficult to pin down: see further in Ch. III sect. 2(c).

[49] See further in Ch. III sect. 5.

[50] This is often referred to as 'the *Lotus* presumption'; however, it was powerfully argued by Ole Spiermann, in a comment on the *Nuclear Weapons* advisory opinion, that the PCIJ applied, not a presumption but a 'residual principle', a principle that applies in the absence of other rules; for the

A further nuance was, however, added by the ICJ advisory opinion on *Accordance with International Law of the Unilateral Declaration of Independence in respect of Kosovo*. In that case the UN General Assembly had asked for an opinion on whether the declaration of independence was 'in accordance with' international law; the Court noted that

[t]he answer to that question turns on whether or not the applicable international law prohibited the declaration of independence. If the Court concludes that it did, then it must answer the question put by saying that the declaration of independence was not in accordance with international law. It follows that the task which the Court is called upon to perform is to determine whether the declaration of independence was adopted in violation of international law. The Court is not required by the question it has been asked to take a position on whether international law conferred a positive entitlement on Kosovo unilaterally to declare its independence or, *a fortiori*, on whether international law generally confers an entitlement on entities situated within a State unilaterally to break away. Indeed, it is entirely possible for a particular act—such as a unilateral declaration of independence—not to be in violation of international law without necessarily constituting the exercise of a right conferred by it.[51]

This appears to recognize the existence of acts that are legally 'neutral'; it does not seem possible to read the ruling as a finding of the existence of a permissory rule, since to do something which is permitted, and which cannot be objected to because it *is* permitted, is indistinguishable from the exercise of a right.

Permissory rules do of course exist; but in most cases they will be found to correspond to the absence of a restrictive rule, or to the existence of a restrictive rule barring interference with the permitted conduct. Thus a State with a coastline may claim certain rights over the waters and seabed off its coasts;[52] the 'reflection' of this is that other States are debarred by law from claiming rights inconsistent with those of the coastal State. In this connection, it has been argued that even if in principle a State has a right to do whatever is not specifically prohibited by international law, there is an ultimate limitation in that the 'residual right does not extend to the doing of things which, by reason of their essential nature cannot form the subject of a right'; and the specific instance that gave rise to this reflection was the asserted right

---

significance of the distinction see '*Lotus* and the Double Structure of International Legal Argument', in Boisson de Chazournes and Sands (eds.), *International Law, the International Court of Justice and Nuclear Weapons* (Cambridge: Cambridge University Press, 1999), 131.

[51] [2010] ICJ Rep 425–6, para. 56.

[52] Some of these are in fact attributed by law automatically, by virtue of the coastal position of the State, but for others, their assertion and their extent are determined (up to a recognized maximum) by the choice of the State, even though in practice every State claims 100% of its entitlement.

to possess and, if necessary, make use of, nuclear weapons.[53] Here we may simply note this extreme case as showing that the *Lotus* principle of freedom of action by States does not necessarily lead to anarchy and disaster.

At a fairly high level of abstraction, we may say that there are in fact only two bases on which a system of legal rules can be established. Either a rule of law can be demonstrated to be such on the basis of, as it were, its pedigree: it came into existence by one of the ways recognized by the legal system concerned as methods of law-creation, and this, as we have seen, is ultimately on the basis that those methods are consensual in origin. Or, alternatively, a suggested rule of law must stand or fall on its own merits, as devised to secure justice and in fact securing it (at least in foreseeable circumstances).[54] At this point, however, an element of individual judgement, and thus of eventual controversy, enters into the discussion: who is to decide what rule secures justice? Who is to decide what *is* justice in particular circumstances? May a subject of law who disagrees with a rule, and considers it an unjust rule, be exempted from it? It is a truism that men and women of goodwill can come to radically different conclusions on matters that the law is or may be called upon to regulate.

This is not to say (to revert to international law) that philosophies other than voluntarism are incapable of providing an adequate basis for the existence of legal rules in international society; but the system of international law as we have it today is, of course, a historical creation. Initially the dominant philosophy was that of *natural law*; the positivist view that succeeded it was, until comparatively recently, virtually unchallenged because it corresponded to the observable growth of, and change in, international law. Some alternative theories will be briefly discussed in Chapter IX.

The third of the recognized sources of international law, however, remains to be briefly considered in this context: what is referred to in the Statute of the ICJ as 'the general principles of law recognized by civilized nations' (Article 38(1)(*c*)). Does this source, in contrast to the two sources already discussed, give rise to law so qualified not by its 'pedigree' but by its intrinsic

---

[53] See dissenting opinion of Judge Shahabuddeen, *Legality of the Threat or Use of Nuclear Weapons* [1996-I] ICJ Rep 392 ff.: 'actions which could destroy mankind and civilization and thus bring to an end the basis on which States exist and in turn the basis on which rights and obligations exist within the international community'. See also the suggested 'distinguishing' of the *Lotus* decision at p. 396.

[54] It should not be overlooked that some rules of law exist simply because society requires that there be *some* rule in place, to prevent chaos, but the rule actually employed may be no more or less 'just' than any other that might be devised. The obvious example is the rule as to which side of the road is to be used by traffic in each direction. See also the use of a similar example by E. A. Roberts, 'Traditional and Modern Approaches to International Law: A Reconciliation', 95 AJIL (2001) 757, and the discussion of this in Ch. IX.

merits as directed to achieving justice? This question will be discussed in more detail in Chapter IV; there has in fact been some development with regard to the recognized scope of this provision. It may here be noted that the text does not refer to 'general principles of law' at large, but to those 'recognized by civilized nations',[55] that is, solely or primarily those that have been found by States to be appropriate for recognition in their internal systems, and (by implication) accepted as suitable for international application. Here too there is a substantial consensual element.

Whether or not one accepts the classic concept of sources, and in particular custom (involving State practice) as a source, there is much to be learned from observing what States in diplomatic exchanges assert to be their legal rights, or accept as their legal obligations, and the justifications offered for their positions.[56] This practice rarely—if ever—throws light on States' conceptions of how international law is made, beyond the assertion in a given dispute that a particular convention is governing, or that there is a clearly established customary rule in support of a position taken. In so far as it is a matter of record, it does seem that the debate proceeds most frequently on the basis of a classical conception of law as source-derived. While the same observation may be true of the decisions of international tribunals, in particular the ICJ, this fact is referable to the requirement of the Court's Statute that the Court apply international law derived from the classic sources; and the language of judicial and arbitral decisions of course has an influence on the language of legal argument in disputes that, at least theoretically, may come to judicial determination.

5. Whose law? States and non-State actors

The classic doctrine of sources was developed in the context of the Westphalian system of international law, in which the only subjects of international law,

---

[55] Objection has been taken to the expression 'civilized' (see e.g. the separate opinion of Judge Ammoun in the *North Sea Continental Shelf* case [1969] ICJ Rep 133–5) as implying that some 'nations' were regarded as 'uncivilized'; but the distinction did make sense at the time (1920) it was originally drafted, and its intention may have been simply to define the *type* of principle contemplated rather than to classify individual States as more or less 'civilised': see further Ch. IV n. 8.

[56] It was even argued by an author hostile to the 'classic' conception of sources, McWhinney, that 'The emphasis today has, in fact, shifted from the old neo-positivist insistence on closed, a priori, formal categories of "sources", to a neo-Realist, Law-as-Fact, approach in which the enquiry, as to a claimed principle or rule of law, is directed to whether the parties involved, expressly or by their conduct, regarded the proposition concerned as normative and legally binding upon them.': *The International Court of Justice and the Western Tradition of International Law*, (Nijhoff, 1987), 31. This seems perhaps an excessively voluntarist view.

in the sense of those who at one and the same time were bound by it and collectively created it, were States.[57] By 1949, however, the ICJ could observe, with reference to the developing international system, that 'The subjects of law in any legal system are not necessarily identical in their nature or in the extent of their rights, and their nature depends on the needs of the community.'[58] As regards the United Nations Organization, the Court came to the conclusion that 'the Organization is an international person'; that it was 'a subject of international law and capable of possessing international rights and duties'.[59] There was thus no longer any doubt that international legal personality was not confined to States, but was henceforth enjoyed also by international organizations of various kinds and dimensions. In the subsequent period, the concept has become recognized of 'non-State actors';[60] this category, somewhat heterogeneous, and perhaps even not truly juridical, appears to comprise international organizations, trade associations, transnational corporations, and perhaps even terrorist groups and transnational criminal organizations.[61] Individuals are also included; according to classical international law, they had no role to play: for example, injury to an individual by a State other than that of nationality could only be redressed if that person's national State chose to exercise diplomatic protection on behalf of its subject; and injury by the individual's own national State was legally without significance.[62] At the present time, the extent to which, and the way in which, a natural person may be a subject of international law is a developing issue, but the individual is no longer totally invisible on the international plane.[63]

---

[57] With a few anomalous exceptions, such as the Order of St John.

[58] *Reparation for Injuries Suffered in the Service of the United Nations* [1949] ICJ Rep 178.

[59] *Reparation for Injuries*, 179.

[60] It has been suggested that this definition was 'intentionally adopted in order to reinforce the assumption that the State is not only the central actor, but also the indispensable and pivotal one around which all other entities revolve': P. Alston, 'The "Not-A-Cat" Syndrome: Can the International Human Rights Regime accommodate Non-State Actors?' in Alston (ed.) *Non-State Actors and Human Rights*, (Oxford University Press, 2005), 3.

[61] In this sense, M. Wagner, 'Non-State Actors', in R. Wolfrum (ed.), *Max Planck Encyclopedia of Public International Law* (Oxford: Oxford University Press, 2012), vii. 742, para. 1; for a different enumeration, see R. McCorquodale, 'Sources and the Subjects of International Law: A Plurality of Law-Making Participants' in Besson and d'Aspremont (eds.) *The Oxford Handbook of the Sources of International Law* (Oxford: Oxford University Press, 2017), 749, 758–60.

[62] The legal philosophy of the monist Georges Scelle (1878–1961) was that the individual was the central element of public international law, which only existed through and for the individual (see his *Précis du droit des gens* (Paris: Dalloz-Sirey, 1932–4), and 'Régles générales du droit de la paix', 46 Recueil de cours (1933) 327).

[63] A separate objection to the 'legitimacy' of international law is that its institutions 'fail to take the legitimate interest of non-State individuals or groups seriously enough and often operate so as to threaten their welfare'; A. Buchanan, 'Legitimacy of International Law', in Besson and Tasioulas (eds.), *The Philosophy of International Law* (Oxford: Oxford University Press, 2010) 86.

Whether non-State actors are or are not to be defined as 'subjects' of international law is not a question that needs to be examined here.[64] However, it was observed earlier that States used to have the monopoly of creation of the law that bound them in their mutual relations. Does the significance now attached to some of these non-States include the possibility of participating in the making of international law, and if so, does our conception of the sources of law need to be adjusted accordingly? The influence of, for example, non-governmental organizations (NGOs) in the codification of a number of areas of law has been very significant, when invited by States to participate in, for example, the Rio Process and the Earth Summit; and the text and adoption of the Rome Statute of the International Criminal Court owes much to NGO participation in the *travaux préparatoires*.[65] The background to the two requests made to the ICJ in 1993–4 for advisory opinions on the legitimacy of nuclear weapons included a very active role for NGOs (approved of by some and deplored by others[66]). The outcome of processes such as these, however, has been, in the first example, an instrument of a treaty nature, binding on States and other subjects of international law, and in the second an international judicial pronouncement, in each case in perfect harmony with Article 38, paragraph 1(a), of the ICJ Statute.

What might call for a reassessment of the doctrine of sources would be if the participation of entities of this kind in international life could be shown to operate in a more direct way, not through the intermediary of treaty, so as to suggest their participation in the creation of quasi-custom, or even some kind of lawmaking activity not fitting into the traditional categories. There is certainly movement in this direction: it has been convincingly contended that for international organizations the question is no longer that of independence and separate personality, now taken practically for granted, but of accountability.[67] As to development of customary international law, some scholars consider that NGOs may contribute directly to the establishment both of practice and of *opinio juris*,[68] the better view appears to be that their

---

[64] A distinction is frequently drawn between the status of 'active' subject of international law (potential 'créateur de normes'), and 'passive' subject ('titulaire de droits'); it is generally recognized that the individual does at least have the latter status.

[65] See e.g. P. Kirsch and J. T. Holmes, 'The Rome Conference on the International Criminal Court: The Negotiating Process', 93 AJIL (1999), 2.

[66] Cf. the opinions of Judges Oda and Weeramantry [1996-I] ICJ Rep 335–6 (Oda) and 438 (Weeramantry).

[67] A. Reinisch, 'Sources of International Organizations' Law: Why Custom and General Principles are Crucial' in Besson and d'Aspremont (eds.) *The Oxford Handbook of the Sources of International Law* (Oxford: Oxford University Press, 2017), 1005, 1012.

[68] e.g. I. R. Gunning, 'Modernizing Customary International Law: the Challenge of Human Rights', 31 Virginia Journal of International Law (1991), 211, 227–34, cited in Lepard, *Customary International Law*, 186. On the other hand, Lepard remains of the view that 'for customary

impact is on the limited level just described. But even if this view is correct, it does not call in question the role of custom as a source, or imply the existence of any additional source.[69] In particular in the field of international humanitarian law and that of international criminal law, the role of non-State actors, particularly armed groups and even individuals, has become increasingly significant.[70]

A special case is that of the United Nations International Law Commission, charged, according to its Statute, both with making proposals 'for the progressive development of international law' and with selecting topics and making proposals for codification.[71] It has frequently been remarked that the Commission does not itself make this distinction clear in its work, and it has itself in fact proposed its abolition.[72] The presentation by the Commission of a field of law for purposes of codification may therefore incorporate rules that strictly have not yet attained recognition as such (or at least remain in a grey area). While the proposals made will normally result in a convention, and thus acquire, in terms of sources, a treaty-basis, in the meantime the authority of the Commission may give some weight or status to its *travaux préparatoires*. In the case concerning *Application of the Genocide Convention*, the International Court treated Article 16 of the ILC Draft Articles on State Responsibility as 'reflecting a customary rule',[73] though there is some doubt whether the ILC itself regarded it as such.[74] In view of the eminence of the Commission's membership, this might, however, be classified as an example of the 'teachings of the most highly qualified publicists' under Article 38, paragraph 1(*d*)!

More generally, however, an increased role of non-State actors in the development and operation of international law, which was at one time heralded

---

international law to retain its character as international law, we must focus on the views and practice of States—acknowledging, however, that these can be shaped by the programs and opinions of nongovernmental organizations and nonstate actors': 'Concluding Reflections' in Lepard (ed.) *Reexamining Customary International Law*, (Cambridge, 2017), 389.

[69] The position of d'Aspremont in this respect is obscured by his individual terminology: he speaks of activities that 'generate communitarian semantics of law-ascertainment' (*Formalism and the Sources of International Law*, 203–17 *passim*), the precise significance of which is, for the present writer at least, difficult to grasp.

[70] See S. R. Ratner, 'Sources of International Humanitarian Law: Warcrimes and the Limits of the Doctrine of Sources' in Besson and d'Aspremont (eds.) *The Oxford Handbook of the Sources of International Law* (Oxford University Press, 2017), 912, 925.

[71] Statute of the ILC, Arts. 16, 18.

[72] *Report of the ILC*, 48th Session (1996), A/51/10, paras. 147(a) and 156–9.

[73] [2007-I] ICJ Rep 27, para. 420.

[74] The Court did not, however, apply Article 16, but rather prayed it in aid for the interpretation of Article III, paragraph 1(*e*) of the Genocide Convention on complicity in genocide.

as an imminent and desirable[75] development, seems not to have come about, despite factors that may be resumed under the heading of 'globalization'.[76] At all events, there is no trace of a new legal philosophy empowering such actors to make a contribution in a form suggestive of the birth of a new source of international law, or a new, non-source-based theory of legal production.

6. Are there additional formal sources, not in Article 38?

The enumeration of formal sources in Article 38 of the PCIJ Statute was presumably then regarded as complete, or sufficiently complete for the purposes of judicial settlement, which probably comes to the same thing. Whether or not it was so in 1920, it has since been questioned whether there may not be today other possible sources of international law. Presumably the International Court, whose powers are circumscribed by its Statute, would not be able to rely on these *eo nomine*; but it should not be overlooked that while decisions of international organizations (for example) are not listed in Article 38, this does not mean that the Court cannot apply such decisions in its reasoning. It must, however, be possible for the process to be analysed as the application of one of the named sources. As candidates for the category of unrecognized sources, a number of possibilities have been mentioned in the literature, but an overall study of the problem, published in 2000, will here be employed as a useful starting-point.[77]

The author enumerates the following possible sources: unilateral acts of States; acts of international lawmaking on the part of international organizations; and agreements between States and international enterprises. In a further category of what may conceivably be sources of international law are listed consent/consensus; international standards; the use of analogy as a source; decisions of international tribunals (these of course are already

---

[75] But which may have a downside: some influential non-State actors have their own agenda, not necessarily in any sense benevolent: see J. Gupta, 'The Role of Non-State Actors in International Environmental Affairs', *Zeitschrift für ausländisches und öffentliches Recht und Völkerrecht* (2003), 459–86, particularly 478ff.

[76] See N. Bhuta, 'The Role International Actors Other Than States can Play in the New World Order', in A. Cassese (ed.), *Realizing Utopia: The Future of International Law* (Oxford: Oxford University Press, 2012), 61, and particularly 66–70. As Cassese points out in the same publication, 'most non-State actors are only tangentially restrained by international rules' and could with advantage be brought under their sway: pp. 675–6.

[77] S. Kratzsch, *Rechtsquellen des Völkerrechts außerhalb von Artikel 38 Absatz 1 IGH-Statut*, Inaugural dissertation, (Tübingen; Köhler-Druck, Tübingen, 2000). Another useful survey of the matter is that of Pellet, in A. Zimmerman et al. (eds.), *The Statute of the International Court of Justice: A Commentary*, 2nd edn. (Oxford University Press, 2012), *sub* Art. 38 paras. 87–110.

recognized as subsidiary sources in Article 38 para. 2 of the ICJ Statute); and some parts of natural law (the *Jus naturale*).

6(a) Unilateral acts

The well-known *Nuclear Tests* cases involved reliance by the International Court on a unilateral act by a State (an announcement by the French Government) as a basis for a legal obligation, and made no attempt in its judgments to link these with any recognized source of law.[78] It is therefore tempting to see these cases as the unavowed recognition of a source outside the Article 38 enumeration. This is, however, by no means a necessary conclusion. The cases will be discussed further in the light also of the 'Guiding Principles Applicable to Unilateral Declarations of States Capable of Creating Legal Obligations', adopted by the International law Commission in 2006.[79] The context chosen for that examination will be in connection with the 'treaties and conventions' of paragraph 1(*a*) of Article 38; the reason being (briefly) that it is here argued that what matters is acceptance by another State, that a unilateral act that prompts absolutely no reaction on the level of international relations is of no legal relevance or significance. The Court had to close its eyes to this evident fact, for reasons—one might say—of judicial convenience.[80] It makes better legal sense, as will be explained further,[81] to see a unilateral act on the international plane as a sort of inchoate treaty, completed by subsequent events. The study of the International Law Commission is non-committal on the question of the source of the obligation.[82]

In its 2014 decision in the case of *Maritime Delimitation between Peru and Chile*, the ICJ considered governmental acts concerning maritime boundaries which were initially unilateral in form, but as to which the question later arose whether, read together they came to have a binding character as in effect constituting an agreement between the author States. Each of the parties had made a Declaration in 1947 in terms suggesting a degree of shared views as to maritime delimitation; but the Court considered that the language of these, 'as well as their provisional nature, precludes an interpretation of them as

---

[78] A fuller account of the case will be given in Ch. II, sect. 4.

[79] See the *Report of the ILC*, 58th Session, A/61/10, pp. 369–81.

[80] The care taken by the Court in those cases *not* to ask the applicant States for their reaction, presumably for fear that it would be unfavourable, means that this approach *in casu* involved certain jurisprudential gymnastics, but it is suggested that this fact does not compromise the principle of the quasi-treaty nature of such acts. See further in Ch. II.

[81] Ch. II sect. 4.

[82] Except perhaps by implication in the use of the word 'creating' in the title of the study: see further in Ch. II sect. 4.

reflecting a shared understanding of the Parties. . . .'[83] On the other hand, the 1962 Santiago Declaration resembled a treaty from the outset, being signed by Chile, Ecuador, and Peru at an international conference. Peru at first considered that it was nevertheless not a treaty; but all three parties in due course ratified it as one, and registered it with the UN, enabling the Court to conclude that it was a treaty.[84]

6(b) Decisions of international organizations

If and to the extent that the taking of binding decisions by and within international organizations does not involve the exercise of powers conferred (ultimately or proximately) by treaty, this possibility is of course a delicate and highly relevant issue. However, if the constitutive treaty of the organization provides for certain decisions of defined organs to be binding on the member States, then their binding force is consensual, however unwelcome a particular decision may be to one or more member States.[85] In view of the reservation to the Security Council of Charter powers to take decisions binding on the Members, the question arises most specifically in relation to resolutions of the General Assembly. We are not here concerned with decisions concerning the internal operation of the Organization (for example, the adoption of the budget), but of decisions purporting to enact or to affect general international law. May these, and resolutions of similar bodies within other international organizations, rank as sources of law in their own right, and if so in what circumstances? There are situations in which for such decisions to have that status would seem to be a way of achieving some end generally regarded as desirable, as in the case of the numerous condemnations by the General Assembly of the South African regime and the position of South West Africa (Namibia) during the post-war period. However, to seek to promote General Assembly resolutions to the rank of a 'source of law' on this basis betrays a confusion of thought: as mentioned earlier, sources theory defines what prescriptions are law in terms of their origins, not of their desirability.[86] The ICJ did of course observe, in the *Namibia* advisory opinion, that 'it would not be correct to assume that, because the General Assembly is in principle vested with recommendatory powers, it is debarred from adopting,

---

[83] [2014] ICJ Rep 23, para. 43   [84] [2014] ICJ Rep 24, para. 47.

[85] Thus the imposition of sanctions imposed by the Security Council is something 'agreed to' by the States affected, *pace* Pellet in Zimmerman et al. (eds.), *The Statute of the ICJ*, sub Art. 38, para. 99. An 'act done under an authority contained in … a treaty' derives its force from the treaty, even if that does not give the act 'a treaty character': cf. joint dissenting opinion of Judges Spender and Fitzmaurice, *South West Africa* [1962] ICJ Rep 490–1.

[86] See this chapter, pp. 19ff. and n. 54.

in specific cases within the framework of its competence, resolutions which make determinations or have operative design'.[87] This is sometimes read as a recognition of general dispositive powers in the Assembly; but as Pellet clearly demonstrates,[88] the point was that the Assembly, representing for this purpose the UN as successor to the League of Nations in relation to the Mandate for South West Africa, had exercised the power to terminate the Mandate on the ground of persistent violations by the other party. This was not a quasi-legislative power, but one conferred by the general law of obligations; the sentence quoted asserted simply that such a power was not excluded because the Assembly, as a constitutional matter, had only recommendatory powers. The decision was binding on South Africa, and on all other States that might be concerned, not as Members of the UN, but as international actors bound to respect an *acte juridique* properly performed by another international actor.

It is also true that decisions of an organ of an international organization not having inherent binding force may in a sense acquire it through the acceptance of the decision by the State or States concerned, as in the example of the creation of jurisdiction through the acceptance by Albania of the Security Council recommendation in the *Corfu Channel* case;[89] but this of course is simply an example of the consensual principle in action, and does not advance the discussion of the substantive point.

In short, decisions of an organ of an international organization may be effectively lawmaking to the extent that the constituent treaty of the organization (or another treaty of similar ranking) confers power to make decisions binding on the member States, and of course subject to compliance with any restrictions or procedures laid down by the authorizing text. Their essentially treaty-law basis also determines to what extent such decisions can depart from or prevail over other existing legal rights and obligations, reserving (as always) considerations of *jus cogens (q.v.)*, or may detract from customary rules or rights. Any conflict with other treaty-rights or obligations is regulated by the provisions of the respective treaties, and in the case of the United Nations, this of course signifies that the Charter, and acts based upon it, prevail (Art. 103).[90] Beyond that, such decision cannot be regarded as an independent

---

[87] [1971] ICJ Rep 50, para. 105.

[88] Pellet, in Zimmerman et al. (eds.), *The Statute of the ICJ*, sub Art. 38, para. 103. In the same sense, R. Higgins, *Problems and Process: International Law and How We Use It* (Oxford: Clarendon, 1994), 26–7.

[89] See *Corfu Channel* [1947–8] ICJ Rep 26; cited by Pellet (previous note).

[90] There is a constitutional debate as to possible limitations on the powers of the Security Council where their use may conflict with other norms, which however need not be gone into here: see the discussion in A. Boyle and C. Chinkin, *The Making of International Law* (Oxford: Oxford University Press, 2007), 114 and 229–33.

technique of lawmaking, thus a 'source' in our terminology.[91] On the other hand, decisions of this kind, made by the General Assembly or, for example, human rights bodies, are of considerable importance for their contribution to customary law; and this aspect will accordingly be treated in Chapter III, devoted to custom (sect. 2(d)).

6(c) Agreements between States and international enterprises

The study already cited[92] mentions these (*Verträge zwischen multinationalen Unternehmen und Staaten*) as a final category of instruments capable, it is suggested, of constituting a source of international law not included in the enumeration of Article 38 of the ICJ Statute. The agreements contemplated are apparently those referred to in the OECD declaration of 21 June 1976.[93] It seems to be established that multinational corporations of this kind do possess, for some purposes, a degree of international legal personality;[94] but whether this is essential for the agreements here considered to be regarded as a source is uncertain. In 1952, the International Court in the *Anglo–Iranian Oil Co.* case refused to see the company's concession contract as a treaty between the United Kingdom and Iran for purposes of the term 'treaties and conventions' in the Iranian declaration of acceptance of jurisdiction;[95] and the same decision would almost certainly still be reached today. For purposes of the present study, furthermore, it is probably sufficient to say that an agreement of this kind is undoubtedly a source of *obligation* (to recall a distinction already mentioned[96]), and to that extent within the scope of the *pacta sunt servanda* principle, but is so only for the parties. Whether for the State party it can be called a source of

---

[91] In this sense the Report of the ILA Committee on the Formation of Customary Law, discussed in Ch. III sect. 2(c), §28 *in fine*, to the effect that 'as a general rule' General Assembly resolutions 'do not *ipso facto* create new rules of international law'.

[92] Kratzsch, *Rechtsquellen des Völkerrechts.*

[93] Kratzsch, *Rechtsquellen des Völkerrechts*, 120–1; the Declaration does not in fact give a formal definition, but speaks of 'companies or other entities established in more than one country and so linked that they may coordinate their operations in various ways': *OECD Guidelines for Multinational Enterprises, I. Concepts and Principles*, para. 4.

[94] For purposes e.g. of settlement of disputes in the context of the International Centre for the Settlement of Investment Disputes (ICSID): see e.g. the 1965 *Convention on the Settlement of Investment Disputes between States and Nationals of other States*, Art. 25.

[95] [1952] ICJ Rep 111–12.

[96] And see further Ch. II, text and n. 7. See also Pellet in Zimmerman et al. (eds.), *The Statute of the ICJ, sub* Art. 38, paras. 84–6.

international law does not seem to be more than a question of terminology without further impact.[97]

6(d) Other proposals

Turning to the less evident candidates suggested in the study referred to: analogy is well established as a method of legal reasoning, but it is difficult to regard it as a source. There are no principles or rules contained within 'analogy' itself; it serves as a lens through which to look at other fields of law—a conduit rather than a source.[98] As regards judicial and arbitral decisions, it is possible to read paragraph 1(*d*) of Article 38 as referring solely to national court decisions (though this clashes with the reservation as to Article 59), and to regard decisions of international tribunals as a source without qualification. All that needs be added here to what has already been said on this is that they are not generally given that rank in subsequent international decisions; the matter will be considered further in Chapter V.[99] Finally as regards 'natural law', this too probably only operates as a synonym for the 'general principles of law' recognized by Article 38, paragraph 1(*c*), and discussed in Chapter IV.

Another suggested candidate is history, defined for this purpose in a leading study as 'the knowledge of the relation between a series of events and realities which reflect the evolution of a social group', also 'the literary analysis of these events and realities'.[100] It is argued that this is a 'source' in the same sense as the judicial decisions and legal writings mentioned in Article 38 (1) (*d*) of the ICJ Statute, namely 'subsidiary means for the determination of the rules of law'. This is stretching the term 'subsidiary' to breaking point: judicial decisions and legal writings are not merely 'what happened'; they offer a more or less specific (and more or less reliable) glimpse of legal prescriptions.

The currently accepted system of sources is also often criticized for incompleteness, without a specific suggestion necessarily being made for an identifiable 'new' source. This is particularly likely to be based on the plethora of

---

[97] A different question, which is of practical import and well known in commercial arbitration, is whether some 'internationalization' of the agreement protects the non-State partner from conduct on the part of the State as sovereign (e.g. new legislation) that would prejudice the performance of the agreement; but this is outside the scope of the present study.

[98] See H. Thirlway, 'Concepts, Principles, Rules and Analogies: International and Municipal Legal Reasoning', 294 Recueil des cours (2002), 267 at 287.

[99] Sect. 2(a).

[100] R. Kolb, 'Legal History as a Source of International Law: from Classical to Modern International Law' in Besson and d'Aspremont, *The Oxford Handbook of the Sources of International Law* (Oxford: Oxford University Press, 2017), 279, 281.

international 'legal' texts which to a greater or lesser degree regulate, or purport to regulate, State action: not merely conventions but resolutions, declarations, model codes, decisions, recommendations *et hoc genus omne*: it is difficult to find a term sufficiently all-embracing. It is against this background that Matthias Goldmann has presented his concept of 'standard instruments for the exercise of international public authority', which will be further considered in Chapter IX.

In theory, the ultimate basis for the legal authority of these, as already indicated, would appear to be 'treaties and conventions' and thus Article 38, paragraph 1(*a*) of the ICJ Statute, as they constitute different degrees of 'delegated legislation': the treaty empowers a governing body to take such action, that body resolves to authorize a commission to implement it, that commission adopts regulations, under which a decision is taken at some lower level, and that decision authorizes the issue of a notice ....[101] It would often be a wearisome task to trace such an instrument to its ultimate treaty-source; but it must always be possible to do so for the ultimate end product to have the force of 'law'. The problem is familiar in the specialized field of European Community law, which recognizes a principle of 'positive legality' in this connection.[102] It is only by such a 'constitutionalization' approach that one can find a firm basis for instruments of this kind consistently with the requirements of Article 38.[103]

This may not, however, be the whole of the story. It has also been pointed out that in some circumstances there may be such a thing as legislation by bureaucracy. It has been suggested that there is a possible movement towards limitation of State autonomy, even in the context of a regime established by non-binding instrument, through institutional 'routine', which signifies 'the potential for reiterated interaction through which networks of specialized government officials, international civil servants and private actors establish common norms and identities—a process which may lead to even greater dissociation of the respective institutional bodies from the will and interests of state governments'.[104]

---

[101] For an extreme example, note the argument that States concluding a taxation treaty might be taken to have incorporated silently, not merely a Model Convention prepared by OECD, but also the Commentary published by OECD upon it: see S. Douma and F. Engelen (eds.), *The Legal Status of the OECD Commentaries* (Amsterdam: IBFD, 2008).

[102] See A. von Bogdandy, 'General Principles of International Public Authority', 9 German Law Journal (2008), 1934–5.

[103] Bogdandy, 'General Principles of International Public Authority', 1936.

[104] J. Friedrich, 'Legal Challenges of Non-Binding Instruments: The Case of the FAO Code of Conduct for Responsible Fisheries', 9 German Law Journal (2008), 1541; see also T. Piiparinen, 'Law versus Bureaucratic Culture: The Case of the ICC and the Transcendence of Instrumental Rationality', in J. Klabbers and T. Piiparinen (eds.), *Normative Pluralism in International Law: Exploring Global Governance* (Cambridge: Cambridge University Press, 2013).

7. Religious law as a rival or additional source

As we have already observed, the unity and universality of international law implies that, unless the contrary can be shown, all subsystems or specialized fields of international law will operate on the basis that they derive their force from the established sources of Article 38 of the ICJ Statute. That universality also implies that, in principle, the individual legal, political, or religious system of a State does not impinge on its acceptance of, and compliance with, general international law. It is well established that on the international plane a State may not rely on the provisions of its internal law to evade its international obligations;[105] while a State's domestic courts may apply, or be obliged by internal law to apply, provisions of that internal law that are clearly not consistent with general international law,[106] any deleterious effect that this may have on other States' interests will raise questions of State responsibility—at which point, as already stated, the provisions of internal law afford no defence.

A particular philosophy or religion existing within a given State may, however, be regarded as of such primacy as to be legally unchallengeable, to such an extent that the State will be reluctant to accept the principle just outlined, and will seek to regulate any conflict between its obligations under international law and the dictates of that philosophy or religion by allowing the latter to prevail. At one time this was, broadly speaking, the case as regards Marxism in the Soviet system. One aspect of this approach was the theory that, alongside general international law there existed a form of 'particular international law', socialist internationalism, which governed the relationship between Soviet bloc States, to the exclusion of conflicting rules of general law. This did not, however, mean a rejection of general international law as operative outside the Soviet system. The generally accepted doctrine of treaty and custom as sources was accepted, but customary law, because of its roots in the pre-Marxist past, was regarded as regressive, and as binding only by virtue of

---

[105] It was stated by the ICJ as a 'fundamental principle of international law that international law prevails over domestic law': *Application of the Obligation to Arbitrate under Section 21 of the UN Headquarters Agreement* [1988] ICJ Rep 34, para. 57.

[106] This may cause complications if it is suggested that customary law is in the process of changing, and the courts of one or more States are, as it were, ahead of the trend; particularly if the constitution of the State concerned provides for the direct internal application of international law. See the position of Italy in relation to the law of State immunity in the case of *Jurisdictional Immunities of the State*, and the *Reflection* in the ESIL Newsletter (January 2013) by G. Cataldi: 'The Implementation of the ICJ's Decision in the *Jurisdictional Immunities of the State* case in the Italian Domestic Order: What Balance should be made between Fundamental Human Rights and International Obligations?'

individual State consent. The collapse of the Soviet system has rendered these contentions largely obsolete.[107]

Since the waning of the influence of the teachings of the Catholic Church on moral and legal concepts, it has become possible for at least half a century to say that international law is now free from any religious input—that it is 'laicized'.[108] There is, however, one system of law operating on a supranational or international level that presents problems that are not easily soluble by application of the principles just stated: Islamic law. This system is supranational of its nature, being addressed, as a minimum, to all who accept Islam, and supranational in its operation, being adopted and applied by a considerable group of sovereign States.[109] Nor is it simply a question of belief or morals: the *Shari'ah* is a system of law.[110] The potential for collision with general international law, at least as understood by lawyers of the Western liberal tradition, becomes evident when certain aspects of the *Shari'ah* are compared with particular norms of human rights law;[111] but there are other legal matters in respect of which Islamic States are reluctant to see general international law applied, and for that reason prefer not to see any intervention of the ICJ.[112] The absolutist claims made for the *Shari'ah* also make it difficult to classify it as a form of local or regional customary law.

The problem will be examined in more detail under the heading of 'Human rights law', in Chapter VIII. It is mentioned here because it is possible to see the intervention of the *Shari'ah* by Islamic States in controversies over their

[107] But not entirely so, as the Marxist approach is still alive in e.g. China: on this and other aspects of the current situation, see B. Chimni, 'Marxism', in Wolfrum (ed.), *Max Planck Encyclopedia*, vii. 11, paras. 31–5. See also this chapter, n. 22.

[108] See e.g. Guggenheim, 'Principes de droit international public', 80 Recueil des cours (1952-I), 32; J. Salmon, 'Le droit international a á l'épreuve au tournant du XXIème siecle', Cursos Euromediterráneos Bancaj de Derecho Internacional (2002), 153–6.

[109] There are at the present time forty-three Muslim majority States, of which twenty-three have declared Islam as state religion: N. A. Shah, 'The Use of Force under Islamic Law', 24 EJIL (2013), 343 at 363.

[110] Two terms are used to refer to Islamic law: *Shari'ah*, which means 'path to be followed', and *Fiqh*, meaning 'understanding', a term used for the *methods* of Islamic law. For simplicity, *Shari'ah* will be used here without making this distinction: see M. A. Baderin, *International Human Rights and Islamic Law* (Oxford: Oxford University Press, 2003), 33.

[111] A delicate question is whether there is a divergence between the laws of war as understood in the Islamic world and in other nations: Mahmoudi, 'Islamic Approach to International Law', in Wolfrum (ed.), *Max Planck Encyclopedia*, vi. 390–4, paras. 21–43, suggests that this may have been so in the past, but no longer; in the same sense, Shah, 'The Use of Force under Islamic Law', 343. A different view is advanced by A. F. Marx and N. K. Modizzadek, 'Ambivalent Universalism? *Jus ad Bellum* in Modern Islamic Legal Discourse', 24 EJIL (2013), 367.

[112] See the very thorough study of E. Powell, 'The International Court of Justice and Islamic Law States: Territory and Diplomatic Immunity' in K. J. Alter et al. (eds.), *International Court Authority* (OUP, 2018), 277. ff, who also provides a very useful enumeration of 'Islamic Law States'.

obligations under major human rights conventions, and even more so in so far as it is claimed that these obligations also exist—for all States—in customary law, as the assertion of the existence of a *source* of law not merely additional to the classical sources, but capable, to some degree, of overriding them. As will be explained, efforts are being made, particularly among Islamic States, to reach an accommodation on delicate issues (freedom of religion, rights of women), but the potential for disputes involving the question of principle remains, though unlikely, for jurisdictional reasons, to require judicial, and therefore authoritative, settlement.

In its most extreme form, the view might be advanced that an Islamic State cannot be held bound to an international legal obligation that contradicts Islamic law; this is in fact implied in the constitutions of certain Islamic States.[113] Does this amount to the assertion of the existence of an additional source of international law? If a constitutionally Islamic State becomes a party to a convention, for example a human rights convention, that imposes requirements incompatible with Islamic teaching, the implementation of the convention obligations might be challenged in the domestic courts of that State as being unconstitutional.[114] The problem can be initially avoided as regards treaty obligations by accepting them subject to appropriately drawn reservations, and as will be explained, this has been done. It then arises at a second stage, however, if it is suggested that such reservations are invalid as contrary to the object and purpose of the relevant convention. In its most acute form, it could result from an extension in this respect of the jurisprudence of the *Loizidou* and *Bellilos* cases before the ECHR, to the effect that an invalid reservation can simply be severed, leaving the State party to the convention unprotected by its reservation.[115] This jurisprudence is now less favoured, and it is suggested that it should not be followed in relation to a reservation on such a sensitive and delicate point.

If, however, it were asserted, for example, that for an Islamic State to authorize men only to practise polygamy was in breach of a customary rule of human rights law, and that State asserted the primacy for this purpose of the *Shari'ah*, on what basis could that assertion be upheld without doing violence to the recognized doctrine of sources? It is tempting to turn to the 'general principles of law' of paragraph 1(*c*) of Article 38; these are generally recognized to include the principles applied in municipal systems. However, as explained in Chapter IV, when transferred to the international plane they undergo an internationalization, broadly substituting States for individual

---

[113] See further in Ch. VIII sect. 2(c).
[114] See Shah, 'The Use of Force under Islamic Law', 343 at 363–4.
[115] See Ch. II, text and n. 32.

subjects of law, and operating by analogy. The fact that the domestic legal systems of a substantial group of States incorporate *Shari'ah* law is therefore not legally significant on the international plane.

8. Is the theory of sources still sufficient?

A major criticism of the traditional doctrine of sources is that it is no longer capable of accounting for, or regulating, the immense mass of quasi-legislative activity that makes up the international law of which States must now take account in their day-to-day relations and activities. A categorization of the 'instruments by which international institutions exercise public authority' would include, in descending order of degree of binding authority, 'international treaties, periodic treaty amendments, decisions on individual cases with binding effect or decisions having the potential to become binding by way of domestic recognition'; 'various types of soft, i.e., non-binding legal instruments' including 'product standards or codes of conduct'; 'instruments containing non-binding rules that are foremost aimed at facilitating consultation, or soft private law instruments'; and 'non-legal instruments that are devoid of any deontic elements, but nevertheless have a high legal or political impact on the affected policy area', including such things as 'reports on implementation and compliance'.[116] Certainly the concept advanced by the author of the study quoted, of a system of 'standard instruments for the exercise of international public authority', into which all these could be fitted in an orderly and consistent manner, is one highly to be recommended; but it does not—as the title of the article cited might lead one to suppose—involve a re-thinking of the concept of sources. It is an essay in *constitutional* thinking, which does not necessarily involve abandonment of what are regarded as the bases on which the edifice must stand.[117]

Many modern theories 'of' international law are in fact not directed to the question to which the concept of sources was traditionally supposed to supply the answer, namely, why is international law binding upon international actors (primarily States), and how does it relate to the 'sovereignty' with which States are, equally traditionally, endowed? Answers to that question may be of two kinds: first 'external' justification, appealing to a standard outside and above sovereignty, primarily one of an ethical or divinely decreed nature, but possibly also based upon historical necessity. Secondly, 'internal'

---

[116] M. Goldmann, 'Inside Relative Normativity: From Sources to Standard Instruments for the Exercise of International Public Authority', German Law Journal (2008), 1866–908.
[117] See further Ch. IX sect. 1(c).

justification, whereby sovereignty is self-limiting, that its acceptance implies acceptance of its limitation to the extent that the sovereign entity abides by what it has agreed to, explicitly or implicitly.[118] The problem of the first justification is that it implies, if not the existence and nature of a deity, a degree of shared recognition of the relevant ethical principles that is hard to come by— or a fragmentation of law in parallel to differences of ethical background.

A number of present-day scholarly studies in international law bypass or set aside this problem, to concentrate, for example, on a more sociological approach: rather than ask why States are bound by international law, they ask how States see themselves as bound, and how they can best devise a system that satisfactorily integrates and co-ordinates their conflicting interests. At best, these plans have a certain unreality, given that the present system, with all its faults, is both an existing fact and the only vehicle for change; and they may even incur the charge of lack of realism or appropriateness to international society.[119] Some features of studies of this kind will be briefly noted at a later stage (Ch. IX).

One circumstance that has, it is suggested, cast doubt on the adequacy of the traditional concept of sources to comprehend modern international law in all its variety is the evident phenomenon, already noted, of the 'fragmentation' of international law, the appearance of more and more specialized areas of international law, to which—it is suggested—different rules apply than would be applicable in 'mainstream' international law.[120] This phenomenon has been the subject of a very thorough examination by a study group of the International Law Commission.[121] Do any of these special rules also purport to be based upon a source or sources other than, or independent of, the traditional triad of treaty, custom, and general principles? The study group did not tackle this question directly; it noted that 'One aspect that does seem to unite most of the new regimes is that they claim binding force from and are understood by their practitioners to be covered by the law of treaties.'[122] It therefore approached the matter adopting as 'conceptual framework' the Vienna Convention on the Law of Treaties. It did consider the

---

[118] It is in this sense that the present writer understands M. Koskenniemi, 'International Legal Theory and Doctrine', in Wolfrum (ed.), *Max Planck Encyclopedia*, v. 979–80, para. 15.

[119] Some may remember the traditional tale of the man who discovered a miracle cure, but was unable to discover the corresponding disease.

[120] The term 'fragmentation' does have some question-begging implications, as a specialization may remain within the corpus of general law, rather than constituting a 'fragment' apart from the rest.

[121] *Fragmentation of International Law: Difficulties Arising from the Diversification and Expansion of International Law, Report of the Study Group*, A/CN.4/L682. See further Ch. VIII n. 5.

[122] *Fragmentation of International Law*, 15, para. 17.

question whether there was some exclusivity of the individual special regimes in relation to each other; that is, whether each of them could be said to be self-contained, so that, for example, '[a] human rights body, for example, should have no business to apply a WTO covered agreement', and rejected this view.[123] The group does not, however, appear to have thought worth examining any contention that a special regime might derive some of its rules from a non-traditional source.[124]

A number of subsystems will be studied more closely in Chapter VIII, where attention will also be paid to the idea of 'special regimes'.

---

[123] *Fragmentation of International Law*, 28–9, paras. 44–5, and 91ff., paras. 172ff.

[124] Note in this respect that in the operation of as up-to-the minute domain of international law as that governing the environment, what is novel is not the appearance of a new 'source', but the complex interplay of the traditional Article 38 sources (including the unmentioned but implied presence of soft law): see Ch. VIII, sect. 5, and the important articles of Catherine Redgwell and Jutta Brunée in Besson and d'Aspremont (eds.), *The Oxford Handbook of the Sources of International Law* (Oxford: Oxford University Press, 2017), 939 and 960.

II

Treaties and Conventions as a Source of Law

1. *Pacta sunt servanda*

Whatever objections may be taken to the positivist view associated with the traditional doctrine of sources of international law, invoking State consent as the ultimate basis for the creation of law, it cannot be doubted that consent is the foundation for law deriving from the second of the sources mentioned in Article 38 of the ICJ Statute, namely 'international conventions, whether general or particular, establishing rules expressly recognized' by States. The significance and effect of treaties is expressed in the principle *pacta sunt servanda*. The whole point of making a binding agreement is that each of the parties should be able to rely on performance of the treaty by the other party or parties, even when such performance may have become onerous or unwelcome to such other party or parties. A treaty is therefore one of the most evident ways in which rules binding on two or more States[1] may come into existence, and thus an evident formal source of law. The 1969 Vienna Convention on the Law of Treaties, which is, as the International Court has observed in a number of cases,[2] to a very large extent the codification of pre-existing general law on the subject, states the principle in Article 26, under the heading '*Pacta sunt servanda*': 'Every treaty is binding upon the parties to it and must be performed by them in good faith.'[3]

---

[1] For the possibility of unilateral obligations assumed by a process in some respects parallel to treaty-making, see sect. 4.

[2] See e.g. *Application of the Convention on the Prevention and Punishment of the Crime of Genocide (Bosnia and Herzegovina* v. *Serbia and Montenegro)* [2007-I] ICJ Rep, 109–10, para. 160; *Territorial Dispute (Libyan Arab Jamahiriya/Chad)* [1994] ICJ Rep, 21–2, para. 41; *Questions of Mutual Assistance in Criminal Matters* [2009] ICJ Rep 222, paras. 123, 124; 229, para. 145; 232, para. 153; *Pulp Mills on the River Uruguay* [2010] ICJ Rep 46, para. 65; 67, para. 145; *Questions Relating to the Obligation to Prosecute or Extradite (Belgium* v. *Senegal)* [2012] ICJ Rep 457, 460, paras. 100, 113.

[3] The treaty only binds to what has been agreed to be binding; thus it is not inconsistent with this principle for a treaty to contain, or even be wholly composed of, commitments that are loosely defined, or contain a voluntaristic element: see the discussion of 'Soft Law' in Ch. VII.

What, however, is the precise status of the principle itself? Is it no more than a customary law principle, as has been suggested?[4] This would seem to imply that it can be set aside by a treaty, but the binding effect of a treaty is itself based on the *pacta sunt servanda* principle. Another modern author has suggested that it is a principle of *jus cogens* (peremptory norms), that is one that cannot itself be derogated from by agreement, and overrides any contrary rule of law.[5] Certainly, as regards conflict of treaties, it is the principle itself which ensures that, for example, a subsequent treaty will override an earlier one. But more generally, since the essence of *jus cogens* is that it constitutes an exception to the principle of *pacta sunt servanda*, it may be simpler not to view the latter as an example of the former. Is the principle then one of the 'general principles of law recognized by . . . nations', also mentioned in Article 38 as a source of the law to be applied by the Court? What this category of sources may entail will be discussed further in Chapter III; but it is odd if the basis for one of the listed sources should be another of these, listed as on the same level, as it were.[6] What is clearly true is that

[T]he rule *pacta sunt servanda* . . . does not require to be accounted for in terms of any other rule. It could neither not be, nor be other than what it is. It is not dependent on consent, for it would exist without it. There could not be a rule that *pacta sunt non-servanda* or *non sunt servanda*, for then the *pacta* would no longer be *pacta*. Nor could there be a rule that *pacta sunt interdum servanda et interdum non sunt servanda*. The idea of *servanda* is inherent and necessary in the term *pacta*.[7]

The same author suggests that a treaty is better understood as a source of *obligation*, and that the only rule of *law* in the matter is the basic principle

---

[4] A. T. Guzman, *How International Law Works: A Rational Choice Theory* (Oxford University Press, 2008), 204–5; B. Chimni, 'Customary International Law: A Third World Perspective', 112 AJIL (2018) 1, Guzman observes that while it is declared in the Vienna Convention on the Law of Treaties, 'states expect one another to follow the rule even if, like the United States, they are not party to the [Vienna] convention'; it 'thus meets *my* definition of CIL [customary international law]' (emphasis added). The author's definition of CIL is individual; more traditionally, customary law would be regarded as something that can be departed from by treaty (save in the case of *jus cogens*), and if the principle *pacta sunt servanda* can be so departed from, there is either a *circulus inextricabilis*, or the principle becomes meaningless. See further in Ch. VII sect. 1(*a*).

[5] See P. Fois, 'I valori fondamentali del "nuovo" diritto internazionale e il principio *pacta sunt servanda*', Rivista di diritto internazionale (2010), 15.

[6] See also the discussion in Ch. VII of the relationship between the enumeration of sources in Article 38 and the rules of law designated *jus cogens*.

[7] G. G. Fitzmaurice, 'Some Problems Regarding the Formal Sources of International Law', in *Symbolae Verzijl* (The Hague: Nijhoff, 1958), 164. For a critical gloss on the semantics, see H. Thirlway, *International Customary Law and Codification* (Leiden: Sijthoff, 1972), 37–8. While Fitzmaurice does not give the rule such status, the approach resembles that of Kelsen, whose *Grundnorm*—the basic norm underlying all others—was the assumption by the subjects of law of what amounted to law in the society of which they are members.

that treaties must be observed.[8] Certainly the content of, let us say, a bilateral customs treaty, setting rates of duties and tariffs on various goods, does not look much like 'law'. Still less resemblance to 'law' may be seen in a treaty that lays down no absolute rules or requirements at all, but merely enunciates guidelines, principles, or shared aspirations towards which the parties intend to work together. Texts of this latter kind fall into one category of what is generally known as 'soft law', and are indeed regarded by some scholars as not constituting law at all; the problem will be examined in Chapter VII, where the various types of 'soft law' will be described.

At the other extreme, there are more and more examples in modern law of so-called 'lawmaking' treaties: multilateral conventions that lay down for the parties to them a whole regime, as for example the Geneva Conventions in the field of humanitarian law, the Genocide Convention, or the Vienna Convention on the Law of Treaties itself. The principle in each case is, however, the same: that the States' parties accept a commitment to certain behaviour that would not be legally required of them in the absence of the treaty. They may indeed by treaty vary or set aside the rules that general international law imposes on all States, though such variation or exclusion is only effective between the parties; and this power is subject to the limits imposed by *jus cogens*.[9] The traditional approach that treaties are sources of law is therefore recommended by logic and convenience.

A treaty, particularly a multilateral treaty, which is as such a direct source of law, may provide for the creation of further instruments (e.g. regulations affecting the implementation of the treaty), and the formal source of these is of course the main treaty. It may also provide for the creation of organs or other international bodies, as for example the United Nations Security Council and General Assembly, and these may be endowed, by the basic constitutional treaty, with powers to make decisions, or to issue regulatory documents. So far as the contents of such instruments, or of such decisions, are part of international law, their basis in terms of sources continues to be the original multilateral treaty. If they have a legally binding effect, it is the treaty ultimately that confers this; if they do not, they may be 'soft law' (discussed in Ch. VII), still on the basis of the original treaty. Even if non-binding, they

---

[8] Fitzmaurice, 'Some Problems Regarding the Formal Sources of International Law'; in the same sense, I. Brownlie, *Principles of Public International Law*, 7th edn. (Oxford: Oxford University Press, 2008), 513; distinguishing treaties creating legal obligations 'the observance of which [does or] does not dissolve the treaty obligation'; 'a treaty for the joint carrying out of a single enterprise is not lawmaking, since fulfilment of its objects will terminate the obligation'. For a different view, see M. Mendelson, 'Are Treaties Merely a Source of Obligation?', in W. E. Butler (ed), *Perestroika and International Law* (Dordrecht: Nijhoff, 1990).

[9] Discussed more fully in Ch. VII sect. 1.

may influence or contribute to the formation of customary law, in a manner to be discussed below.

In principle, the source of what is sometimes called 'international legislation' is simply an underlying multilateral treaty; by acceding to that treaty each State party has consented to every legitimate use of the powers of law-creation contemplated by the treaty; while this sometimes looks like signing a blank cheque, the situation fits without difficulty into the positivist theory of sources. However, the international scene has seen such a proliferation of organizations, sub-organizations, organs, subordinate organs, commissions, committees, etc., and such a welter of resolutions, decisions, directives, regulations, principles, guidelines, and similar lawmaking or apparently lawmaking instruments, that individual governments may be unable to discern at just what point consent to law-creation was given; and to any observer the pattern may look much more like legislative activity than the product of a meeting of minds and an informed consent embodied in a treaty.

In relation to our study of sources, the question is whether in respect of some of this international institutional furniture, and some of this mass of legislative or quasi-legislative material, it has ceased to be realistic to attribute the founding legal authority to 'treaties and conventions in force'; and if so, what other source can be found by way of foundation. Some scholars have regarded developments of this kind in international law over the last twenty years or so as 'constitutionalization', defined as 'an evolution from an international order based on some organizing principles such as State sovereignty, consensualism, non-use of force to an international legal order which acknowledges and has creatively appropriated principles and values of constitutionalism'.[10] There remains the question, by what process have these principles and values been appropriated and incorporated into the international legal system? The same writer suggests that '[j]us cogens norms can be said to operate as constitutional law because they establish a normative hierarchy based on material factors' and 'the "trumping effect" of peremptory norms over contrary "ordinary" law would indeed resemble the supremacy of a written constitution in a (national) legal order ...'.[11] This, of course, throws us back to the problem of the source of peremptory norms themselves.

---

[10] A. Peters, 'Are We Moving towards Constitutionalization of the World Community?', in A. Cassese (ed.), *Realizing Utopia: The Future of International Law* (Oxford: Oxford University Press, 2012), 119. See also J. Klabbers, A. Peters, and G. Ulfstein, *The Constitutionalization of International Law* (Oxford: Oxford University Press, 2009); A. Fischer-Lescano, 'Die Emergenz der Globalfassung', 63 Zeitschrift für ausländisches öffentliches Recht und Völkerrecht (2003), 717–60.

[11] Peters, 'Are We Moving towards Constitutionalization?', 123, conceding, however, that in principle such a trumping effect of *jus cogens* is 'doubtful and controversial'.

The Vienna Convention, as already noted, applies only to treaties and conventions concluded between States; and if we are guiding our study of the sources of international law by the light of the definitions expressed in Article 38 of the PCIJ/ICJ Statute, we should note that reference is made to treaties as defining 'rules recognized by the contesting States'.[12] Many agreements are however concluded between one or more States and an entity or entities that do not rank as such: do these also constitute sources of international law? The wording of Article 38, just quoted, is no bar to this: there is no apparent reason why two States in dispute should not together recognize the applicability of a text to which entities other than States are parties. In principle, it must surely be the case that a *pactum* is a *pactum*, and therefore must be respected and complied with by the parties to it, whatever their individual nature. When the PCIJ declared in the *Wimbledon* case that 'The right of entering into international engagements is an attribute of State sovereignty',[13] this did not imply that such a right cannot be exercised by any other body than a State.[14] The Vienna Convention will not itself apply to such an engagement, but customary law may do so; and it would be difficult to show in this respect any divergence between the treatment of an inter-State treaty in relations between one or more States non-parties to the VCLT (thus also customary)[15] and that of a treaty to which one or more parties are not States.

2. The limits of treaty-law: *jus cogens* and the relative effect of treaties

On this basis, any group of two or more States, or to some degree other entities, can create 'law'; are there limitations on this power? One such limitation is evident: that 'law' is created only for those who accept it, primarily the parties; this is the principle of the relative effect of treaties,[16] to be examined in a moment. But it has come to be recognized that there may be some areas of law in which it is not appropriate that States should be free to legislate as they will, even with such limited effect. More precisely, there are some

[12] The word 'contesting' limits the scope of the term to the parties before the Court, who are by definition States (Article 34 (1)).

[13] *PCIJ Series A, No. 1*, 25.

[14] In this sense T. Grant, 'Who can make treaties? Other subjects of international law', in D. B. Hollis (ed.) *The Oxford Guide to Treaties*, (Oxford University Press, 2012) 125.

[15] For a recent example, cf. the Memorandum of Understanding between Somalia and Kenya (both non-parties to the VCLT) in *Maritime Delimitation in the India Ocean* [2018] ICJ Rep 3, particularly p. 21, para. 42.

[16] See further Ch. VII.

principles or rules of international law of such overriding importance that, it is felt, compliance with them cannot be escaped nor non-compliance excused even by the consent of other States affected or potentially affected. A principle or rule of this kind is referred to as a 'peremptory norm', and is classified as *jus cogens* as distinguished from *jus dispositivum*, the latter being law that may be excluded or varied in the relations between two or more States by the simple consent of all concerned. The greater part of international law falls into this latter category. Article 53 of the Vienna Convention on the Law of Treaties offers the classic definition of a 'peremptory norm':

A treaty is void, if at the time of its conclusion, it conflicts with a peremptory norm of general international law. For the purposes of the present Convention, a peremptory norm of general international law is a norm accepted and recognized by the international community of States as a whole as a norm from which no derogation is permitted and which can be modified only by a subsequent norm of general international law having the same character.

The content of the category of *jus cogens* is, however, a hotly disputed issue, as is the operation of the concept; in Chapter VII we shall consider some points of this kind, in the context of the question whether rules of *jus cogens* derive from the regular sources of Article 38, or come into existence in some other way.

If it is axiomatic that a party to a treaty is committed to what has been agreed in the treaty, it is equally axiomatic that a State that is not a party to a treaty is under no such obligation. The principle *res inter alios acta nec nocet nec prodest*[17] is as valid as *pacta sunt servanda* and can in fact be regarded as a corollary of that principle. As the Vienna Convention on the Law of Treaties (Art. 34) expresses the point: 'A treaty does not create either obligations or rights for a third State without its consent.' The Vienna Convention being itself a treaty, its codifying provisions, even those that codify pre-existing customary law, are themselves only applicable *as treaty-law* to the States that have ratified it; but the same rule exists as a general principle.[18]

There are two apparent exceptions to this principle—but they are only apparent. First, the situation in which an obligation stated in a treaty is or becomes an obligation of general customary law (a process to be examined further), in which case the non-party State may be bound by the same substantive obligation, but as a matter of customary law, and not by the effect of

---

[17] 'No benefit is conferred, and no obligation imposed, by a transaction between third parties.'

[18] A more general study by Kolb concludes that the principles and rules judicially applied to the interpretation of treaties are standard for all treaties, and do not vary according to the subject-matter of the treaty: see R. Kolb, 'Is there a subject-matter ontology in interpretation of international legal norms?' in E. Madenas and E. Bjorge, *Farewell to Fragmentation: Reassurance and Convergence in International Law* (Cambridge: Cambridge University Press, 2015), 473–85.

the treaty. As already noted, this is in fact the case of the Vienna Convention on the Law of Treaties itself; its provisions have frequently been applied by the International Court, on the basis that such provisions state rules that apply to all States as customary law, to a State not party to the Convention.[19]

Secondly, it is possible for a State not a party to a treaty to accept an obligation defined in the treaty, or to derive a benefit from the treaty, if all States concerned—the parties to the treaty and the outsider State—are so agreed. In effect a new treaty is concluded extending the scope of the original treaty, or of certain identified provisions of it, to the third State.[20] A bilateral treaty may thus impose obligations upon, or create, or purport to create, rights for a third State. In accordance with the principle of consent, the consent of that State is, however, required just as much for the creation of a right as it would be for the imposition of an obligation. However, the Vienna Convention goes on to provide, reasonably enough, that the assent of the third State to the conferral of a right or benefit 'shall be presumed so long as the contrary is not indicated, unless the treaty otherwise provides'.[21]

The principle of the relative effect of treaties does not normally give rise to difficulties in practice, since the function of many treaties is to deal only with matters of interest to the parties, so that the potential impact on third States is limited, if not non-existent. An example of a context in which the principle does, however, acquire importance is in relation to delimitation of maritime areas over which coastal States may claim rights: territorial sea, continental shelf, and exclusive economic zone. In an area of sea surrounded on many sides by different States, such as the Caribbean for example, the ideal method for determining the areas over which each of them enjoy such rights would, of course, be a multilateral treaty, to which all coastal States of the region would be parties; but this seems rarely to prove possible. Bilateral treaties, between different pairs of States, may produce apparent overlaps; legally no such overlaps exist, by virtue of the principle that each treaty is *res inter alios acta* for non-parties, but there are, or may be, two or more conflicting views of the legal situation, held by different pairs (or even groups) of States.[22] Such a bilateral delimitation may also have been effected by judicial decision, as in the case of the ICJ decision between Nicaragua and Honduras,[23] which was

---

[19] For a recent example, see the ICJ decision in *Sovereign Rights and Maritime Space* [2016-I] ICJ Rep 19, para. 15.

[20] See Vienna Convention on the Law of Treaties, Arts. 35 and 36.

[21] Vienna Convention, Art. 36(1).

[22] For an early example, see the conflicting bilateral delimitations of the North Sea indicated on Map 2 attached to the ICJ Judgment in the *North Sea Continental Shelf* cases [1969] ICJ Rep 15.

[23] *Territorial and Maritime Dispute between Nicaragua and Honduras in the Caribbean Sea* [2007-II] ICJ Rep 659.

then an element to be taken into account in the subsequent proceedings be-tween Nicaragua and Colombia.[24] Like a treaty, a judicial or arbitral decision is *res inter alios acta*, and thus also without effect for non-parties (this will be considered further in Ch. V); in the context of, for example, maritime delimi-tation it therefore ranks no higher than a bilateral treaty.[25]

3. Commitment to the treaty-obligations

Article 38 of the ICJ Statute refers to 'treaties and conventions in force', thus excluding, logically enough, treaties that have not, or not yet, come into force, or which have ceased to be binding on the parties. The normal way in which a State becomes bound by the obligations provided for in a treaty is by becoming a party to it.[26] Where the treaty is a multilateral convention of the 'lawmaking' type, it has been suggested that a State could, simply by conduct, indicate its acceptance of the regime of the convention as applicable to itself. In the *North Sea Continental Shelf* case, the ICJ did not accept the argument of Denmark and the Netherlands that Germany, which had signed but not ratified the 1958 Geneva Convention on the Continental Shelf, had 'by con-duct, by public statements and proclamations, and in other ways ... unilat-erally assumed the obligations of the Convention'.[27] The Court rejected this contention on the facts of the case, but did not, however, absolutely rule out any possibility of such a process occurring.[28]

The question whether a particular provision of a treaty is 'in force' be-tween a particular pair of States is not simply a matter of checking that each

---

[24] See ICJ Press Release 2013/21 (17 September 2013).

[25] Though it seems that for the Court itself it may have a higher status; see further in Ch. V.

[26] This may involve internal legal processes leading to ratification, with which we are not here concerned; but note the comments of the ICJ on the interim situation, in its judgment on the *Territorial Dispute (Burkina Faso/Niger)* [2013] ICJ Rep, paras. 41–59; and on the possibilities of making ratification or mere signature sufficient, *Maritime Delimitation in the Pacific Ocean (Somalia v. Kenya)* [2018] ICJ Rep 3, at 23–4, paras. 47–9.

[27] *North Sea Continental Shelf* [1969] ICJ Rep 25, para. 27.

[28] The Court did, however, make it clear, first that 'only a very definite, very consistent course of conduct on the part of [the] State' could have the effect suggested, and secondly that there could be no question of a State being permitted to claim rights or benefits under a treaty 'on the basis of a declared willingness to be bound by it, or of conduct evincing acceptance of the conventional regime': *North Sea Continental Shelf* [1969] ICJ Rep 25, para. 28. Underlying the distinction is of course the question of the consent of the original parties: they may be presumed to have no objection to other States accepting the *obligations* of the Convention, but if other States are to enjoy *benefits* under it there must be positive consent of the original parties, as indeed the Vienna Convention requires. This point also was made by the ICJ in that case.

of them is named as a party,[29] and has signed[30] and ratified the treaty. A new State may be bound by certain treaties concluded by its predecessor, without a formal act of accession thereto, on the basis of State succession. The 1978 Vienna Convention on Succession of States in Respect of Treaties, which entered into force on 6 November 1996,[31] was intended to deal primarily with States emerging from colonization, and the extent to which its terms reflect current customary law is obscure,[32] particularly as most recent instances of the appearance of new States have been outside the colonial context.[33] In the special field of human rights treaties, it has been argued that the obligations arising from such a treaty are not affected by a succession of States, and that State practice supports this view.[34]

A further complication arises from the possibility of reservations. A reservation may be made by a party when signing or ratifying the treaty; it amounts to a unilateral modification of one or more terms of the treaty, desired by the reserving party. The Vienna Convention on the Law of Treaties indicates as follows the nature and effect of a reservation:

1. A reservation [by one party] established with regard to another party ...
    (a) modifies for the reserving State in its relations with that other party the provisions of the treaty to which the reservation relates to the extent of the reservation; and
    (b) modifies those same provisions to the same extent for that other party in its relations with the reserving State.
2. The reservation does not modify the provisions of the treaty for the other parties to the treaty *inter se*.[35]

[29] For an exceptional problem, see the case of the 1995 Interim Accord between Greece and the Former Yugoslav Republic of Macedonia (ILM 1995, p. 1497) which does not name either party; for explanation, see A. Aust, *Modern Treaty Law and Practice*, 2nd edn. (Cambridge: Cambridge University Press, 2000), 332 n. 1.

[30] Though the Vienna Convention on the Law of Treaties does not mention this as a requirement, and some instruments amounting to treaties are merely initialled: Aust, *Modern Treaty Law*, 24.

[31] UN Treaty Series vol. 1946, p. 3.

[32] The 1978 *Restatement (Third) of the Foreign Relations of the United States*, §210 (3), Reporter's Note 4, took the view that a successor State is not bound by its predecessor's treaties. On the other hand, the Arbitration Commission of the Conference on Yugoslavia has held that succession of States is 'governed by the principles of international law embodied in' (inter alia) the Vienna Convention: Opinion no. 9, 92 ILR 203.

[33] See P. Pazartsis, 'State Succession to Multilateral Treaties: Recent Developments', 3 Austrian Review of International and European Law (1998), 397.

[34] M. T. Kamminga, 'State Succession in Respect of Human Rights Treaties', 7 EJIL (1996), 469–84; for a more cautious view, M. N. Shaw, 'State Succession Revisited', 5 Finnish YIL (1994), 34 at 84.

[35] This text is generally accepted as representing the customary law on the subject. The view was at one time widely held that 'no reservation was valid unless it was accepted by all the contracting parties without exception, as would have been the case if it had been stated during the negotiations' (*Reservations to the Genocide Convention* [1951] ICJ Rep 21). This view was rejected by the ICJ in its

For one State party's reservation to be 'established' in relation to another State party, the latter must specifically have accepted the reservation or failed to object to it within twelve months of being notified of it.[36]

Reservations to bilateral treaties are uncommon, since it is to be supposed that between two parties all matters will have been settled in the course of the negotiation of the treaty, and that its text will represent what both States are prepared to accept.[37] In the case of a multilateral treaty, however, there may in effect be a number of parallel regimes operating between different pairs of States, depending on the extent to which any given State may have excluded certain provisions of the treaty by reservation, and the extent to which the reservation has been accepted (or more precisely, not objected to) by other State parties. Thus a single formal source—the treaty—may involve several different versions of its content, the material source, depending on the identity of the two States whose relations are under consideration.

Reservations imply a variation of the rights and obligations under the treaty; to secure this is, of course, their function. This has given rise to concern when States have sought to make their adhesion to multilateral conventions in the field of human rights subject to reservations, since it is of the essence of the rights protected by such conventions that they be universally and integrally recognized. A controversy that should be mentioned here arose from an attempt by the UN Human Rights Committee to regulate the matter and from two decisions of the European Court of Human Rights.

In these cases the Court gave decisions difficult to reconcile with the basic law of treaties, and this stand has received some endorsement from the UN Human Rights Committee. The specific issue was the validity of reservations to a multilateral convention, or more precisely the effect of invalidity. The established rules on the point derive ultimately from the ICJ advisory opinion in the case of *Reservations to the Genocide Convention* in 1951.[38] If objection is taken to a reservation made to a convention by another party, and *a fortiori* if such a reservation is invalid as contrary to the convention itself, the result is dictated by the principle that it is consent that makes treaty obligations. The reserving State does not become a party to the convention (and therefore able to invoke it) vis-à-vis the State or States objecting, or, in the case of an impermissible reservation, at all. Where the convention is one designed to further

---

advisory opinion in that case, and this paved the way for developments, in the ILC and elsewhere, leading to general recognition of the position stated in the Vienna Convention.

[36] Vienna Convention, Art. 20 (where appropriate, the 12-month time-limit may begin from the date on which the potentially objecting State consented to be bound by the treaty).

[37] In fact the matter is not quite so simple: see Aust, *Modern Treaty Law*, 106–7.

[38] *Reservations to the Convention on the Prevention and Punishment of the Crime of Genocide* [1951] ICJ Rep 15.

such a worthy purpose as human rights, the maximum participation of States is clearly desirable. It does not seem possible, in the light of the principle of consent, to insist in such a case that the reservation, being invalid, simply falls away, and the reserving State becomes a party to the convention on the same terms as if it had never made the objectionable reservation.

This, however, was what was decided by the European Court of Human Rights in 1988 in the case of *Bellilos* v. *Switzerland*;[39] and the same course was followed in 1995 in the case of *Loizidou* v. *Turkey*.[40] The UN Human Rights Committee in 1994 expressed its view as being in the same sense;[41] and more recently the Inter-American Court of Human Rights has followed the same line of reasoning.[42] The view of the UN Committee was tersely expressed:

Because of the special character of a human rights treaty, the compatibility of a reservation with the object and purpose of the Covenant must be established objectively, by reference to legal principles, and the Committee is particularly well placed to perform this task. The normal consequence of an unacceptable reservation is not that the Covenant will not be in effect at all for a reserving party. Rather, such a reservation will be severable, in the sense that the Covenant will be operative for the reserving party without benefit of the reservation.

The only justification for this ruling appears to be 'the special character of a human rights treaty', which apparently makes 'the object and purpose' thereof something analogous to *jus cogens*: attempt to contract out at your peril![43]

Must these decisions be treated as simply erroneous, despite the authority attaching to the institutions that handed them down? Or must they be regarded as examples of a divergence of general rules of international law, as they apply in the specific context of human rights, from such rules as they apply in all other fields?[44] Let us be clear as to relevance of the problem to the present study. It does not appear that the human rights tribunals, or the UN Committee, were purporting to draw their law from a source other than those generally recognized. They were in effect asserting that at least certain rules of treaty-law (that is, the rules relating to the effects of treaties) were subject

---

[39] ECHR (1988) Ser. A no. 132.

[40] ECHR (1995) Ser. A no. 310. Cf. also *Gradinger* v. *Austria* (1995) Ser. A no. 328-C.

[41] In a document with the magnificent title, garnished with initial capitals, of 'General Comment No. 24 on Issues Relating to Reservations Made upon Ratification or Accession to the Covenant or the Optional Protocols Thereto, or in Relation to Declarations under Article 41 of the Covenant'.

[42] *Benjamin* et al. v. *Trinidad and Tobago*, IACHR Ser. C no. 81 (1 September 2001); *Constantine* et al. v. *Trinidad and Tobago* Ser. C no. 82 (1 September 2001).

[43] It is interesting to compare this approach with that underlying Art. 53 of the Vienna Convention on the Law of Treaties, on treaties conflicting with peremptory norms.

[44] In this sense B. Conforti, 'The Specificity of Human Rights and International Law', in U. Fastenrath et al. (eds.), *From Bilateralism to Community Interest: Essays in Honour of Judge Bruno Simma* (Oxford: Oxford University Press, 2011), 433 at 434–6.

to exceptions where appropriate; and that in the context of reservations to human rights treaties, such an exception was justified. This might appear to be no more than a degree of variation within the effective law based on traditional sources.

In 1997, the International Law Commission (ILC) considered the question of 'Reservations to normative multilateral treaties including human rights treaties'. Its 'Preliminary Conclusions' were tactfully worded, recognizing the competence of monitoring bodies established under treaties of this kind to 'comment upon and express recommendation with regard to, *inter alia*, the admissibility of reservations by States'.[45] However it went on to make clear that 'in the event of inadmissibility of a reservation, it is the reserving State that has the responsibility for taking action',[46] that is it disapproved the 'severability' argument.

But what is at stake is no mere detail of the legal operation of treaties. To claim that—even exceptionally—a State may be bound by a convention in a form to which it has not assented, in fact in a form to which it has expressly made objection, cannot easily be reconciled with the basic idea of treaties as a source of law—that consent makes obligation, and non-consent signifies absence of obligation. From what source then does the exceptional *Bellilos* rule derive? While not putting the question in those terms, the ECHR and the UN Committee would no doubt respond: the interest of the international community in securing widespread recognition of rules fundamental to human dignity, and thus the fullest participation in conventions aimed at achieving this.[47] The *Loizidou* judgment indicated that the ECHR 'must bear in mind the special character of the Convention as an instrument of European public order ("*ordre public*") for the protection of individual human beings and its mission, as set out in Article 19 [of the Human Rights Convention] "to ensure the observance of the engagements undertaken by the High Contracting Parties" '.[48] The special character of the Convention, its 'object and purpose', could justifiably be invoked to support a particular interpretation of its text; but the question whether a

---

[45] *Yearbook of the ILC* (1997), ii. 57, para. 5.

[46] *Yearbook of the ILC* (1997), ii. 57, para. 10: such action might include 'the State's modifying its reservation so as to eliminate the inadmissibility, or withdrawing its reservation, or *forgoing becoming a party to the treaty*' (emphasis added).

[47] In passing be it noted that there is something of a contradiction in asserting, as some scholars do, that the contents of the International Covenant corresponds to customary law, and is therefore in any event binding on all; and yet seeking participation in conventions that, on that basis, add no fresh obligation.

[48] *Loizidou* v. *Turkey* (40/1993/435/514), para. 93.

particular State is or is not a party to it does not depend on the terms of the Convention (though these may be relevant as, for example, prescribing the procedure for accession to it), but upon general international law.[49] In short the contention must be that it is not only customary law, but also treaty-law, for which the law-creating process has somehow to be 'bent' to meet the demands of human rights thinking: views may differ as to the legitimacy of this in each case.

However, in 2011 the ILC produced a Guide to Practice on Reservations to Treaties, in which it stated the position as follows, in paragraph 4.5.3:

1. The status of the author of an invalid reservation in relation to a treaty depends on the intention expressed by the reserving State or international organization on whether it intends to be bound by the treaty without the benefit of the reservation or whether it considers that it is not bound by the treaty.
2. Unless the author of the invalid reservation has expressed a contrary intention or such an intention is otherwise established, it is considered a contracting State or a contracting organization without the benefit of the reservation.

This seems to represent a solution that respects, inter alia, the regular doctrine of sources.

The obligations imposed on a party by a treaty continue in principle to bind so long as the treaty has not been validly terminated (unless of course the treaty itself provides otherwise). Such termination will of course have to be consensual, either through the treaty itself providing for its own termination, unilaterally or otherwise, or because the parties at some stage decide to put an end to it. It may be that a forgotten treaty will lapse through what has been termed desuetude or obsolescence, but there is little practice in this respect. The matter has been raised several times before the ICJ with respect to the 1928 General Act for the Pacific Settlement of International Disputes, which had not been effectively implemented before it was replaced—or possibly supplemented—by a revised General Act in 1949. The 1928 Act was put forward by a party to it as basis of ICJ jurisdiction in three successive cases, but in each of them the Court was able to dispose of the case on other preliminary grounds, and did not therefore have to venture to rule on the issue

---

[49] In this sense Pellet and Müller, 'Reservations to Human Rights Treaties: Not an Absolute Evil ...', in Fastenrath et al. (eds.), *From Bilateralism to Community Interest*, 521 at 525. There is a curious argument in the *Loizidou* decision that Turkey, by depositing a declaration containing the reservation, was taking the risk that it might be ruled invalid, and 'should not now seek to impose the legal consequence of this risk on the Convention institutions' (para. 91). This argument assumes its conclusion, namely that the risk being run was that the reservation would be declared invalid *and severable*.

of whether the Act had ceased to be in force.[50] The ILC, when examining the law of treaties, considered that in circumstances of this kind the conduct of the parties to the treaty might be considered to show a shared intention to abandon it.[51] In addition to the complications of reservations, already mentioned, there is of course also the possibility that the State that is a party may cease to exist,[52] as in the case of the German Democratic Republic, but on these rare occasions arrangements are generally made for succession, ensuring continuity of treaty commitments, other than those which of their nature would only apply to the extinct party. In default of such arrangements, the provisions of the 1978 Vienna Convention for total or partial succession, as appropriate, may be applicable by analogy or as customary law.[53]

If some obligation under the treaty depends on an independent acceptance by a party, such an acceptance creates a separate special regime within the general treaty-relationship; this may of course terminate, or be denounced separately in accordance with its terms, and with the relevant provisions of the treaty itself. The evident example of this is Article 36, paragraph 2, of the ICJ Statute, whereby a State party to the Statute may make a declaration recognizing the jurisdiction of the Court as compulsory for legal disputes, either in general, or falling within one or more specified categories. The effect of this provision is to give rise to an 'inner circle' of States parties who have recognized such compulsory jurisdiction; their relations, and their rights and duties, *inter se*, are additional to those existing between all parties, including those that have not made such a declaration. As in the case of reservations, however, the varying terms of these acceptances result in the existence of a multiplicity of separate regimes, all within the overall treaty system.[54] Such declarations can in principle be amended or withdrawn without affecting the status as a party to the treaty itself.

---

[50] In the *Nuclear Tests* cases, the Court made the controversial finding that the claims no longer had any object, on the basis of France's unilateral commitment to cease atmospheric testing. In the case concerning *Trial of Pakistani Prisoners of War* the parties reached agreement and the case was removed from the list: [1973] ICJ Rep 347. In the *Aegean Sea Continental Shelf* case, the Court found that a reservation made by one party at the time of acceding to the Act would exclude the case before it from the Court's jurisdiction, so that 'a finding on the question whether the Act is or is not a convention in force today ceases to be essential for the Court's decision regarding its jurisdiction': [1978] ICJ Rep 17, para. 40.

[51] *Yearbook of the ILC* (1966), ii. 237.

[52] Compare the elegant drafting of the reported terms of subscription to a British publication: 'A subscription implies that this journal will be sent to the subscriber until one of the three expires.'

[53] Vienna Convention on Succession of States in Respect of Treaties, Art. 34.

[54] See Zimmermann et al. (eds.), *The Statute of the International Court of Justice*, 2nd edn. (Oxford: Oxford University Press, 2012), 676ff., paras. 68ff.; H. Thirlway, *The Law and Procedure of the International Court of Justice: 50 Years of Jurisprudence* (Oxford: Oxford University Press, 2013), i. 777ff.

4. Unilateral acts as inchoate treaties?

It will be convenient here to deal with what was mentioned earlier as having the appearance of constituting an additional source of international law, not mentioned in Article 38, paragraph 1 of the ICJ Statute: unilateral acts. There are certain categories of unilateral acts of States that have legal effect because there exists a rule of international law attributing specified results to their performance: for example, the act of ratification of a treaty is unilateral, but it produces the effect of being bound by the treaty; the making of a protest is unilateral, but has the effect of excluding acquiescence, or, in the context of international practice, even impeding the formation of a custom. These cases present no particular problem of analysis; but it is now recognized that in some circumstances a specific legal act by a State may lead to specific legal results that are not dictated in advance by a rule of law.[55] Mention has already been made of the example in the *Peru Chile* Delimitation case of an act with several States as parties which was, as it were, an 'almost-treaty', and subsequently became recognized by all parties as a 'real' one.[56] Here we are concerned with acts that are and continue to be purely unilateral in form and substance. If such acts are to be brought within the enumeration in Article 38, it is perhaps as a sub-division of 'treaties and conventions', or a special case akin to them. If a commitment as to specified future conduct is offered by a State, not repudiated by the offeree, and acted upon, can it be said that there is here an agreement, one that looks one-sided because it is concluded by one party silently, and that it is capable of having the same effects as an openly bilateral treaty? The (very limited) judicial authority in the field is however not entirely consistent with such an approach.

The inclusion of unilateral acts in the category of sources of obligation, and thus (in the absence of an attributable underlying source) as a possible source of law, is in fact based essentially on no more than the decisions of the International Court in the two *Nuclear Tests* cases, which are (so far as relevant) in identical terms,[57] and which have been mentioned, but not developed, in subsequent decisions.[58] The subject has subsequently been studied by the ILC, which in 2006 adopted a set of guiding

---

[55] See H. Thirlway, 'Concepts, Principles, Rules and Analogies: International and Municipal Legal Reasoning', 294 Recueil des cours (2002), 334 ff.

[56] *Maritime Delimitation between Peru and Chile*, [2014] ICJ Rep 3, discussed in Ch. I, p. 19.

[57] For a lengthy examination of the case in terms of a categorization of arguments as 'hard' or 'soft', see D. Kennedy, 'The Sources of International Law' (1987) 2 Am UJILP 45–57.

[58] *Frontier Dispute* [1986] ICJ Rep 573, para. 39: *Armed Activities on the Territory of the Congo (DRC v. Rwanda)* [2006] ICJ Rep 26–9, paras. 45–55.

principles;[59] these of course are not binding as they would be if incorporated in a convention, and their wording is clearly inspired by the *Nuclear Tests* decisions. Before the ILC principles are examined, those decisions should be recalled in some detail.

Australia and New Zealand each brought proceedings against France complaining of radioactive fall-out on their respective territories emanating from the French nuclear tests in the atmosphere at Mururoa. The principal jurisdictional title relied on was the General Act for the Pacific Settlement of International Disputes of 1928. On the level both of the jurisdictional issues and of the merits of the case, the problems presented to the Court were of the thorniest. The General Act was apparently still in force, but had been virtually forgotten as a jurisdictional basis, which is probably why France, which had taken care to attach to its acceptance of jurisdiction under the optional clause of the Court's Statute a reservation excluding 'activities connected with national defence', had not attached any comparable exclusion to its acceptance of the General Act.[60] There was some force in France's argument that the General Act was obsolete,[61] and could no longer be relied on; but to dismiss this contention and uphold jurisdiction would bring the Court face to face with the very contentious issue of the legality of atmospheric nuclear tests. Even twenty-two years later, when the Court was asked for an advisory opinion on the *Legality of the Threat or Use of Nuclear Weapons*, it found in effect that the law on that issue was still unsettled; and if the use of nuclear weapons could not be said to be unlawful, the testing of them was presumably also lawful.[62] There was in 1974 however a strong ground-swell of opinion opposed to the nuclear arm, and at the least the Court would be likely to be drawn into political storms.

When therefore the French Government announced—unilaterally, and purportedly without reference to the pending litigation—that it would not be carrying out any more tests in the atmosphere, but solely underground tests, this must have looked like a way for the Court to escape from a painful dilemma. The announcement was made outside the ICJ proceedings, in

[59] See the Report of the Working Group on the question, UN document A/CN.4/L/703, and the subsequent *Report of the ILC* A/61/10, 2006; the UN General Assembly 'took note of' these principles by resolution 61/34 of 4 December 2006.

[60] This was presumably either because it was overlooked, or—more probably—because this could strictly only be done by denunciation of the Act and re-accession, and there would be a six-month period before denunciation would become effective, during which proceedings might be instituted by any State whose attention had been drawn to the possibility by France's own action!

[61] See the discussion of possible lapse of treaties through obsolescence, at sect. 3, text and n. 43.

[62] Whether this was so if the testing produced harmful effects on another State's territory is, of course, another matter.

which France was taking no part, and after the two Applicant States had concluded their arguments; the cases were not withdrawn, but neither did the Applicants take any initiative to inform the Court, as they might have chosen to do, that the French concession made no difference, and that they maintained their claims.[63] If it could be argued that France had undertaken a binding legal obligation for the future to refrain from atmospheric testing (even if it continued to assert in principle its right to carry out such tests), and if that obligation was owed to the two Applicant States, then it could be said that the litigation had achieved its object, and there was no further need of a judgment.

But was there such a binding legal obligation? If the French change of policy had come about in the context of negotiations with the Applicants, and particularly if the Applicants had gone on record as saying that the change met their wishes, and satisfied them, then even in the absence of a formal discontinuance of the proceedings,[64] it could be said that there was no dispute still subsisting before the Court.[65] The attitude of Australia and New Zealand however remained officially—or at least procedurally—unknown, and the Court did not take any initiative to ask them to indicate it. The Court may well have suspected that, as became apparent after the judgment had been given, the Applicants' response to such an enquiry would have been that they did *not* find the French announcements sufficient to meet their claims.

The Court proceeded to give judgment to the effect that there was no longer any dispute before it, on the basis of the following finding.

It is well recognized that declarations made by way of unilateral acts, concerning legal or factual situations, may have the effect of creating legal obligations. Declarations of this kind may be, and often are, very specific. When it is the intention of the State making the declaration that it should become bound according to its terms, that intention confers on the declaration the character of a legal undertaking, the State being thenceforth legally required to follow a course of conduct consistent with the declaration. An undertaking of this kind, if given publicly, and with an intent to be bound, even though not made within the context of international negotiations, is binding. In these circumstances, nothing in the nature of a *quid pro quo* nor any subsequent acceptance of the declaration, nor even any reply or reaction from other

---

[63] The Australian Solicitor-General had towards the close of his argument invited the Court to indicate if there were any aspects of the question of the admissibility of the case that Australia had not dealt with: *ICJ Pleadings, Nuclear Tests*, i. 472. For the Court's unhelpful response, see i. 514.

[64] This is provided for in Arts. 88 (agreed discontinuance) and 89 (unilateral discontinuance) of the ICJ Rules of Court.

[65] An argument that has been deployed in a number of cases, but never yet accepted by the ICJ: see H. Thirlway, 'Quelques observations sur le concept de *dispute* (différend, contestation) dans la jurisprudence de la C.I.J.', in *Liber Amicorum Raymond Ranjeva* (Paris: Pedone, 2013). See also, however, *Frontier Dispute (Burkina Faso/Niger)* [2013] ICJ Rep, paras. 46–8.

States, is required for the declaration to take effect, since such a requirement would be inconsistent with the strictly unilateral nature of the juridical act by which the pronouncement by the State was made.[66]

The judgment was adopted by a majority, and four of the dissenting judges attached a powerful joint dissent.[67] However, only one, Judge de Castro, expressed doubts on the question of principle, whether a simple, unaccepted, statement of intent could give rise to a legal obligation; he pointed out that while there was 'not a world of difference between the expression of an intention to do or not do something in the future and a promise envisaged as a source of legal obligations ... the fact remains that not every statement of intent is a promise. There is a difference between a promise which gives rise to a moral obligation (even when reinforced by oath or word of honour) and a promise which legally binds the promiser. This distinction is universally prominent in municipal law and must be accorded even greater attention in international law.'[68]

He rejected the Court's view that nothing was required in exchange for the promise in order that it should be binding, and observed that in municipal law at least, for a promise to be legally binding, except for a few special cases, 'the law generally requires that there should be *a quid pro quo* from the beneficiary to the promiser'. Nothing of this kind had been shown or alleged in the case before the Court.

The finding quoted was therefore adopted without specific dissent, other than that of Judge de Castro, but in view of the terms of the joint separate opinion, it does not follow that it was regarded by all Members of the Court as correct. The initial declaration that this doctrine of unilateral acts 'is well recognized' is a skilful piece of camouflage, as there does not seem to be any clear precedent for a binding obligation to become established without *some* recognition or acceptance by the beneficiary, precisely what was lacking in the specific circumstances.

Nor has the case been followed in the subsequent jurisprudence of the Court itself or of other international tribunals, which is perhaps not surprising in view of the very unusual nature of the facts on which the decision was

---

[66] [1974] ICJ Rep 267, para. 42; 372, para. 46.

[67] Judges Onyeama, Dillard, Jiménez de Aréchaga, and Waldock: [1974] ICJ Rep 312 and 494. However, they did not choose to comment on the statement of principle cited, as their objections proceeded on the basis that, even if it were correct in principle, the statement actually made by the French Government did not mean that the Applicants had obtained all they were asking for. In particular, the dissenters disagreed with the Court's finding that what was being asked for was cessation of the tests, and the declaration also sought from the Court was no more than a means to this end.

[68] [1974] ICJ Rep 373–4.

based.[69] An attempt was subsequently made to rely on the concept of binding unilateral acts in the *Territorial Dispute* between Burkina Faso and Mali; when the determination of a frontier was entrusted to a Mediation Commission, the Malian Head of State was quoted as saying that his Government would accept the line so arrived at, even if it ran through his country's capital! The ICJ had little difficulty in rejecting this attempt to raise a mere *boutade* to the level of a commitment.[70] The ICJ had also briefly to refer to its *Nuclear Tests* statement when, in the *Armed Activities* case,[71] it was suggested that a rather vague indication by the Minister of Justice of Rwanda of an intention to withdraw reservations to human rights conventions amounted to a withdrawal of Rwanda's reservation to the Genocide Convention. This claim was, unsurprisingly, dismissed; it was unnecessary for the Court to consider the general question of the legal force of unilateral declarations, since it is well established that the making and withdrawal of reservations to a multilateral convention is a necessarily unilateral act recognized by the law of treaties, and its legal effect depends on the reaction of the other contracting States.

The consideration of the question embarked on in 1996 by the ILC was clearly desirable, since, as the Commission noted, 'it is important for States to be in a position to judge with reasonable certainty whether and to what extent their unilateral behaviour may legally bind them on the international plane'.[72] The Commission excluded from consideration a category, already noted, of 'unilateral acts ... formulated in the framework and on the basis of an express authorization under international law', mentioning as examples 'laws establishing the extent of the territorial sea, or reservations to treaties',[73]

---

[69] A further instalment of the story nevertheless occurred when New Zealand returned to the Court in 1995 in consequence of France's announced intention to carry out further nuclear tests in the South Pacific; these were not to be atmospheric tests, but New Zealand argued that the 1974 judgments had effectively applied to all tests causing any kind of fall-out. Those judgments had contained a unique clause providing that the Applicants could return to the Court 'if the basis of this Judgment were to be affected', with the implication that this would be so if France went back on the undertaking it had been found to have given. After some procedural convolutions, the Court rejected the request of New Zealand on the basis that the 1974 judgment 'dealt exclusively with atmospheric nuclear tests', so that the basis of that judgment had not been affected: [1995] ICJ Rep 306, para. 63.

[70] See the judgment at [1986] ICJ Rep 573–4, paras. 39–40; and the discussion in Thirlway, *The Law and Procedure of the International Court of Justice*, i. 18–19.

[71] *Armed Activities on the Territory of the Congo (New Application, 2002), DRC v. Rwanda* [2006] ICJ Rep 28, para. 50.

[72] ILC, *Report of the Working Group on Unilateral Acts of States*, A/CN.4/L.703, Introductory Note, para. 2. This is particularly relevant to States with a monist approach to the relationship between international and domestic law (including France: cf. E. Decaux, 'Déclarations et conventions en droit international', Cahiers du Conseil constitutionnel 21 (January 2007), 1): if a treaty is legally effective in the municipal sphere without the need for intervening legislation, and a unilateral declaration ranks as a treaty for this purpose, then it similarly has immediate internal effects.

[73] ILC Working Group Report, para. 3.

the effect of which was not in any doubt; they are also immaterial to the question of sources, since for each there is an established basis in one of the recognized sources. It noted the difficulty (inherent in the wording of the *Nuclear Tests* decisions) that 'in practice, it is often difficult to establish whether the legal effects stemming from the unilateral behaviour of a State are the consequence of the intent that it has expressed or depend on the expectations that its conduct has raised among other subjects of international law'.[74] The key principle identified by the Commission, and stated by it in terms closely following those of the *Nuclear Tests* decisions, was to the effect that

> Declarations publicly made and manifesting the will to be bound may have the effect of creating legal obligations. When the conditions for this are met, the binding character of such declarations is based on good faith; interested States may then take them into consideration and rely on them; such States are entitled to require that such obligations be respected.[75]

The conditions referred to were spelled out in a further set of principles: they relate to the factual circumstances, the capacity of the author of the statement, revocation, etc. The Commission, and its Working Group, had had some difficulty defining the terms of its mandate, which (as eventually adopted by consensus[76]) did not include any assessment of the status of unilateral acts as forming a possible independent source of international law.[77] In that respect, the Commission's Principles appear not to take the matter further than the original *Nuclear Tests* decisions.

A key point is that of withdrawal of a declaration: if the declaration alone creates an obligation, before or independently of any acceptance, does that mean that it cannot be withdrawn? In the *Nuclear Tests* cases, the Court made this a question of intention of the declarant State: the French statements 'cannot be interpreted as having been made in implicit reliance on an arbitrary power of reconsideration'.[78] The ILC picked up the use of the term 'arbitrary' and stated the rule as being that 'A unilateral declaration that has created legal obligations for the State making the declaration cannot be revoked arbitrarily', with an explanation of what might be considered

---

[74] ILC Working Group Report, 4th recital.
[75] ILC Working Group Report, Principle 1.   [76] See A/CN.L/646.
[77] The point was not completely lost sight of: in the debates in 2006, 'Some members remarked that the unilateral acts par excellence that ought to be examined, were autonomous acts qualifying as sources of international law and not as those stemming from a customary source' (A/60/10, 137, para. 316).
[78] [1974] ICJ Rep 270, para. 51; 475, para. 53.

as relevant to the 'arbitrariness' of a given revocation, namely the terms of the declaration, or subsequent events (reliance on the declaration by the addressee, or 'a fundamental change in circumstances').[79] This, however, does not take any further the question in what way and on what basis such a declaration 'has created legal obligations'; and the relevance of reliance on the declaration by the addressee supports the idea that we are here dealing with an incomplete contract (or treaty) rather than something essentially unilateral.

To return to the main question: if the 1974 judgments in these cases, and the ILC Principles reflecting them, accurately represent the state of international law,[80] does this involve recognition of a source of international law additional to those of Article 38 of the ICJ Statute? The Court did not express itself in those terms; but it was emphatic that what was involved was a legal obligation on the part of France, and it was careful to exclude any element of agreement that might have justified regarding that obligation as essentially treaty-based. Could it be said that there exists a rule of customary law to the effect that a unilateral promise, involving no counterparty or exchange of consents, gives rise to a legal obligation according its terms? This would seem a somewhat artificial construction, inviting the attentions of Occam's razor; no one would contend, it is suggested, that the obligation to comply with a treaty results from a customary rule, that *pacta sunt servanda* is a customary rule, and no more. But it would also be necessary to find some support for such a rule in the practice and *opinio juris* of States. One specialized field in which it has been argued that there is such practice is that of international investment law, where it has been suggested that 'the practice of states making unilateral undertakings within the frame of *national investment legislation*' is 'rather challenging for the theory of sources of international investment law'.[81] This suggestion will however be considered later, in the context of the relation generally of the theory of sources to that field of law.[82]

---

[79] Principle 10.

[80] Which is by no means universally accepted: see the opinion of Judge de Castro, already cited, and e.g. J. Salmon, 'Le droit international à l'epreuve au tournant du XXième siècle', Cours Euro-Méditerraneéens Bancaja (2002), vi. 37 at 70: 'Le raisonnement de la Cour n'est convaincant ni en droit, ni en fait.'

[81] M. M. Mbengue, 'National Legislation and Unilateral Acts of States', in T. Gazzini and E. de Brabandere, *International Investment Law: The Sources of Rights and Obligations* (Leiden: Nijhoff, 2012), 183 at 185 (italics original; fn. omitted).

[82] Ch. VIII sect. 4.

If then the decision in the *Nuclear Tests* cases is to be regarded as anything other than an anomaly, a judicial device to escape a politico-legal difficulty, it must perhaps be regarded as based on something analogous to *pacta sunt servanda*. There is much to be said for the view of Franck:

Intentionality, as the Court said, must be the test. But the intention cannot be determined solely by reference to the speakers' state of mind but must also take into account that of the listeners. A spokesman for state policy—like the President of France, who speaks with the solemn voice of 'acts of the French state,'—must be taken to intend the natural consequences of his words just as actors are assumed, in law, to intend the natural consequences of their acts. If a state speaks, through an ostensible agent, and the statement contains an express commitment to a course of future conduct by that state, it should not be necessary to inquire whether the state intends to be bound, but merely whether the states with an interest at stake could reasonably assume that the statement constituted a commitment.[83]

The present writer, concluding in 1989 a detailed study of the decisions, suggested that

the *Nuclear Tests* judgments may be said to have contributed to the corpus of international law the development of the idea of a unilateral *servandum*, a legally enforceable obligation assumed purely unilaterally. The use of the concept of 'good faith' as a peg on which to hang this development is perhaps unfortunate, since what is operative here is a more fundamental principle, allied to the philosophical basis of *pacta sunt servanda*. Furthermore, in order to apply the principle of the unilateral obligation to the particularly recalcitrant facts of the case, the Court had to state the principle in a dangerously wide formulation—excluding any need for any acceptance of the unilateral undertaking, or indeed any sort of two-way relationship, or any *cause* in the sense of Continental law.[84]

In other words, a *pactum*—an agreement—is necessarily *servandum*—something that has to be complied with, as Fitzmaurice emphasized, but something does not have to qualify as a *pactum* in order to have the quality of being *servandum*.[85]

---

[83] T. Franck, 'World Made Law: The Decision of the ICJ in the Nuclear Tests Cases', 69 AJIL (1975) 612, 616–17.

[84] H. Thirlway, 'The Law and Procedure of the International Court of Justice, 1960–1989', BYIL (1989) 16–17: reproduced in *The Law and Procedure of the Internal Court of Justice*, i. 16–17.

[85] The distinction made by Fitzmaurice, cited earlier (text and n. 7) between sources of law and sources of obligation might also be borne in mind. It is difficult to regard a major multilateral convention (the UN Convention on the Law of the Sea, for example) as anything other than a *law-creating* act; but a unilateral act of a State merely creates an obligation for that State, even if it may be addressed to several States, or the 'international community' (ILC Report, Principle 6).

Since the jurisprudential possibilities that the decisions appeared to open up have not subsequently been judicially explored, nor (so far as is known) relied on in international practice,[86] this may perhaps serve as sufficient explanation of the place of the decision in the structure of sources, without the need to postulate an additional source ranking with those generally recognized.

---

[86] The ILC did trace a number of international unilateral declarations that were recognized to be legally effective, but the circumstances surrounding them do not appear to cast further light on the basis for such effectiveness: the Truman Proclamation concerning the continental shelf (28 September 1945); Declaration by Egypt concerning the Suez Canal (24 April 1957); Declaration by the King of Jordan waiving claims to the West Bank Territories (31 July 1988); Statements by Switzerland concerning privileges and immunities of UN staff.

III

Custom as a Source of International Law

1. Introduction

It is debatable whether custom or treaty can claim to be the oldest form of international law. In human societies generally, custom ranking as something amounting to law can be traced back to preliterate societies, where indeed it was virtually the only form of law possible.[1] More relevant to our study is the fact that the relations between such an early society and other similar groups may have been by some form of agreement, but could not by definition be written instruments.[2] As observed earlier, it is probably a universal characteristic of human societies that many practices that have grown up to regulate day-to-day relationships imperceptibly acquire a status of inexorability: the way things have always been done becomes the way things *must* be done. It is certain at least that throughout the history of the various civilizations, custom has played a central role in defining mutually accepted rights and obligations. In the international sphere as in domestic legal systems, it is as well to bear in mind, first, that this is a form of development of law of which the outcomes are often not as 'tidy' as those that a far-seeing lawgiver might lay down;[3] and

---

[1] A note of caution, however: 'Preliterate peoples understood that a practice might be observed in a community, but still did not rise to the level of a binding and obligatory custom': D. J. Biederman, *Custom as a Source of Law* (Cambridge: Cambridge University Press, 2010), 12. The same dilemma faces international lawyers today. For the existence of a customary law of warfare in ancient India (around 200 BC), see N. Singh, 'Human Rights in India', in *International Law at the Time of its Codification (Mélanges Ago)* (Milan: Giuffrè, 1987), i. 527ff.

[2] See generally the treatment of 'Custom in Pre-literate Societies', in Biederman, *Custom as a Source of Law*, 3 ff.

[3] Here Mr. Justice Holmes' celebrated dictum has relevance: 'The life of the law has not been logic; it has been experience', in *The Common Law* (London: Macmillan, 1881), 1. He continued: 'The law embodies the story of a nation's development through many centuries, and it cannot be dealt with as if it contained only the axioms and corollaries of a book of mathematics.' Cf. the observation of the ILC Special Rapporteur: '[C]ustomary international law as a source of law inherently denies exact formulations': Fifth Report of the Special Rapporteur on Identification of Customary International Law, A/CN4/717, para. 20.

secondly it is the interests of the entities participating in the custom, and those alone, that shape the outcome—more on this later.[4]

In treating custom as a source of legal rules, international law thus does not deviate from the pattern discernible in municipal legal systems.[5] Historically, at the international level, once the authority of natural law, in the sense of what was given by God or imposed by the nature of an international society made up of independent princes, had weakened, it was natural to derive legal obligations from the legitimate expectations created in others by conduct. The precise nature and operation of the process have, however, always presented obscurities.

One approach is to regard all custom as a form of tacit agreement: States behave towards each other in given circumstances in certain ways, which are found acceptable, and thus tacitly assented to, first as a guide to future conduct and then, little by little, as legally determining future conduct.[6] The difficulty of this analysis is that if agreement makes customary law, absence of agreement justifies exemption from customary law. On that basis, a given rule would be binding only on those States that had participated in its development, and so shown their assent to the rule. Yet it is generally recognized that, subject to two exceptions to be indicated in sections 5 and 6, a rule of customary international law is binding on all States, whether or not they have participated in the practice from which it sprang. The problem has arisen in the case of new States: during the period of decolonization after the Second World War, some attempt was made by the newly independent States to argue that they began life with a clean slate so far as rules of customary law were concerned.[7] They claimed to be able to choose which established rules of law they would accept, and which they would reject. This view was not accepted by other States, and later quietly abandoned by its adherents. It was

---

[4] See below pp. 77–8.

[5] Many of the difficulties and debates concerning international customary law can be closely paralleled in the legal controversies of 13th to 14th-century Europe: see E. Kadens and E. A. Young, 'How Customary is Customary International Law?', 54 William & Mary LR (2013) 885–920. There was even a proposal, anticipating Bin Cheng (see n. 65), for a sort of 'instant custom' (Kadens and Young, 'How Customary?', 891)!; cf. also R.-J. Dupuy, 'Coutume sage et coutume sauvage', in *Mélanges offerts à Charles Rousseau* (Paris: Pedone, 1974), 75ff.

[6] For a parallel in a specialized international field, cf. Art. 9 of the Vienna Convention on Contracts for the International Sale of Goods, whereby the parties to such a contract are bound not only by the usages to which they have agreed, but also by usages 'of which the parties knew or ought to have known and which in international trade [are] widely known to, and regularly observed by, parties to contracts of the type involved in the particular trade concerned'.

[7] Cf. Separate opinion of Judge Ammoun in *Barcelona Traction, Light & Power Co. Ltd.* [1970] ICJ Rep 329–30. A similar claim was made by Russia during the Communist period, to have created a 'socialist international law' distinct from that of the capitalist West see G. Tunkin, 'Remarks on the Juridical Nature of Customary Norms of International Law', 49 Cal.LR (1961) 419 at 428.

probably realized that it could have been a two-edged sword; that most rules of general custom are such that a State which rejects one of them today in one dispute may find it needs to invoke the same rule in its favour tomorrow in a different dispute.

It is of course a natural progression from following a given practice for convenience, or because it is seen as 'fair' and appropriate, to regarding it as 'what we always do', and therefore required by convention, or by something more than convention—by law.

The evident problem is to determine when this stage has been reached; when is it appropriate to expect all participants in the society within which the custom has grown up, perhaps including some who have, for one reason or another, not participated in it, to abide by it even when, for those particular participants, or one of them, it is undesired.

Custom as a source of law in any society poses something of a philosophical problem, well expressed by Finnis:[8] how is it that 'an authoritative rule can emerge (i.e. begin to regulate a community) without being made by anyone with authority to make it, and even without the benefit of an authorised way of generating rules'; and in order to examine this problem, he selects the international community as the context in which it most frequently arises.[9] His analysis makes a number of carefully defined distinctions, and the following simplified summary may do it less than justice, but will perhaps serve to indicate its originality. The key element is the identification of the underlying adoption by the community of a meta-principle. The psychological element (the *opinio juris*[10]) involves two beliefs accepted by States: that in the relevant field of law, it is desirable that there be 'some determinate, common and stable pattern of conduct and corresponding authoritative rule'; and that a particular pattern, 'is (or would be, if generally adopted and acquiesced in)' appropriate for that purpose. Alongside these beliefs, States note, empirically, first that 'there is a widespread concurrence and acquiescence in this desirable pattern of conduct', and secondly that the *opinio juris* (as just defined) 'is widely subscribed to by States'. For these to add up to the existence or recognition of a customary rule, and for the beliefs comprised in the *opinio juris* (as defined) not to be baseless, or as Finnis puts

---

[8] J. Finnis, *Natural Law and Natural Rights* (Oxford: Clarendon, 1980).

[9] Finnis, *Natural Law*, 238–45. Note, however, the useful distinction of Louis Henkin: customary law is not made, is not created, but results from an accretion of practices: it is 'rooted not in the consent of States but in the consent of the system': L. Henkin, 'International Law: Politics, Values and Functions', 216 Recueil des cours (1989-IV) 54.

[10] Reference is here made to this concept as understood by Finnis; the significance of the term in general usage will be explored in sect. 2(c).

it, 'a complete *non-sequitur*', it must be recognized that there exists, accepted by States, this meta-principle:

The emergence and recognition of customary rules (by treating a certain degree of concurrence or acquiescence in a practice and a corresponding *opinio juris* as sufficient to create such a norm and to entitle that norm to recognition even by states not party to the practice or the *opinio juris*) is a desirable or appropriate method of solving interaction or co-ordination problems in the international community.[11]

Finnis concludes that 'the general authoritativeness of custom depends on the fact that custom-formation has been *adopted* in the international community as an appropriate method of rule-creation'.[12]

An important difference between customary law and law derived from treaties is that, as already observed, in principle customary law is applicable to all States without exception, while treaty-law is applicable as such only to the parties to the particular treaty. A State which relies in a dispute on a rule of treaty-law has to establish that the other party to the dispute is bound by the treaty; whereas if a claim is based on general customary law, it is in principle sufficient to establish that the rule exists in customary law, and there is no need to show that the other party has expressly accepted it, or participated in the practice from which the rule derives.[13] There are two exceptions to this. First, it is in principle possible for a State which does not accept a rule that is in the process of becoming standard international practice to make clear its opposition to it, in which case it will be exempted from the rule when it does become a rule of law, having the status of what is generally called a *persistent objector*: see section 5. Secondly, alongside general customary law there exist rules of *special* or *local* customary law (or in the more recent terminology of the ILC, *particular customary law*), which are applicable only within a defined group of States, and when a claim is based upon an asserted custom of this kind it is necessary to show that the respondent State had accepted the custom as one binding upon it by appropriate acts of practice indicating *opinio juris*: see section 6.[14]

---

[11] Finnis, *Natural Law*, 243.   [12] Finnis, *Natural Law*, 243–4.

[13] If the dispute is subjected to arbitration or judicial settlement, there is theoretically no need even to establish the existence of the rule; according to the principle *jura novit curia* (the court knows the law), no proof of general rules of law is required. However, in practice litigant States do endeavour to prove the existence of the rules of law on which they base their claims.

[14] Dealt with in the final Conclusion 16 of the ILC as 'whether regional, local or other'; not covered in the Report of a Committee of the ILA (see this chapter, text and n. 19) (in accordance with its mandate).

2. Constituent elements of custom

2(a) Two elements or one?

The first edition of this book took note of the work of the International Law Commission (ILC) on the 'Identification of Customary International Law', then in progress. That work has now been completed, in sixteen carefully worded 'Conclusions'.[15] As a convenient document of reference, these supersede, and with greater intrinsic authority, the 2000 Final Report of the Committee set up by the International Law Association (ILA) on the 'Formation of Customary (General) International Law', referred to in the previous edition of this book.[16] Nevertheless, as will appear, some of the observations made by that Committee, retain their usefulness alongside the later work of the Commission.

To some extent, therefore, the subject can be said to have been 'codified'; but this term should not be read too literally. The vehicle of the ILC's statements of the law employed, on its proposal, is a resolution of the General Assembly, primarily 'welcoming' them, annexing them to the resolution and bringing them to the attention of States and all who may be called upon to identify rules of customary international law.[17]. Such a resolution is of course not endowed by the Charter with binding force, or indeed any legal effect; nor does it, in itself, have the status of customary law, or of an element of it. In the *Nicaragua* v. *US* case, the International Court considered that an essential element of custom, '*opinio juris*[,] may, though with all due caution, be deduced from *the attitude of . . . States* towards certain General Assembly resolutions'[18]. Thus the 'code' of law concerning custom may in the future, if it finds general favour, itself acquire the force of custom; but that time is not yet.

The text of the ILC Conclusions is annotated in detail in the ILC Commentary upon it, read together with comments in the earlier Reports

---

[15] Even before final adoption, the impact of these was already being felt in municipal court jurisprudence: see the judgment of the UK Court of Appeal in *Freedom and Justice Party and Ors.*, [2018] WLR (D) 460, para. 18.

[16] The ILA does not have any official status of the kind possessed by the United Nations International Law Commission, but its membership is, and in particular the membership of this Committee was, such as to give the Report the weight of 'teachings of the most highly qualified publicist of the various nations', as contemplated by Art. 38 of the ICJ Statute.

[17] For the full details of the ILC's recommendations, see the decision taken by it at its 3444th meeting (6 August 2018); and for the General Assembly's action, resolution 73/203 of 20 December 2018 (A/RES/73/203).

[18] [1986] ICJ Rep 14, at 99–100, para.188.

of the ILC. Rather than reproducing the Conclusions *in toto,* it is proposed here to discuss the substance thereof in a more general way, referring to the Conclusions and supporting Reports when appropriate.[19]

The traditional criteria in international law for the recognition of a binding custom, endorsed in the ILC Conclusions, are stated in what is known as the 'two-element theory', which requires that there should have been sufficient practice (i.e. sufficient examples of consistent conduct in harmony with the alleged custom),[20] and that this should have been accompanied by, or be backed by, evidence of what is traditionally called *opinio juris* or *opinio juris sive necessitatis.*[21] An adequate translation of this term into English, in the light of its application in law, requires rather more words than the economical Latin: it signifies 'the view (or conviction) that what is involved is (or, perhaps, should be) required by the law, or by necessity'. A practice might have been followed consistently, and even for a lengthy period, but without any suggestion in any quarter that there was any obligation to do so; the stock example is that of the courtesies involved in diplomatic relations,[22] and in such case the *opinio juris* would be lacking, and one State could not suddenly insist that the custom be followed if another State chose to take a different course in a particular case.[23] Much ink has been spilt on the question whether the situation could not equally well, or better, be defined by a 'single-element theory', seeing these two aspects as facets of one and the same reality;[24] with both the

---

[19] The conclusions are set out in UN doc A/CN./L.908 and A/RES/73/203.

[20] The nature of *opinio juris* as underlying custom-creating practice is discussed further in sect. 2(c). A point that remains somewhat obscure is whether an international organization which engages in a potentially custom-creating practice must, if the practice is to be regarded as relevant, similarly be inspired by *opinio juris*, and if so, what form this might take. The ILC Conclusions limit custom-creating practice to States (Conclusion 4, para. 3), though ascribing certain possible effects to resolutions of international organizations (Conclusion 12). The question was raised, but not answered, by a Legal Adviser of Unesco, A. A. Yusuf, in the 2003 Geneva Colloquium on *La Pratique et le droit international* (Paris: Pedone, 2004), 255, who observed that what is more important is that the practice should be in conformity with the constitution of the organization. A similar problem is that of the practice of entities not universally recognized as States. Should the participation of e.g., 'South Ossetia', or 'Abkhazia', in a relevant practice be excluded for purposes of assessing the generality of the practice?

[21] I. Brownlie, *Principles of Public International Law,* 8th edn. (Oxford University Press, 2008) uses the expression *opinio juris et necessitatis,* thus 'and' rather than 'or', but it is not clear whether this is intended to indicate that the belief must be that the practice is both a matter of law and necessary in some way. Note the discussion of the possible effect of considerations of necessity at text and nn. 114, 115 below.

[22] See the passage from the *North Sea Continental Shelf, Judgment* [1969] ICJ Rep 44, para. 77, cited below, text and n. 104.

[23] 'A general practice that is accepted as law (opinio juris) is to be distinguished from mere usage or habit': ILC Conclusion 9 (2).

[24] A classic study is that of P. Haggenmacher, 'La doctrine des deux éléments du droit coutumier dans la pratique de la cour international', RGDIP (1986) 5, revivified and endorsed, under the

ILC and (as will be shown) the ICJ endorsing the 'two-element theory', we can afford to put aside its rival.[25]

The classic definition of the relationship between the practice and the *opinio* is to be found in the ICJ judgment in the *North Sea Continental Shelf* cases; the Court was discussing the process by which a treaty provision might generate a rule of customary law, but its analysis is applicable to custom-creation generally:

> Not only must the acts concerned amount to a settled practice, but they must also be such, or be carried out in such a way, as to be evidence of a belief that this practice is rendered obligatory by the existence of a rule of law requiring it. The need for such a belief, ie, the existence of a subjective element, is implicit in the very notion of the *opinio juris sive necessitatis*.[26]

There is some controversy over whether this statement of principle was in fact required to support the decision that the Court took in the case, since if this was not so the statement would in principle rank only as an *obiter dictum*.[27] However, it has been widely quoted as defining the classical position (both by those who support that position and by its opponents), and the Court has quoted it, and followed the same reasoning in subsequent decisions, so that its authority is indisputable.

Both constitutive elements evidently leave considerable room for differing assessments, and the whole definition is sometimes criticized as being circular. The evident questions that arise are, for example: how much is sufficient practice? How widespread must it have been? What is relevant practice, and what is not? How can sufficient *opinio juris* be shown? The ILC has now provided much guidance and authoritative direction toward the answers to these questions, but they will continue to be asked. The most direct evidence is, of course, what States have in fact done, and what they have themselves indicated as to their reasons for doing it—or not doing it. In the course of the history of international relations, on many issues the practice, in itself evidence of an *opinio*, has been so built up that no one seriously doubts the existence of numerous customary rules. They will often have been recorded

---

appellation of a 'legal fiction' by B. K. Schramm, *La fiction juridique et le juge: contribution à une autre herméneutique de la Cour international de justice* (Bruylant, 2018).

[25] The ICTY has also endorsed the two-element view in *Hadžihasanovich and Kabura, Case No.IT-01-47-T*, 15 March 2006.

[26] *North Sea Continental Shelf, Judgment* [1969] ICJ Rep 3, para. 77. See also *Continental Shelf (Libya/Malta), Judgment* [1985] ICJ Rep 13, para. 27; *Military and Paramilitary Activities in and against Nicaragua (Nicaragua v. United States of America)*, Merits, Judgment [1986] ICJ Rep 14, paras. 183 and 207.

[27] See in particular Haggenmacher (n. 23 above) at 101ff., para. 45; and Thirlway in *Max Planck Encyclopedia of International Procedural Law, s.v. 'Obiter dictum'* (in press).

and defined in scholarly writings or in judicial or arbitral decisions that, it will be recalled, are—in precisely this way—subsidiary sources of international law under Article 38, paragraph 1(*d*), of the ICJ Statute.[28] In more modern times, the increased use of multilateral conventions to define internationally accepted law means that such conventions may point to the existence of customary rules, which as such will be binding on States not parties to the relevant convention. Since however non-participation may signify opposition to the rule, this may sometimes be a delicate question. As the International Court expressed the matter in a dictum which it has found it appropriate to repeat in a subsequent decision:

It is of course axiomatic that the material of customary international law is to be looked for primarily in the actual practice and *opinio juris* of States, even though multilateral conventions may have an important role to play in recording and defining rules deriving from custom, or indeed in developing them.[29]

One thing that can be stated with certainty is that unanimity among all States is not a requirement, either in the sense that all States must have been shown to have participated in it, or in the sense that there is evidence that the *opinio*, the view that it is a binding custom, is held by all States. The ILC, in Conclusion 8, found that 'The relevant practice must be general, meaning that it must be sufficiently widespread and representative . . .'.

It is the general 'untidiness' of the apparent structure (or the lack of it) in customary law that has inspired a number of analyses that aim to replace the classic system of sources with a new and more rigorous analysis, or to reconsider the classic system in a more rigorous way; some of these will be surveyed in Chapter IX. Here it may just be noted that when a system has arisen (one can hardly say 'has been devised') to enable disputed issues to be debated and settled on the common-sense basis of what States usually do, and usually require of each other, it does not necessarily stand up well to analysis in terms of logical construction. When the scholar (analyst) asks, 'How does customary international law work?', the question raised is, in effect, 'How—on what theoretical basis—can a system of customary international law operate?', whereas the practitioner (and the judge) asks 'What does customary law indicate on this issue?'—with, of course, the possible corollary 'if anything'!

A further question to which the answer is not entirely clear is this: when it is sought to establish the existence of a rule of general customary law by

---

[28] See further in Chapter V.
[29] *Continental Shelf (Libya/Malta), Judgment*, I.C.J. Reports 1985, pp. 29–30, para. 27, quoted in *Jurisdictional Immunities of the State (Germany v. Italy, Greece intervening)* [2012] ICJ Rep 122–3 para. 55.

surveying the practice of States (and possibly of international organizations), whose practice, and whose *opinio juris*, is relevant to the enquiry? This is not a matter of level of authority, that is whether the findings of municipal courts are relevant, for example, but of identification of the participants in the practice and *opinio* at State level.[30] To take an obvious example, in the establishment of the law of maritime delimitation, States not possessing a coastline clearly cannot participate in the practice of delimitation, from which a customary rule might be built up; does it follow that they do not or cannot have an *opinio* on the subject? Since it is difficult to imagine circumstances in which the choice of delimitation method by two opposite or adjacent States would have any incidence on the interest of a landlocked neighbour, the point may appear to be of purely hypothetical interest. However, where the exclusion of some States from custom-creating practice is not based on a fact of nature of this kind, the problem is more practical.

The definition of *opinio juris* adopted in the ILC Conclusions throws light on the participants in the practice: it requires 'that the practice in question must be *undertaken* with a sense of legal right or obligation' (Conclusion 9 (1)). This links the definition of potential possessors of *opinio juris* with that of those engaged in the practice, from which it seems to follow that a State that, for whatever reason, cannot take part in the practice, cannot have a relevant *opinio* on the matter. However acts amounting to a practice may impinge on those unable to indulge in it themselves; thus the ILC, following the ICJ's decision in the *Military and Paramilitary Activities* case, explains that it is 'the States taking [the relevant] action [and] those in a position to react to it'[31] who are to be regarded as the participants in an *opinio juris*.

When the ICJ was asked for an advisory opinion on the *Legality of the Threat or Use of Nuclear Weapons*, it had to consider whether there was any rule of customary law either forbidding the use of such weapons, or expressly authorizing their use in some circumstances. The Court's finding was that there was, as yet, no 'customary rule specifically prohibiting the use of nuclear weapons as such',[32] and possibly (by implication) that there was also no rule specifically authorizing their use.[33] In reaching this conclusion, it considered international practice and the possible existence of an *opinio juris*. But whose *opinio juris* was to count? The majority of States in the world did not possess nuclear weapons, and therefore could neither choose to use them

---

[30] Cf. the problem, already mentioned, of entities not universally recognized as States, e.g. Abkhazia.

[31] [1986] ICJ Rep 14 at 109 and the ILC Report on the Work of the Seventieth Session, A/73/10, Commentary on Conclusion 3, para. 7.

[32] [1996-I] ICJ Rep, p. 255, para. 73.

[33] On this, cf. the views of Judge Simma in the *Kosovo* case, already mentioned.

nor consciously and deliberately refrain from using them. They might well have—indeed most of them did have—strong views to the effect that the use of such weapons was, or ought to be, illegal;[34] but did these views have any more weight than the view of a landlocked State as to the rules of maritime delimitation? Did they put those States in the category of being 'in a position to react' to the policy?

The Court's finding was not specific on this point, but was expressed in terms that are suggestive. Having noted the practice of deterrence, it continued: 'Furthermore, the Members of the international community are profoundly divided on the matter of whether non-recourse to nuclear weapons over the past fifty years constitutes the expression of an *opinio juris*. Under these circumstances the Court does not consider itself able to find that there is such an *opinio juris*.'[35] Rather curiously, the Court here does not raise and answer the question, 'Does the practice show the existence of *opinio juris*?' but rather the question, 'Do the members of the international community think that there is an *opinio juris*?' This is to raise the psychological element in custom from one level to another; more significantly, it suggests a divorce of *opinio juris* from practice, in the sense that the views of States that do not possess nuclear weapons become relevant, if not as *opinio juris*, then as *opinio* as to the existence thereof, a sort of *opinio opinionis juris*. The practice associated with this sort of *opinio* would presumably be opposing or supporting the freedom of the nuclear States to possess nuclear weapons; and the Court in fact examined resolutions of the General Assembly on the basis that such resolutions 'can, in certain circumstances, provide evidence important for establishing the existence of a rule or the emergence of an *opinio juris*'.[36]

Is this sufficient? Can a State that is, for whatever reason, debarred from taking part in the relevant practice nevertheless possess an *opinio* that is relevant when it comes to 'counting heads'? In the case of the law of maritime delimitation, landlocked States took part in the successive conferences on the law of the sea, and were not debarred from expressing a view as to offshore delimitation; but would those views be relevant as *opinio juris* for determining a customary rule on the matter? There is the evident difference between the two cases that the actual use of nuclear weapons would probably have very serious repercussions for many States not members of the nuclear 'club', and which might well be neutrals in the conflict in which such weapons were resorted

[34] There is a useful table of the voting by nuclear and non-nuclear States on General Assembly resolutions on nuclear disarmament in the dissenting opinion of Judge Oda in the *Legality of the Threat or Use of Nuclear Weapons* [1996-I] ICJ Rep 366–7.

[35] *Legality of the Threat or Use of Nuclear Weapons* [1996] ICJ Rep 254, para. 67.

[36] *Legality of the Threat or Use of Nuclear Weapons* [1996] ICJ Rep 254–5, para. 70, reflected in ILC Conclusion 12.

to.[37] The problem is also, and again, one of the nature of what is called '*opinio juris*': the anti-nuclear States in the General Assembly clearly believed that international law *should* outlaw nuclear weapons; but could they credibly assert a belief that it *did*, in the face of the retention of the weapons by all those in a position to do so?[38]

Whatever the merits of this approach expressed in the passage quoted (text and n. 32 above), it seems inconsistent with an examination of the significance of *inaction* on the part of the nuclear States. The Court seemed reluctant to uphold the simple contention that a negative practice, the non-use of nuclear weapons, does not support *opinio juris*, because it is far from being manifestly attributable to a belief in the unlawfulness of such use; it constitutes what has been termed an 'ambiguous omission'.

We have noted the landlocked States in maritime delimitation as an example of States who are, for physical reasons, specially excluded from particular kinds of custom-generating practice. May there also exist a category of States who are, for similar or other reasons, specially to be *included* in such practice, that is to say that such that the practice must comprise their participation? There is a category of States referred to by the ICJ as that of 'States specially affected'. In the *North Sea Continental Shelf* case, the Court was being asked to find that the equidistance method of maritime delimitation was a matter of customary law, either through 'widespread and representative participation' in the Continental Shelf Convention, or passage of time, and in each respect it emphasized that the participation would have to include 'that of States whose interests were specially affected'.[39] Since the Court did not find it necessary to determine whether there were any such States in that case, it gave no clue to what such 'special affecting' might involve; the point will be further considered.[40]

---

[37] For the legal relevance of this consideration, see the dissenting opinion of Judge Shahabuddeen, [1996-I] ICJ Rep 387–9 and 392ff.

[38] A different analysis that has been offered is, briefly stated, that not all general practices are in fact desired by States in general, and the *opinio juris* serves to distinguish those that are so desired, and therefore rank as custom. An example of such an undesired practice is the retention of nuclear weapons; all States (it is argued) would prefer that no State should possess them, but the well-known 'prisoner's dilemma' (see explanation in Ch. IX n. 15) operates to defeat this: see C. Dahlman, 'The Function of *Opinio Juris* in Customary International Law', 81 Nordic JIL (2012) 327–39. This is certainly consistent with the ICJ's finding that no *opinio juris* at present exists, either way, on the point: [1996-I] ICJ Rep 264, para. 67. The case of nuclear weapons (and of CO_2 emissions, also mentioned by Dahlman) may, however, be exceptional; in other cases, it may be much more difficult to show that those States whose acts constitute a general practice would much rather be refraining from it. A disturbing contemporary parallel is however that of activities contributing to global warming: cessation or modification of activities of this kind is desperately needed, but in view of their competitive commercial nature could, if unilateral, amount to economic suicide.

[39] *North Sea Continental Shelf*, [1969] ICJ Rep 42, para. 73; 43, para. 74.

[40] Below, text and n. 61.

Practice and *opinio juris* together supply the necessary information for it to be ascertained whether there exists a customary rule, but the role of each—practice and *opinio*—is not uniquely focused; they complement one another.

The two elements are thus so intertwined as concepts that they need to be studied together, or in tandem.[41] When a State acts (or refrains from acting) in a legally significant way, it is contributing both to the body of State practice[42] in the relevant field, and to the manifestations of *opinio juris*; yet the State (or those directing its acts) may well not be conscious of doing either. However, an attempt will be made to discuss them in two sections, each concentrating on one element without losing sight of the other.

2(b) State practice

(i) In general

At the outset, let us note a divergence to which attention has been called of late, between State practice as it actually happens, and State practice as reported, summarized, or assumed in academic discussion and (in particular) judicial decisions. The International Court in particular has been criticized for basing its conclusions as to the existence (or non-existence) or content of a rule of customary law less on actual events in the relations between States than on assumptions or deductive reasoning from postulates.[42] It has been pointed out by commentators that the Court's own reasoning on a question of custom does not always start with the raw material of practice, but is itself already at one remove from reality. This has been seen as a trend which results in the propagation of what has even been dubbed 'fake custom'.[43] One explanation, or justification, offered for this practice, so far as it is a practice, lies in the need for the ICJ to demonstrate impartiality, which might seem to be compromised by an examination, as a basis of a decision on custom, of the practice only of certain States.[44]

---

[41] This does not, however, justify the construction of a sort of 'custom calculus', whereby nsufficiencies in practice may be balanced against significant evidence of *opinio juris*, or vice versa. See F. L. Kirgis, Jr., 'Custom on a Sliding Scale', 81 AJIL (1987) 146, and the discussion in Ch. IX, sect. 2(b).

[42] See for example A. Roberts, 'The Theory and Reality of the Sources of International Law', in Evans (ed.) *International Law* 5th edn. (Oxford University Press, 2018) 106–7, 111.

[43] F. Tesón, 'Fake Custom', in Lepard (ed.), *Reexamining Customary International Law* (Cambridge, 2017) 86–110; but see the fuller and more nuanced analysis of S. Yee, 'Article 38 of the Statute and Applicable Law', Journal of International Dispute Settlement (2016) 472. Section 3, 479ff.

[44] See Petersen, 'The International Court of Justice and the Judicial Politic of Identifying Customary Law', 28 EJIL (2017) 157–86. On the question of the availability of information as to the practice of the 'weaker' States, see below, text and n.84. (States which avoid involvement in ICJ

More generally, it should be observed that it does not necessarily follow that a court that is economical in this way in its reasoning was unaware of, or chose to disregard, the unstated material. An academic thesis may set out *all* the case-law relevant to the subject, however extensive; a judge is expected to be more economical. Still less does it follow that the conclusion reached by the Court in an economically worded decision must then be unsound; and it is in any event the function of the judge to *interpret* the material before him into law.[45]

Since international law, including custom, regulates essentially the relationships between States, the practice that is relevant for establishing a rule of customary law is therefore the practice (action or inaction) of States in relation to each other; also capable of custom development is practice of States acting through international organizations composed of States constituting international actors.[46] This follows from the nature of the process whereby custom grows from action by one subject of law and the reaction of other subjects of law concerned: acceptance, rejection, or toleration. Conduct of what the ILC terms 'other actors' (individuals, corporations, etc.) does not contribute, 'but may be relevant when assessing the practice' that does so contribute (para. 3.)

Consequently, the practice of a State in relation to its own citizens, being a matter of 'domestic jurisdiction' within the meaning of Article 2(7) of the United Nations Charter, was, at one time, in principle without significance for the establishment of a customary rule.[47] This may appear to be inconsistent with the corpus of the modern law of human rights, which prescribes numerous limitations on the freedom of States in this domain. The matter will be examined in more detail,[48] but here it may be observed that human rights law has grown very largely through the adoption of wide-ranging

proceedings—e.g. by declining to accept optional jurisdiction—are thus, it might be said, missing an opportunity to influence the direction of customary law!)

[45] Cf. Venzke, *How Interpretation Makes International Law: On Semantic Change and Normative Twists* (Oxford University Press, 2012), 70–1; see also the discussion in *EJIL Talk*, http://www.ejiltalk.org/the-international-court-of-justice-and-customary-international-law-a-reply-to-stefan-talmon/.

[46] The ILC Conclusions express the point by defining relevant practice as being that 'of States as expressive or creative of rules of customary international law' (Conclusion 4, para. 1), then adding reference—'with the qualification [i]n certain cases'— to the contribution of international organizations (para. 2).

[47] The treatment of foreign nationals, in particular those resident or present in the State's territory, may give rise to a claim of diplomatic protection by the national State, and is thus very relevant to the development of customary law in this field.

[48] Cf. Simma, '*Der Einfluss der Menschenrechte auf das Völkerrecht*' in *International Law between Universalism and Fragmentation (Hafner Festschrift) (Brill 2009)*; and further in Ch. VIII, sect. 2.

international conventions, precisely because of the difficulty in establishing a practice-based customary law.[49] Since many of these conventions have been ratified by almost all States, and taking into account the moral authority of the principles that they embody, it is widely argued that the conventional provisions, or some of those principles, are binding also on non-parties, and one of the grounds for this contention is that there is, despite the theoretical problem just noted, a customary law of human rights.[50] The question remains controversial, though there are signs that many States recognize a compromise approach which is workable, even if it may be difficult to define legally.[51]

To be invoked as practice, an act has to be something the State has done, or is doing, in its capacity as a State (and not, for example, as an investor) the ILC Conclusions recognize as such any activity 'in the exercise of its executive, legislative, judicial or other functions' (Conclusion 5).[52] Furthermore, '[p]ractice may take a wide range of forms. It may include both physical and verbal acts as well as deliberate inaction' (Conclusion 6, para. 1). The key word with regard to *non*-action is 'deliberate', and it may not always be easy to distinguish masterful restraint leading to significant inaction from unconcern (or even bureaucratic ineptitude). After providing a catalogue of examples of relevant practice (see Conclusion 6, para. 2), the ILC indicates that 'There is no predetermined hierarchy among the various forms of practice' (para. 3). A single act by a single State could not serve in itself as sufficient evidence of State practice for purposes of establishment of a custom, nor would the consistent acts of a mere minority of States,[53] though in either case this result might follow if such act or acts were coupled with the acceptance of a number

---

[49] See generally on this, T. Meron, *Human Rights and Humanitarian Norms as Customary Law* (Oxford: Oxford University Press, 1989). The problem is of course not merely whether other States may legally object to actions by a State regarded as contrary to human rights, but also whether they will have any interest in doing so, and thus in carrying out acts creative of State practice; the situation is very different in the field of e.g. international trade.

[50] The controversy over customary human rights law also involves the problem of whether non-binding resolutions of international bodies, particularly the United Nations General Assembly, rank as State practice: on this see sect. 2(d).

[51] See M. Byers, *Custom, Power and the Power of Rules* (Cambridge: Cambridge University Press, 1999), 43–5.

[52] Decisions of national courts (the State acting in its 'judicial capacity'—see ILC Conclusion 5) may be relevant as acts of practice (see for example *Arrest Warrant of 11 April 2000* [2002] ICJ Rep 24, para. 58; *Jurisdictional Immunities of the State* [2012-I] ICJ Rep 131–5, paras. 72–4; and text and n. 85 below) but they may also be relevant as 'judicial decisions', and thus 'subsidiary' sources as contemplated by Article 38 (1) *(d)* of the ICJ Statute (cf. the ILC Secretariat 2016 Memorandum on the matter, A/CN.4/691, Observation 23).

[53] As roundly stated by Judge Abraham in *Obligation to Prosecute or Extradite* [2012-II] ICJ Rep 479, para. 36.

of other States affected by the act.[54] However, in principle the essence of a practice is that it involves consistent repetition, by a number of actors; international judicial decisions have spoken of a 'constant and uniform practice'.[55] This implies that a certain passage of time is required, though what matters is consistency in the way a particular matter is handled: the ILC concluded that 'Provided that the practice is general, no particular duration is required' (Conclusion 8, para. 2). If the issue to be resolved arises frequently, and is regulated in essentially the same way on each occasion, the time required may be short; if the issue arises only sporadically, it may take a longer time for consistency of handling to be observable.[56] (It has sometimes been argued that very long-standing practice alone may suffice to create custom, in the same way as a path is created by successive walkers adopting the same route, without regard to their state of mind (the *opinio juris*),[57] but this is a form of the 'single-element theory' rejected by the ILC.) It is in fact the consistency and repetition rather than the duration of the practice that carries the most weight. In the *North Sea Continental Shelf* case, the ICJ explained that

the passage of only a short period of time is not necessarily, or of itself, a bar to the formation of a new rule of customary law ... [yet] an indispensable requirement would be that within the period in question, short though it might be, State practice, including that of States whose interests are specially affected, should have been both extensive and virtually uniform ... and should moreover have occurred in such a way as to show a general recognition that a rule of law or legal obligation is involved.[58]

---

[54] The stock example is the launching of the first satellite, coupled with the lack of objection by other States to this infringement of traditional sovereignty *usque ad coelum*. ILC Conclusion 10 (3) observes that 'Failure to react over time to a practice may serve as acceptance as law (*opinio juris*) provided that States were in a position to react and the circumstances called for some reaction.'

[55] *Right of Passage over Indian Territory* [1960] ICJ Rep 40; *Advisory Opinion of the Arbitral Tribunal constituted in virtue of the Compromise signed at Rome on 30 June 1964 (USA/Italy)*, RSA xvi. 100.

[56] The point was well put by the Federal Republic of Germany in the *North Sea Continental Shelf* case: '[T]he shorter the length of time in which a rule of customary law is said to have been developed, the stricter are the requirements for consistency and uniformity of usage and for proof of an underlying legal conviction in support of this usage. It is not the length of time alone which is decisive, but rather ... whether or not during this time "specific usage", supported by legal conviction, can be proved': Memorial of Germany, *ICJ Pleadings, North Sea Continental Shelf*, i. 58. The ILC's assessment is that 'Provided the practice is general, no particular duration is required': Conclusion 8, para. 2.

[57] See the authors (and the poem!) cited by M. Kohen, '*La pratique et la théorie des sources du droit international*', in *Société française pour le droit international, La Pratique et le droit international, Colloque de Genéve* (Paris: Pedone, 2003), 82. For a similar poem, with a similar moral, from New England, see S. W. Foss in 32 Cornell Quarterly (1946) 137; *quoted in* R. E. Megarry, *Miscellany-at-Law* (London: Stevens, 1955), 285–7.

[58] [1969] ICJ Rep 43, para. 74. The Court was contemplating the particular case of a custom developing 'on the basis of what was originally a purely conventional rule' (Art. 6 of the 1957

It will be noted that the Court, dealing here with an alleged general practice, does not indicate as a requirement that the practice be universally, or even 'generally', followed: what that practice must also feature (as already noted) is the participation of States 'whose interests are specially affected', and it should be such as to show the existence of 'general recognition' that a rule of law is involved. The definition of 'general' offered by the ILC is that the practice 'must be sufficiently widespread and representative, as well as relatively uniform'.[59] The recognition is required to be general; but it may be based on, or treated as implied in, a practice that is less than general.

The concept of States 'specially affected' has provoked considerable controversy in recent years, sparked by the inclusion of that concept in the studies prepared by the ILC Special Rapporteur on the Identification of Customary International Law, who proposed, on the basis of international case-law and established doctrine, its mention in the draft conclusions of the Commission. Vociferous opposition by a number of States led ultimately to such mention being excluded from the draft Conclusions presented in 2018.[60] Essentially, the opposition was based on the belief that 'specially affected States' meant, or would be interpreted to mean, the more powerful States, those of the 'global North' as distinct from those of the 'global South', even though the historical source of the expression (the ICJ decision in *North Sea Continental Shelf*) was free of any such connotations.[61] However the concept remains available for

---

Geneva Convention on the Continental Shelf), but its statement is generally recognized not to be limited to that situation. The final phrase quoted refers of course to the requirement of *opinio juris*.

[59] Conclusion 8, para. 1.

[60] But a paragraph in the Commentary (Conclusion 8, para. 4) explains that 'in assessing generality [of practice], an indispensable factor to be taken into account is the extent to which those States that are particularly involved in the relevant activity or are most likely to be concerned with the alleged rule ("specially affected States") have participated in the practice. While in many cases all or virtually all States will be equally affected, it would clearly be impractical to determine, for example, the existence and content of a rule of customary international law relating to navigation in maritime zones without taking into account the practice of relevant coastal States and flag States, or the existence and content of a rule on foreign investment without evaluating the practice of the capital exporting States as well as that of the States in which investment is made. It should be made clear, however, that the term "specially affected States" should not be taken to refer to the relative power of States.'

Cf. also *Mondev International Ltd.* v. *USA* (ICSID Award, 11 Oct 2002).

[61] For a recent controversy around the concept, see the US Response to the ICRC Study on International Humanitarian Law (J. B. Bellinger, III and W. J. Haynes, II, 'A U.S. Government Response to the International Committee of the Red Cross Study Customary International Humanitarian Law', 89 Int'l Rev. Red Cross (2007) 443, 446); and the debate in the *AJIL* between K. J. Heller, 'Specially Affected States and the Formation of Custom', 112 AJIL (2018) 191, and S. A. Yeini, 'The Specially-Affecting States Doctrine', *ibid.* 244–253.

use in negotiation over the validity of a particular alleged customary rule, and may well be judicially re-endorsed in due course.[62]

A further indication as to the required generality and consistency of practice is given by the ICJ decision in the case of *Military and Paramilitary Activities in and against Nicaragua*. The Court observed that '[i]t is not to be expected that in the practice of States the application of the [customary] rules in question should have been perfect, in the sense that States should have [acted] with complete consistency . . .'. It went on to explain that it did not consider that,

for a rule to be established as customary, the corresponding practice must be in absolute rigorous conformity with the rule. In order to deduce the existence of customary rules, the Court deems it sufficient that the conduct of States should, in general, be consistent with such rules, and that instances of State conduct inconsistent with a given rule should generally have been treated as breaches of that rule, not as indications of the recognition of a new rule.[63]

While frequent repetition lends weight to a custom, the degree of frequency has to be weighed against the frequency with which the circumstances arise in which the action constituting practice has to be taken, or is appropriate. If the circumstances are such that they only present themselves from time to time, all that can be required is that the response to them has been, overall, consistent; and the fact that there have in sum been only a handful of instances is irrelevant. To take an extreme example: if in the case of the *United States Diplomatic and Consular Staff in Tehran* the Court had ruled that the United States' attempt to retake the Embassy by force was a legitimate response to its seizure by Iranian militants,[64] this would be a consecration of a practice occurring on only one occasion, and one that was, if not unique, highly uncommon; but the action, coupled with the reaction of other States to it, would nevertheless contribute to the corpus of international law.

In the view of most authors, and on the basis of ICJ jurisprudence, while the formation of a custom normally requires a more or less lengthy period

---

[62] A suggested (but questionable) interpretation of 'specially affected' in the context of humanitarian law would apply it to 'States that have contributed more practice than others because they have been involved more often in armed conflict', see Henckaerts and Debuf, 'The ICRC and Clarification of Customary International Humanitarian Law', in Lepard (ed.), *Reexamining Customary International Law* (CUP, 2017), Section 6.4.3, 183–4.

[63] [1986] ICJ Rep 98, para. 186. The Court does not specifically mention the possibility that the inconsistent conduct, while not being sufficiently consistent to add up to the 'recognition of a new rule', might still throw sufficient doubt on the existing rule for it to be regarded as obsolescent, if not obsolete. Unlike nature, customary law does not, it is suggested, abhor a vacuum.

[64] The Court had in fact no jurisdiction to rule on the point, but in its judgment it went as far as it could to condemn the United States' action: see [1980] ICJ Rep 43–4, paras. 93–4.

of development, the transition from 'regular practice not yet binding as a custom' to 'binding rule of customary law' is something that happens at a particular moment, and in that sense is instantaneous.[65] The word 'crystallization' is often used to refer to this decisive moment. It has, however, been suggested that the normativity of a rule *in statu nascendi* (coming to birth) could be a matter of degree: that its binding quality could 'harden', as it were, as time went by.[66] This may be conceivable, or even probable, as a matter of theory; but the function of law being to settle disputes, at any moment it ought to be possible to say whether a rule in course of formation does or does not exist as a binding rule. Relevant practice (together with *opinio juris*) in principle emerges from the clash of States' interests, and therefore does so particularly clearly when the interests on each side are in conflict. The essence of custom, in the traditional view, is that its provisions have been hammered out in the resolution of conflicts of interests, or disputes, between States in their day-to-day relations. As has been well observed by Simma and Alston: '[A]n element of interaction—in a broad sense—is intrinsic to, and essential to the kind of State practice leading to the formation of customary international law ... [T]he processes of customary international law can only be triggered, and continue working, in situations in which States interact, where they apportion or delimit in some tangible way.'[67] If a practice is equally convenient for both sides, its continuation does not involve any consultation by one party of the wishes of the other; and it is only when, for some reason, one of them prefers to act in another way, and the other objects, that the question of custom-forming practice arises.[68] This view is supported by the treatment by the International Court in the *Asylum* case of the question of the grant of safe-conduct for the beneficiary of the grant of asylum to leave the country. The Court recognized the existence of a practice whereby such a safe-conduct was regularly requested by the Embassy granting asylum, and usually granted

[65] This of course is a distinct question from the creation of 'instant customary law' associated with the famous study by Bin Cheng (mentioned in n. 5), suggesting that in some circumstances the long gestation period would be unnecessary: see B. Cheng, 'United Nations Resolutions on Outer Space: "Instant" International Customary Law?', 5 Indian Journal of International Law (1965) 23. For the theory of 'Grotian moments', periods of fundamental change, technological, in international relations, or otherwise, during which customary law may change much more rapidly, and with a less demanding requirement of State practice, than at other times, see M. P. Scharf, *Customary Law in Times of Fundamental Change* (Cambridge: Cambridge University Press, 2013).

[66] See F. L. Kirgis, 'Custom on a Sliding Scale', 80 AJIL (1987) 146; J. Tasioulas, 'In Defense of Relative Normativity: Communitarian Values and the Nicaragua Case', 16 Oxford Journal of Legal Studies (1996).

[67] 12 *Australian YIL* (1988–9) 82 at 99.

[68] A possible exception to this is where a custom is deduced from the successive practice of states in the adoption of treaties (normally bilateral) consistently containing a particular provision: see Subsection (ii).

by the receiving State. However, the Court pointed out that such a procedure suited both sides—the receiving State on the basis that it 'desires in a great number of cases that its political opponent who has obtained asylum should depart'—and held that '[t]his concordance of views suffices to explain the practice ... but this practice does not and cannot mean that the [receiving] State ... is legally bound to grant' safe-conduct.[69] This is clearly not an argument that may be pressed too far: it would be too much to ask that, for a practice to create a custom, at least one of the States involved should always be acting with reluctance, or against its own interests. What the Court had in mind was probably the question of the presence of *opinio juris*; as explained in the next section, this usually involves a belief that the practice under consideration is binding as a matter of law.

As already observed, the settled practice required to establish a rule of customary law does not need to be the practice of every single State of the world, as long as it is widespread and consistent.[70] Two special problems may however be mentioned: that of the divergence between States' assertion of the existence of a particular rule of customary law, and their practice inconsistent with it; and that of what we may call undemocratic custom.

Taking the first question, in the field of human rights law, for example, it is probably the case that the municipal law of practically every State of the world prohibits torture, and States are generally agreed, in theory, that there is a rule of international law forbidding it; yet there is no doubt that torture continues to be widely practised. Can a rule that flies in the face of consistent practice still be said to have existence as one of customary law? An observation of the International Court in the case of *Military and Paramilitary Activities in and against Nicaragua*, already quoted, is in point here. The Court observed that for the recognition of the existence of a customary rule, it is sufficient that 'the conduct of States should, in general, be consistent with such rules, and that instances of State conduct inconsistent with a given rule should generally have been treated as breaches of that rule, not as indications of recognition of a new rule'.[71] The Court was in fact dealing with customary rules forbidding the use of force or intervention; while the use of torture may be, and usually is, surreptitious, the use of force is in most cases very visible. If, however, instances of torture come to light, one may hope that neither the

---

[69] [1950] ICJ Rep 279 (a case involving a local custom: see this chapter, sect. 5(b)).

[70] For an example where this requirement was conspicuously not met, see the Asylum case: 'The facts brought to the knowledge of the Court disclose so much uncertainty and contradiction, so much fluctuation and discrepancy ... and the practice has been so much influenced by considerations of political expediency, that it is not possible to discern in all this any constant and uniform usage, accepted as law ...': [1950] ICJ Rep 277.

[71] *Military and Paramilitary Activities in and against Nicaragua* [1986] ICJ 98, para. 186.

State involved nor the international community is likely to suggest that it indicates 'recognition of a new rule'! In the case of the use of force, the tendency is to seek excuses, as for example that force was needed in self-defence; and on this the Court commented further:

> If a State acts in a way prima facie inconsistent with a recognized rule, but defends its conduct by appealing to exceptions or justifications contained within the rule itself, then whether or not the State's conduct is in fact justifiable on that basis, the significance of that attitude is to confirm rather than to weaken the rule.[72]

The Court here rules that conduct inconsistent with an existing rule is not necessarily an indication of the recognition, or even the emergence, of a new rule; but it does at the same time recognize that this is a way in which a new rule may be discerned. If it were not so, it is difficult to see how customary rules, once established, could ever change and develop to meet changing circumstances, or the developing needs of the international community and its members. Later in the same decision, discussing the principle of non-intervention, the Court observed that 'Reliance by a State on a novel right or an unprecedented exception to the principle might, if shared in principle by other States, tend toward a modification of customary international law.'[73] To anticipate for a moment our discussion of *opinio juris*, a paradoxical element in its workings is here emphasized: if a State decides to act in a way inconsistent with a recognized rule of custom, it will no doubt have good and sufficient reason for doing so, and perhaps even for thinking that its approach should be generalized—that the rule needs to be modified along lines that are consistent with its action. It will however, almost by definition, not be acting because it is convinced that there is already a new rule. The process by which customary rules change and develop thus presents theoretical difficulties; but it is a process which does occur. Customary law, in the traditional conception of it, is not a rigid and unchangeable system, though it is sometimes criticized as being such.

Where is practice, or rather evidence of practice, to be found? In the context of the ILC study on Identification of Customary International Law, a valuable Memorandum was prepared by the UN Secretariat on: 'Ways and means for making the evidence of customary international law more readily available'[74], which goes a good way to answer this question. In many States official or semi-official digests are regularly published summarizing the practice

---

[72] *Ibid.*

[73] *Military and Paramilitary Activities in and against Nicaragua* [1986] ICJ 98, para. 207 Compare the attempt of Italy to establish a modification of the customary rules on State immunity, in the case of *Questions concerning Jurisdictional Immunities of the State* (this chapter, text and n. 128).

[74] A/CN.4/710.

of the State, classified under various appropriate headings.[75] To the extent that the events and positions recorded involve other States (as by definition most of them do) these give a valuable snapshot of elements of practice; when the context is customary law, they are also valuable as indicating what the State concerned regards as relevant and significant as practice. Decisions of international tribunals, particularly the ICJ, on disputed questions of customary law are similarly significant as showing not merely what the Court finds to be the relevant customary rule, but also what it regards as the practice supporting it, and thus the kind of practice that may contribute to custom-formation. For a number of years now, however, there have been fewer decisions available that furnish materials of this kind: so much customary law has been, or is in the process of being, codified by multilateral conventions that the judge no longer has to ascertain from the practice what the alleged rule requires; he merely considers whether the rule, as conveniently defined by the convention, is or is not binding on the respondent State.[76] In theory this question too requires a study of the practice of non-parties, but this tends to be dispensed with; the 'pull' of the conventional provision creates, it seems, something of a presumption in favour of the rule's having customary force, however lacking in logic that may appear.[77]

Turning to the second problem mentioned above, the concept of custom suggests that its rules emerge from the interaction of all States, all sovereign and equal, contributing to its establishment by their action or their reaction (or lack of it): a democratic means of arriving at rules applicable, and acceptable, to all. Even today, this is not necessarily an accurate picture, and that it has been less so in the past is notorious. Certain States have at all times been more powerful and influential, and have been able either to control the practice to

---

[75] See e.g. the 'United Kingdom Materials on International Law' in the *British Yearbook of International Law*; the survey of 'Contemporary Practice of the United States Relating to International Law' in the American Journal of International Law; the annual summary of 'Völkerrechtliche Praxis der Bundesrepublik Deutschland' in the *Zeitschrift für ausländisches öffentliches Recht und Völkerrecht*; etc. A wider view is implied by the title of the 'Chronique des faits internationaux' in the *Revue générale de droit international public*.

[76] Where the convention text corresponds with a previous custom, the correspondence may, for various reasons, not be exact, but unless the difference tends to be disregarded unless it is marked, and relied on in argument.

[77] A striking example is to be found in the recent ICJ Judgment in the *Territorial and Maritime Dispute between Nicaragua and Colombia*: a disputed question was whether an island composed solely of coral debris was an 'island' for purposes of maritime delimitation. The Court rejected Nicaragua's argument that it was not, on the ground that '[i]nternational law defines an island by reference to whether it is "naturally formed" and whether it is above water at high tide, not by reference to its geological composition' ([2012] ICJ Rep 645, para. 37), without mentioning that the quoted words are taken from Art. 121, para. 1, of the United Nations Convention on the Law of the Sea, which was not, as a convention, in force between the parties to the case.

be noted as relevant to custom, or to dominate the prevailing *opinio*, so as to influence what becomes established as 'international custom': custom is not necessarily democratic.[78] It has been suggested that the practice hitherto invoked to support the assertion of the existence of a customary rule, has been too limited, being confined to the practice of a certain category of States, and neglecting that of the remainder.[79] But is the fact of bias due the influence of powerful States necessarily a reason for challenging what is law, essentially merely because the observer would have preferred it to be otherwise? A customary norm is, of its nature, not a rule devised by and for an ideal community; it was devised by and for an actual community, and necessarily took into account (inter alia) the power relations within that community.[80]

The relevant distinction between States is sometimes defined in terms of 'strong/weak', but a key element is also whether the practice of the State comes to the attention of the international community, in particular through its recording in the publications of, or within, the State itself.[81] The contention is that this leads to an unbalanced picture of what the *general* international practice comprises, thus distorting the consequent vision of the law (and, incidentally, conflicting with the principle of sovereign equality of States). There is justice in this criticism, but it is perhaps over-simple. State practice is normally bilateral (at least): if action by a State does not have any impact on its fellows, this is probably because it is within its sovereignty, or at any rate is of no particular significance for the development of the law. If there is contact—not to say conflict—between an 'invisible' State and a 'visible' State, the outcome (which is what matters for custom-development) will become visible in the publications of the 'visible' State.[82] What may remain invisible is the contention of the 'losing' side in the controversy (which will not necessarily be the 'invisible' State), but if it was put forward to no avail it does not

---

[78] See, for example, J. P. Kelly, 'Customary International Law in Historical Context: the Exercise of Power without General Acceptance', in B. D. Lepard (ed.), *Reexamining Customary International Law* (CUP, 2017), 47ff.

[79] B. S. Chimni, 'Customary International Law: A Third World Perspective', 112 AJIL (2018) 1, at 21ff. For a fuller and more nuanced study of TWAIL (Third World Approaches to International Law), see A. Bianchi, *International Law Theories* (Oxford University Press, 2016), Chapter 10.

[80] Can, or should, the relevance of the practice of States be 'weighted' according its extent or nature? In the field of air law, for the purpose of custom-development, it has been suggested that such a 'sliding scale' should be applied according to the extent of the activity of the carriers of each State: see S. Michaelides-Mateou, 'Customary International Law in Aviation', in B. Lepard (ed.), *Reexamining Customary International* Law (CUP, 2017), 309, 314, who rejects the suggestion.

[81] As the ILC observed. 'In order to contribute to the formation and identification of rules of customary international law, practice must be known to other States (whether or not it is publicly available)': Commentary to Conclusion 5, para. (5).

[82] If the dispute remains unresolved, it may still appear in publications of the 'visible' State, with the argument of the 'invisible' State necessarily referred to as explanatory of the dispute.

generate 'practice'. It is only in the relations between two (or more) 'invisible' States that significant practice might develop, yet remain out of view.

An indication of the significance in this respect of municipal court decisions was given in the recent case of the *Jurisdictional Immunities of the State*. It has, of course, only limited application as a general statement, being one directed to the particular kind of customary rule contended for, namely the duty of State authorities, particularly domestic courts, to respect recognized immunities:

> State practice of particular significance is to be found in the judgments of national courts faced with the question whether a foreign State is immune, the legislation of those States which have enacted statutes dealing with immunity, the claims to immunity advanced by States before foreign courts and the statements made by States, first in the course of the extensive study of the subject by the International Law Commission and then in the context of the adoption of the United Nations Convention.[83]

With regard to practice, what matters is not merely what is done, but— perhaps more importantly—why it is done. One possible reason is of course the existence of *opinio juris*, but if the existence of another reason sufficient in itself, is shown, then the act may be an element of practice, but *opinio juris* will not be present.[84] If *opinio juris* is present, since it is a state of mind, there is an evident difficulty in attributing it to an entity such as a State; and it thus has to be deduced from the State's pronouncements and actions, particularly the actions alleged to constitute the 'practice' element of the custom. It has already been emphasized that State practice is (at least) two-sided; one State asserts a right, either explicitly or by acting in a way that impliedly constitutes such an assertion, and the State or States affected by the claim then react either by objecting or by refraining from objection.[85] The practice on the two sides adds up to imply a customary rule, supporting the claim if no protest is made, or excluding or weakening the claim if there is a protest. The accumulation of instances of the one kind or the other constitutes the overall practice required for establishment of a customary rule.

(ii) *The relevance of treaties*

An act that in normal circumstances is essentially bilateral or multilateral is the conclusion of a treaty, or accession to an existing multilateral

---

[83] *Jurisdictional Immunities of the State* [2012] ICJ Rep 122–3, para. 55.

[84] Cf. the analysis of Judge Abraham in *Obligation to Prosecute or Extradite*, cited in n. 54 above.

[85] As the present writer has suggested elsewhere, 'Claims may be made in the widest of general terms, but the occasion of an act of State practice contributing to the formation of custom must always be some specific dispute or potential dispute': *International Customary Law and Codification*.

treaty. In what circumstances might an act of this kind also be legally relevant as an act of State practice contributing to, or confirming, the formation of a customary rule? The ILC, in Conclusion 6 first included as State practice 'conduct in connection with treaties', a wide expression which clearly may include the negotiation, adoption, ratification, and implementation of a treaty, but would also include less formal action.[86] In Conclusion 11, the ILC considered the matter *ex post*, by indicating the significance of a treaty already in existence, for the determination of customary law: this might be by way of codification or crystallization of pre-existing custom, or its generation, by way of giving rise 'to a general practice that is accepted as law (*opinio juris*) thus generating a new rule of customary international law'.

In the case of a bilateral treaty that forms one of a pattern of treaties concluded by various States in similar or identical terms, there is an evident ambiguity. On the one hand, States are indicating by their actions that a certain rule, which they are imposing upon themselves by the treaties, would be generally desirable; or even that it exists but should be explicitly backed by a treaty commitment. On the other hand, they may also be taken to be implying the opposite, that however desirable the rule might be, *because* it is not yet a customary rule, if they want it to apply to their relations they will need to incorporate it in a treaty.[87] Or again, at some point the true interpretation (if that expression means anything in the context) of the situation may at some point have to flip over from 'no customary rule yet discernible' to 'accumulation of practice confirms the existence of a customary rule'.

In Conclusion 11, paragraph 2, the ILC stated that 'The fact that a rule is set forth in a number of treaties may, but does not necessarily, indicate that the treaty rule reflects a rule of customary international law.' The ILA Committee on the Formation of Customary Law had come to a similar conclusion in

---

[86] There is a teasing theoretical problem here: normally, practice in relation to custom-formation is doing something that is capable of being required by a rule. What exactly is the State indicating by its act in relation to a treaty? The treaty requires it do *X*; if the State already thought that it was required by a customary rule to do *X*, why the treaty? Can a State be required not merely to do *X*, but to enter into a treaty to do *X*? D'Amato suggested that the act of entering into a treaty should be taken into account as an act of State practice because a treaty is 'a binding commitment to act': A. d'Amato, 'Treaty-based Rules of Custom', in *International Law Anthology* (Cincinnati: Anderson, 1994); but there seems no reason why this element should be essential for the act to constitute practice.

[87] An example is the speciality rule in extradition treaties (the rule that a person extradited may only be prosecuted in the requesting State for the offence for which extradition was granted). This is 'incorporated in almost every treaty and statute' even though it is 'considered as a rule of general international law' (T. Stein, 'Extradition', in Zimmermann et al. (eds.), *Max Planck Encyclopedia of International Law* (Oxford: Oxford University Press, 2012), iii. 1061 (para. 19)).

1985,[88] and the ICJ decision in the *Diallo* case (cited by the ILC)[89] was to the same effect. The ILC Committee had excluded the possibility in the case of extradition treaties, but recognized the possibility in connection with bilateral investment treaties. Maritime delimitation agreements also suggest themselves in this context, but as noted elsewhere,[90] it is striking that the International Court, in its successive decisions on maritime delimitation, has not drawn any conclusions from similarities in the various agreements of this nature drawn to its attention. As regards State practice, there is some trace of a consistency, that might suggest growth of a regional custom, in maritime delimitations concluded between States of Latin America,[91] but even for a regional custom, the small number of States involved, and the absence of evidence of *opinio juris*, rather militate against such a conclusion. A more promising example may be that advanced by Brownlie, of the provisions for the nationality of populations in treaties involving succession of States, from the Versailles Treaty onward.[92]

2(c) The *opinio juris*

At the outset, we may note that the question whether a given practice is accompanied by the required *opinio juris* may sometimes be resolved quite simply by showing that the practice is, in the case of some or most of the States engaged in it, demonstrably to be attributed to a different motive, or may have been regarded by those States as *justifiable* under international law, but not *required* by it.[93]

A frequent objection taken to the classical doctrine that custom derives from accumulation of practice accompanied by appropriate *opinio juris* is

---

[88] International Law Association, Final Report of the Committee on Formation of Customary (General) International Law, Pt. IV(B), p. 48, para. 25, responding to, in particular, the contention that certain provisions in bilateral investment protection treaties, 'especially the arrangements about compensation or damages for expropriation', have come to constitute customary international law.

[89] *Ahmadou Sadio Diallo (Republic of Guinea* v. *Democratic Republic of the Congo), Preliminary Objections* [2007] ICJ Rep 582, at 615, para. 90.

[90] H. Thirlway, *The Law and Procedure of the International Court* (Oxford: Oxford University Press, 2013), ii. 1196.

[91] In this sense H. I. Llanos Mardones, *The Delimitation of Maritime Areas between Adjacent States in the Southeastern Pacific Region*, Thesis, Graduate Institute of International Studies, Geneva, 195ff. This work was drawn to my attention by Professor Yoshifumi Tanaka, who also doubts the existence of a custom of this kind (personal communication).

[92] See I. Brownlie, *Principles of Public International Law*, 7th edn. (Oxford University Press, 2008), 655–6.

[93] See the observations of Judge Abraham in his separate opinion in *Obligation to Prosecute or Extradite* [2013-II] ICJ Rep 479, paras. 37 and 38.

addressed to the theoretical situation accompanying the initial establishment of a custom, or its early stages. States or other international actors, it is said, must behave in a particular way in order to conform to, and in the belief that they are conforming to, an established practice amounting to a general custom; but how can that be so before the practice has come into existence? The fact that other States are behaving in the same way may inspire the appropriate belief, but a practice has to begin somewhere. Although one swallow proverbially does not make a summer, it is recognized that to show the appropriate practice of one State may be sufficient to establish a general custom to do so, if backed by a more widespread *opinio*; but how can that State then be acting in the belief that it is conforming to an existing custom, and how can that *opinio* be held, if that custom does not yet exist? Or must we say that the *erroneous* belief that there is an established practice is sufficient to contribute to bringing that practice into existence? But in that case what of inconsistent practice? If two States at more or less the same moment, and in similar circumstances, are faced with the decision whether to do *X* or *Y*, and the one does *X* because it believes (wrongly) that there is an established practice of so doing, amounting to a custom, and the other does *Y* in the (correct) belief that there is no such practice, why should the one practice prevail over the other?

A first question is the nature of the subjective element itself. The ILA Committee already mentioned observed, in its 2000 Report, that 'the subjective element means, for some, *consent or will* that something be a rule of customary law, and for others a *belief* that it is a rule'.[94] This distinction clearly has implications for the chronological question: one may consent or will that something be a rule, while recognizing that, at the time of the act of consent or will, it is not yet so; but a belief that something is a rule is either a correct belief or an erroneous one. The ILC, however, defined *opinio juris* in relation to practice, as signifying 'that the practice in question must be undertaken with a sense of legal right or obligation',[95] that is *existing* right or obligation, not a future or desirable one—but existing in the mind of the State performing the act or practice, in other words, a belief. There is no requirement that the belief, at the time that it comes to be held, correspond to the then existing legal situation. Thus an act done in the conviction that it is legally required (or legally justified), at a time when it could be shown that no such requirement or justification yet exists in customary law, is nonetheless an act of State practice accompanied by *opinio juris*. The ILC Rapporteur would

---

[94] ILA, Final Report, Pt. III, p. 30, para. 3.   [95] Conclusion 9 (1).

have found the expression 'accepted as law', as used in the ICJ Statute (Article 38 (1) *(b)*), preferable for precisely this reason.[96]

Mention has already been made of the study carried out by a Committee of the ILA in 1985; though in most ways superseded by the work of the ILC, it contains some interesting reflections in the domain of legal logic, or philosophy of law. It made extensive use of the logical distinction between a necessary condition and a sufficient condition.[97] In particular, the distinction appears as part of the Committee's conclusions on the formation of customary law, where it is argued that:[98]

if the existence of a belief that there is such-and-such a rule of customary international law is not proved, that of itself does not disprove the existence of that rule; it may still exist, even if the belief in it has not been demonstrated by proof (not a necessary condition). But if it *is* shown that the belief exists, then this proves the existence of the rule (a sufficient condition). The recourse to logical terminology does not, however, seem to ease matters for the decision-maker: if not satisfied that the belief has been shown to exist, how can a judge (for example) uphold the existence of the customary rule? Logically the possibility that it exists cannot be denied; yet surely he must rule against it, on the basis of a sort of *Not proven* verdict.[99] There is, of course, another possibility: that the existence of the belief that the rule exists as one of customary law can be *disproved*: this would be so if it could be shown that in all cases that might otherwise be treated as examples of practice supporting the rule, there was a belief that the practice was *not* required by custom, but was one of 'courtesy, convenience, or tradition'.

Problems arise as soon as one tries to use these essentially negative requirements in a positive way, as a question of degree. If there is *no* practice, then there is no customary rule; if there is some, but not much, is there a rule? If States do not regard a practice as required by a legal rule, there is no customary rule; if some States regard, or have come to regard, the matter as one of rules, when does this become sufficient for a rule of law to 'crystallize'? The

---

[96] See the ILC Second Report on Identification of Customary International Law, A/CN.4/672, para. 68.

[97] 1. A condition A is said to be necessary for a condition B, if (and only if) the falsity (/nonexistence/non-occurrence) [as the case may be] of A guarantees (or brings about) the falsity (/nonexistence/non-occurrence) of B.2. A condition A is said to be sufficient for a condition B, if (and only if) the truth (/existence/occurrence) [as the case may be] of A guarantees (or brings about) the truth (/existence/occurrence) of B.

[98] ILA, Final Report, Pt. III, p. 38, para. 18, italics original.

[99] Elsewhere in the Committee's report the point is put slightly differently: 'The view has already been expressed in this Statement that the subjective element is not in fact usually a necessary ingredient in the formation of customary international law ...' (Part III, p. 40, para. 19(a)). Here it is not the demonstration of a subjective element that is sufficient but not necessary, but (apparently) the existence of that element. The context suggests, however, that this is merely an inadvertent curtailing of the stated requirement.

two conclusions cited are therefore perfectly coherent *as far as they go*, even if in practice they are not always easy to apply.

However the ILA Committee went further than this; apparently still basing itself on the distinction between a sufficient condition and a necessary condition, it took the view that, 'where practice exists which satisfies the conditions [specified in the Report], it is not necessary to prove the existence of an *opinio juris*'.[100] This leaves somewhat obscure the exact role of the *opinio*: is it a component part of the custom-creating process, but one that can, in certain circumstances, be *presumed* to exist; or is it an optional extra, so that custom would be created by practice (of an appropriate kind) alone? Or is it that the practice, *as defined by the ILA*, is practice accompanied by belief, that is incorporating *opinio juris*, so that it is the presence or absence of *opinio* in the minds of *other* States that is irrelevant.

Where the Committee did recognize the role of an *opinio* is where the circumstances of the practice relied on are those referred to above as amounting to *disproof* of a customary rule: where they are such as to suggest that the parties concerned were acting in the belief, or with the intention, that the acts performed should not constitute a precedent or contribute to a practice capable of being generalized into customary law. As the ICJ observed in a classic dictum in the *North Sea* case,

[To establish a custom,] [n]ot only must the acts concerned amount to a settled practice, but they must also be such, or carried out in such a way, as to be evidence of a belief that this practice is rendered obligatory by the existence of a rule requiring it . .The frequency, or even habitual character of the acts is not enough. There are many international acts, e.g., in the field of ceremonial and protocol, which are performed almost invariably, but are motivated only by considerations of courtesy, convenience, or tradition, and not by any sense of legal duty'.[101]

This is what the Committee refers to, neatly enough, as 'a sort of *opinio non juris*'.[102] The same view was of course taken (without recourse to that term) by the ILC.[103]

---

[100] ILA, Final Report, Pt. III, p. 31, para. 4. Similarly, the Report continues, 'If it can be shown that States generally believe that a pattern of conduct fulfilling the conditions [stated later in the Report] is permitted or (as the case may be) required by the law, this is sufficient for it to be law; but it is not necessary to prove the existence of such a belief'. What then is the distinction between 'it can be shown that . . .' and proving the existence of the same situation?

[101] [1969] ICJ Rep 44, para. 77.

[102] ILA, Final Report, Pt. III, p. 35, sub para. 17(i). It devotes a lengthy section (sect. 17) to the different scenarios in which this is the conclusion to be drawn.

[103] See Commentary to Conclusion 9, paras. 2 and 3, citing the *Asylum* case, [1950] ICJ Rep 266, at 277 and 286. What matters is the view of the States concerned in the transaction that is under examination (by a court or otherwise): if they act, react, or refrain from reacting 'with a sense of legal right or obligation', then the transaction may count for the formation or identification of a

An example of this is where the act in question was required of the State performing it by its treaty obligations. In the same *North Sea* case, the ICJ considered whether the delimitation rules in the Geneva Convention on the Continental Shelf might have entered customary law through State practice subsequent to the adoption of the Convention. For this purpose, it excluded from consideration the delimitation practice not merely of those States who were parties to the Convention—since their compliance with it revealed nothing indicating their views as to the possible customary status of its provisions—but also those who became parties to the Convention shortly after an act of delimitation that might otherwise have shown *opinio juris*. In the Court's view, '[f]rom their action no inference could legitimately be drawn as to the existence of a rule of customary international law'.[104]

A decision of the ICJ subsequent to the Committee's Report contains a classic example of practice that falls into this category contemplated in the *North Sea Continental Shelf* decision. In the case concerning *Jurisdictional Immunities of the State*, Italy was arguing for a qualification of the immunity recognized for States in respect of acts *jure imperii*, and relied on alleged practice in support. The Court observed:

While it may be true that States sometimes decide to accord an immunity more extensive than that required by international law, for present purposes, the point is that the grant of immunity in such a case is not accompanied by the requisite *opinio juris* and therefore sheds no light upon the issue currently under consideration by the Court.[105]

Various suggestions have been made to get round the chronological difficulty. It has been argued, for example, that, as a matter of philosophy of law, the

---

rule of customary international law, even if it is the first, or only, one of its kind (the generality will or may come later).

[104] [1969] ICJ Rep 43, para. 76. The implication is thus that there are two sorts of *opinio juris*: the view that the State is bound by a treaty to act in a certain way, and the view that it is so bound by a customary rule. This idea is vigorously rejected by Abi-Saab: 'il n'y a pas deux types de sentiment d'obligation juridique, l'un généré par voie de coutume, l'autre par voie de traité: soit on a la conviction d'être juridiquement obligé soit on ne l'a pas': 'Cours general de droit international public', 207 *Recueil des cours* (1987), 200. This, however, is in the context of the question whether widespread participation in a convention can generate customary law binding on non-parties. A rather startling view is that taken by Judge Cançado Trindade in the *Nuclear Disarmament* cases: the conclusion of a series of international conventions banning certain weapons, coupled with the failure of attempts to secure a similar convention banning nuclear weapons, implied that the latter weapons were illegal under customary international law: see his Dissenting Opinion in *Nuclear Arms and Disarmament (Marshall Islands* v. *United Kingdom)* [2016] ICJ Rep 937, paras. 74–75. A more sober conclusion would be to read the pattern as clearly signifying a negative *opinio juris*, in the sense that banning weapons was something that could only be achieved by treaty, i.e. that customary law was, at most, neutral on the matter.

[105] [2012] ICJ Rep 122–3, para. 55.

'so-called chronological paradox rests on two confusions, the first regarding the process whereby a customary rule comes to exist, and the second regarding the process whereby that customary rule becomes law'.[106] According to this view, 'the evolution of a new customary rule does not require that the agents'—that is, those persons in the State apparatus whose action involves the potential rule—'believe *truly* that they are subject to the rule prior to their actually being bound by it ... the rule-guided judgment regarding the legal validity of a customary norm is conceptually distinct from the process whereby that customary norm comes to exist'.[107] However, this seems to be based on a somewhat obscure distinction between 'the actors whose conduct and beliefs give rise to the existence of a customary rule, and the vast majority of the officials in the international legal system whose adherence to the rule of recognition leads them to deem some of those rules legally valid'.[108]

Furthermore, for the lawyer it is difficult to grasp the nature of a 'customary norm' that does not (yet) possess legal force. That force validity must be acquired at a moment in time that is theoretically determinable, even if it is factually unascertainable: at that moment it is impossible to apply a 'rule of recognition' that depends on a (correct) belief that the legal validity already exists. What the argument seems to amount to is to say that States may recognize that a consistent practice has come into existence (stage 1) and later that that consistent practice has hardened into a rule of law, that is to say has become binding (stage 2). The riddle remains, however, as to how this transition occurs: if for it to occur requires the presence of a *justified* belief that it has already occurred, it can in fact never occur. The problem is not solved by being dressed up in philosophical language, it is merely rephrased or displaced.

It is, of course, normal that at one moment a practice may exist that is not regarded as involving a binding customary rule, and at some subsequent moment it may be generally considered to be such a rule. In practice this is something that is noted retrospectively, usually in the context of a dispute: one State asserts that there is a custom, the other concedes this, perhaps after first arguing the contrary; or a tribunal decides that a customary rule, contested by one party, does indeed exist. To this extent the chronological

---

[106] D. Lefkowitz, 'The Sources of International Law: Some Philosophical Reflections', in S. Besson and J. Tamioulas (eds.), *The Philosophy of International Law* (Oxford University Press, 2010), 187–203 at 202.

[107] Lefkowitz, n. 106 above. The picture is complicated by the fact that, as the author recognizes, 'states have historically comprised both the actors whose conduct and beliefs give rise to the existence of a customary rule and the vast majority of officials in the international legal system whose adherence to the rule of recognition leads them to deem some of those rules legally valid' (p. 203).

[108] Lefkowitz, n. 106 above, 203.

problem, whatever its validity as a philosophical conundrum, does not pose a direct difficulty.

To what extent must *opinio juris* be identically based among different actors? It has been suggested that if there is a 'convergence of beliefs' that a particular norm exists, but that these beliefs are based on different grounds (regarded as 'substantively just' or on the basis of an authoritative declaration etc.), this is not 'rule-guided'. There must be more than an agreement that an act in violation of the norm is illegal; there must be 'a shared understanding of what makes [the] customary norm legally valid'.[109] This may perhaps be too fine a distinction. It would not seem to split possible *opinio juris* into more than two categories: the view that the rule *is* law, and the view that the rule *should be* law.

The controversy over whether the *opinio* required is essentially a belief that the customary rule exists, that is an opinion as to a matter of fact (or mixed fact and law), or may include a belief or conviction that such a rule *ought to* exist leads on to the wider question of the role—if any—of moral or ethical considerations in the development of customary law. An initial distinction is required: considerations of equity, or at least of fairness, *as between States actors*, can be traced in the earliest international law. There has always been an element of 'do as you would be done by' in international relations, as is indeed likely to be the case within any society, even one of a comparatively primitive degree of organization. Whether we should be right in attributing this, in the inter-State context, to something of a customary-law nature, is less certain; as will be explained in Chapter IV, considerations of this kind may more appropriately be attributed, in terms of Article 38 of the ICJ Statute, to the 'general principles of law'. It is noteworthy that the areas in which the strongest case can be made for the relevance of ethical considerations are those relating to human rights and to humanitarian law, that is those in which natural persons—human beings—are involved directly. It is worth considering whether the more traditional areas of international law, involving pure State-to-State relations, had no room for ethical issues: that *par in par non habet imperium* had the corollary that *par in parem non habet misericordiam*, that there was no need for either party to need the protection of considerations of conscience!

The ILC Conclusions, and the Commentary on these, leave no room for considerations of what *ought* to be the law, on the basis of ethical or moral considerations; they concentrate, as already noted, simply on what States

---

[109] Lefkowitz, n. 106 above, 200.

believe to be already required by customary international law. Academic support for ethics or morality to enter the equation has probably become more widespread, but it existed when the Special Rapporteur was preparing his text, and was noted, but apparently not regarded as significant.[110]

Although the standard expression is *opinio juris sive necessitatis*, it is almost always quoted as *opinio juris*; and this fact has its own significance. What is generally regarded as required is the existence of an *opinio* as to the law, that the law is, or is becoming, such as to require or authorize a given action. But the phrase in its entirety signifies that it is or may be sufficient if there is an *opinio* to the effect that the action (or refraining from it, as the case may be) is required as being, in some sense, necessary. The possible application of this view was illustrated at the time of the interventions in the situation in Kosovo, examined in particular in the columns of the *European Journal of International Law*.[111] The question there discussed was whether a new customary rule might be in the process of formation, namely—subject to certain stringent conditions—a rule legitimizing the use of forcible countermeasures by groups of states in the event of failure by the UN Security Council to respond to egregious violations of international humanitarian law. The author considered first whether States, while recognizing a moral and political necessity to act,[112] consider also that there is a crystallizing legal rule authorizing action (and concludes that this is not so), and secondly whether the *opinio* as to the necessity of action suffices. On this, he concluded that, though the *opinio* is widespread, a contrary view is held by other States, and that a rule of humanitarian law is not established on these grounds. The interest of the study is, however, to indicate the importance that may attach to the mention of *necessitas*, long disregarded;[113] this is, however, an avenue that has subsequently remained unexplored.

---

[110] See the Second Report on Identification of Customary International Law, A.CN.4/672. para. 66, pp. 46–7 and fn. 210.

[111] See A. Cassese, 10 EJIL (1999) 23 and 791.

[112] Or even taking the view that to act would, if not 'legal', be in some sense 'legitimate' on ethical grounds, and that such legitimacy is in itself sufficient justification: on this, see J. Klabbers, 'Normative Pluralism: an Exploration', in J. Klabbers and T. Piiparinen (eds.), *Normative Pluralism and International Law* (Cambridge: Cambridge University Press, 2013), 29ff; and on the concept of legitimacy generally, I. Clark, *Legitimacy in International Society* (Oxford: Oxford University Press, 2005).

[113] A possible earlier example, mentioned by Professor Cassese, was the 1945 Truman Proclamation which set in motion the modern law of the continental shelf: see Cassese, 10 EJIL (1999) 797; and M. Mendelson, 'The Formation of Customary International Law', 272 Recueil des cours (1998) 271.

2(d) The role of international organizations

Resolutions of the United Nations Security Council have of course their own special entitlement to create legal rights and duties, by virtue of the provisions of the Charter. In terms of sources, this of course comes under the heading of treaties, so far as the parties to the Charter are concerned. It has been suggested that in respect of matters, such as global warning and climate change, where changes in international law are required too urgently to be left to the leisurely processes of custom, the powers of the Security Council to issue binding resolutions might be put to use.[114]

The manner in which *non-binding* resolutions of the United Nations General Assembly might be considered sources of law in their own right, so to speak, has already been briefly considered in Chapter I, section 6(b). They may, however, be of considerable importance in the possible establishment of a customary rule, whether as evidence of *opinio juris*, or of practice, or even arguably of both. In its advisory opinion on the *Legality of the Threat or Use of Nuclear Weapons*, the Court observed that

General Assembly resolutions, even if they are not binding, may sometimes have normative value. They can, in certain circumstances, provide evidence important for establishing the existence of a rule or the emergence of *opinio juris*. To establish whether this is true of a given General Assembly resolution, it is necessary to look at its content and the conditions of its adoption; it is also necessary to see whether an *opinio juris* exists as to its normative character.[115]

The use of the word 'also' in the last phrase is slightly puzzling: if a customary rule exists on the basis of practice and *opinio* before the adoption of a resolution which states it, whether States then view the resolution as codificatory or not would seem to be irrelevant; but the point is probably only of academic interest.

The view of the matter taken by the ILA Committee on the Formation of Customary Law[116] was:

28 ....[R]esolutions of the United Nations General Assembly may in some instances constitute evidence of the existence [of] customary international law; help to

---

[114] F. Boyle, 'International Law-Making: Towards a New Role for the Security Council', in Cassese (ed.) *Realizing Utopia: the Future of International Law* (Oxford: Oxford University Press, 2012), 172–84, and works cited. However, his argument is not so revolutionary as it appears: it does not equate with raising certain decisions to the level of sources of law in their own right, as it were, but setting them in a general procedural framework that would bring them into the category of those on which the Charter confers binding quality.

[115] [1996-I] ICJ Rep 254–5, para. 70.

[116] ILA, Final Report, Part V, where it also noted that 'resolutions of other universal intergovernmental organizations' might have a similar effect: Introduction, para. 4.

crystallize emerging customary law; or contribute to the formation of new law. But as a general rule, they do not *ipso facto* create new rules of customary law.

The subsequent examination of the question by the ILC led to a more reserved approach: while 'A resolution adopted by an international organization or at an intergovernmental conference cannot, of itself create a rule of customary international law,' such a resolution 'may provide evidence for determining the existence and content of a rule of customary international law'[117] (Conclusion 12, paras. 1 and 2).

The essential role of resolutions was seen by the ILA as possibly supplying the subjective element, the *opinio juris*, or rather as supplying evidence of it. This aspect was also considered by the ILC, which concluded that a provision in a resolution 'may reflect a rule of customary international law if it is established that the provision corresponds to a general practice that is accepted as law (*opinio juris*)',[118] in other words, merely as supportive evidence.

However, the ILC thus did not follow the ILA Committee in considering that voting for General Assembly resolutions, as a 'verbal act', can 'constitute a form of State practice'. For the ILA Committee, 'for States lacking the material means for concrete activity in the field in question (e.g. States lacking weapons of mass destruction, or landlocked States), verbal acts may be the only form of practice open to them'.[119] It may, however, be objected that if the mere verbal expression of an *opinio* may also constitute State practice, a custom could, *semble*, become established without any 'concrete activity' at all. The classic ICJ definition of custom-generating practice referred to acts 'amounting to a settled practice' which 'must also be such, or be carried out in such a way, as to be evidence of a belief that *this practice* is rendered obligatory by the existence of a rule of law requiring it'.[120]

When States vote in favour of a purportedly law-declaring resolution, should one be asking whether they did so because they believed themselves legally bound to do so, because the resolution constituted a statement of the law, law which in itself would be binding on them?[121] Or should one not merely ask whether, by voting in favour, they were merely affirming, in a public and social context, what they believed to be a correct statement of the law, but did not think that that law *obliged* them to join in asserting

---

[117] This wording followed that of the ICJ in the *Legality of the Threat or Use of Nuclear Weapons* case, [1996] ICJ Rep 226, at 254–5, para. 70, save that the ICJ included the phrase 'in certain circumstances', as noted in para. 5 of the Commentary to Conclusion 12.

[118] *Ibid.*, para 3.   [119] ILA, *Final Report*, Pt. V(A), pp. 60–1, para. 59.

[120] *North Sea Continental Shelf*, quoted at text and n. 26 above.

[121] An approach postulated by Higgins, but not regarded by her as equivalent to *opinio juris*: R. Higgins, 'The United Nations and Law-Making: The Political Organs', 64 ASIL Proceedings (1970) 37; reprinted in R. Higgins, *Themes and Theories* (Oxford University Press, 2009), i. 63.

it? The first possibility is probably an unrealistic scenario; a negative vote on such a resolution surely cannot constitute a breach of the declared rule, even if it is one classified as *jus cogens*. Even taking the second possibility, is it legitimate to assume that a State voting for a resolution of this kind necessarily holds the view of the law declared in it, without reservation? Unless there is reason to believe that none of the affirmative votes were cast, for example, with reservations, or out of a desire not to be 'isolated in the sole company of certain political undesirables',[122] such a resolution may point to, but not constitute of itself proof of, *opinio juris*, and still less constitute State practice.

That said, there is no doubt that any examination of the state of customary law on any given issue may legitimately take into account any pronouncements on the subject contained in General Assembly resolutions as affording some evidence of the existence of *opinio juris*. The ICJ reference to 'in certain circumstances' may be read as including the degree of support for the resolution, since 'the normal rules for the formation of *general* customary law require *widespread and representative* acceptance of the rule'.[123] This is, in fact, the transposition to the *opinio* question of a criterion stated by the ICJ for the element of practice.[124] It is suggested that the widespread and representative support for the resolution would at least have to be backed by consistent actual practice, limited though it might be, among those States 'whose interests are specially affected'.

3. Changes in customary law

As many commentators have pointed out, some with concern, some with relish, according to their respective standpoints, it is particularly when customary law is alleged to have changed that a teasing intellectual problem arises. If it is difficult to establish *opinio juris* in the sense of States' belief that a particular practice *is*—already—sanctioned by a customary rule, still more difficult is the establishment of such *opinio* in favour of a new rule that, by definition, contradicts an established rule. This is exemplified by the argument of Italy in the case of *Jurisdictional Immunities of the State*. It

---

[122] Higgins, *Themes and Theories* (n. 123), who clearly had in mind the successive resolutions concerning South Africa and South West Africa.

[123] ILA, *Final Report*, Pt. IV(A), para. 32(f), referring to Pt. IV(c), paras. 12–15.

[124] '[A]n indispensable requirement would be that . . . State practice, including that of States whose interests are specially affected, should have been both extensive and virtually uniform . . .': *North Sea Continental Shelf* [1969] ICJ Rep 43, para. 74.

was generally agreed that, as a matter of established customary law, it had long been the case that a State was entitled to invoke immunity if sued before the courts of another State; this is a necessary consequence of the doctrine of State sovereignty: *par in parem non habet imperium*. Subsequently, at some date unascertained, the customary rule had become modified so as to confine immunity to actions arising out of acts performed by the respondent State as a State, defined as acts *jure imperii*.[125] If the dispute arose out of acts defined as *acta jure gestionis*, then there was no reason why the State should enjoy an immunity not available to other persons or entities engaged in similar activities but not being sovereign States. In the contention of Italy, the universal scope of sovereign immunity had subsequently undergone a further limitation: 'immunity as to acts *jure imperii* does not extend to torts or delicts occasioning death personal injury or damage to property committed on the territory of the forum State'.[126] In order to show that such a change had occurred, Italy would have had to point to acts of State practice consistent with such a limitation; but it would also have had to show that such acts were inspired or accompanied by the sentiment that the practice corresponded to the current state of customary law. When it is suggested that new practice has brought about a change in an established customary rule, the importance of the *opinio* is increased, because it may be that the (or some) States that have acted in a manner not in conformity with the established practice did so, surreptitiously or shamefacedly, while aware that they were out of line, so that their *opinio* remains as it was.[127]

While the difficulty in changing custom by embarking on a new practice, and at the same time possessing the appropriate *opinio juris*, is well known as a matter of international law, there may also be a problem with municipal

---

[125] These are acts performed as a sovereign State, which no other entity would have the power to perform, as contrasted with *acta jure gestionis*, 'acts in right of management or business', i.e. when a State corporation engages in trade, for example, in the same way as a private corporation might have done.

[126] Italy also claimed that immunity was not available because the acts complained of 'involved the most serious violation of rules of international law of a peremptory character for which no alternative means of redress was available', i.e. matters of *jus cogens* (ICJ Judgment of 3 February 2012, para. 61). This contention will be examined elsewhere (Ch. VII sect. 1(a)).

[127] This has been suggested as the situation with regard to torture: that it is recognized as contrary to customary international law, *even by the States that practise it*, so that no new custom, making it permissible, can become established: see R. Higgins, *Problems and Process: International Law and How We Use It* (Oxford: Oxford University Press, 1994), 21–2. This analysis, however, assumes that torture was at some point already contrary to customary law. A parallel may be seen with the situation in which a State openly goes beyond existing law in special circumstances, while stating that it does not intend to create a precedent: e.g. the attitude of Germany and Belgium in relation to intervention in Kosovo, mentioned by Cassese in 10 EJIL (1999), 798.

law. Mention has been made above of the observation by a recent commentator, with reference to the ICJ decision in the *Jurisdictional Immunities* case, that the Italian constitution provides that 'The Italian legal system complies with the generally recognized rules of international law', thus introducing customary international law rules into the domestic legal system.[128] For Italy and other States that have a similar constitutional provision (written or unwritten), it would seem that they are constitutionally debarred from beginning a new practice inconsistent with current customary law (as Italy was doing when it excluded the immunity of Germany in cases brought by victims of the Nazi regime).

Against this criticism of customary law that it is rigid, inasmuch as a custom that has once become settled can only be changed by a process that repeats, in more intensified form, the difficulty of its original creation, it has been contended that custom is 'a fluid source of law', because '[t]he content of custom is not fixed; it can develop and change in light of new circumstances'.[129] This author links this view with an approach called 'the reflective interpretative approach' which will be examined in more detail in Chapter IX. Generally, the fact that custom *can* develop in the light of new circumstances does not prevent it being categorized as a rigid system: it all depends on how readily such development can occur, or does in practice occur. The example given in the article quoted is the question of the legality of the NATO intervention in Kosovo, which (as the author concedes) was regarded by most commentators as illegal under existing international law.[130] Nevertheless there were voices raised in favour of its legality, and significance may be attached to, for example, the rejection of a draft Security Council resolution condemning the use of force. The author urges the relevance of 'the substantive aims of international law', and the need for consideration of how these 'should be prioritized when they conflict'.[131] It does not appear, however, that in the system of sources as it stands anything other than the development of a new practice, accompanied by appropriate *opinio juris*, can achieve change.[132]

---

[128] See G. Cataldi, 'The Implementation of Germany v. Italy', European Society of International Law 'Reflection' (February 2013).

[129] E. A. Roberts, 'Traditional and Modern Approaches to Customary International Law: A Reconciliation', 95 AJIL (2001) 757 at 784.

[130] Roberts, 'Traditional and Modern Approaches', 785–6; also Cassese, 10 EJIL (1999), 23 and 791, and see this chapter, text at n. 81.

[131] Roberts, 'Traditional and Modern Approaches', 786–7.

[132] With the assistance of time, which has the 'power/To o'erthrow law, and in one self-borne hour,/To plant and o'erwhelm custom.' (Shakespeare, *The Winter's Tale*, Act IV, Sc. 1, ll. 7–9).

4. The relevance of ethical and similar principles to customary law

State practice indicates what States, considered as a group, consider to be a useful and desirable system for regulating their respective rights and duties, and has in principle to be accepted for what it is, and not judged according to any preconceived assessment of its appropriateness or propriety. [133] Fortunately the international maritime practice caricatured by Voltaire in *Candide*, if it ever existed, is not part of modern customary law;[134] and in general it is not the role of the judge or other interpreter of existing law to deny recognition to an established practice, accepted and created by States, as somehow improper.[135] An interesting conundrum is the value of participation in a practice by a State which, by doing so, commits a breach of a treaty binding upon it; it could be argued that, as regards *opinio juris*, this is an *a fortiori* case!

As for the *opinio juris*, as soon as its definition shifts from being strictly a conviction that the law *is* to this or that effect, to a belief that at any rate the law *ought to be* to that effect, an element of judgment is introduced. Traditionally, this was limited to an assessment of the posited rule as desirable because of its convenience, its *necessitas*, because of its consistency with other rules and principles, and—*à la rigeur*—because of its fairness, as between international actors, that is. (Such fairness has, however, never until recently[136] ventured to correct, for example, the inequalities of nature the vast differences between the endowment of natural resources enjoyed by each State.) As regards the possible relevance to custom-development of ethical or

---

[133] On the possible relevance of ethical principles, see also Chapter VIII, sect. 3(b).

[134] Voltaire, *Candide, ou l'Optimisme* (1759), ch. XI, where the power of custom is adduced as justifying extremely intimate searches of women passengers on a vessel captured by corsairs I acknowledge my debt to Professor Condorelli for drawing attention to this literary precedent, though I do not share the conclusions he draws (see next note).

[135] *Contra* Condorelli in *La Pratique et le droit international*, Colloque de Genéve, 2003 (Paris: Pedone, 2004), 287, who condemns 'la conception d'apr è s laquelle les "lois du droit des gens" consacreraient ce que les nations font habituellement, que ce soit moral ou immoral, agréable ou désagréable, juste ou injuste', and contends that 'La pratique ... est d'abord l'objet de l'évaluation par la règle de droit. Le droit évalue la pratique des États, et la juge, la qualifie de valide, licite, illicite, opposable, génératrice de responsabilité, etc.'

[136] The United Nations Convention on the Law of the Sea may have achieved what custom probably never could have done, with its provisions for land-locked States to share in 'the surplus of the living resources of the exclusive economic zones of coastal States of the same region or subregion' (Art. 69, para. 1), and the recognition of the 'Area' ('the seabed and ocean floor and subsoil thereof, beyond the limits of national jurisdiction') as 'the common heritage of mankind' (Art. 1, para 1(1), Art. 136).

moral principles governing the treatment of human beings,[137] there has undoubtedly been a change in the attitude of international lawyers, and possibly
also of States. It has been suggested that in recent years the concept of

opinio juris has broadened to include the impetus 'to follow the norm out of a sense
of legal or moral obligation'. For instance, international tribunals have found 'existing customary international law' when actual practice has been absent, but morally
compelling reasons have led the court to rule on the illegality of certain atrocities.[138]

A similar view is taken by Lepard, who argues that when assessing the question of the existence of a customary rule, 'it is appropriate to relax the state
practice requirement in . . . cases involving norms that states reasonably believe
directly further fundamental ethical principles'.[139] He offers three reasons for
this approach. 'One reason is that States, although believing a norm setting
high ethical standards to be desirable, may find it challenging to comply perfectly with the norm. States might not wish their own imperfect behaviour
to undermine recognition of the legal rule.'[140] The logic of this is hardly compelling. A State is, it is suggested, uncertain that it can comply with a rule
that has been mooted, but still wishes its *attitude* towards the rule to be given
weight in forwarding it as a binding rule, so that it will, in due course, find
itself obliged to comply with the rule.

A second reason offered is more openly paternalistic: that 'judged from the
standpoint of the global community of states, it is intrinsically desirable to
recognize legal norms that directly advance fundamental ethical principles',
even if states have not given any indication by their behaviour that this is how
they view the interest of the 'global community'. State practice, we are told,
has simply not yet 'caught up' with the norms—or rather with the wisdom
of academic internationalists. What matters, however, is how States see their
interests, not how a scholar may view them from the sidelines.

The third reason offered is, briefly stated, that some compliance with the
ethical norm, that is to say compliance by some States, is better than none;
that this is not a situation in which 'widespread compliance is a prerequisite
for the realization of any benefit from the norm'.[141] From the observer's point

---

[137] And indeed the treatment of animals (wildlife), and possibly the global environment; but
these matters would take us too far afield.

[138] N. Arajärvi, 'The Lines Begin to Blur? Opinio Juris and the Moralisation of Customary
International Law', 1–2 (<http://www.academia.edu/544738/>).

[139] B. D. Lepard, *Customary International Law: A New Theory with Practical Applications*
(Cambridge: Cambridge University Press, 2010), 224.

[140] Lepard, *Customary International Law*, 224.

[141] Lepard, *Customary International Law*, 224: the author offers a detailed analysis of what he
calls 'co-ordination problems' elsewhere in the book, and this will be briefly noted in Ch. IX, text
and n. 108.

of view, and at that moment in time, this may well be so; but the function of rules of general customary law is not to favour an uncooperative minority. Moreover, the suggestion encounters the same objection as the first reason mentioned: the growth of a rule that will require a State to modify its current behaviour in an unwelcome way is not something that that State will regard as a benefit.

In sum, the view here taken is well expressed in a recent paper: 'Even if political, social and moral considerations are integral in the underlying rationales of law in general, they are best to be retained as implicit elements of law developing through changing circumstances, rather than accepting them as explicitly influencing law—or as grounds for tilting the applicable law one way or the other.'[142]

5. The extent of application of a rule of customary international law

5(a) General customary law and the 'persistent objector'[143]

It is fundamental to the concept of law created by custom that once a rule has 'crystallized' as an established custom, it is binding not merely on those States that participated in the practice from which it sprang, but on all members of the international community, both those existing at the moment of crystallization, and States coming into existence subsequently. In principle, this also includes the States that expressed doubts about the rule during its formative stages. The one exception to this generality of applicability is the possibility for a State, by its conduct during the development of the rule, to acquire the privileged status of the 'persistent objector'.

The ILC recognized the rule known by this title in Conclusion 15 (1) and (2) of its Conclusions on the Identification of Customary International Law, in the following terms:

Where a State has objected to a rule of customary international law while that rule was in the process of formation, the rule is not opposable to the State concerned for so long as it maintains its objection.

---

[142] N. Arajärvi, 'The Lines Begin to Blur? Opinio Juris and the Moralisation of Customary International Law', European University Institute; Tilburg University—Department of European & International Public Law March 2011, p. 20. Online at <http://papers.ssrn.com/sol3/papers.cfm?abstract_id=1823288>, accessed November 2013.

[143] For an earlier, brief but lucid, treatment of this subject, see M. Byers, *Custom, Power and the Power of Rules* (Cambridge: Cambridge University Press, 1999), 102–5.

The objection must be clearly expressed, made known to other States, and maintained persistently.[144]

[145]The notion of the *'persistent objector'* has been identified in the case-law of the ICJ in its reasoning in the *Asylum* case;[146] but the idea is usually regarded as exemplified by the earlier *Fisheries* case between the UK and Norway, which concerned the legality of the baselines drawn by Norway around its coasts in order to calculate the breadth of its territorial sea. The UK argued that the Norwegian baselines were inconsistent with a rule of customary law referred to as the 'ten-mile rule', but the Court was not satisfied that any such general rule of customary law existed. However, it then added, 'In any event the ten-mile rule would appear to be inapplicable as against Norway inasmuch as she has always opposed any attempt to apply it to the Norwegian coast.'[147]

As a result of, in particular, a very influential argument advanced by Sir Gerald Fitzmaurice,[148] it became accepted by most scholars that a State that objected consistently to the application of a rule of law while it was still in the process of becoming such a rule—in other words, while practice consistent with the possible rule was still accumulating, but before the rule could be regarded as established—could continue to 'opt out' of the application of the rule even after it had acquired the status of a rule of general customary law.

This is an attractive theory, since if there were no possibility of dissent from a nascent rule, customary law would always be created by the majority of States and imposed willy-nilly on the minority; there is more State practice to support it than is commonly thought,[149] (and if it exists, it is itself

---

[144] A third paragraph was included to the effect that the text 'is without prejudice to any question concerning peremptory norms of international law', simply because the ILC was planning to deal with *jus cogens* as a separate project: Fifth Report of the ILC Special Rapporteur, A/CN.4/717, p. 48, paras. 109–10.

Cf. the similar statement in the ILA Committee's Report on the Formation of Customary Law, already referred to: 'If whilst a practice is developing into a rule of general law, a State persistently and openly dissents from the rule, it will not be bound by it.' ILA, Final Report Pt. II(C), p. 27, para. 15.

[145] ILA, *Final Report* Pt. II(C), p. 27, para. 15.

[146] Examining a claim for the existence of a local custom, the Court noted that 'even if it could be supposed that such a custom existed between certain Latin-American States only, it could not be invoked against Peru which, far from having by its attitude adhered to it, has, on the contrary repudiated it ...' [1950] ICJ Rep 277–8.

[147] *Fisheries* [1951] ICJ Rep 1167 at 131.

[148] G. G. Fitzmaurice, 'The Problem of the Single Recalcitrant State', 92 Recueil des cours (1957-II) 131; see also 'Law and Procedure of the International Court, 1951–1954', 30 BYIL 1 at 21, repr. in G. G. Fitzmaurice, *The Law and Procedure of the International Court of Justice* (Cambridge: Grotius, 1986), i. 132 at 154–6.

[149] Cf. A. Green, *The Persistent Objector in International Law* (Cambridge University Press, 2016).

a rule of customary law established by practice), and its very existence has been questioned by commentators,[150] as has its purpose.[151] What is certain is that customary law is not made by simple majority:[152] if a sufficient number of States manifest their opposition to a developing rule—particularly if they include States with a special interest in the matter—the rule will not come into existence at all, even to apply to the States that do favour it. In the case of *Legality of the Threat or Use of Nuclear Weapons*, the Court accepted that the opposition of the handful of nuclear States to any customary rule prohibiting such weapons blocked the creation of such a rule, even though it was favoured by a substantial majority of the States of the world.[153] In theory, there might thus be a tipping point at which a custom whose development has been blocked by dissentients becomes established, but leaving the dissentients as 'persistent objectors'; but this could hardly be so in the case of nuclear weapons, as only a total ban, universally accepted, would be thinkable.[154]

On the other hand, the development of the law of the sea has seen a number of persistent dissentients ultimately brought into line. The successive extensions of the rights claimed by coastal States over the waters and the seabed off their coasts have been opposed by States who regarded their interests as threatened, in particular the United States, the United Kingdom, and

---

[150] See e.g. A. d'Amato, *The Concept of Custom in International Law* (Ithaca, NY: Cornell University Press, 1971), 261, who suggested that the rule could only be operative in relation to special or local custom (see this chapter, sect. 6); T. L. Stein, 'Approach of the Different Drummer: The Principle of the Persistent Objector in International Law', 26 Harvard Int'l LJ (1985) 457; J. Charney, 'The Persistent Objector Rule and the Development of Customary International Law', 58 BYIL (1987); J. Charney, 'Universal International Law', 87 AJIL (1993) 529; J. P. Kelly, 'Customary International Law in Historical Context', in Lepard (ed.), *Reexamining Customary International Law* (Cambridge, 2017), 47, 80: 'If the persistent objector principle is accepted, then customary international law theory is inconsistent and incoherent.'

[151] It has even been presented as a means by which the powerful States can 'have it both ways': imposing rules that suit them, and evading those that do not: see B. S. Chimni, 'Customary International Law: A Third World Perspective', 118 AJIL (2018) 1 at 46, who also draws attention to the point that is the practice of the same States that is fully reported, and thus lends bias to any analysis of State practice in general.

[152] Though, in a sense, customary law *is* 'made by weighted majority': in this sense, J Charney, 'The Persistent Objector Rule and the Development of Customary International Law', 56 BYIL (1985) 18–21, replying to the views of M. Akehurst to the effect that international society cannot be run on the basis of weighted majorities: M. Akehurst, 'Custom as a Source of International Law', 47 BYIL (1974–5).

[153] *Legality of the Threat or Use of Nuclear Weapons* [1996] ICJ Rep 236, para. 73.

[154] For slightly different reasons, it is perhaps doubtful how far divergent regimes could be tolerated in the law governing the rights of the coastal State over the waters and seabed off its shores. The *Fisheries* case itself shows that there may be exceptions to the generality of rules as to delimitation techniques, but the existence and nature of continental shelf and similar rights must apparently be uniform.

Japan, but their opposition has ultimately proved ineffective to retard these developments. A similar scenario appears to have been observed in the field of compensation for expropriation of foreign assets. The conclusion reached in a study of the matter was that, in these cases, the persistent objector rule does not appear to have significantly helped the State or States that have resisted the new developments.[155]

Once a general rule of customary law has become established, however, it seems that there is no possibility to become a belatedly persistent objector, and opt out of the rule for the future (other than in bilateral relations with such partners as are willing to agree by treaty to put the rule aside).[156] If the rule were to be embodied in a lawmaking convention, it would be possible for any State party to the convention to denounce it and thus withdraw from it (subject to any contrary provision in the convention itself), but this would leave unaffected its obligations under the customary rule.[157]

As explained in section 3, changes in customary law normally occurred simply through practice, which by definition took a certain amount of time to accumulate, and therefore gave the opportunity for any dissentient State to make its disagreement known. Nowadays changes in customary law may be effected, or at least attempted, by General Assembly resolution, for example; what is the position of States that vote against, or abstain, on such an occasion? A recent authoritative study has suggested that 'Even if such resolutions can change the law for states which were in favour, it is clear that they do not do so for the dissenting minority.'[158]

---

[155] Charney, 'The Persistent Objector Rule', 15. There may however be some significance in the fact that Norway in the *Fisheries* case was a 'persistent objector' to the application of a new general rule to its own coasts, whereas the United States and other dissenters were objecting to the application of the new rule by other States to *their* own coasts, to the detriment, it was argued, of the generality of States, most of whom had not objected—if indeed they were not already enthusiastically adopting the rule.

[156] See the controversy on this point in C. Bradley and M. Gulati, 'Withdrawing from International Custom', 120 Yale LJ (2010) 202; A. Roberts, 'Who Killed Article 38(1)(b)? A Reply to Bradley and Gulati', 21 Duke Journal of Comparative and International Law (2010) 173; J. P. Trachtman, 'Persistent Objectors, Cooperation and the Utility of Customary International Law', 21 Duke Journal of Comparative and International Law (2010) 221–33.

[157] Cf. the position in the *Military and Paramilitary Activities* case, where the ICJ had no jurisdiction to rule on alleged breaches by the US of the Charter, but could still determine whether it was in breach of customary rules that were also embedded in the Charter. This is discussed in Ch. VI, sect. 2, text and n. 38.

[158] A. Boyle and C. Chinkin, *The Making of International Law* (Oxford: Oxford University Press, 2007), 226, citing the *Texaco* v. *Libya* arbitration (1977) 53 ILR 422, and referring to the dissent on the point of Charney, 'The Persistent Objector Rule'.

5(b) Particular[159] customary law

If the practice and the *opinio juris* underlying a rule of customary international law is not general, but confined to States belonging to an identifiable group, or otherwise linked by a common interest, a custom may still come into existence, but it will apply only between members of that group, and cannot be enforced upon, or relied upon in relation to, other States. As the ILC expresses it (Conclusion 16), 'A rule of particular customary international law, whether regional, local or other, is a rule of customary international law that applies only among a limited number of States.' Perhaps the only clear and well-known example of such local customary law is that relating to the practice of diplomatic asylum in Latin America, whereby the States of the region recognize the right of the embassies of other States of the region to give asylum to political fugitives.[160] The rule is purely local in that it is not asserted in favour of, or against, States outside the region: as has become clear in the case of Julian Assange, the right of the Embassy of Ecuador in London to offer asylum of this kind is not recognized by the UK Government,[161] which similarly would not claim it for the British Embassy in Quito. The International Court had to consider the detailed application of the rule in the *Asylum* and *Haya de la Torre* cases, in which Colombia relied, against Peru, on 'an alleged regional or local custom peculiar to Latin-American States'. In the *Asylum* case the Court observed that:

The Party which relies on a custom of this kind must prove that this custom is established in such a manner that it has become binding on the other Party. The Colombian Government must prove that the rule invoked by it is in accordance with a constant and uniform usage practised by the States in question, and that this usage is the expression of a right appertaining to the State granting asylum and a duty incumbent on the territorial State.[162]

---

[159] This is the term preferred by the ILC: in the past the term 'special' or 'local' has generally been used, but of course the group of States affected is not necessarily geographically defined.

[160] Another alleged rule of regional customary law was pleaded in the *Dispute regarding Navigational and Related Rights between Costa Rica and Nicaragua*, but the ICJ found it unnecessary to decide whether such a rule existed: [2009] ICJ Rep 233, paras. 34–6.

[161] See the statement made by the UK Foreign Secretary on 16 August 2012: 'The UK does not accept the principle of diplomatic asylum. It is far from a universally accepted concept: the United Kingdom is not a party to any legal instruments which require us to recognise the grant of diplomatic asylum by a foreign embassy in this country.'

[162] [1950] ICJ Rep 276. This is in contrast to the accepted convention, as regards general customary law, of *jura novit curia* (the law is known to the court), so that a litigant is not expected to prove the existence of any general rule. In practice, however, unless the rule relied on is so well established as to be virtually unchallengeable, counsel usually offer proof in support of a customary rule—or of their interpretation of the rule.

Further on in its judgment, the Court held that 'even if such a custom existed between certain Latin-American States only, it could not be invoked against Peru which, far from having by its attitude adhered to it, has on the contrary repudiated it ...'.[163] As already noted, this has been held by some commentators to constitute a finding that Peru had the status of 'persistent objector'; but it can also be understood as a finding that the regional custom, at least on the specific point in dispute, applied to a group of States that did not include Peru.

It has even been held that a special custom may exist between two States only: in the *Right of Passage over Indian Territory* case, Portugal relied on such a custom as regulating the relationship between itself and India concerning access to certain Portuguese enclaves in Indian territory. The Court held that:

It is difficult to see why the number of States between which a local custom may be established on the basis of long practice must necessarily be larger than two. The Court sees no reason why long continued practice between two States accepted by them as regulating their relations should not form the basis of mutual rights and obligations between the two States.[164]

It would seem evident that two must be the minimum number of States to be subject to a special custom: if a single State claimed (otherwise than as a 'persistent objector'—see this chapter, section 5) to be entitled in certain respects to rely on rules different from those generally in force, such a claim could only be maintained as the result of a general acceptance making it a matter of general customary law. Thus the suggestion that has from time to time been made that the USA, by reason of its position as sole remaining superpower and self-appointed global policeman,[165] is not necessarily bound by such rules as that of non-intervention, cannot rest on the assertion of a special custom.

A local custom will not necessarily deviate from a general custom, as it may well be that the local custom applies to a regional geographical situation, for example a closed sea or a river, or provides for an institution that does not exist under general international law. In so far as there might be conflict between the requirements of a local custom and those of general customary law, it would seem evident that the local custom prevails, the special prevailing

---

[163] [1950] ICJ Rep 277–8.

[164] *Right of Passage over Indian Territory, Merits, Judgment* [1960] ICJ Rep 6 at 39. Cases of this kind are likely to be rare, since it would normally be more appropriate to analyse such a situation as one of tacit agreement, i.e. in effect governed by treaty-law. In the *Right of Passage* case this interpretation would have raised problems of succession, the arrangement dating back to the Mughal period, and left undisturbed by the successive British and independent Indian governments.

[165] Cf. the views of McDougal on hydrogen bomb testing, and (more recently) D. Murswiek, 'The American Strategy of Pre-emptive War and International Law', XIII FBYIL (2003) 195.

over the general, unless of course the general customary rule is one of *jus cogens*. It is possible also that a local custom may exist between a limited group of States, yet with its attributes and its operation conforming to a pattern existing by virtue of a general custom. In the *Dispute concerning Navigational and Related Rights* on the San Juan River, between Costa Rica and Nicaragua, Costa Rica suggested that a possible example of this is the regime of international rivers; it argued for the existence of 'rules of general international law that are applicable, even in the absence of treaty provisions, to navigation on "international rivers" '.[166] The rights conferred by such a regime would belong solely to riparian States, so that such a custom would be, in that respect, local, but scattered over a number of localities, even if the pattern of rights were set by a general custom. The ICJ decided that in the case before it, the relevant rights were regulated wholly by applicable treaty provisions, so that it did not have to 'take a position ... on whether and to what extent there exists, in customary international law, a regime applicable to navigation on "international rivers" '.[167]

[166] [2009] ICJ Rep 232–3, para. 32.
[167] [2009] ICJ Rep 232–3, para. 32. Note also the Declaration appended to the judgment by Judge ad hoc Guillaume, expressing the view that there are no such rules of general international law: [2009] ICJ Rep 290–1, para. 3.

IV

General Principles of Law as a Source of Law

1. What are the 'general principles of law'?

When Article 38 of the Statute of the Permanent Court[1] was being drafted, the Advisory Committee of Jurists was concerned that in some cases the future Court might find that the issues in dispute before it were not governed by any treaty, and that no established rule of customary law could be found to determine them. It was thought undesirable, and possibly inappropriate in principle, that the Court should be obliged to declare what is known as a *non liquet*. This is a judicial finding that a particular claim can neither be upheld nor rejected, for lack of any existing applicable rule of law: the concept will be examined in more detail further on in this chapter.

The extent to which international legal relations were governed in the 1920s, at the time of the Committee's work, by anything beyond treaties and custom, was obscure; the positivist approach, recognizing the role of State consent in treaties and custom, left little room for a further source.[2] The Commission was, however, able to agree that, failing one of those sources, the Court should apply 'the general principles of law recognized by civilized nations'. Up to the present, while there have been judicial mentions of certain principles, which will be discussed further, it seems that neither the ICJ nor its predecessor has based a decision entirely and directly on such general principles.[3] There are some decisions by arbitral bodies (to whom, of course,

---

[1] Article 38 is central to the discussion of 'general principles' even more than it is to that of the other sources listed, and the discussion is even more focussed on the jurisprudence of the two International Courts, because the use of such principles in direct State-to-State relations is rarely visible. This does not signify that Article 38 was in this respect creative any more than in any other respect: see the discussion of the arguments of d'Aspremont in Chapter I.

[2] See, however, later in this section as to the background—and return—of 'natural law'.

[3] The only possible candidate may be the decision in the *Corfu Channel* case, referring to 'certain general and well-recognized principles' including 'elementary considerations of humanity': [1949] ICJ Rep 22; this has recently been reinterpreted as possibly based on an interpretation of the Hague Convention of 1907, and thus treaty-based; see text and nn. 42, 43.

Article 38 of the ICJ Statute has no direct application) which have relied on the concept.

A word should be said as to the nature of 'principles' of law. No system of law can consist solely of specific rules, covering every situation that could possibly arise. Unforeseen cases are bound to be encountered, and if there is no higher principle to be called on, either a *non liquet* would have to be declared, or the judge would have to exercise a discretion. That law consists of more than rules has been demonstrated by Dworkin, who has shown that not only must there also be principles, but that they are neither case-specific nor automatic in their operation, and may even conflict.[4] This latter aspect is characteristic; as observed by (for example) Higgins, a judicial decision is often a choice between two or even more conflicting principles,[5] while rules, at least in theory, do not conflict but form a structure. Fitzmaurice expresses the distinction vividly: 'By a principle, or a general principle, as opposed to a rule, even a general rule, of law is meant chiefly something which is not itself a rule, but which underlies a rule, and explains or provides the reason for it. A rule answers the question "what"; a principle in effect answers the question "why".'[6] This does not mean that a principle is on too elevated a plane to be capable of being applied to a legal problem, but it does mean that the principle will, by being applied to the case, in effect generate a rule for solving it.

The general principles now under consideration are those contemplated by Article 38 of the ICJ Statute as additional to, and therefore independent of, the other sources enumerated in that Article. Customary law, for example, is not merely made up of rules; it also contains established principles—established, that is, in the same way as rules (by practice and *opinio juris*) or derived by extrapolation or analysis from such rules. The application in argument, or in a judicial or arbitral decision, of such principles, is an application of customary law, not of Article 38, paragraph 1(*c*), of the ICJ Statute. It is clear that a legal principle may be termed a 'general' one in other senses: for example, that of the intangibility of boundaries inherited from decolonization (*uti possidetis*) is

---

[4] R. Dworkin, 'Is Law a System of Rules?' from 'The Model of Rules', 14 University of Chicago LR (1967), reprinted in Dworkin (ed.), *The Philosophy of Law* (Oxford: Oxford University Press, 1977).

[5] R. Higgins, *Problems and Process: International Law and How We Use It* (Oxford: Oxford University Press, 1994), 3.

[6] G. G. Fitzmaurice, 'The General Principles of International Law Considered from the Standpoint of the Rule of Law', 92 Recueil des cours (1957), 7. A slightly different approach is for e.g. that of Weil: 'Régles et principes sont des termes juridiquement synonymes, sous la réserve que l'on a l'habitude de qualifier de principes des normes de caractère plus général et plus fondamental, relevant plus ou moins de la technique des standards': P. Weil, 'Le droit international en quête de son identité', 237 Recueil des cours (1992), 150.

often termed a 'general principle',[7] but it is rather a principle that is custom-based (and is not in fact universally and consistently applied).

There is broad agreement but no unanimity among scholars as to the nature of the principles that may be invoked under this head. The members of the Advisory Committee of Jurists who prepared the draft of the PCIJ Statute were themselves divided.[8] There are in effect two possible interpretations.

According to one interpretation, the principles in question are those which can be derived from a comparison of the various systems of municipal law, and the extraction of such principles as appear to be shared by all, or a majority, of them.[9] This interpretation gives force to the reference in Article 38 to the principles being those 'recognized by civilized nations'; the term 'civilized' is now out of place, but at the time it was apparently included inasmuch as some legal systems were then regarded as insufficiently developed to serve as a standard of comparison.[10] In line with this interpretation, parties to cases before the ICJ have at times invoked extensive comparative studies of municipal law.[11] It is perhaps significant that other international tribunals who are not specifically endowed by their creators with the power to apply general

---

[7] See for example *Frontier Dispute (Burkina Faso/Niger)* [2013] ICJ Rep 73, para. 63, where it was also relevant that it was jointly invoked by the parties rather than applying of its own force.

[8] For a convenient brief summary of the views expressed, see G. Gaja, 'General Principles of Law', in R. Wolfrum (ed.), *Max Planck Encyclopedia of International Law* (2012), iv. 371–2, paras. 1–3; also the separate opinion of Judge Cançado Trindade in *Pulp Mills on the River Uruguay* [2010] ICJ Rep 139–42.

[9] A pioneering and influential work on this subject was H. Lauterpacht, *Private Law Sources and Analogies of International Law* (London: Longmans, 1927). A clearer statement of the derivation of general principles from national systems is to be found in the Rome Statute of the International Criminal Court: 'general principles of law derived by the Court from national laws of legal systems of the world' (Article 21(1)(c)).

[10] In the *Abu Dhabi* arbitration in 1951, 18 ILR 144, the arbitrator found that the law of Abu Dhabi contained no legal principles that could be applied to modern commercial instruments, and could not therefore be applied to an oil concession. See also the arbitrations in the cases of *Sarropoulos v. Bulgarian State*, AD 4 (1923–4), no. 173, *Goldenberg & Sons v. Germany*, AD 4 (1927–8), no. 369. It is now generally recognized that no State's legal system may be disregarded on the ground that it is not a 'civilized nation': for the disquiet caused by the term, see separate opinion of Judge Ammoun in *North Sea Continental Shelf* [1969] ICJ Rep 132–3; the fierce criticism by S. Yee, 'Arguments for Cleaning-up Article 38(1)(b) and (1)(c) of the ICJ Statute', 4 Romanian Journal of International Law (2007), 34; and cf. V.-D. Degan, 'General Principles of Law', 3 Finnish Yearbook of International Law (1992), 54.

[11] In the case of *Right of Passage over Indian Territory*, Portugal argued that general principles of law supported its right to passage from the coast to its enclaves of territory, and adduced a comparative study of the provisions in various legal systems for what may be called 'rights of way of necessity'. When for the first time an application was made by a State (Malta) to intervene in a case between two other States (Tunisia and Libya) on the basis of having an interest which might be affected by the decision in the case (a possibility referred to in Art. 62 of the Court's Statute), Malta similarly relied on a comparative law study showing the conditions and modalities of intervention in judicial proceedings in various national courts.

principles of law, nevertheless have been known to do so, without objection from States and others concerned; this suggests that the need for the possibility of ultimate resource to such principles is generally recognized.[12]

An alternative interpretation of the intention underlying Article 38 (1) (c) is that, while the Committee of Jurists may have had primarily in view the legal principles shared by municipal legal orders, the recognized principles also include general principles applicable directly to international legal relations, and general principles applicable to legal relations generally.[13] As already noted, many of these find expression in customary law, and therefore exist as rules derived from that source; others are in effect assertions of secondary rules, for example the principle *pacta sunt servanda*. Some are applied unquestioningly as self-evident: for example the principles that have already been referred to in Chapter II as appropriate for determining the relationship between successive treaties (and possibly successive legal rules generally)—the principles that the special prevails over the general, and that the later prevails over the earlier.

The derivation of general principles from systems of municipal law has been the subject of critical examination by Jaye Ellis. She suggests that there are three lines of thought, or 'assumptions', advanced as justifying treating principles found in such systems as appropriate for employment at the international, thus inter-State level.

The first possible assumption is one rooted in natural law thinking, namely that the presence of a rule in many legal systems is evidence of its belonging to the objective idea of law. The second is based on a voluntarist approach to positivism, namely that the presence of the rule in many systems is evidence of State consent. The third flows from concerns about the democratic validity of international law, particularly in a postcolonial context, and takes national adoption of a rule as a kind of warrant for its production through democratic processes.[14]

Professor Ellis recognizes that on the voluntaristic approach, the source of the validity of a principle can, 'by a somewhat circuitous route, be anchored in State consent rather than in the judge's authority'.[15] Nevertheless she does

---

[12] See e.g. the *Argentina/Chile Boundary Dispute*, award, para. 68, citing the principle of *res judicata*; the ICSID arbitration in *Amco Asia Co* v. *Indonesia*, award para. 267, citing the principles of damages for *damnum emergens* and *lucrum cessans*.

[13] Still less compatible with the intentions of the draftsmen of the PCIJ Statute is the idea that the 'general principles' also include such concepts as the value of the human person (human rights), or of the preservation of the environment, in 1920 not yet seen as a problem. On the concept of 'intergenerational equity' in the separate opinion of Judge Cançado Trindade in the *Pulp Mills* case [2010] ICJ Rep, see this chapter, text and n. 20.

[14] J. Ellis, 'General Principles and Comparative Law', 22 EJIL (2011), 949 at 970.

[15] 'General Principles and Comparative Law', 953–4.

not regard the positivist approach (nor, for that matter, either of the other two approaches mentioned) as 'particularly convincing'.[16] Her conclusion takes the form of a recommendation, and is apparently thus offered as *lex ferenda*; it is broadly to regard the current 'quest for a universally shared body of legal rules or concepts' as 'probably futile'; that the 'pretence' of 'demonstrating the commonality or representativeness of a legal rule' should 'fall away'; and that 'the validity of a general principle would have to be grounded in the soundness and persuasiveness of legal argumentation rather than in claims about the objective nature of law or implicit state consent'.[17] In other words, this would involve the familiar movement, already mentioned,[18] from source-theory, grounding the legal validity of a rule in its history and means of production, to something approaching natural-law theory, grounding such validity in the perceived justice of the rule, with all the potential that this involves for personal judgment being substituted for observation. Similarly, d'Aspremont draws attention to 'the difficulty of collecting representative data of domestic traditions', the convergence which is or should be relied on to deduce the existence of such principles.[19]

A further question, relevant in particular to the possible application of general principles by the International Court, is whether the phrase 'general principles of law' is to be interpreted as referring to such principles as were understood to exist at the time of drafting of the Statute, or as more open-ended and capable of comprising principles that were not thought of in 1920, or even in 1946, when the ICJ Statute was adopted. A case in point is the principle of 'inter-generational equity': the idea that there is a legal duty to protect and preserve the natural order and the environment, for the benefit of future generations. The origin of this concept can be dated fairly accurately to 1988, when the Advisory Committee to the United Nations University issued its 'Guidelines on Intergenerational Equity'.[20] In 2010 Judge Cançado Trindade apparently saw no difficulty in applying the principle in the case of *Pulp Mills on the River Uruguay* under the general heading of the 'general principles of law' which, in his understanding 'emanate ... from human conscience, from the universal judicial conscience, which I regard as the ultimate material "source" of all law'.[21] The Court did not see the need to recognize or

---

[16] 'General Principles and Comparative Law', 970.

[17] 'General Principles and Comparative Law', 970.   [18] Ch. I sect. 4.

[19] J. d'Aspremont, *Formalism and the Sources of International Law* (Oxford University Press, 2011), 171.

[20] See the extensive quotation, and references to the whereabouts of the complete text, in the separate opinion of Judge Cançado Trindade in the case of *Pulp Mills on the River Uruguay* [2010] ICJ Rep 178–9, para. 118.

[21] [2010] ICJ Rep 156, para. 52.

apply such a principle, or indeed any 'general principles', but if it had done so, it seems unlikely that it would have felt restrained by any intertemporal law principle. Yet there is about the concept of 'general principles' such an air of permanence, of stability, of having been selected for their evident and perpetual rightness, that an interpretation of the phrase as meaning 'whatever principles may in future come to be regarded as general principles' is somehow disquieting.

A more wide-ranging enquiry into municipal law analogies was undertaken by Judge Simma in his separate opinion in the *Oil Platforms* case, in connection with the United States' counterclaim for economic damage caused by Iranian mine-laying activities during the Iran–Iraq war. He dissented from the Court's rejection of the counter-claim, but was troubled by the *extent* of Iran's responsibility, and therefore of its liability to compensate, in view of the participation of Iraq (not a party to the case) in the injurious activities. He had therefore, he explained, engaged in some research 'in comparative law to see whether anything resembling a "general principle of law" within the meaning of Article 38, paragraph 1 (*c*), of the Statute of the Court can be developed from solutions arrived at in domestic law to come to terms with the problem of multiple tortfeasors'.[22] After examining a number of municipal law systems (common law, and Canadian, French, Swiss, and German law[23]), he concludes that 'the principle of joint-and-several responsibility common to the jurisdictions I have considered can properly be regarded as a "general principle of law ...".'[24] It is also striking that it is only *after* reaching this conclusion that he invokes the ILC draft article on State Responsibility, adopted in 2001,[25] which is to the same effect: this emphasizes the importance apparently attributed by Judge Simma to the municipal-law background of general principles of law.

The learned editors of the 9th edition of Oppenheim saw general principles of law as a source of international law that (1) 'enables rules of law which can fill gaps or weaknesses in the law which might otherwise be left by the operation of custom or treaty', and (2) 'provides a background of legal principles in the light of which custom and treaties have to be applied and as such it may act to modify their application'. However, they go on to say that '[g]eneral principles of law ... do not just have a supplementary role, but

---

[22] [2003] ICJ Rep 354, para. 66.

[23] These systems appear to have been chosen for convenience of reference: there is no indication that the judge regarded any other systems as not being those of 'civilized nations'!

[24] [2003] ICJ Rep 358, para. 74.   [25] [2003] ICJ Rep 358, para. 75.

may give rise to rules of independent legal force' (as is, of course, suggested by their place in Art. 38 (1)).[26]

The fact that a court may apply general principles of course implies that appeal may be made to such principles in support of a claim presented for judicial settlement—or indeed a claim presented in any context as founded upon international law. There is, however, a striking lack of evidence in international practice and jurisprudence of claims to a specific right of a concrete nature being asserted or upheld on the basis simply of the general principles of law; some examples have already been mentioned. As far as the ICJ is concerned, throughout its history it has given only one judgment apparently relying on a general principle of law (though without invoking Art. 38, para. 1(*c*)), namely that in the *Corfu Channel* case[27] mentioned earlier; and in only a handful of cases has the Court been asked by a party to base its decision on a general principle.[28] It may be that this dearth of examples is consistent with the nature of such principles; in any event, this particular source of law appears to be of less practical importance in determining the rights and obligations of States in their regular relations.

A positivist approach would suggest that there are limits to the type of general principles of law that a court, including the ICJ, is authorized to apply, and which, on that basis, are to be taken to be part of general international law. The possible impact of ethical or moral considerations in this domain remains to be considered; but even equity or equality is not necessarily entailed in such an approach. In a novel field such as space law, a judicial body called upon to determine the issue might well have asserted the same principle as was to be embodied in the 1967 Treaty, that 'Outer space, including the moon and other celestial bodies, shall be free for exploration and use by all States without discrimination of any kind, on a basis of equality and in accordance with international law …'. But, however admirable, this is by definition a novelty, which raises the intertemporal law point: could it be a 'general principle of law' in the sense of Article 38, paragraph 1(*c*), of the ICJ Statute?

---

[26] R. Jennings and A. Watts (eds.), *Oppenheim's International Law*, 9th edn. (London: Longman, 1992), i. 40.

[27] See this chapter, n. 41.

[28] The claim by Portugal in the case of *Right of Passage over Indian Territory* [1960] ICJ Rep 43; an argument from 'necessity' as basis for the claim of entitlement to invoke the breach of Mandate in *South West Africa* [1966] ICJ Rep 44–7, paras. 80–8; the German claim to a 'just and equitable share' of the continental shelf in *North Sea Continental Shelf* [1969] ICJ Rep 21, para. 17; an alleged procedural principle excluding evidence improperly obtained, advanced by Mexico in *Avena and other Mexican Nationals* [2004-I] ICJ Rep 61, para. 127.

The principles contemplated by that text are, or at all events include, those principles without which no legal system can function at all,[29] that are part and parcel of legal reasoning. The fact that they are to be drawn from municipal systems, as contemplated when the Statute was drawn up, is less a criterion in itself than a guide to the nature of the principles to be looked for.[30] An evident example is the principle *pacta sunt servanda*; as we have seen in the context of sources theory, and of the role of treaties and conventions as a source, that principle is one that cannot but exist in any legal system, because to say that 'binding commitments are not binding' is mere nonsense.[31] The same applies to the related principle *pacta tertiis nec nocet nec prodest*; and similarly, the principle that *res judicata pro veritate habetur* is necessary and inevitable in any system of dispute-*settlement*, since if a dispute is settled it is terminated, by definition.[32] It may be significant that principles of this kind can often be expressed in a Latin formula, which reveals their antiquity in legal thinking generally. None of the principles in this category have, as such, an ethical or moral significance.

Good faith as a general concept may be a candidate for inclusion in the category of international legal principles, though it is, in isolation, a highly flexible concept. In the *Nuclear Tests* cases, the ICJ referred to the principle of good faith as a 'basic principle', but invoked it only in the special context of the 'creation and performance of legal obligations',[33] and omitted any reference (deliberately or otherwise) to Article 38, paragraph 1(*c*) of the Statute. This placed the reasoning of the decision in a treaty or quasi-treaty context,

---

[29] An interesting question is whether judicial review of decisions of political bodies, as found in municipal systems, could be regarded as a general principle of law transposable to the international plane, so as to justify ICJ review of Security Council decisions: see E. de Wet, 'Judicial Review as an Emerging General Principle of Law and its Implications for the International Court of Justice', Netherlands ILR (2000), 181, who, however, sees the principle as only a 'tenuous' basis for such ICJ action (p. 208).

[30] The difficulties resulting from inconsistencies in usage and application, as between different national systems, of what may look like the same principles, should not be underestimated: see the observations of Prosper Weil on the difficulties involved in 'transplantation': P. Weil, 'Le Droit international en quête de son identité', 237 Recueil des cours (1992-VI), 145ff.; and the present writer's lectures, H. Thirlway, 'Concepts, Principles, Rules and Analogies: International and Municipal Legal Reasoning', 294 Recueil des cours (2002).

[31] Though the principle is regarded by David Kennedy, curiously enough, as 'soft law': D. Kennedy, 'The Sources of International Law' 2 AM UJILP (1987), 25; cited in A. Boyle and C. Chinkin, *The Making of International Law* (Oxford: Oxford University Press, 2007), 14, and it has even been suggested (e.g. by A. T. Guzman, *How International Law Works: A Rational Choice Theory* (Oxford: Oxford University Press, 2008), 183), that it is a principle of customary law, but this raises problems in connection with the notion of hierarchy of sources: see Ch. I sect. 3.

[32] See the extensive consideration of the principle in the judgment in *Application of the Genocide Convention (Bosnia v. Serbia)* [2007-II] ICJ Rep 89ff., paras. 114ff.

[33] [1986] ICJ Rep 268, 473.

referable more appropriately to paragraph 1(*a*) of that text.[34] The principle of interpretation of treaties in good faith also suggests itself as appropriate for the category of self-evident general principles of law, and one that might be thought to govern treaty-law rather than being contained within it.[35] It is therefore unexpected that the ICJ has treated the good faith principle in this context as a matter of 'customary international law as expressed in Article 31 of the Vienna Convention on the Law of Treaties',[36] rather than a general principle. The implications of this categorization are rather strange; since there is nothing pre-ordained or logically *necessary* about a rule of customary law, the dictum seems to suggest that things might have been otherwise, that a legal system might exist in which it was *not* required to interpret treaties in good faith, that it was legitimate to interpret them in bad faith—*quod est absurdum*. A more appropriate (and more respectful) conclusion is that the Court is very reluctant to appeal to general principles if another source can be cited.

This is also suggested by two recent cases before the ICJ: first, the case of *Application of the Interim Accord of 13 September 1995*,[37] in which Greece asserted the existence in international law, and relevance, of the *exceptio non adimpleti contractus*, the rule that a party who has not performed his side of a contract may not insist on compliance by the other party. The judgment found on the facts that, since Greece had failed to show that the conditions for the *exceptio* 'which it had itself asserted' were not met, it was 'unnecessary for the Court to determine whether that doctrine forms part of contemporary international law'.[38] Judge Simma would have upheld the application of the *exceptio*, but took the view that it had in effect been excluded by Articles 42 and 60 of the Vienna Convention on the Law of Treaties: the latter text sets out the means of terminating or suspending the operation of a treaty 'as a consequence of its breach', and the former provides that termination or suspension 'may take place only as a result of the provisions of the treaty or of

---

[34] See the discussion in Ch. II, sect. 4.

[35] In this sense Oppenheim's *International Law*, 9th edn., i. 37–8; and cf. the dictum of the ICJ in *Border and Transborder Armed Actions* [1988] ICJ Rep 105, para. 94: 'The principle of good faith is, as the Court has observed, "one of the basic principles governing the creation and performance of legal obligations" (*Nuclear Tests, ICJ Reports 1974*, p. 268, para. 46; p. 473, para. 49); it is not in itself a source of obligation where none would otherwise exist.'

[36] *Oil Platforms (Preliminary Objections)* [1996-II] ICJ Rep 812, para. 23. The reference to the Vienna Convention suggests that it was overlooked that not everything that is codified by a convention was necessarily customary law up to that time, that general principles may also conveniently be included even though they existed and were operational prior to the conclusion of the codifying treaty.

[37] *Former Republic of Macedonia v. Greece* [2011] ICJ Rep 644.

[38] [2011] ICJ Rep 691, para. 161.

the present Convention'.[39] At first sight this raises the question whether a general principle can be excluded by treaty;[40] but in fact Article 60 of the Convention preserves and enacts the essence of the principle, merely leaving out the specific application of it favoured by Judge Simma. The *exceptio* as a principle says no more than that you cannot have the benefit of a contract if you don't fulfil your side of the bargain; nor does the Vienna Convention say otherwise.[41]

The second case of interest in this connection is that of *Questions concerning the Obligation to Extradite or Prosecute*.[42] In that case, the Court found that the principle that a State cannot invoke its internal law to justify a failure to comply with international law, a principle which one might have thought was equally a general principle of law, 'reflects customary law'.[43] Again, it is difficult to imagine an international regime in which this principle did not hold sway; and this, it is suggested, casts doubt on the categorization of the principle as one of custom, since custom is of its nature adaptable and tending to vary from society to society. If this principle does indeed rank as a general principle, it does not seem that it might *also* be part of customary law; the fact that general principles are mentioned in a separate clause of Article 38 shows that this is not how they were envisaged.

The examples of express reliance by the International Court on a 'general principle' are thus sparse, and in no case did the Court expressly link the principle adumbrated with Article 38, paragraph 1(c), of the Statute. Mention has already been made of the *Corfu Channel* case, in which the Court based its finding that Albania had failed in a duty to warn ships approaching a minefield, on 'certain general and well-recognized principles, namely: elementary considerations of humanity ...; the principle of the freedom of maritime communication; and every State's obligation not to allow knowingly its territory to be used for acts contrary to the rights of other States'.[44] This has been widely understood as in substance an appeal to the 'general principles' contemplated by Article 38, paragraph 1(c), of the Statute.[45] A recent

---

[39] See separate opinion of Judge Simma [2011] ICJ Rep 703, para. 19.

[40] A question going to the problem of the hierarchy of sources (Ch. VI). It would seem that a treaty may operate to effect an exception to such a principle, but perhaps not exclude it altogether.

[41] Cf. also the Court's treatment of the principle underlying the *exceptio non adimpleti* in the 1971 *Namibia* opinion, cited in the *Interim Accord* case by Simma [2011] ICJ Rep 706, para. 24, where it treated the Vienna Convention (not yet in force) as 'a codification of existing *customary law* on the subject'. Note also Judge Simma's remarks on the *Gabčíkovo* case ([2011] ICJ Rep 706, para. 25).

[42] *Belgium* v. *Senegal* [2012] ICJ Rep 422.   [43] [2012] ICJ Rep 460, para. 113.

[44] [1949] ICJ Rep 22.

[45] *Contra*, Meron, *Human Rights and Humanitarian Norms as Customary Law* (Oxford: Oxford University Press, 1989), 109–10, who regards the finding as an application of customary law.

study, however, examining the dictum against the background of the parties' pleadings in the case, has suggested that the Court did not have in mind the principles of paragraph 1(*c*), but was referring to principles existing under customary law, and to a rule 'extracted ... by reference to treaty provisions', namely the Hague Convention of 1907.[46]

In the case of *Reservations to the Genocide Convention*, the ICJ advised that 'the principles underlying the Convention are principles which are recognized by civilized nations as binding on States, even without any conventional obligation', and that '[t]he object of the Convention is "to confirm and endorse the most elementary principles of morality"'.[47] The Court did not, however, derive any legal conclusion directly from these observations; they led up to the finding that the Genocide Convention 'was manifestly adopted for a purely humanitarian and civilizing purpose', that it was intended to advance a 'common interest' and that accordingly 'it was the intention ... that as many States as possible should participate'.[48] Again, no reference was made to Article 38, paragraph 1(*c*), nor would such reference have been appropriate.

Mention of a 'general principle' can be found in a number of other ICJ decisions, but that formula does not necessarily indicate reference to one of the principles contemplated by Article 38, paragraph 1(*c*), as a basis of decision independent of the operation of other sources.[49] We have also noted a number of cases in which States have invoked general principles before the ICJ, but in which the Court has decided the case on a different basis, or has found it unnecessary for other reasons to rule on the applicability or otherwise of a general principle. One further field in which the existence of a general principle of law has been asserted is on the controversial question of the binding effect of provisional measures indicated by the ICJ under Article 41 of its Statute. When the question was examined in the *LaGrand* case, the Court dealt with it purely as a question of interpretation of the Statute, without recourse to 'general principles'.[50]

Several recent ICJ cases have raised the question of the existence and scope of general principles of law in the context of judicial proceedings (those of

---

[46] See A. Shihata, 'The Court's Decision *in silentium* on the Sources of International Law: Its Enduring Significance', in K. Bannelier, T. Christakis, and S. Heathcote (eds.), *The ICJ and the Development of International Law* (London: Routledge, 2012), 201.

[47] [1951] ICJ Rep 23.   [48] [1951] ICJ Rep 23–4.

[49] A very full enumeration of such references will be found in the separate opinion of Judge Cançado Trindade in the *Pulp Mills on the River Uruguay* case [2010] ICJ Rep 143–5, paras. 20–5 of the opinion.

[50] *LaGrand (Germany v. United States of America), Merits, Judgment* [2001] ICJ Rep 466, para. 99.

the Court itself, and by implication more generally in international litigation).[51] A principle laid down in this context, but having wider scope, is the classic, and long-established principle 'that reparation must, as far as possible, wipe out all the consequences of the illegal act and reestablish the situation which would, in all probability, have existed if that act had not been committed'.[52]

The following principles have also been judicially recognized as being in this category:

The *Monetary Gold* principle, that the ICJ (and by implication anybody having the status of a 'court') cannot adjudicate on the international responsibility of a State not a party before it, and thus not consenting to such adjudication; the ICJ has however ruled in *Application of the Genocide Convention (Croatia/Serbia)* that the principle 'has no application to a State that no longer exists';[53]

- The principle of *res judicata*, declared by the Court in *Delimitation of the Continental Shelf (Nicaragua/Colombia)* to be 'a general principle of law'[54]
- The principle of 'the sound administration of justice', invoked (for example) in support of
  - the principle of the equality of the parties: *Judgment No, 2867 of ILO*;[55]
  - the possibility of joinder of the proceedings in two separate cases (see those brought by and against Costa Rica and Nicaragua);[56]
  - the burden and the standard of proof;[57]
- The right of a party to legal proceedings to confidentiality of communications with its legal advisers, which the Court considered might be derived from the principle of the sovereign equality of States, 'one of the fundamental principles

---

[51] A matter extensively discussed in the lengthy opinions of Judge Cançado Trindade, e.g. [2015-II] ICJ Rep 623–31, paras. 23–40. (The presence of an opinion of this judge in each case is, if not a procedural principle, at least a regular procedural landmark.)

[52] Factory at Chorzów, Merits, 1928, PCIJ, Series A, No. 17, p. 47, recalled in *Certain Activities carried out by Nicaragua (Compensation)*, Judgment of 2 February 2018, para. 29.

[53] [2015-I] ICJ Rep 3, at p. 57, para. 116; criticized by Judge Tomka, *ibid.*, pp. 165–6, paras. 28 ff. In the earlier case, the Court had referred to the point as an aspect of one of 'the fundamental principles of its Statute', hinting at a source in treaty-law rather than general principles, a dubious proposition.

[54] [2016-I] ICJ Rep 125, para. 58; the Court noted that the principle 'protects, at the same time, the judicial function of a court or tribunal and the parties to a case'; this dictum was approved and followed in *Maritime Delimitation in the Caribbean Sea (Costa Rica v. Nicaragua)*, Judgment of 2 February 2018, para, 68.

[55] [2012] ICJ Rep 10.

[56] Two Orders of 17 April 2013 in *Construction of a Road in Costa Rica* and *Activites of Nicaragua in the Border Area* [2013] ICJ Rep 170, para. 18; 187, para. 12. Note however that in *Maritime Delimitation in the Caribbean Sea and the Pacific Ocean*, Order of 5 February 2017, para. 15, the Court claimed that joinder was a matter for its discretion (and cf. Art. 47 of the Rules of Court).

[57] *Genocide Convention (Croatia v. Serbia)* [2015] ICJ Rep 3.

of the international legal order, and ... reflected in Article 2, paragraph 1, of the Charter of the United Nations'.[58]

• The principles relevant to the determination of the compensation due in reparation for an illegal act.[59]

Thus far the discussion has proceeded on the basis of a traditionalist, or, if you will, a positivist viewpoint. Although this has in recent times been the most conspicuous interpretation of international law, yet as was suggested by Fitzmaurice as long ago as 1973, 'the weight of preponderant international law doctrine has continually oscillated between [the] two concepts' of the 'positivist-voluntarist' approach and the 'natural law' approach.[60] The increasing attention paid to legal concepts, such as the law of human rights, that were difficult to derive from voluntarist bases similarly led Dominicé in 1992 to hail a return of the concept of 'natural law'.[61] What was discernible, he suggested, was

non pas l'idée qu'il existerait un système de normes juridiques d'origine transcendante, mais plutôt l'idée que certaines régles du droit international sont identifiées comme telles en raison de la nature de leur contenu—particulièrement important du point de vue éthique—ou encore font l'objet d'un processus de création lui aussi quelque peu différent du mode usuel en raison du poids moral particulier attaché à leur teneur.[62]

However, in the context of the 'general principles of law' referred to in the ICJ Statute, he inclines to the view that while one category of these (including e.g. good faith, *pacta sunt servanda*, the obligation of reparation for injury, etc.) has an ethical significance, it is more their logical necessity that earns them their place in the canon of general principles; and that for the impact of natural law in modern times it is more profitable to look in the field of customary law.[63] This judgment has, it is suggested, been confirmed by developments since Dominicé was writing, with the gloss that it is custom as driven by the pressure of international conventions that has moved so far in

---

[58] *Seizure and Detention of Certain Documents (Timor-Leste v. Australia)* [2014] ICJ Rep 153, para. 27. Cf. Sienho Yee, 'Article 38 of the ICJ Statute and Applicable Law: Selected Issues in Recent Cases' *Journal of International Dispute Settlement*, Vol 7, Issue 2, July 2016.

[59] Most recently declared by the ICJ in *Certain Activites carried out by Nicaragua in the Border Area, (Compensation)*, Judgment of 2 February 2018, paras. 29–31.

[60] G. G. Fitzmaurice, 'The Future of Public International Law and the International Legal System in the Circumstances of Today', Special Report, Institut de droit international, Livre du centenaire (1973), para. 98.

[61] C. Dominicé, 'Le grand retour du droit naturel en droit des gens', Mélanges en l'honneur de Jean-Michel Grossen (1992); repr. in Dominicé, *L'Ordre juridique international entre tradition et innovation* (Geneva: PUF, 1997), 31.

[62] 'Le grand retour du droit naturel' (1997), 33 para. 5.

[63] 'Le grand retour du droit naturel' (1997), 33–7 paras. 6–7.

this direction. General principles, whether or not common to municipal systems, must represent a shared approach to a general need of a strictly legal nature. For ethical principles to influence international law, the filter afforded by the process of the development of custom must allow what is genuinely felt as ethical for all mankind to be distinguished from views (often passionately held) as to what is right which are nevertheless imbued with a particular local, regional, or religious influence.[64]

2. The role of equity

There is no doubt that international law recognizes the concept of equity,[65] that equity is a part of international law; but is it one of the 'general principles of law', or can it be said to operate as a source of law, independent of, or additional to, the sources of Article 38 of the ICJ Statute? That instrument, in paragraph 2, does allot a separate role in judicial decision to one form of equity, by recognizing that the Court has power 'to decide a case *ex aequo et bono*, if the parties agree thereto'. This power has never been exercised, as no parties have yet invited or authorized the Court to do so, but the text is generally understood as meaning that the Court would decide simply on the basis of what it thought was fair in the circumstances, however much the solution so arrived at might depart from what would have resulted from the application of law.[66] While a decision so given would be a judicial one, it would by definition not be a legal one, in the sense of based on law, and in no sense therefore can paragraph 2 of Article 38 be regarded as indicating a source of international law. That particular and idiosyncratic form of equity will therefore be left aside in what follows, which will be devoted to equity as it is more generally invoked.

There are innumerable references to equity, or to considerations analogous to equity, in multilateral conventions, for example in the law of the sea (of

---

[64] See in particular the discussion of the role of Islamic law in Ch. VIII, sect. 2(*c*).

[65] In the context of international law, it is essential to rid one's mind of the specialized meaning of 'equity' in Anglo-American law, deriving ultimately from the historical circumstance of the distinction between the High Court and the Court of Chancery. See, however, the separate opinion of Judge Fitzmaurice in the *Barcelona Traction* case, suggesting that international law would be the richer if it *did* incorporate such a system: [1970] ICJ Rep 85–6, para. 36. For the opposite view, see separate opinion of Judge Ammoun in the same case: [1970] ICJ Rep 85–6, para. 333.

[66] The text raises the question (again, never put to the test) whether, if the Court can, by agreement between the parties, be in effect directed to decide without taking into account the law that would otherwise be applicable, it can similarly be directed to apply a 'tailor-made' law, ignoring, for example, certain texts or rule that the parties both reject, or whether this would be too great a contradiction of the opening words of Article 38 of the Statute.

which more later), international economic law, sustainable development, etc. The application of equity in these contexts raises no problem in relation to the theory of sources, as they are clearly referable to treaty-law as source (Art. 38(1)(*a*) of the ICJ Statute). It remains to be seen, however, whether other examples of recourse to equity are referable to customary law or to the general principles of law, or whether equity has some claim to be considered itself a source.

The role of equity has been judicially considered by the International Court in several cases, of which it is convenient to mention first the *Frontier Dispute* case between Burkina Faso and Mali; although not chronologically the first such decision, it contains a useful analysis of different kinds of equity. The case concerned the position of a land frontier. At the time of the decision, there was in existence a body of judicial and arbitral decisions in maritime delimitation cases involving the employment of 'equitable principles'; these cases will be considered further, but it should be noted here that they involved drawing a delimitation line in an area—but an area of sea—that had never previously been divided. The *Frontier Dispute* case, like most cases involving disputed land boundaries, involved determining the position of a boundary that had at some stage been created (by agreement, or in the case of ex-colonized countries, by administrative decision). Unless the boundary were to be determined *ex aequo et bono*, considerations of fairness—equity in a loose sense—had no role to play.[67] Mali, however, asked the Court to apply 'that form of equity which is inseparable from the application of international law'.[68]

The Chamber distinguished between three forms of equity: *contra legem* (contrary to law), *praeter legem* (additional to law), and *infra legem* (within the law).[69] The first of these apparently equates to decision *ex aequo et bono*: fairness is all, and the otherwise applicable law has no role to

---

[67] As the Chamber observed, no modification of these frontiers 'is necessary or justifiable on the ground of considerations of equity', since 'however unsatisfactory they may be, [they] ... are fully in conformity with contemporary international law': [1986] ICJ Rep 633, para. 149. In some arbitration cases, where it was recognized that the boundary might be difficult to establish in strict law, the tribunal was authorized to go beyond this: see the *Bulama Island* arbitration, J. B. Moore, *History and Digest of the International Arbitrations to which the United States has been Party, together with appendices containing the treaties relating to such arbitrations and historical and legal notes* (Washington: Government Printing Office, 1898); *Chaco* case, *United Nations Reports of International Arbitral Awards* (*UNRIAA*), iii. 1819.

[68] [1986] ICJ Rep 567, para. 27.

[69] [1986] ICJ Rep 567–8, para. 28. There is some inconsistency in the use of these and similar terms: see e.g. Bin Cheng in *Current Legal Problems* (1955), 185; W. Jenks, *The Prospects of International Adjudication* (London: Stevens, 1964), 316ff; V. D. Degan, *L'Équité et le droit international* (The Hague: Nihjhoff, 1970), 25ff.

play.[70] The Chamber did not explain what significance it attached to equity *praeter legem*; what that term may mean will be considered later. The Chamber indicated however that it would 'have regard to equity *infra legem*, that is, that form of equity which constitutes a method of interpretation of the law [in force], and is one of its attributes', and it quoted an earlier judgment to the effect that 'it is not a matter of finding simply an equitable solution, but an equitable solution derived from the applicable law'.[71]

The application of this reasoning came later in its judgment, when the Chamber had to determine the course of the frontier in the region of a small lake known as the pool of Soum; it found it established that the frontier crossed the pool, but where? Its solution was to divide the pool equally between the parties, on this basis:

[I]n the absence of any precise indication in the texts of the position of the frontier line, the line should divide the pool of Soum in two, in an equitable manner. Although 'Equity does not necessarily imply equality' (*North Sea Continental Shelf, I.C.J. Reports 1969*, p. 49, para. 91), where there are no special circumstances the latter is generally the best expression of the former.[72]

This then was an application of equity *infra legem*, 'a method of interpretation of the law in force and one of its attributes'.

What the decision illustrates is one of the principal functions of equity in international law, perhaps indeed its sole function. While rules of international law generally answer the question What? (what are the rights of the parties?) or Whether (was this act a breach of international law?), equity comes into play when the question is How far? How much? A good recent example is the decision of the International Court on compensation in the *Ahmadou Sadio Diallo* case, where there was a claim for compensation for the non-material (i.e. unquantifiable) injury, concerning Mr Diallo's arrest, imprisonment, and expulsion. The Court explained that 'Quantification of compensation for non-material injury necessarily rests on equitable considerations.'[73] The Court cited in this connection the decision of the European Court of Human Rights in *Al-Jedda* v. *United Kingdom*, that for determining damage, the 'guiding principle' is equity, which 'involves flexibility and an

---

[70] A different view is advanced by F. Francioni, 'Equity in International Law', in R. Wolfrum (ed.), *Max Planck Encyclopedia of Public International Law* (Oxford: Oxford University Press, 2012), iii. 636–7, paras. 14–18.

[71] The authoritative French text does not contain anything corresponding to the words 'in force' in the English translation. The citation is from the *Fisheries Jurisdiction* cases [1974] ICJ Rep 33, para. 78, and 202, para. 69.

[72] [1986] ICJ Rep 633, para. 150.   [73] [2012] ICJ Rep 334, para. 24.

objective consideration of what is just, fair and reasonable in all the circumstances of the case'.[74]

Such equity is certainly not *contra legem*, however much in itself a decision on these lines may resemble a decision on a compensation issue taken *ex aequo et bono*. But is equity being applied in this way because a *legal* rule directs this (*infra legem*), or is it operating independently to resolve a question that the law is not equipped to answer (*praeter legem*)? On the latter analysis, it could be said that equity was in some sense an independent source of law, inasmuch as the legal outcome in such cases as the *Diallo* case requires its contribution, the matter not being resolved by rules drawn from the other recognized sources. The dictum in the *North Sea Continental Shelf* case, emphasizing that the 'equitable solution' to be adopted is one 'derived from the applicable law' (i.e. *infra legem*) has been criticized as 'simply a rhetorical device permitting the court to "assume" the existence of a legal norm or principle prescribing the application of equitable principles'.[75]

In the *Barcelona Traction* case, decided the year after the *North Sea* case, an attempt was made by a party to rely on equity *praeter legem*.[76] The Court had found that customary law did not recognize a right for the national State of shareholders in a foreign company to exercise diplomatic protection on their behalf for the losses they suffered through a wrong done to the company by a third State. Belgium, the applicant, had contended that on that basis, 'considerations of equity . . . require that it be held to possess a right of protection'. The Court hinted that if the injury to the company had been done by its own national State, then 'considerations of equity might call for the possibility of protection of the shareholders . . . by their own national State'. It continued, 'In view however of the discretionary nature of diplomatic protection, considerations of equity cannot require more than the possibility for some protector State to intervene, whether it be the national State of the company, by virtue of the general rule . . . or in a secondary capacity, the national State of the shareholders . . .'.[77] For these reasons, the argument that the shareholders should be protected on a basis of 'considerations of equity' was rejected.[78] But when these considerations do operate, simply to ensure that 'some protector

---

[74] Application No. 27021/08, Judgment of 7 July 2011, *ECHR Reports* (2011), para. 114.

[75] F. Francioni, 'Equity in International Law', in R. Wolfrum (ed.), *Max Planck Encyclopedia of Public International Law* (Oxford: Oxford University Press, 2012), iii. 635, para. 10.

[76] *Barcelona Traction, Light and Power Company, Limited* [1970] ICJ Rep 48ff., paras. 92ff.

[77] [1970] ICJ Rep 48ff., para. 94.

[78] Shareholder applicants before the US/Iran Claims Tribunal may, under the Claims Settlement Declaration, assert claims belonging to their corporation; but 'equity requires that they take such claims subject to the defenses and counterclaims that could have been raised as against the corporation': *Harza* et al. v. *Iran*, Award No. 232–97–2, para. 86.

State can intervene', do they operate directly, or are they rather the inspiration for developments, actual or potential, in customary law? In his separate opinion, Judge Jessup mentioned the extension of diplomatic protection to shareholders, and explained that '[t]he rationale seems to be based largely on equitable considerations, and the result is so reasonable it has been accepted in State practice'.[79]

Turning now to the process of maritime delimitation, as it has developed during the period since the end of the Second World War, we may set aside, for the sake of simplicity, the essentially codifying provisions of international conventions (in particular, the United Nations Convention on the Law of the Sea), since (as already noted) the application of equity by virtue of a treaty indication raises no problem of sources theory. It has, however, also become well established that, as a matter of customary law, each coastal State is entitled to certain rights over the sea and the seabed off its coasts, in respect of the territorial sea, the continental shelf, and the exclusive economic zone. Unless these areas are bounded only by the open sea, a question of delimitation arises between the areas subject to the rights of one coastal State and the areas subject to the rights of its neighbours, opposite or adjacent.[80] Such delimitation may be, and usually is, effected by agreement between the States concerned: thus treaty-law determines the legal validity of the outcome. Failing agreement, the delimitation may be effected by judicial or arbitral decision; and the court or arbitrator will (unless otherwise agreed) apply customary law. It would seem to follow that the delimitation that would comply with customary law already exists *in posse* before and behind the treaty-law delimitation that is actually concluded. The latter may well not follow the theoretical customary-law line; for example, one State may make concessions departing from what it believes to be its full entitlement in one area, in exchange for parallel concessions by the other party in a different area. This raises no problem of theory, since treaties may of course modify customary entitlements; and the extent of maritime rights has never been thought to be a matter of *jus cogens*. On the basis that there is a theoretically 'correct' delimitation, what the judge or arbitrator is doing is, so to speak, 'discovering' that 'correct' line; in theory, any judge or arbitrator given the same mandate, and supplied with the same materials, would draw the same line.

This is not, however, what emerges from a study of, for example, the ICJ decisions on maritime delimitation. On the one hand, the Court speaks (for example) of entitlement; on the other it speaks of proportionality, or rather

[79] 191–2.

[80] For an excellent general survey, see Y. Tanaka, *Predictability and Flexibility in the Law of Maritime Delimitation* (Oxford: Hart, 2006).

it seeks to avoid 'disproportionality' in the areas attributed to each party. For example, in the recent case of the *Territorial and Maritime Dispute (Nicaragua v. Colombia)*, the Court explained that, following previous jurisprudence, the third stage in the process of determination of the line would be 'testing the result achieved by the boundary line ... to ascertain whether, taking account of all the circumstances, there is a significant disproportionality which would require further adjustment'.[81] The Court also explains that this does not mean that what is to be achieved is simply 'a correlation between the length of the parties' coasts and their respective shares of the relevant area'.[82] There is, in short, room for the sort of judicial appreciation and weighing-up of factors that cannot be reduced to a formula.[83] The theoretical 'ideal' 'correct' delimitation is not, it seems, already there waiting to be discovered.

Equity, however, is the subject of a more general dictum in the *North Sea Continental Shelf* cases:

The Court comes next to the rule of equity. The legal basis of that rule in the particular case of the delimitation of the continental shelf as between adjoining States has already been stated. It must however be noted that the rule rests also on a broader basis. Whatever the legal reasoning of a court of justice, its decisions must by definition be just, and therefore in that sense equitable. Nevertheless, when mention is made of a court dispensing justice or declaring the law, what is meant is that the decision finds its objective justification in considerations lying not outside but within the rules, and in this field it is precisely a rule of law that calls for the application of equitable principles.[84]

What was the source of the 'rule of law' that, in the view of the Court, effected a *renvoi* to equitable principles? A little earlier in the judgment, the Court refers to 'applying a rule of law which itself requires the application of equitable principles', and spells this out as being 'in accordance with the ideas which have always underlain the development of the legal regime of the continental shelf in this field'.[85] This appears to be an appeal to something closely resembling *opinio juris*, and perhaps thus justifies attributing the role of equity in this field to inchoate or developing customary law.

As the *Nicaragua v. Colombia* and *Costa Rica v. Nicaragua* cases show, the role of equity in maritime delimitation has developed into a final test, an

---

[81] [2012] ICJ Rep 715, para. 239. Cf. also paras. 202-4 of the Judgment of 2 February 2018 in the case of *Maritime Delimitation in the Caribbean Sea and the Pacifi Ocean (Cosat Rica v. Nicaragua)*.

[82] [2012] ICJ Rep 715, para. 240.

[83] It is tempting to illustrate the idea by suggesting that this is a stage in the process that could not be performed by a computer; but the development of AI (artificial intelligence) has achieved so much that this would probably be subject to contradiction!

[84] [1969] ICJ Rep 48, para. 88.   [85] [1969] ICJ Rep 47, para. 85.

ultimate stage in the process of drawing a line, when it is looked at from a point of view of general fairness, and with a view to possible corrective action. Initially, it seems to have been only injustice of a fairly extreme degree that would make it necessary to invoke equity: in the *Gulf of Maine* case, the ICJ chamber was concerned by the possibility that the result of its elaboration of a delimitation, 'even though achieved through the application of equitable criteria' should 'unexpectedly be revealed as radically inequitable, that is to say, as likely to entail catastrophic repercussions for the livelihood and economic well-being of the population of the countries concerned'.[86]

It seems possible to conclude that the great majority of references to 'equity' in international law can be regarded as the invocation of equity, equitable principles, or what is 'just and equitable', though the intermediary of a treaty provision or a rule of customary law, in other words as the operation of equity *infra legem*.[87] To the extent that equity may in some limited contexts appear to operate *praeter legem*, independently, this need not call for the recognition of equity as an independent source; it is better regarded as one of the 'general principles of law' recognized by Article 28 of the ICJ Statute. This indeed was the interpretation of that text adopted by two judges of the Permanent Court as long ago as 1937, in the case concerning *Diversion of Waters from the Meuse*. Judge Hudson noted that '[t]he Court has not been expressly authorized by its Statute to apply equity as distinguished from law', but pointed out that 'Article 38 of the Statute expressly directs the application' of general principles, and that 'in more than one nation principles of equity have an established place in the legal system'.[88] Judge Anzilotti considered the principle *inadimplenti non est adimplendum*[89] to be 'one of those "general principles of law recognized by civilized nations" which the Court applies in virtue of Article 38 of its Statute'.[90]

3. General principles of law and *non liquet*

As has been explained, the general principles of law found their way into the Statute of the Permanent Court as a reserve source to provide a basis for

---

[86] [1984] ICJ Rep 342, para. 237.

[87] Note the development of the 'Fair and equitable treatment' standard in international investment law, derived originally from consistent usage of the term in treaty texts, examined in Chapter VIII, p.217

[88] *PCIJ Series A/B No. 70*, p. 76.

[89] i.e. the *exceptio non adimpleti contractus*, mentioned earlier (n. 38).

[90] 'A party that is not complying with an agreement cannot insist on compliance by the other party': *PCIJ Series A/B No. 70*, p. 50.

decision in the event that neither relevant treaties nor customary law did so. Mention has also been made of what is known as a *non liquet*: a decision by a court or tribunal that the matter in dispute cannot be determined on the basis of law, inasmuch as the law has nothing to say on the question. It should be emphasized that a decision of this kind is different in nature from a decision that the law does not support the claim made, with the consequence that the respondent wins the case. A finding that a particular claim is not supported by a positive rule of law, is tantamount to a finding that there exists a negative rule of law, as is indicated by the decision in the case of the *SS Lotus* before the Permanent Court, already mentioned in Chapter I.[91] Another example is the *Barcelona Traction, Light and Power Co.* case, also mentioned earlier, in connection with the possible application of equity. Belgium's claim for reparation from Spain for loss suffered by Belgian shareholders in a Canadian company—allegedly through unlawful action attributable to Spain, was dismissed, in effect on the ground that States did not make reparation in comparable circumstances to any State other than that of the company. This was a finding that there was no rule of law supporting that claim, but was nevertheless not a *non liquet*, but a finding as to the content of customary law: that in customary law, only the national State of the company (Canada) could seek reparation.

A further case should be mentioned in which, as the ICJ found, no decision at all could be given: the *Northern Cameroons* case.[92] The Court found that 'the proper limits of its judicial function do not permit it to entertain the claim submitted to it';[93] the reason was that the dispute was one 'about the interpretation and application of a treaty ... which has now been terminated, is no longer in force, and there can be no opportunity for a future act of interpretation or application of that treaty in accordance with any judgment the Court might render'.[94] The emphasis was not on the absence of any law that the Court might declare, that is a *non liquet* (since an interpretation of what the treaty used to mean when it was in force would have been a possible intellectual exercise), but on the absence of any purpose that might be served by a declaration of the law: hence the emphasis on the 'proper limits of [the] judicial function'.

The distinction to be emphasized is that between a finding that the right claimed does not exist, and a finding that there is no law on the point, positive or negative. This latter situation is one that is highly uncommon, if not

---

[91] See Ch. I, text and n. 50.

[92] The dispute arose out of the termination of the UN Trusteeship for the Cameroons; following a plebiscite, the territory was incorporated into Nigeria rather than into the Republic of Cameroon.

[93] [1963] ICJ Rep 38.   [94] [1963] ICJ Rep 37.

practically unknown, in municipal law; does it exist in international law, or would it exist if there were no 'general principles of law' to fall back on? The reason why it was only with the drafting of the original Statute of the Permanent Court that the problem surfaced is that it is essentially a judicial problem. For a court called upon to decide a dispute, in the absence of an international custom or an applicable treaty, the outcome of a case might have to be a *non liquet* unless the judge were also empowered to pray in aid general principles.[95] As between the parties to a dispute, however, there is no need for any formal recognition of an absence of law; each side will urge its interests, and from the clash of these—assuming that both parties truly seek a settlement—a compromise or intermediate solution will emerge—or, of course, the dispute may remain unsettled. If a solution is found, this in its turn may well have value as initiating the growth of a customary rule on the point in dispute.[96]

For this purpose, the context of a judicial decision must apparently also include an advisory opinion of the kind that the ICJ is empowered to give. In fact the ICJ decision that is the best candidate for classification as a *non liquet* is such an opinion: that given at the request of the UN General Assembly on the *Legality of the Threat or Use of Nuclear Weapons*. However, independently of whether a tribunal is or may be seised of a dispute, does there exist a correct legal solution to every dispute? If so, either the established sources must be capable of giving an authoritative answer in every combination of circumstances—and municipal legal systems do not support the idea that this is so even in comparatively sophisticated systems—there must be some 'fallback' legal principles to supply an answer when the normal sources fail to do so.[97] But does this prove that such principles actually exist, or must necessarily

---

[95] Cf. the present writer's H. Thirlway, *International Customary Law and Codification* (Leiden: Sijthoff, 1972), citing the discussions of the 1920 Advisory Committee of Jurists on the PCIJ Statute, p. 296; Siorat, *Le Problème des lacunes en droit international: Contribution à l'étude des sources du droit et de la fonction judiciaire* (Paris: Librairie générale de droit et de jurisprudence, 1958), H. Lauterpacht, 'Some Observations on the Problem of *Non Liquet* and the Completeness of the Legal Order', in *Symbolae Verzijl. présentées au professeur J. W. H. Verzijl* (The Hague: Martinus Nijhoff, 1958), 196; J. Stone, '*Non liquet* and the Function of Law in the International Community', 35 BYIL (1959) 124.

[96] The process does, of course, raise the problem of the point in time at which one may speak of *opinio juris*: see Chapter III sect. 2(c).

[97] In the case of a treaty, it is perfectly possible that the parties have failed to foresee every eventuality (cf. the *Haya de la Torre* and *Gabčíkovo/Nagymaros* cases, mentioned in this chapter). Something can be done with extensive interpretation; and if there is customary law on the issue, it will fill the gap. Interpretation carries its dangers, however; the observer must not cross the line between, on the one side, interpreting what the parties did say in order to understand what they thought they were achieving, and on the other, doing their work for them by writing into the text what the observer thinks would have been appropriate: see G. G. Fitzmaurice, '*Vae victis*, or Woe to the Negotiators: Your Treaty or Our "Interpretation" of it?' 65 AJIL (1971) 358. (For a contrary

exist? As Prosper Weil has convincingly observed, not only are some norms of international law too controversial to govern effectively the conduct of States, and others have only remained at the stage of abstract general principles, but '[i]n regard to certain points, international law knows no norm at all, but a lacuna.'[98]

Once again, the example of space law affords a useful illustration. Before the conclusion of the Outer Space Treaty in 1967,[99] was there any international law governing the matter? If the ICJ had been asked, at that time, for an advisory opinion on whether, for example, the moon was capable of appropriation, what reply could it have given (assuming that it did not simply exercise its discretion to decline to give an opinion at all)? It is suggested that the only answer could have been a *non liquet*, a statement that in the then current state of international law, the matter was not regulated by law. (This on the basis that the attitudes of States to the matter, however clear a consensus they seemed to indicate, did not establish a rule of customary law in the absence of practice, in the form of actual exploration of space, or visits to heavenly bodies.[100])

The question arose before the ICJ in a different context when it was asked for an advisory opinion on the legality of the threat or use of nuclear weapons. The Court found that 'In view of the current state of international law, and of the elements at its disposal, the Court cannot conclude definitively whether the threat or use of nuclear weapons would be lawful or unlawful in an extreme circumstance of self-defence, in which the very survival of a State would be at stake ...'.[101] It is striking that the Court did not find it appropriate to apply the doctrine of the *Lotus* decision,[102] that an act can only be unlawful in international law if it contravenes a legal prohibition, that is that it is not required that the act be authorized by a positive rule. At least in

---

view, see M. McDougal, J. Lasswell, and J. C. Miller, *The Interpretation of Agreements and World Public Order* (Boston: Martinus Nijhoff, 1994), Introduction, p. xlviii.).

[98] P. Weil, 'Towards Relative Normativity in International Law?', 77 AJIL (1983), 413, 414.

[99] Treaty on Principles Governing the Activities of States in the Exploration and Use of Outer Space, including the Moon and other Celestial Bodies, 610 UNTS 205.

[100] See Chapter III sect. 2(*b*), and the concept of 'instant custom' (Ch. III n. 65).

[101] [1996-I] ICJ Rep 33, para. 105. For the view that this is a case of *non liquet*, see e.g. Weil, '"The Court Cannot Conclude Definitively ...".': *Non Liquet* Revisited', 36 Columbia JIL (1997), 109; an alternative view might be that the Court was indicating that, although the law was complete, it had insufficient facts before it to apply it: see D. Bodansky, '*Non liquet* and the Incompleteness of International Law', in L. Boisson de Chazournes and P. Sands (eds.), *International Law, the International Court of Justice and Nuclear Weapons* (Cambridge: Cambridge University Press, 1999), 153, who nevertheless considers that 'a straightforward and plausible reading of the Court's opinion is as a *non liquet*'.

[102] See Ch. I sect. 4. Judge Shahabuddeen would have taken this course: see next paragraph.

the field of international responsibility, if the *Lotus* rule were one of universal application, it seems there would be no need for a doctrine of *non liquet*.

For Judge Shahabuddeen, who voted in favour of the finding quoted, it was, however, not a *non liquet*: on the basis of the *Lotus* rule, there was no prohibitory rule; alternatively, if an authorizing rule was absent, then States do not have a right to use nuclear weapons.[103] Judge Higgins, on the other hand, who voted against, took the view that it could not be doubted that 'the formula chosen is a *non liquet*'; she objected to it because for her it was 'an important and well-established principle that the concept of *non liquet* ... is no part of the Court's jurisprudence'.[104] In her view, '[t]he fact that principles are broadly stated and often raise further questions that require a response can be no ground for a *non liquet*'.[105] The need for a doctrine of *non liquet* is thus assessed by different schools of legal thinking, according to the degree that a measure of 'filling-in' or extrapolation of established law is considered to be legitimate, or the degree to which a given principle is deemed potentially generative of rules.

Another example, this time in the field of maritime delimitation, of an apparent hiatus in the law, though hardly a substantial one, is to be found in the ICJ judgment in the case of *Maritime Delimitation and Territorial Questions between Qatar and Bahrain*. The Court was faced with competing claims over 'low-tide elevations', areas of land covered at high tide, but clear at low tide. Qatar maintained that a low-tide elevation cannot legally be appropriated by a State; Bahrain maintained that it could be so appropriated.[106] Since these areas had been of no particular interest or importance until exploitation of the seabed made coastal delimitation an important issue, it is hardly surprising that the Court found that '[i]nternational treaty law is silent on the question whether low-tide elevations can be considered to be "territory". Nor is the Court aware of a uniform and widespread State practice which might have given rise to a customary rule which unequivocally permits or excludes appropriation of low-tide elevations ....'[107] The Court did not however have to allocate the elevations in question to the one State or the other; they were

---

[103] [1996-I] ICJ Rep 389–90.   [104] [1996-I] ICJ Rep 590, para. 30; 591, para. 36.

[105] [1996-I] ICJ Rep 591, para. 32.

[106] The Court observed that if a low-tide elevation lay within the territorial sea of a coastal State (which would normally be the case) then the sovereignty enjoyed over the territorial sea meant that the coastal State also had sovereignty over the low-tide elevation: [2001] ICJ Rep 101, para. 204. The question there was whether sovereignty over a low-tide elevation situated in an area of overlapping claims to territorial sea by two States could be obtained by appropriation.

[107] [2001] ICJ Rep 101–2, para. 205. The Court went on to consider in the following paragraph whether low-tide elevations could be treated for legal purposes as 'islands' and decided that they could not.

situated in an area where the claims of the two parties to territorial sea over-lapped, and what the Court was asked to decide was whether either (and if so, which) State could use the low-water mark of the low-tide elevation as baseline for determining the extent of the territorial sea. Its conclusion was the sensible one of disregarding the low-tide elevations altogether for the purpose of drawing the equidistance delimitation line.[108] Was this decision a *non-liquet?*

The possibility of lacunas in international law only poses a conceptual problem in the case of customary law. It is perfectly possible for a treaty to fail to cover every eventuality among those intended to be within its reach, and this does not imply any weakness in the theory that attributes the status of source of law to such instruments. In the *Haya de la Torre* case, the International Court had to decide the legal position under a Convention to which the States concerned were parties; it found that that Convention did not 'give a complete answer' to the question of how asylum, once lawfully granted, could be terminated.[109] Similarly, when dealing with the complex situation following the breakdown of the treaty arrangements between Hungary and Slovakia for the *Gabčíkovo/Nagymaros Project*, the Court was ultimately ob-liged to tell the parties to work out their own destiny, effectively on the basis that the situation was one contractually unforeseen.[110] In neither of these cases was there any role for the general principles of law to fill the gap.

---

[108] [2001] ICJ Rep 102–3, para. 209.

[109] [1951] ICJ Rep 80. The whole proceedings in this and the preceding *Asylum* case were conducted in the context of the parties' rights and obligations under the Havana Convention on Asylum; the Court regarded its mandate as limited in this respect ([1951] ICJ Rep 83). Whether customary law had anything to say on asylum, and if so whether it contained a similar hiatus, was not examined.

[110] [1997] ICJ Rep 83, para. 155(2)(B).

V

The Subsidiary Sources

1. Introduction

Paragraph 1(*d*) of Article 38 of the ICJ Statute makes a clear distinction[1] between, on the one hand, the sources mentioned in the preceding paragraphs, and on the other, judicial decisions and teachings, inasmuch as it refers to the latter as being merely 'subsidiary means for the determination of rules of law'.[2] The reason for this has already been mentioned: if a rule of international law is stated in a judicial decision, or in a textbook, it will be stated as a rule deriving either from treaty, custom, or the general principles of law. The decision, or the textbook, will not assert that the rule stated is law *because* the judge or the author has stated it; it will be so stated because the judge or the author considers that it derives from one of the three principal sources indicated in paragraphs (*a*) to (*c*) of Article 38.[3] The first three sources of Article 38 are formal sources; those of paragraph (*d*) are material rather than formal sources, but material sources having a special degree of authority. It does remain the case, though, that an informed observer may take the view that the source relied on does not supply the authority required for the finding, and that the decision constitutes judicial legislation decorously concealed under a

---

[1] Which is, it is suggested, misleading, as the distinction is less abrupt: A. Roberts and S. Sivakumaran, 'The Theory and Reality of the Sources of International Law', in M. Evans (ed.), *International Law* 5th edn., (Oxford: Oxford University Press, 2018), 106.

[2] It has been suggested that 'subsidiary' implies that 'lawyers are not *required* to resort to a source so designated: a strange interpretation when the implication is rather that frequently a lawyer may not *need* to resort to that source, because one of the non-subsidiary sources supplies the answer': A. Papaux and E. Wyler, 'Legal Theory as a Source of International Law', in *Oxford Handbook on the Sources of International Law* (Oxford: Oxford University Press, 2017) 513, 520 (italics added). That does not mean that, if such a need appears, every relevant publication must be scanned (see Sect. 3).

[3] In this sense also, Ingo Venzke (who, however, regards the doctrine of sources as a benevolent myth): 'The idea that international courts can confine themselves to applying the law hinges on the fact that the law is made by someone else': I. Venzke, 'The Role of International Courts as Interpreters and Developers of the Law: Working Out the Jurisgenerative Practice of Interpretation', 34 Loyola of Los Angeles International and Comparative Law Review (2011) 99.

fig-leaf of authority.[4] Nor would anyone suggest that there is never any 'added value' obtained when a court decides that a particular consequence results from a rule deriving from a recognized source; but as Sir Robert Jennings has observed, 'Even where a court creates law in the sense of developing, adapting, modifying, filling gaps, interpreting, or even branching out in a new direction, the decision must be seen to emanate reasonably and logically from existing and previously ascertainable law. A court has no purely legislative competence.'[5] This does not detract from the fact that a judicial decision, in almost all cases, by definition adds something to the corpus of law on the subject of the dispute: if the law had been crystal clear before the decision, it is reasonable to suppose that the case would never have been fought.[6] Some observers therefore regard the principle that a judicial body does not create law as a pious fiction, and insist that courts do have, in effect, a legislative role and competence; this will be discussed further, in relation to the ICJ itself, in section 2(*a*).[7]

This derivative character of judicial decisions and, in particular, of legal writings was clear even in the early days of the development of international law, when the opinions of eminent legal writers carried much more weight than do the authors of even the most respected textbooks of today. Those classical authors based their views much more on natural law than on State practice or judicial decisions.[8] Natural law is, by definition, as it were, only visible in the form stated by legal authors; and the greater the authority of the author, the more trust is to be placed in the definition there given of what natural law prescribes. Nevertheless, the authority of the law stated as natural law rested on what would now be called the general principles of law, and not on the say-so of the writer, of however great an eminence.

---

[4] This seems to be the underlying reason for the views of Judge Shahabuddeen, explained in sect. 2(*a*) of this chapter, as to the effect of two successive decisions of (e.g.) the ICJ adding up to law with only a judicial source as basis.

[5] R. Y. Jennings, 'The Role of the International Court of Justice' 68 BYIL (1997) 43.

[6] One might perhaps make exceptions for cases in which the respondent State does not appear (a course the possibility of which is contemplated by Art. 53 of the ICJ Statute). In the few cases where this has occurred (the two *Fisheries Jurisdiction* cases and the merits phase of the *Military and Paramilitary Activities* case), some, but not all, of the law declared by the Court might have been predicted by a competent observer.

[7] For a more general approach on these lines, see I. Venzke, *How Interpretation Makes International Law: On Semantic Change and Normative Twists* (Oxford: Oxford University Press, 2012), particularly pp. 69–71 and 144–7, and his conclusions on judicial development of GATT/WTO law, pp. 190–5.

[8] Nor should the influence, for much of the period, of an underlying coupling of natural law with the Christian religion be underestimated—sometimes with effects repugnant to the modern approach, as in the treatment of those referred to as 'the heathen'.

Now that there exists a much greater body of judicial and arbitral decisions enunciating rules of law, the emphasis in practice has shifted to the
contribution made by such decisions, and away from the views of 'the most
highly qualified publicists of the various nations'.[9] Furthermore, the judges
and arbitrators are more often than not themselves eminent scholars and
practitioners, so that the distinction between judicial precedent and teachings is not a sharp one. The two categories practically converge or overlap in
relation to the separate and dissenting opinions that Members of the ICJ are
authorized to attach to a decision, under Article 57 of the ICJ Statute. These
are written by judges, in that capacity, and to the extent that their authors
share the overall view of the Court must be regarded as judicial pronouncements. More delicate is the case of a dissenting opinion, or a separate opinion
indicating how the judge reaches the same conclusion as the majority of the
Court, but on different grounds.[10] To the extent that these may be regarded
as contradicted by the majority judgment, can they be regarded as judicial
decisions? At the same time, since they set out conclusions reached after considering the arguments presented by the parties on each side, they may be
regarded as having more weight than a simple 'opinion' of a publicist.[11] Still
further along the spectrum from the judicial to the academic are opinions, or
parts thereof, that deal with questions outside the scope of the decision, on
which the parties may or may not have expressed views.[12]

In any event, despite the principle *jura novit curia*,[13] States involved in a
dispute, or their counsel, will cite judicial precedents, judges' opinions, and
the leading textbooks and monographs in support of their claims, as will arbitrators and individual judges of the ICJ in separate or dissenting opinions.
The Court itself formerly avoided quoting scholarly publications, despite
the justification for doing so offered by Article 38;[14] the Chamber judgment

[9] In this sense also Roberts and Sivakuman in Evans (ed.), *International Law* 5th edn.
(Oxford: Oxford University Press, 2018), 107.

[10] The phenomenon may be less familiar to lawyers from a continental system, in view of the
general European practice whereby courts give a single judgment in the name of the court, as an entity. British lawyers are used to the subtle gradings of authority of observations made in the distinct
judgments of members of the Court of Appeal or the Supreme Court.

[11] This is not to say that such opinions may not have an interpretative function in relation to the
judgment, as indicating what views may have been examined in deliberation.

[12] To be deprecated therefore is the practice indulged in by certain Members of the ICJ, past and
present, of employing the right to attach an opinion as an opportunity to make public views on legal
(and sometimes political) questions bearing little or no relation to the issues before the Court in the
case. For a restrictive view of the extent of the judge's rights under Art. 57, see the declaration of
President Spender in *South West Africa* [1966] ICJ Rep 52–5, paras. 5–22.

[13] The principle that a court is presumed to know the law, and therefore is not restricted in its
decision to the legal issues presented in argument: see Ch. III sect. 1 n. 13.

[14] Two convincing explanations offered for this policy are that 'writers vary considerably in skill,
diligence, intellectual honesty, independence and eminence, but it may be thought invidious to

in the *Land, Island and Maritime Frontier* case (mentioning Oppenheim, Lauterpacht, and Gidel),[15] seemed to signal a relaxation of this policy, but the example has not been followed in subsequent cases.

2. Judicial decisions

2(a) International tribunals

The judicial decisions referred to in Article 38 of course include the decisions of the ICJ, as being of the highest authority: the ILC Conclusions refer to '[d]ecisions of international courts and tribunals, *in particular* of the International Court of Justice' as a subsidiary means for determining rules of customary international law (Conclusion 13 (1), emphasis added). It is in respect of these decisions in particular that the cross-reference in Article 38 of the Statute to Article 59 is relevant. The latter article states expressly that '[t]he decision of the Court has no binding force except between the parties and in respect of that particular case'.[16] The established jurisprudence of the Court has, of course, considerable weight, and is regularly relied on in argument before it, but no decision can simply be applied automatically to another case, however similar, even if one or both of the parties are the same.[17] The ICJ has, however, made clear that, even for the Court itself, previous decisions are not in the nature of binding precedents. In a recent case in which one of the points in issue was directly covered by an earlier decision, the Court said in relation to that decision: 'It is not a question of holding [the parties to the

---

distinguish between them' or that 'the Court is itself composed of eminent jurists who may be reluctant to treat others as "authorities" '; M. Mendelson, 'The ICJ and Sources of International Law', in V. Lowe and M. Fitzmaurice (eds.), *Fifty Years of the International Court of Justice: Essays in Honour of Sir Robert Jennings* (Cambridge: Cambridge University Press, 1996), 63 at 84.

[15] [1992] ICJ Rep 593, para. 394.

[16] The significance of the final phrase was emphasized in a recent case in which the Court had, in an interlocutory judgment, in effect decided (though implicitly) a jurisdictional issue that had not then been argued. When subsequently the issue was raised specifically, the Court held that the earlier judgment was *res judicata* and could not be reopened: see *Application of the Genocide Convention (Bosnia and Herzegovina v. Federal Republic of Yugoslavia)*, Judgment of 11 July 1996 [1996-II] ICJ Rep 595, and Judgment of 26 February 2007 [2007-II] ICJ Rep 93–102, paras. 121–40.

[17] This must be valid even when separate cases turning on the same facts are brought by one State against several others, as e.g. the *Use of Force* cases brought by Yugoslavia (Serbia) against the Member States of NATO. These could theoretically have been decided differently from each other, though their simultaneous presentation and virtually simultaneous decision would have made this hypothesis somewhat absurd (except in so far as there were any factual differences between the cases). Yet if the decision in some (or one) of them had been delayed, and a change in the composition of the Court had intervened, a decision inconsistent with the earlier ones could have been the result; and Arts. 38 and 59 would deprive the earlier decisions of any *automatic* authority.

current case] to decisions reached by the Court in previous cases. The real question is whether, in this case, there is cause not to follow the reasoning and conclusions of earlier cases.'[18] This judiciously worded indication suggests that to suppose that the rule of *stare decisis* (on Anglo-American lines) is excluded by Article 59[19] is going too far, though there may be more scope before the ICJ for the technique of 'distinguishing' earlier cases.

What is meant by the expression 'judicial decisions' in Article 38? In one sense, the 'decision' of the ICJ or of another international court is what is contained in the *dispositif,* the 'operative clause', as distinct from the reasoning leading up to it. The classic formula for that clause is that the Court 'decides', 'for these reasons/*pour ces motifs*'. It is in this sense that the 'decision' is declared by Article 59 to be 'binding' on the parties: the reasoning is not in itself binding.[20] However, when the 'decisions' of a court are being referred to as a source of law, it is evident that it is primarily the reasoning that is being contemplated. The decision in the sense of the operative clause, may be, for example, no more than 'The Court dismisses the claim' of the applicant party, which is in itself no guide to any court subsequently seeking the *ratio decidendi*. Here the 'decision' is the reasoning, which may cause the case to become a precedent, *faire jurisprudence*.

The extent to which this law-creative effect attaches to the separate and dissenting opinions has already been discussed; but is the whole text of the reasoning in a judgment authoritative as a 'judicial decision' in the sense of Article 38; or does international law recognize the distinction drawn in some municipal legal systems between essential reasoning and *obiter dicta*, observations by a judge in his decision that are not essential to the chain of reasoning leading to the ultimate finding?[21]

In the *Arrest Warrant* case[22] this distinction appears prominently. The Court re-asserted 'the rule according immunity from criminal jurisdiction and inviolability to incumbent Ministers for Foreign Affairs' relied on by the Applicant. The Court then observed that immunity was not the same as

---

[18] *Land and Maritime Boundary between Cameroon and Nigeria* [1998] ICJ Rep 275, para. 28.

[19] In this sense e.g. A. Pellet in A. Zimmermann et al. (eds.), *The Statute of the International Court of Justice: A Commentary*, 2nd edn. (Oxford: Oxford University Press, 2012), sub Art. 38, para. 307, p. 855.

[20] Though it is difficult to see how a party to the case could act, in that context, inconsistently with the reasoning without thereby also contravening the operative decision.

[21] There seems little scholarly comment on the point, but note the reference to the distinction by H. Lauterpacht, *The Development of International Law by the International Court* (Cambridge University Press, 1958), who argues for the desirability of ICJ Judgments being more wide-ranging than necessary for the determination of the issues in the case, in the interests of development of the law: see pp. 37 ff.

[22] *Case concerning the Arrest Warrant of 13 April 2000 (DRC v. Belgium)*, [2002] ICJ Rep 3.

impunity: '[i]mmunity from criminal jurisdiction and individual criminal responsibility are quite separate concepts'.[23] It went on to deduce, and specify,
four sets of circumstances in which the immunities of a Foreign Minister 'do
not represent a bar to criminal prosecution'.[24] Since none of these circumstances was present,[25] this paragraph of the judgment is unnecessary for the
decision, and was probably inserted as a general guide to the extent of the
immunities in question. But as an evident *obiter dictum*, what is its value as
such a guide if it does not rank as a precedent?[26] Simply, one must suppose,
the weight given to it by the general authority of the ICJ.

The ICJ is, of course, not the only international tribunal judging according
to public international law. While in principle operating in the field of international criminal law, the International Criminal Courts, the ICTY, and
similar bodies, may in the course of their work be called upon to decide
questions going beyond the application and interpretation of their respective
statutes and the definition of the crimes that they are called upon to deal
with, and thus contribute to stating the law.[27] In the case of the ICC, the
Rome Statute expressly states that 'The Court may apply principles and rules
of law as interpreted in its previous decisions'; but because of the operation of
the Court in separate chambers, it is difficult to say whether its practice has
tended to follow, or to diverge from, previous case-law.[28]

At the time of the ending of the Cold War in 1989 the number of permanent
international courts was six, plus the GATT system of non-compulsory settlement of disputes; and between 1945 and 1989 these courts handed down a
total of 373 judgments. According to an informed observer, today there are at
least twenty four such courts, and they have between them issued more than
37,000 binding judgments.[29]

There are also the numerous courts of arbitration set up, particularly under
the auspices of the Permanent Court of Arbitration, whose decisions are made

---

[23] [2002] ICJ Rep 25, para. 60.   [24] *Ibid.*, para. 61.
[25] Though, curiously, the Court did not expressly say so, possibly by oversight.
[26] There has been some reliance on it by international criminal courts: see for example the *Charles Taylor* case, Special Court for Sierra Leone, Appeals Chamber, Case No. SCSL-2003-01-I. Decision on Immunity from Jurisdiction, 31 May 2004; and the successive (and somewhat inconsistent) rul-ings of the Pre-Trial Chamber of the ICC in 2011, 2013, and 2017 in the *Al-Bashir* case.
[27] For an example of divergence of views between the ICJ and the ICTY see *Application of the Genocide Convention (Bosnia v. FRY)* [2007-I] ICJ Rep 209, paras. 402–3.
[28] See Bitti, 'The ICC and its Applicable Law, Article 21 and the Hierarchy of Sources before the ICC', in C. Stahn (ed.), *The Law and Practice of the International Criminal Court*, (OUP, 2015).
[29] K. J. Alter, *The New Terrain of International Law: Courts, Politics, Rights* (Princeton University Press, 2014) 68. The same author considers that as a result of, or in parallel to, this increase, the whole field of present-day international law has been transformed, as is implied by the title of her book.

public and are often highly influential as statements of the law as applied to the cases in hand. As in the case of the ICJ, the authors of the decisions, the arbitrators, are almost invariably internationalists of established reputation and high qualifications, so that in this respect also the distinction between judicial decisions and opinions of publicists is somewhat blurred.[30] There are numerous international judicial decisions in the context of the WTO and GATT, in the specialized field of economic relations.[31]

Against this background, it was observed in 2011 that

The increasing number of international judicial institutions, producing an ever-growing stream of decisions, has been one of the dominant features of the international legal order of the past two decades. The shift in quantity has gone hand in hand with a transformation in quality. Today, it is no longer convincing to only think of international courts in their role of settling disputes. While this function is as relevant as ever, many international judicial institutions have developed a further role in what is often called global governance. Their decisions have effects beyond individual disputes. They exceed the confines of concrete cases and bear on the general legal structures. The practice of international adjudication creates and shifts actors' normative expectations and as such develops legal normativity.[32]

On this basis, the authors argue that 'the generation of legal normativity in the course of international adjudication should be understood as judicial lawmaking and as an exercise of public authority'. Their approach is not made from the standpoint of the traditional doctrine of sources. Nevertheless, the phenomenon to which they draw attention raises the question, in the context of that doctrine, whether it is still true that international judicial decisions rank as no more than subsidiary sources of international law.

An earlier study of this issue is that of Judge Shahabuddeen, who devoted a chapter of his work on *Precedent in the World Court* [33] to 'The possibility of judge-made international law'; his study was, however, narrower, focusing (as

---

[30] Note also the recent limitation imposed by the ICJ on the extent to which its Members may, during their term of office, sit as arbitrators, ending a situation which was reaching the dimensions of a scandal: See address to the UN General Assembly, 73rd Session, by the President of the Court, H. E. Judge Yusuf, 25 October 2018.

[31] '[F]ormally of course, the WTO system has no *stare decisis*, but ... there is unquestionably the use of authority of past decision-making as to the means by which adjudication takes place': D. Unterhalter, 'What Makes the WTO Dispute Settlement System Procedure Particular?', in R. Wolfrum and I. Gätzschmann (eds.), *International Disputes Settlement: Room for Innovations?* (Heidelberg: Springer, 2012), 10.

[32] A. von Bogdandy and I. Venzke, 'Beyond Dispute: International Judicial Institutions as Lawmakers', 12 German LJ (2011), 979. For a more recent book-length study of the phenomenon and its implications see K. J. Alter, *The New Terrain of International Law: Courts, Politics, Rights* (Princeton University Press, 2014).

[33] (Cambridge: Cambridge University Press, 2007), ch. 7.

his title indicates) on the International Court. He puts forward as 'arguable' an interpretation of Article 38 according to which 'the reference in Article 38, paragraph 1 (*d*) of the Statute to "the determination of rules of law" may be read as including a determination of new rules of law by a decision of the Court itself which is based on earlier judicial decisions or the writings of publicists'.[34] This is based on the idea that Article 38 'visualises that decisions of the Court may operate in two ways':

First, they may serve as material for the determination of a rule of law by a later decision. Judicial decisions (including those of the World Court and of other courts) which serve in that way constitute 'subsidiary means for the determination of rules of law'. The second way in which judicial decisions (now restricted to decisions of the Court itself) may serve is by effecting the determination of rules of law on the basis of earlier decisions. The new decision by which a rule of law has been determined on the basis of earlier decisions is not a subsidiary means; it is the source of a new rule of international law; it is made by the Court alone.[35]

What is not clear, however, is the basis for the earlier decision: clearly if it was based on a treaty or a custom or other regular source, the second decision will presumably be able to rest on that same source, without there being a need for it to rely on the earlier decision as creative of law. If, on the other hand, the earlier decision is not so based, it is not apparent how it can have justified its own existence.

At all events, the Court itself does not seem ever to have claimed a lawmaking competence on the lines put forward by Judge Shahabuddeen; and the generally accepted view continues to be that judicial decisions, including those of the Court itself, are not in themselves sources of law comparable to those listed in sub-paragraphs (*a*) to (*c*) of Article 38, paragraph 1.

One specialized field in which it appears that the decision of an international tribunal can be regarded as creative of law is in the domain of the tribunal's own procedure.[36] This is normally regulated by a constitutional text: the Statutes of the ICJ, the ICC, and the various specialized criminal tribunals are obvious examples. Characteristically the provisions of a Statute are enlarged and applied by Rules, the power to make these being conferred by the Statute.[37] Sometimes these are extended further by sub-subsidiary 'legislation', for example the Practice Directions issued by the ICJ and the

---

[34] *Precedent in the World Court*, 78.   [35] *Precedent in the World Court*, 76.

[36] In this sense Shahabuddeen, *Precedent in the World Court*, 72: 'it seems that a new procedural principle may come into being as a result of the precedential authority of the Court's decisions'. Procedure for this purpose does not include jurisdiction, which is dependent on a finding of consent of the parties, i.e. in effect, a treaty basis.

[37] e.g. Art. 30 ICJ Statute.

Resolution concerning the Internal Judicial practice of the Court. The grant of rule-making power to a tribunal carries with it an implied authorization to interpret the constitutional text—the Statute—either by such subsidiary general texts, or by such decisions in specific cases as may be found necessary.

A striking example of this procedure in operation is afforded by the finding of the ICJ in the *LaGrand* and *Avena* cases that provisional measures indicated by the Court under Article 41 of the Statute create a binding international obligation. The text of Article 41 is ambiguous, to say the least, on the subject; and scholarly opinion has been divided on the correct interpretation of the text practically from the beginning. In 2001, in its judgment in the *LaGrand* case, the Court decided that provisional measures are, at least if expressed in categorical terms, binding on the State or States to which they are addressed, and State responsibility is incurred if they are not complied with; this responsibility being intellectually distinct from the responsibility that may be found to exist on the basis of the substantive claims made in the proceedings. In the present context, the importance of the decision (which has been unchallenged in subsequent cases[38]) is that even if its legal basis was open to question,[39] it is essentially unappealable and, as a precedent, irreversible, so that it is arguable that an important rule of State responsibility has in effect been created by judicial *fiat*.[40] The Court could, of course, in a future case decide that the measures there indicated were *not* binding, but would be highly unlikely to reverse its finding of principle in *LaGrand*;[41] and if it did, this would be an assertion of the power to undo confirming its power to do, thereby confirming that it had been legislating.

---

[38] e.g. *Armed Activities on the Territory of the Congo (DRC v. Uganda)* (2005) ICJ Rep 258, para. 262; *Temple of Preah Vihear (Interpretation)* (2011) ICJ Rep 554, para. 67.

[39] See the present writer's criticisms in H. Thirlway, *The Law and Procedure of the International Court of Justice: Fifty Years of Jurisprudence* (Oxford: Oxford University Press, 2013), i., 956–58.

[40] If a decision of this kind were displeasing to the 'clientele' of the Court generally it would, of course, be possible to introduce an amendment of the Statute to reverse it; but this is a wholly unrealistic scenario. Generally on the position of States in relation to possible judicial innovation, see Thirlway, 'Unacknowledged Legislators: Some Preliminary Reflections on the Limits of Judicial Lawmaking', in Wolfrum and Gätzschmann (eds.), *International Disputes Settlement. Room for Innovations?* (Springer, 2013) 311.

[41] That the Court should indisputably have powers to preserve the situation *pendente lite* is in itself an excellent thing; it is merely the manner in which it arrogated these powers to itself that may be regrettable. Although provisional measures were not originally conceived with this in mind, they have come to constitute also a contribution by the Court to the maintenance of international peace and security, which is probably to be welcomed: see K. Oellers-Frahm in Zimmerman et al. (eds.), *The Statute of the International Court of Justice* (Oxford: Oxford University Press, 2012) 1072–3. Note also the Order of 18 July 2011 in the case of *Request for Interpretation of the Judgment of 15 June 1962 in the* Temple of Preah Vihear *case* [2011] ICJ Rep 537 in which the Court arguably went beyond the usual limitation of provisional measures to protection solely of the rights claimed in the main proceedings, in the interests (*semble*) of the maintenance of peace.

2(b) Municipal courts

The application of the rule of law expressed in Article 38(1)(*d*) of the ICJ Statute is, however, not limited to the decisions of international courts and tribunals; the reference to decisions includes those of municipal courts also. In this respect the ILC was however cautious: in paragraph 2 of Conclusion 13 it stated that 'Regard may be had, *as appropriate*, to decisions of national courts concerning the existence and content of rules of customary international law.'[42] Such decisions may play a dual role: on the one hand they may contain a useful statement of international law on a particular point (thus constituting a material source);[43] on the other, the courts of a State are organs of the State and their decisions may also rank as State practice on a question of customary law. In fact, a development noticeable in (for example) the reports of the decisions of the International Court is that the nature of the disputes submitted for judicial settlement is more and more frequently such that the decisions of national courts furnish much material relevant to the quest for the applicable law.

In the ICJ case concerning the *Arrest Warrant*, the question was whether Heads of State and Foreign Ministers enjoy absolute immunity from prosecution for crimes allegedly committed during their period of office, and whether there is an exception to this rule in the case of war crimes or crimes against humanity. The parties (Belgium and the Democratic Republic of the Congo) both relied on decisions on the point by the UK House of Lords in the *Pinochet* case[44] and the French *Cour de cassation* in the *Qadaffi* case.[45] The statements of international law in those decisions could have been regarded as 'subsidiary means' for the determination of the customary law on the subject; they were, however, presented as evidence of State practice, and the Court dealt with them as such.[46] The Court referred to the 'few' decisions of national courts on the question; the paucity of practice was obviously relevant to the question whether a customary rule had become established (as explained in

---

[42] Emphasis added. See the explanatory comments of the Special Rapporteur in UN doc A/71/10, p. 110, paras. (6) and (7).

[43] A national court is in the position of having to apply public international law (on the basis of whatever directives are to be found in national constitutional law), but, at least in theory, being unable to develop it as it might when applying national law. For the difficulties thus raised, see M. Kloth and M. Brunner, 'Staatenimmunität im Zivilprozess bei gravierenden Menschenrechtsverletzungen', 50 Archiv des Völkerrechts (2012), 218–43 at 238–9.

[44] *R. v. Bow Street Metropolitan Stipendiary, ex parte Pinochet Ugarte (Amnesty International Intervening) (No 3)* [1999] UKHL 17; [2000] AC 147; [1999] 2 All ER 97.

[45] *SOS Attentat and Castelnau d'Esnault v. Qadaffi, Head of State of the State of Libya*, France, Court of Cassation, criminal chamber, 13 March 2000, no. 1414.

[46] *Arrest Warrant of 11 April 2000 (Democratic Republic of Congo v. Belgium), Preliminary Objections and Merits, Judgment, ICJ Reports 2002*, p. 3, paras. 57, 58.

Ch. III). But if the decisions had been classified as 'subsidiary means' under Article 38(1)(*d*), the only question would have been whether they correctly stated the law, which statement might in turn be based on an assessment of international practice *outside* the domestic courts, not whether the decisions themselves represented a widespread practice of national judicial bodies.[47]

Similarly in the case concerning *Jurisdictional Immunities of the State*, the Court noted that

the notion that State immunity does not extend to civil proceedings in respect of acts committed on the territory of the forum State causing death, personal injury or damage to property originated in cases concerning road traffic accidents and other 'insurable risks'. The limitation of immunity recognized by some national courts in such cases was treated as confined to *acta jure gestionis* ...[48]

In this context, it is not the authority of the domestic court as a court that is relevant; it is the fact that the nature of the rule of law contended for was such that it would be the decisions of domestic courts that would constitute the relevant practice to support the existence of a custom. In the same paragraph the ICJ turned to national legislation (and its application by national courts) as showing the existence of a qualification to the rule it was examining, equally on the basis that the legislation, as thus authoritatively interpreted, constituted practice of the States concerned.[49] This is even more clear from a later passage in the Judgment in which the decisions of numerous national courts are cited; the material is introduced by a paragraph to the effect that 'there is a substantial body of State practice ... which demonstrates that customary law' is as declared by the International Court.[50]

In that case, however, the Court also had to determine the correct interpretation and interrelation of articles of the European Convention on State Immunity and the United Nations Convention on the Jurisdictional Immunities of States and their Property. It noted that courts in Belgium, Ireland, Slovenia, Greece, and Poland had all reached the same conclusion as to the effect of the relevant article.[51] Here the question was not a simple matter

---

[47] However, since they would only be subsidiary means of proving the law, it would have been necessary to show that there was **other** State practice supporting a customary rule.

[48] [2012] ICJ Rep 127, para. 64, citing the judgment of the Supreme Court of Austria in *Holubek v. Government of the United States of America (Juristische Blätter* (Wien), 84 (1962), 43; ILR, vol. 40 p. 73).

[49] Citing the Supreme Court of Canada in *Schreiber v. Federal Republic of Germany* [2002] Supreme Court Reports (SCR), vol. 3, p. 269, paras. 33–6.

[50] [2012] ICJ Rep 137, para. 84.

[51] [2012] ICJ Rep 129, para. 68, citing Judgment of the Court of First Instance of Ghent in *Botelberghe* v. *German State*, 18 February 2000; Judgment of the Irish Supreme Court in *McElhinney v. Williams*, 15 December 1995 [1995] 3 Irish Reports 382; ILR, vol. 104, p. 69; Slovenia Constitutional Court, case no. Up-13/99, para. 13; Greece, *Margellos* v. *Federal Republic of Germany*,

of customary law, however, but the interpretation of a multilateral treaty: the decisions of national courts could not qualify as practice under Article 31, paragraph 3(*b*), of the Vienna Convention on the Law of Treaties, since the decision of a court of one party could not be said necessarily to 'establish the agreement of the parties' to the treaty regarding its interpretation. It is perhaps the presence of a foreign State as a party to the proceedings that suggests an interpretation as practice; but this feature is, strictly speaking, irrelevant so long as there is no agreement between that State and the forum State as to the international law rule. The existence of the case would suggest disagreement over the interpretation of the relevant text; and the decision of the national court would necessarily be contrary to the interpretation advanced by one of the two States concerned. The 'practice' would in that sense be ambiguous. If a case before a national court concerns a rule of international law but neither of the parties is a foreign State, the decision may rank as practice of the State of the forum. If the decisions of the national courts had weight, therefore, were they to be taken for what they were worth under Article 38, paragraph 1(*d*)? The Court did not present them in these terms; but it is suggested that this will be how paragraph 1(*d*) might operate.

Clearly to the extent that the decisions of national courts are a subsidiary source of international law, there is no reason to limit the choice of such decisions on any regional or national basis: it must be assumed that the courts of every State are equally competent to interpret international law. Yet as Professor Roberts has shown, this is not the case in practice. An analysis of citations in international law textbooks published in various countries shows 'a primary focus on the practices of Western States in general and core English-speaking common law States in particular'[52] where Court decisions are being considered as State practice. Similarly, 'when looking laterally at foreign case law' that is when looking at the foreign decision as a subsidiary source rather than as practice, 'Western and non-Western States alike turn primarily to the case-law of Western States'.[53] The phenomenon may be attributable in large part to the predominance of the English language as the most widely spoken second language, but it does indicate the difficulty that non-Western ideas in international law may have in being heard.[54] A similar distorting factor is the role played, in United States domestic case-law involving international

---

case no. 6/2002; ILR, vol. 129, p. 529; Judgment of the Supreme Court of Poland, *Natoniewski* v. *Federal Republic of Germany*, Polish YIL (2010), xxx. 299.

[52] A. Roberts, *Is International Law International?* (OUP, 2017), p.166.   [53] *Ibid.*, 167.

[54] It would however be morbidly over-sensitive to detect an echo of the repudiated term 'civilised nations' in Article 38, paragraph 1 (*c*), of the ICJ Statute! Cf. the problem of unreported, or under-reported, State practice where the State in question is 'third world' or non-Western, noted in the context of practice relevant to the growth of a custom in Chapter 3, text and n. 83.

law, by previous United States domestic case-law on the point: US courts are often content to cite, as sufficient authority for a norm of international law, earlier decisions of US courts rather than the classic non-subsidiary source that may underlie the norm in question; and this process is of course a self-reproducing one.[55]

3. The teachings of publicists

It is worth pausing a moment to consider the original context in which the Permanent Court was directed by its Statute to consider 'the teachings of the most highly qualified publicists of the various nations' as a subsidiary source of international law. First of all, those teachings would be written almost exclusively either in French (the *lingua franca* of international relations) or in English, whatever the nation from which they came. Secondly, they would take the form either of books or of lectures (possibly transcribed), and only to a lesser extent of articles in learned journals, of which there were then very few.[56] The international legal world was much smaller; most of its practitioners would be known to each other; and the number of published pages each year was such as to make researching any particular point a task to be contemplated without particular qualms, and completed without nagging doubts whether some thesis of particular originality or convincingness had been overlooked.

The contrast with the flood of published writings today in the field of international law (and indeed in virtually every scholarly or scientific field) does not need to be underlined.[57] It might once have been possible to expect that a publicist would take into account, when expressing a view, virtually all the teachings of his contemporaries; this is evidently now impossible (without taking into account the existence of writings in a wider range of languages than most scholars would be likely to be able to read). Even the limitation to the work of 'the most highly qualified publicists', while putting

---

[55] In the foreword to her book, cited in n.52, Prof. Roberts gives an entertaining account of her first startled encounter with this phenomenon: at, pp. xvii–xviii.

[56] Most of the well established and highly respected journals of today did not then exist: the pioneers were the *Journal Clunet* (founded in 1874); the *American Journal of International Law* (1907); and the *Transactions of the Grotius Society* (1915; merged in 1938 with what became the British Institute of International and Comparative Law). *International Affairs* followed in 1924, the *British Year Book of International Law* in 1929, the *Cambridge Law Journal* in 1931, the *Netherlands International Law Review* in 1953, etc.

[57] For a light-hearted survey of the problem of 'publish or perish' in the scientific context, see G. Wright, *Academia Obscura* (Unbound Publishing, 2017).

aside Ph.D. theses and the like, would not sufficiently reduce the extent of the task.[58]

For the PCIJ or ICJ judge, the conclusion is clear: Article 38(1)(*d*) of the Statute does not—cannot—impose any obligation to read everything published on a point submitted for decision, nor (it is suggested) to take up every reference discovered by the industrious research of a party appearing before him. In the context of the reference to 'writings' as a subsidiary source for consultation outside the courtroom it has probably an indicative role: that a 'highly qualified' international lawyer has expressed a particular view is relevant to the question whether that view is a correct one.[59] But it remains a view, not an authority, for the following reason.

It was suggested earlier (Ch. I sect. 3 *in fine*) that, like judicial decisions, 'the teachings of the most highly qualified publicists of the various nations', being a subsidiary source, would only carry weight in so far as they referred back to one of the three principal sources.[60] There is now resistance to this view in some scholarly quarters, with the suggestion being made that doctrine may be constitutive of international law:[61] creating rather than recording. It must be doubted however, whether States, as the direct subjects of law, would accept a dictum on the lines of 'This is international law, because I say so', and what is intended as such an assertion will be disguised in such a way as to contradict the essence of such a claim.

Whatever may have been the position in the past, today a legal consultation offered with only the weight of the reputation of the scholar giving it would have little or no value;[62] reference would be made to treaties interpreted in that sense, or customary law that had, in the author's opinion, developed in that way. With that qualification, there are a number of scholarly publications in specialized fields that have obtained the status of being *the* book on that particular subject, cited by counsel and by tribunals with almost the authority of one of the three sources of international law;[63] and the major general treatises still carry weight.

---

[58] A more dramatic limitation would be achieved by reading the definition as contemplating only traditional paper publication, thus at a stroke excluding not only internet blogs (such as *EJIL Talk!*), but material digitally published but intended for more lasting readership.

[59] How to choose the 'most highly qualified' jurists? On the basis of 'intellectual superiority'? A. Papaux and E. Wyler, 'Legal Theory as a Source of International Law', in *Oxford Handbook on the Sources of International Law*, (Oxford University Press, 2017) 522. But in whose judgment? So far as journal articles are concerned, the reputation of the journal must also come into the equation.

[60] Cf. the comments of the ILC Special Rapporteur, UN doc. A/71/10m p. 111, para (2).

[61] This is the sub-title of the article by A. Papaux and E. Wyler quoted in n. 59.

[62] Though there is no shortage of confident scholarly assertions that international law in a particular field *ought to be* such-and-such!

[63] e.g. in international investment law, 'a unique position has been achieved by Christoph Schreuer's *The ICSID Convention: a Commentary*, which was cited in 60 separate [arbitral] awards': T. Cole,

A legal opinion or publication would be valuable as indicating why the treaty or customary-law rule referred to should be held to determine the point, but this would still be an operation on a 'subsidiary' level. How much weight, one might ask, would teachings of this kind carry, in association with actual evidence of practice and *opinio juris*? If such evidence were very limited, to the point where a court might not consider itself authorized to find the existence of a customary rule, would the view of the publicists tip the scale? The answer here suggested is that, as a psychological phenomenon, it probably would; but that a judge would be unlikely to express himself in these terms. At the level of the participants in an international dispute, it is certain that pleadings may, and indeed do, often invoke scholarly opinion to bolster the arguments advanced; which suggest that litigants expect them to have *some* effect on the decision-maker's approach.

There remains, of course, the more general and continuing influence that may be attributed to international scholarly opinion in relation to the development of law, that is, not in respect of the factors to be weighed up to determine a specific point of law, but in relation to the process of lawmaking by States. Such influence is visible when a general lawmaking convention is elaborated;[64] less so when States may—or may not—adjust their conduct in a particular field in such a way as to affect the course of practice capable of giving rise to custom, or modification of custom. A scholarly opinion cannot constitute of itself *opinio juris*, since that is a psychological attribute of States themselves, or rather of those directing their affairs, but there is no doubt that the one contributes to the other.[65] A special case, but one that is here relevant, is that of the collective Reports and other publications of the UN International Law Commission, which combine the input of individual scholars, working collectively, and the reaction of States. The result is that

---

'Non-Binding Documents and Literature', in T. Gazzini and E. de Brabandere (eds.), *International Investment Law: The Sources of International Rights and Obligations* (Leiden: Nijhoff, 2012), 289 at 305. One might think also of Rosenne's work on the International Court, Crawford on State Responsibility, etc., and perhaps multi-author works such as that on the Charter (ed. Simma) and on the Statute of the ICJ (ed. Zimmerman et al.), and on international law generally, that edited by Sir Malcolm Evans (5th edn., 2018).

[64] Note the input of individual jurists to the work of the International Law Commission, either as Members (ILC Statute, art. 2 (i)), or as experts consulted (art. 16 (e)).

[65] Similarly, in the context of a very different approach to the sources of law, J. d'Aspremont does not regard legal scholars as 'law-applying authorities', since 'they do not apply the law but interpret and comment upon it': J. d'Aspremont, *Formalism and the Ascertainment of International Law* (Oxford: Oxford University Press, 2011), 210. Might they even at times create it? Cf. the suggestion, by the same author, that a particular concept may have been invented by scholars 'to provide themselves with extra raw material to work with, and therefore reduce the number of scholars focusing on the same object of study': J. d'Aspremont, 'Softness in International Law: A Self-Serving quest for New Legal Materials', 5 EJIL (2008), 1090.

such texts are, for example, cited judicially as expressing the law on the point even if they have never been embodied in a treaty or other instrument identifiable as a true 'source'.[66]

It is, however, possible to hold very different views as to the actual weight that international legal writers carry in the determination or guiding of international law. On the one hand, the presence has been detected of an 'invisible college' of international lawyers that in this respect has a significant function: that it 'play[s] a role in the process of creating new law and in extending existing law to meet emerging needs'.[67] On the other, a more recent writer has assessed the position more soberly, and (it is suggested) more accurately:

[I]nternational legal scholars, although they are not at the origin of a practice of law-ascertainment ... undoubtedly participate in the fine-tuning and streamlining of the formal criteria of law-ascertainment which, in turn, are picked up by the social actors involved in the application of international legal rules. In other words ... legal scholars come to play the role of grammarians of formal law-ascertainment who systematise the standards of distinction between law and non-law.[68]

Always to be borne in mind, however, is the fact that 'writers ... do not always distinguish clearly between the law as it is and the law as they would like it to be'.[69]

[66] See A. Papaux and E. Wyler, 'Doctrine as Constitutive of International Law', in Besson and d'Aspremont (eds.), *The Oxford Handbook on the Sources of International Law* (Oxford University Press, 2017), 513 at 532–3, who offer this as an example of *doctrine savante*.

[67] O. Schachter, 'The Invisible College of International Lawyers', 72 New York University LR (1977–8), 217. See also S. Villalpando, 'The "Invisible College of International Lawyers" Forty Years Later', *European Society of International Law, 5th Research Forum: International Law as a Profession* (May 2013).

[68] d'Aspremont, *Formalism and the Sources of International Law*, 209.

[69] ILC Commentary on the Work of the 68th Session, p. 111, para. (3).

VI

Interaction or Hierarchy between Sources

Since international law derives from more than one source, and these sources operate, initially at least, independently of each other, a not infrequent situation is that the same transaction or relationship attracts the operation of norms deriving from more than one source. The norms in question may in fact not conflict: a treaty or convention may, for example, impose the same duties, and accord the same rights, as pre-existing customary law: this will be the first case considered. If, however, the two sets of norms are not in agreement, a problem may arise—one that has given rise to much scholarly debate, but does not seem to have caused much difficulty in practice. The concept is that referred to as the hierarchy of sources. Primarily, this refers to the question whether a norm deriving from one of the recognized sources prevails over a norm from a different source solely for that reason, that is that norms from source A *always* outrank norms from source B; but there is also the possibility that a particular norm, because of its content or nature, has an over-riding quality in relation to all other norms: this goes to the concept of *jus cogens*, examined in Chapter VII.

A separate question is whether conflicts, or apparent conflicts, between norms of international law may arise in other ways: for example between a norm that developed or appeared later in time than a conflicting one (*lex prior* and *lex posterior*); or a law of limited application (*lex specialis*) diverging from a general rule.[1] Conflicts of this kind however are not resolved on the basis of identification of the source or sources of the relevant norms, and will not be treated here.

[1] On this see, for example, E. de Wet, 'Sources and the Hierarchy of International Law', in Besson and d'Aspremont (eds.), *The Oxford Handbook of the Sources of International Law* (Oxford University Press, 2017), 628–30.

1. Simultaneous and identical obligations under treaty and under customary law

An obligation that is stated in a treaty may exist for a State that is not party to the treaty if, as already explained, that obligation is also one of customary law.[2] There are three possible sets of circumstances in which this situation may be observed.[3] First, a treaty (normally a multilateral convention) may have been drawn up specifically in order to codify, or place on record, obligations that the States concerned already regarded as imposed on them by customary law; or, more frequently, such a convention may be intended partially to innovate, to declare rules that are not yet part of customary law (or whose status in that respect is uncertain), and within the general schema of the convention it is appropriate to mention unchallenged rules, as part of the overall pattern of obligation.[4] When this is the case, it is immaterial—as regards the customary law obligations—whether the convention, as a treaty, is binding on the parties to a dispute, or indeed ever comes into force at all. In such a case it must, however, be clear that the convention relied on was codifying in its effect, and one of the indications for or against this conclusion may be the number of ratifications that the convention received. In the *Asylum* case, Colombia relied on the 1933 Montevideo Convention on Asylum as a codification of the rules on diplomatic asylum recognized in Latin America, even though the respondent State (Peru) was not a party to the Convention. The ICJ not only found that '[t]he limited number of States which have ratified this Convention reveals the weakness of this argument', but also that even if the custom asserted by Colombia 'existed between certain Latin-American States only, it could not be invoked against Peru, which, far from having by its attitude adhered to it, has, on the contrary, repudiated it by refraining from ratifying the Montevideo Convention'.[5] Similarly in the

---

[2] For simplicity, the discussion here takes the treaty as a unit, as though the whole of its contents corresponded, in one of the ways indicated, to a customary rule or set of rules. In practice, of course, the situation will be more complex. Note that the ILC, when drafting its Conclusions on the Identification of Customary International Law, deliberately left aside any question of the relationship between customary international law and other sources of law: see *Fifth Report* on the subject, A/CN.4/717, para. 27.

[3] These are stated, in slightly different terms, in Conclusion 11 of the ILC's Conclusions on the Identification of Customary International Law.

[4] Many lawmaking treaties develop from the work of the ILC, whose mandate, derived from Art. 13(1)(*a*) of the UN Charter, is directed to 'the progressive development of international law and its codification'. The Commission does not always indicate in its reports and drafts which of its proposals are seen as simple codification of existing law, and which as 'progressive development'.

[5] [1950] ICJ Rep 277, 278. Colombia also relied on a later Montevideo Convention, of 1939, which had only received two ratifications. Peru's attitude could be interpreted as that of the 'persistent

North Sea Continental Shelf case, the Court regarded apparent lack of enthusiasm among States for ratification of an allegedly codifying convention as evidence casting doubt on the existence of the customary rule which, it was said, the convention was destined to codify.[6]

A second case (which is intellectually distinct from the first case, but may in practice hardly be distinguishable) is where a customary practice has arisen before the treaty was concluded and is widely followed, but an observer would be hard put to say whether or not it had achieved the status of a rule of law. The adoption of a 'codifying' convention may have a crystallizing effect, with the paradoxical result that its mere adoption will make the rules it contains binding on all States, so that signature and ratification could, to that extent, be considered otiose.[7]

The third case is, of course, where this crystallizing process takes place at some date after the adoption of the convention, as a result, perhaps, of more and more widespread participation in the practice indicated in the convention by States not parties to it, or by clearer and clearer evidence that States generally regard that practice as a matter of customary obligation: again, the relationship between practice and the psychological element of the *opinio juris* for custom-creation has been examined in Chapter III. There is here, however, another difficulty, noticed by the ICJ in the *North Sea Continental Shelf* case. To recall what has been indicated in Chapter III as to the establishment of custom, what needs to be shown is widespread and consistent participation in the relevant practice, viewed as indicating the *opinio* that there is or should be a rule prescribing it. The Court was considering whether there had been such practice since the adoption of the Geneva Convention on the Continental Shelf, adopting the principles there laid down for the delimitation of the shelf. The Court noted that

> over half the States concerned ... were or shortly became parties to the Geneva Convention, and were therefore presumably, so far as they were concerned, acting actually or potentially in the application of the Convention. From their action no inference could legitimately be drawn as to the existence of a rule of customary international law in favour of the equidistance principle.[8]

---

objector' (see Ch. III sect. 5 (a)); but this was also a local or regional custom, which cannot be relied on against a State that has not expressly accepted it (it does not have to expressly 'repudiate' it).

[6] [1969] ICJ Rep 42, para. 73.

[7] A very unusual provision is to be found in the Rome Statute of the ICC, Art. 10, whereby the Statute is expressly declared to be incapable of affecting 'existing or developing rules of international law' except for the purposes of the Statute itself. This was to avoid any possibility of affecting the development of customary law relating to war crimes: see the explanation by L. van den Herik, in *Custom's Future* C. A. Bradley (ed.), (Cambridge: Cambridge University Press, 2016), Ch. 9, 240–1.

[8] [1969] ICJ Rep 43, para. 76.

The more States became parties to the Convention, the fewer there would be whose actions could be looked at to determine whether or not there was a customary rule. In this way, it seems that the adoption of a multilateral co-difying convention might have a paralysing effect on the development of the rule or rules it is intended to codify.[9] This line of argument may perhaps be over-rigorous; it has not been repeated or recalled in later decisions.

In practice, it will often not be easy to say just when, at what moment in time, a treaty-provision has become accompanied by an identical obligation of customary law. If a claim by one State against another can be based upon the provisions of a treaty in force between them, the question whether an identical obligation may exist in customary law is of course irrelevant on the international plane (though it may have implications in domestic law[10]). The ICJ tends to be guarded in its approach to this temporal problem, confining itself to the question whether the customary rule existed at the moment relevant to the case before it. For example, in *Armed Activities on the Territory of the Congo*, the Court stated flatly that provisions of the Declaration on Principles of International Law Concerning Friendly Relations and Cooperation among States (GA Res. 2625 (XXV)) 'are declaratory of customary international law'.[11] But did it mean that at the moment when the resolution was adopted, it declared customary law (which might be controversial); or that what it declared had at any rate by the date of the decision in 2005, become customary law, so that it was applicable to the acts of the parties in issue in the case?[12] In the same decision it referred to 'customary international law, as reflected in Article 42 of the Hague Regulations of 1907';[13] again, the time-element is left

---

[9] There may also be some inconsistency between this argument, and the argument used by the Court in the same breath, that a limited number of ratifications of a multilateral convention weighs against the contention that it was intended to be codifying of a customary rule: see the continuation of the paragraph cited.

[10] It appears that many national constitutions incorporate international customary law into the law of the land (sometimes with superior force), while treaties merely rank alongside national statutes: see B. Simma and P. Alston, 'The Sources of Human Rights Law', 12 Australian Yearbook of International Law (1988–9) 82, citing A. Verdross and B. Simma, *Universelles Völkerrecht: Theorie und Praxis*, 3rd edn. (Berlin: Duncker & Humblot, 1984), sect. 1234.

[11] [2005] ICJ Rep 227, para. 162.

[12] The French text of this passage in the judgment: 'revêtent un caractère déclaratoire du droit international coutumier', however, seems nearer to a statement that the resolution was, when adopted, declaratory.

[13] [2005] ICJ Rep 226–7, p. 229, para. 172. The Court there also refers to 'a well-established rule of a customary nature, as reflected in Article 3 of the Fourth Hague Convention' ([2004] ICJ Rep 1345, p. 242, para. 214). The same phrase—'customary law as reflected in'—is used e.g. in *Legality of the Use of Force (Serbia v. UK)* [2004] ICJ Rep 1345, para. 98.

out of the equation: did it then reflect, or has it come to reflect? In contrast, in *Legal Consequences of the Construction of a Wall in the Occupied Palestinian Territory*, the Court said that 'the provisions of the [1907] Hague Regulations have become part of customary law',[14] that is they were not so, or not necessarily so in 1907, but were at the time, and for the purposes, of the facts of the case.[15] A court has normally, of course, only to decide what was the state of the law at the moment relevant to the case before it, and can afford to leave open the question of when it attained that state, however interesting that question may be for scholars—or, indeed, for the settlement of other disputes.

If a multilateral convention is adopted in a field already covered to some extent by customary law, is the operation of the convention in that field to be regarded as fixed in terms corresponding to customary law as it stood when the treaty was concluded? If customary law continues to develop, must the law of the convention be regarded as frozen, and therefore diverging more and more from the developing customary standard? An example of a problem of this kind has arisen in the context of International Investment Agreements: that of the interpretation of the 'FET standard', the standard of fair and equitable treatment by one State of the property in its territory or control of nationals of another. As noted by UNCTAD, 'the reference to fair and equitable treatment in IIAs has created a controversy about whether the FET standard is autonomous, that is, has a content of its own, or whether it is limited to the minimum standard of treatment of aliens under customary international law' as it exists at the time of a decision. It was noted that in arbitral decisions there had been 'a noticeable trend in arbitral practice away from the classic customary international law standard of treatment of aliens [i.e. the standard frozen in the Convention] towards a less stringent reading of the standard.'[16]

---

[14] [2004] ICJ Rep 172, para. 89, cited in *Armed Activities* [2005] ICJ Rep 243, para. 217; cf. also 244, para. 219.

[15] This is an example of the phenomenon whereby lack of theoretical orderliness in the process of creation of customary law, which makes the moment of creation of law difficult or impossible to pin down, is often of no importance for the function of dispute settlement, where the question is whether the law has developed, not when.

[16] UNCTAD, 'Fair and Equitable Treatment: A Sequel', Series on Issues in International Investment Agreements II, (2012), p. 6. This publication does not claim to offer resolution of the issue, noting that the practice is 'in a state of development' and making suggestions as to how States might influence such development.

2. The 'hierarchy of sources'

This term is used in more than one sense. Most frequently it refers to the question whether a rule deriving from one of the recognized sources over-rides, on that basis, a rule derived from another. Two other uses of the term will be noted at the end of the present section.

Let us suppose that two or more norms, deriving from separate sources are applicable, or appear to be applicable, between the same parties, to the same question arising in some particular field of law. Theoretically the norms involved might be customary norm and a treaty norm; a treaty norm and a general principle; and a customary norm and a general principle. In practice, it is only the first situation which may raise problems. A treaty may contain provisions which do not match general principles, but unless the general principle involved has a *jus cogens* character, the treaty will prevail; it will probably have been prepared to meet a specific situation where the general principle would not give satisfactory results. The interaction between custom and general principles is more difficult to analyse *in abstracto*; but the reciprocal State interaction that is the basis of custom gives to it a 'reality' that renders the development of an allegedly contradictory 'general principle' unlikely.[17]

Even in the custom/treaty collision, a conflict is not necessarily the result: the ILC noted that 'It is a generally accepted principle that when several norms bear on a single issue they should, to the extent possible, be interpreted so as to give rise to a single set of compatible obligations';[18] and it may be found that one norm simply 'assists in the interpretation of the other'.[19]

Article 38, paragraph 1, of the Statute of the International Court lists the sources in the familiar order: treaties, custom, general principles, subsidiary sources, but does not indicate specifically whether the order in which they are mentioned also indicates the order in which they are to be applied.[20]

---

[17] This suggestion takes into account the recent very thorough study by T. Kleinlein, 'Customary International Law and General Principles: Rethinking Their Relationship', in Lepard (ed.), *Reexamining Customary International Law* (Cambridge: Cambridge University Press, 2017), 131–58, but does not correspond precisely to the conclusions there offered.

[18] *Conclusions of the Study Group on the Fragmentation of International Law: Difficulties Arising from the Diversification and Expansion of International Law* (2006), in *Report of the ILC* (A/61/10), para. (4).

[19] *Report of the ILC* (A/61/10), para. (2).

[20] For some, this should generally be the case, but sometimes not, leaving it obscure just when, and why, a different order should be followed: e.g. Judge Moreno Quintana, dissenting opinion in the *Right of Passage* case [1960] ICJ Rep 90; I. Brownlie, *Principles of Public International Law*, 6th edn. (Oxford: Oxford University Press, 2003), 5.

In the more recent convention, the Rome Statute, establishing the International Criminal Court (ICC), a different course was followed,[21] possibly to leave the new Court less scope for discretion. In normal circumstances, however, it seems clear that a rule, or an obligation, derived from a specific treaty excludes, *as between the parties to that treaty*, the operation of any inconsistent customary rule that would otherwise govern the matter.[22] The whole doctrine of *jus cogens*, which teaches that certain obligations, principally of *customary* law, are exceptional in that they cannot be contracted out of by treaty,[23] is built on the assumption that all other obligations of customary law can be so ousted; and indeed, if a treaty did not modify the legal situation as between the parties to it there would normally be no point in making a treaty at all.

In the *Rainbow Warrior* case between Australia and France, arising out of the sinking of the Greenpeace vessel of that name by French agents, it was suggested that there was a conflict between treaty-law—applicable to the question whether there had been a breach of treaty—and the law of international responsibility, applicable to the determination of the consequences of the breach. On this basis, it was argued that France could not defend itself against a claim of breach of treaty by invoking circumstances recognized as excluding responsibility, in that field of law. The arbitral tribunal, however, rejected this contention, holding that 'for the decision of the present case, both the customary Law of Treaties and the customary Law of State Responsibility are relevant and applicable'.[24] In the *Gabčíkovo/Nagymaros* case, however, the ICJ ruled that 'the law of treaties and the law of State responsibility' were 'two branches of international law [that] obviously have a scope that is distinct';[25] in the circumstances, however, the fact that 'Hungary chose to place itself ... within the ambit of the law of State responsibility' had implications for its position as regards non-performance of treaty obligations.[26] In general,

---

[21] This provides that the ICC shall apply '(a) In the first place, this Statute, Elements of Crimes and its Rules of Procedure and Evidence; (b) In the second place, where appropriate and the principles and rules of international law ...'; and '(c) Failing that, the general principles of law ...'. There is an additional qualification that 'the application and interpretation of law pursuant to this article must be consistent with internationally recognized human rights ...' (Article 21(3)).

[22] Cf. the provision of the French *Code civil* quoted in Ch. I n. 32. In the case of the *Dispute concerning Navigational and Related Rights* on the San Juan river, the ICJ observed that if the river were an 'international river', which 'would entail the application of [certain] rules of customary international law', nevertheless 'such rules could only be operative, at the very most, in the absence of treaty provisions that had the effect of excluding them': [2009] ICJ Rep 233, para. 35.

[23] As explained further in Ch. VI.   [24] UNRIAA, XX. 251, para. 76.

[25] [1997] ICJ Rep 38, para. 47.

[26] [1997] ICJ Rep 39, para. 48. This part of the decision is far from clear: for comment see Thirlway, 'Treaty Law and the Law of Treaties in Recent Case-Law of the International Court', in M. Craven and M. Fitzmaurice (eds.), *Interrogating the Treaty: Essays in the Contemporary Law of Treaties* (Nijmegen: Wolf Legal, 2005), 13–20.

where two norms demand to be applied, both of which derive from the same source, no question of conflict should arise. However, a problem does appear more likely to arise where the same issue involves an overlapping of two different subsystems or specializations of international law, and the norm which the first system would apply derives from a source other than that which the second system would apply. It has been proposed that a system of 'dialogue' originally outlined for application in the field of private international law, should be invoked in such cases.[27]

According to this proposal, in contrast to the 'vertical', hierarchical, relationship between norms characterized by the concept of superior norms—*jus cogens*—the 'dialogue' is designed to operate horizontally. It is based on a presumption against conflict between norms of the international system that was formulated in doctrine many years ago in the context of lawmaking treaties.[28] This becomes a presumption that States, when a norm-creating process occurs, take into account the rules already in force, in an endeavour to secure harmony between the old and the new law.[29] Such a presumption would, it is suggested, chime with the International Court's dictum in the *Right of Passage* case that '[i]t is a rule of interpretation that a text emanating from a Government must, in principle, be interpreted as producing and as intended to produce effects in accordance with existing law and not in violation of it'.[30] This was, of course, not a case of conflict of norms belonging to two separate systems: the Court was rejecting an interpretation of Portugal's acceptance of jurisdiction that would have involved Portugal trying to do, or rather to reserve the right to do, the impossible, namely evade the Court's jurisdiction after it had become validly seised of a claim against Portugal. In the context of present-day international relations, the possibility of a government simultaneously committing itself to two mutually inconsistent obligations is not at all unlikely, since as between different Ministries and offices, it is increasingly difficult for the right hand to know what the left hand is doing. With the

---

[27] The only study devoted wholly to the subject appears to be A. de Amiral Júnior, 'El "dialogo" de las fuentes: fragmentación y coherencia en el derecho internacional contemporaneo', *Revista Española de Derecho Internacional*, 62/1, (2010), 61. On the reconciliation of economic law with environmental law, see e.g. E.-U. Petersmann, *International and European Trade and Environmental Law after the Uruguay Round* (Boston: Kluwer, 1995), 3–5; J. A. Peters, 'How to Reconcile Trade and Environment', in W. P. Heere (ed.), *International Law and The Hague's 750th Anniversary*, (The Hague: T. M. C. Asser, 1999), 309.

[28] W. Jenks, 'Conflict of Law-making Treaties', 30 BYIL (1953), 401.

[29] do Amiral, 'El "dialogo" de las fuentes', 73.

[30] [1957] ICJ Rep 142. do Amiral also cites the *Certain Expenses* case: 'When the Organization takes action which warrants the assertion that it was appropriate for the fulfilment of one of the stated purposes of the United Nations, the presumption is that such action is not *ultra vires* the Organization': [1962] ICJ Rep 168.

saving words 'in principle' in the passage quoted, the presumption of consistency may be a useful tool.[31]

Do Amiral considers that the international legal system is not a heterogeneous collection of norms, but contains structural rules, of varying degrees of hierarchical superiority, which define the relationships between norms. Criteria have long been established, on the basis of a logical rule of non-contradiction, such as chronological and hierarchical relationship, and the principle of speciality, which operate to maintain the coherence of the system by the suppression of one of the conflicting norms.[32] Notwithstanding the intrinsic value of these, the present conjunction, with the implicit risks of the fragmentation of international law, suggests the adoption of a different approach: that of seeking to identify convergences between rival norms, and applying the traditional criteria of conflict-regulation only where absolutely necessary. A 'dialogue' is the reciprocal relationship between norms that each supply a solution to the case in question; the purpose served by each will be a guide to the identification of shared propositions. Rather than opting for a single solution on the basis of the classic principles for resolving inconsistencies, the interpreter will apply two or more norms simultaneously.[33] The possible dialogues are defined by their objectives as being directed to coherence, to co-ordination and adaptation, and to complementarity.[34] These objectives will no doubt be generally regarded as desirable, but there is less clarity in description of how in practice they are to be attained: most of the examples adduced relate to the specialized field of GATT and WTO law, and lie outside our field of reference at this point.

A striking example of the interrelationship between norms deriving from two apparently separate and self-contained regimes is that of the operation of human rights law, on the one hand, and international law relating to protection of the environment, on the other. In a powerful article, Alan Boyle has raised the question 'Why should environmental protection be treated as a human rights issue?', and answered that 'Most obviously, and in contrast to the rest of international environmental law, a human rights perspective directly addresses environmental impacts on the life, health, private life, and property of individual humans rather than on other states or the environment

---

[31] Cf. the treatment of the right to life (embodied in Art. 6 of the International Covenant on Civil and Political Rights) in relation to the laws of war, in the advisory opinion on *Legality of the Threat or Use of Nuclear Weapons* [1996-I] ICJ Rep 239–40, paras. 24–5.

[32] do Amiral, 'El "dialogo" de las fuentes', 86.

[33] This is, of course, already an established practice of municipal courts (where in principle all norms by definition will derive from the same source), e.g. constitutional courts called upon to balance such rights and liberties as non-discrimination, security, protection of the family, etc.

[34] *Do Amiral*, 76–80.

in general.'[35] As long ago as 1994, the UN Human Rights Council produced a study report and draft declaration, which, however, did not secure the backing of States; but since then both UNHRC and the United Nations Environment Programme have continued studying the question.[36] What is here involved, however, would seem to be more an interrelationship tending towards shared goals rather than a conflict; other interactions between special regimes may be less immediately capable of reconciliation.

There is, however, perhaps more to be said in this particular context on the general relationship between customary law and treaty provisions. A treaty may of course re-enact, as it were, an existing rule of customary law, and thus make it applicable to the parties to the treaty as a conventional rule; this is a common phenomenon in the case of multilateral, so-called 'lawmaking' conventions. The fact that a treaty embodies a rule of customary law does not of course signify that there is any obligation on States to become parties to it, even if the rule in question is one of *jus cogens*. Similarly, the International Law Commission noted, in its 'Guide to Practice' on Reservations to Treaties, that 'The fact that a treaty provision reflects a rule of customary international law does not in itself constitute an obstacle to the formulation of a reservation to that provision.'[37]

When, on the other hand, a treaty is concluded that excludes a rule of customary law, that rule of course continues to exist, and to bind States other than the parties to the treaty, a point already made. It may also be that, to a greater or lesser extent, a treaty 're-enacts' rules of customary law, so that the parties are bound to comply with them on two distinct bases. Normally, on the basis that a treaty takes the place of customary law between the parties, the application of the customary rule is wholly notional. In one case before the ICJ, however, a jurisdictional anomaly produced a situation in which the Court interpreted and applied the customary law, between the parties to a treaty, which existed 'behind' the treaty, as it were. The Court found that where both custom and treaty appeared to be relevant in the relations between two or more States, then 'even if two norms belonging to two sources of international law appear identical in content, and even if the States in question are bound by these rules both on the level of treaty-law and on

---

[35] A. Boyle, 'Human Rights and the Environment: Where Next?', 23 EJIL (2012), 613.

[36] In August 2012 Mr John Knox was appointed by the UN Human Rights Council as the first Independent Expert on human rights obligations relating to the environment; he was recently replaced (August 2018) by Mr David R. Boyd. A joint project was established by UNHRC and UNEPF, with the Independent Expert in 2013. For work in progress in this context, see the UNHRC Report on Framework Principles in this context, UN doc. A/HRC/37/59.

[37] 2011 Guidelines, Art. 3.1.5.3. The situation may be different if the reservation is 'incompatible with the object and purpose of the treaty': see the discussion in Chapter II.

that of customary international law, these norms retain a separate existence'.[38] The circumstances in which this pronouncement was made were unusual; the Court was debarred by the terms of the United States' acceptance of jurisdiction from deciding whether or not that State had committed breaches of international treaties, including the United Nations Charter, but could determine whether it was in breach of customary law.[39] These circumstances were always unlikely to recur, and have not in fact recurred before the Court.

Two more recent cases have, however, raised questions of interest as regards the interrelation of treaty and customary law, though in the first of these, that of *Maritime Delimitation in the Area between Greenland and Jan Mayen*, the point is by no means evident, and is not referred to in the judgment; it may have been overlooked by all concerned. Briefly,[40] the parties to the case, Denmark and Norway, were parties to the 1958 Geneva Convention on the Continental Shelf, but not to the 1982 United Nations Convention on the Law of the Sea, which, furthermore, was not yet in force. In 1958, the extent seawards of the continental shelf, as a concept, was identical in customary law and in the law of the Convention. The customary law on the point could of course develop; but in principle those States that had become parties to the 1958 Convention had agreed on a conventional definition that could only be varied by agreement between them, and—again in principle—would not be affected by subsequent developments in customary law.

If the areas of continental shelf appertaining to the parties were to be determined according to the criterion of the 1958 Geneva Convention, 200 miles from the coastline, there would be no need for a delimitation, since the shelf of neither coast would extend far enough offshore to encounter the shelf of the other.

The parties seem to have taken it as axiomatic that they were entitled at customary law to continental shelves of the greater extent defined by the 1982 Convention; nor does it appear to have worried them that they were making such a claim while at the same time recognizing that they were bound by the 1958 Geneva Convention. The Court held that the 1958 Convention 'governs the continental shelf delimitation to be effected', but passed over in silence the question whether that Convention also governed the definition of what it was that was to be delimited. What it effected was a delimitation of continental shelf avowedly according to the 1958 Geneva Convention

---

[38] *Military and Paramilitary Activities in and against Nicaragua* [1986] ICJ Rep 14.

[39] See further Thirlway, *The Law and Procedure of the ICJ*, i. 132 ff.

[40] For a fuller account of the case, see Thirlway, 'The Law and Procedure of the International Court of Justice', 76 BYIL (2005) 84–6, reproduced in Thirlway, *The Law and Procedure of the International Court of Justice: Fifty Years of Jurisprudence* (Oxford: Oxford University Press, 2013), ii. 1180–2.

of continental shelf, but in truth continental shelf as defined by 1993 customary law. Clearly the existence of the conventional bond created by the 1958 Convention could not prevent Denmark and Norway from becoming entitled under customary law to a full 200-mile continental shelf.[41]

From a different angle, the *Oil Platforms* case before the ICJ is also of interest as regards the relationship between treaty obligations between two States and the background of customary law equally binding upon them. Under Article XX, paragraph 1 (*d*) of a 1955 Treaty of Amity, that Treaty was not to 'preclude the application of measures ... necessary to fulfil the obligations of a High Contracting Party ... necessary to protect its essential security interests'. The United States claimed that the attacks by its forces on Iranian oil platforms were such measures; it had also contended, in particular in communications to the Security Council, that they were justified as an exercise of the inherent right of self-defence.

The Court's jurisdiction was derived from the compromissory clause (Art. XXI, para. 2) of the 1955 Treaty, and the United States contended that the Court need not (and should not) address the issue of self-defence.

[The United States] does not however contend that the Treaty exempts it, as between the parties, from the obligations of international law on the use of force, but simply that where a party justifies certain action on the basis of Article XX, paragraph 1(*d*), that action has to be tested solely against the criteria of that Article, and the jurisdiction conferred on the Court by Article XXI, paragraph 2, of the Treaty goes no further than that.[42]

The Court rejected this contention, as a matter of interpretation of the Treaty. However it also argued as follows:

Moreover, under the general rules of treaty interpretation, as reflected in the 1969 Vienna Convention on the Law of Treaties, interpretation must take into account 'any relevant rules of international law applicable in the relations between the parties' (Article 31, paragraph 3(*c*)). The Court cannot accept that Article XX, paragraph 1(*d*),

---

[41] Cf. the ruling in the *Military and Paramilitary Activities* case, just referred to. One possible view of the situation in the *Jan Mayen* case would therefore be that the physical shelf off the coast of the two States was governed, as far out as the 200-metre depth line (or the exploitation limit contemplated by the 1958 Convention, whatever that might be), by the terms of the 1958 Convention, and beyond that limit by customary law. On that basis, the delimitation provisions of Art. 6 the 1958 Convention would have no application between the two States, since, as already noted, their 'Convention-shelves' were at no point contiguous. The delimitation of the 'custom-shelves' would of course be governed by customary law. There is of course a certain awkwardness in contemplating two different meanings of the expression 'continental shelf' in international law; Judge Shahabuddeen, in his separate opinion, took the view that 'the same facts cannot at one and the same time be subject to two contradictory rules': [1993] ICJ Rep 134.

[42] [2003] ICJ Rep 181, para. 39.

of the 1955 Treaty was intended to operate wholly independently of the relevant rules of international law on the use of force, so as to be capable of being successfully invoked, even in the limited context of a claim for breach of the Treaty, in relation to an unlawful use of force. The application of the relevant rules of international law relating to this question thus forms an integral part of the task of interpretation entrusted to the Court by Article XXI, paragraph 2, of the 1955 Treaty.[43]

The problem posed was in a sense the mirror-image of that which arose in the *Military and Paramilitary Activities* case. In that case, the Court was unable to apply the conventional law that it knew existed between the parties, and had to apply the general customary law on the same subject even though in the actual relations between the parties that customary law had been overlaid, or ousted, by the conventional law. In the *Oil Platforms* case, the Court was only empowered to judge whether or not the United States actions constituted breaches of the Treaty; it could not declare them a breach of customary law on the use of force, however flagrant a breach they might appear to be. The passage quoted is one of the hinges of the process by which the Court nevertheless managed to assess and reject the United States plea that its use of force was in self-defence; but that aspect of the case is not here our concern.[44]

What these cases do re-confirm is that the codification of a customary rule by its incorporation into a treaty does not lead to the abrogation or disappearance of the rule as part of customary law, even in the relations between two States that are party to the relevant treaty. On the basis of general relationship between treaty-law and customary law already outlined, it is normally the provisions of the treaty that govern any question arising in this context. The background of customary law is relevant to any question on which the treaty does not speak, and may well be of service in the interpretation of the treaty, on the basis, for example, of Article 31, paragraph 3(*c*), of the Vienna Convention on the Law of Treaties.[45] Otherwise, the customary rule remains invisible, but alive and present.

---

[43] [2003] ICJ Rep 182, para. 41. Cf. also the finding in the *Greenland/Jan Mayen* case, that the Geneva Convention on the Continental Shelf could not be interpreted and applied 'without reference to the customary law on the subject'([1993] ICJ Rep 58, para. 46). Judge Higgins dissented from this part of the *Oil Platforms* judgment, in particular from the Court's reading of the Vienna Convention, Art. 31, para. 3 as 'incorporating the totality of the substantive international law ... on the use of force': [1993] ICJ Rep 58, 237, para. 46.

[44] See D. H. Small, 'The *Oil Platforms* Case: Jurisdiction through the (Closed) Eye of the Needle', 3 Law and Practice of International Tribunals (2004) 113; Thirlway, *The Law and Procedure of the ICJ*, (n. 40 above), ii. 1636–7.

[45] For treaty interpretation, '[t]here shall be taken into account, together with the context ... (*c*) any relevant rules of international law applicable in the relations between the parties'. It was by invoking this provision that the Court in the *Oil Platforms* case was able to deal with the customary law on self-defence; for a well-argued criticism of its reasoning see the separate opinion of Judge Buergenthal [2003] ICJ Rep 279, para. 22.

Finally we should note that in some circumstances a conflict, or apparent conflict, may be resolved by observing that one norm constitutes a recognized exception to the other. A good example is that of the collision between the principle of territorial jurisdiction and that of sovereign immunity that arose in the leading case of *The Schooner Exchange* v. *Mcfaddon*.[46] The conflict was between the sovereign rights of the United States over its territory, including the port where the ship lay, and the State immunity asserted by France for one of its warships. The US court (Justice Marshall) based its decision on treating State immunity as a matter of 'relaxation' of the jurisdictional authority based on territorial sovereignty, thus as an exception to the principle of such sovereignty.[47]

What then of the third recognized source of international law, general principles? As principles they presumably have a certain importance: if a treaty, or a custom, is contrary to such a principle, is it so far void? The answer depends on the kind of general principles that are contemplated by Article 38, paragraph 1(c): these have already been discussed in Chapter IV and here we may simply note that essentially they are called upon only when the rules derived from treaty or custom do not resolve the legal issue. In disputes submitted to third-party settlement this has very rarely occurred,[48] and in no case have the principles been in contradiction with other applicable rules.

A second usage of the term 'hierarchy' refers to the situation in which there are norms, emanating from the same source, that conflict: for example, a State may simultaneously be party to a multilateral convention and to a bilateral treaty, the requirements of the two instruments being incompatible, or indeed both parties to the bilateral treaty may be in this position. There are some criteria for giving the one or the other instrument preference: for example, a norm of *jus cogens* may be expressed in one of two conflicting treaties, and must on that basis prevail. In some cases, preference may be given to the later in date of the two instruments, on the basis of a presumed intention of the parties.[49] Conflicts between requirements of customary law are less likely, since the way in which customary law is formed theoretically involves awareness of, and lack of objection to, developments in the field on the part of the whole international community. Local or regional custom derogates from general custom, and therefore prevails, as between the

[46] 11 US (7 Cranch) 116 (1812).

[47] See the detailed analysis of the case in Caplan, 'State Immunity, Human Rights, and *Jus cogens*: A Critique of the Normative Hierarchy Theory', AJIL 2003, 741 at 749ff.; and the discussion of the alleged 'tort exception' to the law of State immunity in *Jurisdictional Immunities of the State (Germany* v. *Italy)* [2012] ICJ Rep 127, para. 64.

[48] For references, see Ch. IV, text and nn. 27, 28.

[49] See Art. 59 of the Vienna Convention on the Law of Treaties.

members of the community in which it is established, as indicated in Chapter III section 6. Some writers argue for the existence of specialized 'subsystems' within international law, and suggest that the norms existing within one of these may conflict with those existing within another, or with general international law; this matter will be examined in Chapter VIII section 1.

A third usage is to see as a hierarchy the relationship between norms of a greater or lesser degree of 'hardness', with peremptory norms (*jus cogens*) at one end of the scale, and 'soft law' provisions at the other.[50] These concepts will be examined in Chapter VII; at this point we need only recall that a peremptory norm is one from which no derogation is permitted, so that any agreement between States to act in contravention of the norm is void;[51] and that 'soft law' is the appellation given to agreements between States or other international actors which, either because of the form and procedure adopted for their conclusion, or because of the language used, do not commit the parties to any specific action or inaction, but merely (for example) to 'use their best endeavours' to secure some named objective. A conflict in this last case is perhaps difficult to conceive. A State might be bound by one instrument to 'use its best endeavours' toward some objective, and be bound by another treaty to act in such a way as would frustrate or impede that objective; but a 'best endeavours' obligation could not be read as implying a duty to commit a breach of a firm obligation in another direction.[52]

---

[50] In this sense, D. Shelton, 'Normative Hierarchy in International Law', 100 AJIL (2006), 291.

[51] See Vienna Convention on the Law of Treaties, Arts. 53, 64.

[52] Particularly since this form of 'soft' obligation may also be seen as an 'obligation of conduct', or 'obligation of means', as distinct from an 'obligation of result', and as such rather 'hard' than 'soft': this was the approach of R. Ago as ILC Rapporteur on State Responsibility: see J. Crawford, *The International Law Commission's Articles on State Responsibility: Introduction, Text and Commentaries* (Cambridge: Cambridge University Press, 2002), 20–2.

VII

Specialities: *jus cogens*, Obligations *erga omnes*, Soft Law

1. Superior norms and their sources: *jus cogens* and obligations *erga omnes*

The debate over the sources of international law involves also a controversy between what are termed 'absolute' and 'relative' concepts of law as applicable on the international level. As explained by a commentator some years ago,

Absolute positions make a categorical distinction between (binding) law and (non-binding) non-law. A rule is either part of (binding) law or it remains in the penumbra of politics or morals. Relative positions however assume that different grades of legal normativity are conceivable. In the case of international law, some relativists suggest a continuum ranging from non-law to *ius cogens*.[1]

The expression 'relative normativity' was coined by a scholar, Prosper Weil,[2] who (in these terms) took an absolute view. Despite his powerful arguments, a relativist viewpoint seems to be generally adopted in most legal writing today;[3] and among States there is at least a wide measure of support for the notion of *jus cogens* (and its stable-mate the obligation *erga omnes*).

---

[1] Goldmann, 'Inside Relative Normativity: From Sources to Standard Instruments for the Exercise of International Public Authority', 11 German LJ (2008), 1865–1908 at 1872 (fns. omitted). At the extreme lower end of this continuum, there may be some distinctions still to be made: cf. F. Johns, *Non-Legality in International Law: Unruly Law* (CUP, 2013), who notes at the outset (p.1) that 'International lawyers make law as they go about their daily work, but they also make non-law', and points to the possibility of distinguishing between 'illegality, extra-legality, pre- and post-legality, supra-legality and infra-legality' *(ibid.)*. Illegality, in the sense of contrariness to a legal precept, would seem to have a source, namely that precept; but to the other categories the idea of a source does not seem appropriate; or at least the relationship does need to be studied here.

[2] P. Weil, 'Vers une normativité relative en droit international', RGDIP (1982), 5; P. Weil, 'Towards Relative Normativity in International Law', 77 AJIL (1983), 413.

[3] And it is recognized that some of his consequent gloomy prophecies have come to pass: see S. Besson, 'Theorizing the Sources of International Law', in S. Besson and J. Tasioulas (eds.), *The Philosophy of International Law* (Oxford: Oxford University Press, 2012), 174.

The existence and nature of what is termed 'soft law', one category of which would occupy the opposite end of the relativity spectrum, is perhaps more controversial, even though examples of texts that would seem to merit that designation are far more numerous than is the case for *jus cogens*.

A comparatively recent development in international law, but one that has to a considerable extent remained in the domain of theory, has in fact been this recognition, or the belief, that not all international rules belong to the domain of *jus dispositivum*, that is to say, rules that apply failing agreement to the contrary, but which can be set aside in the relationship between two or more States, by agreement between those concerned.[4] In contrast to these, it is recognized that there is a category of *jus cogens*, rules that continue to apply notwithstanding any agreement to the contrary. In the domestic legal order, the phenomenon is so evidently necessary that it is often not explicitly recognized as a legal category, or at least not with the Latin title. The present-day international community recognizes, at least in general terms, the existence of rules of this kind, also known as 'peremptory norms'; the clearest and earliest effective example of such recognition is Article 53 of the Vienna Convention on the Law of Treaties. This text provides that '[a] treaty is void if, at the time of its conclusion, it conflicts with a peremptory norm of international law'; and the latter term is defined as meaning 'a norm accepted and recognized by the international community of States as a whole as a norm from which no derogation is permitted, and which can be modified only by a subsequent norm of general international law having the same character'.[5] As a provision of the Vienna Convention, this is binding only on the parties to that Convention, but it has become generally recognized that a comparable rule exists for all States, as a matter of customary law or of 'general international law'.[6] Such recognition, while generating a considerable literature, has not

---

[4] For an early recognition of the concept in international law by a national court, see the 1965 decision of the German Federal Constitutional Court discussed by S. Riesenfeld, '*Jus dispositivum* and *jus cogens* in the Light of a Recent Decision of the German Supreme Constitutional Court', 60 AJIL (1966), 511. The appearance of, in particular, the concept of obligations *erga omnes* can be associated with the growth of the idea of an international community of States, as is well demonstrated by S. Villalpando, *L'Émergence de la communauté internationale dans la responsabilité des États* (Paris: Presses universitaires de France, 2005), particularly 293ff.

[5] Art. 64 of the Convention provides for the emergence of a new peremptory norm: any existing treaty which is in conflict with that norm 'becomes void and terminates'—in absolute terms, apparently, not even *pro rata*. Similar provisions appear in the parallel Convention on Treaties between States and International Organizations.

[6] There is also a class of, as it were, imprescriptible international law that may or may not also be appropriately categorized as *jus cogens*. Generally, norms recognized as *jus cogens* owe their status to a quasi-ethical character: obtaining concessions by the use of force, or committing genocide, is generally recognized as 'wrong', to use the simplest term. There are, however, rules of law that apply automatically to States simply as part of the recognized structure of modern legal relations: a good example is the rule that every coastal State is exclusively entitled to certain rights over the continental

however been supported by very much practice in the form of frequent application in inter-State relations.[7] The concept has however been endorsed by the ICJ in the context of allegations of genocide;[8] and there has been sufficient practice for the subject to be thought ripe for consideration by the International Law Commission.[9]

The significance of the quality of a norm as *jus cogens*, on the basis of Article 53 of the Vienna Convention, is simply to invalidate any agreement purporting to contradict or evade that norm. There has inevitably been a temptation for scholars to attach wider effects to the concept, since by definition a norm of *jus cogens* is a benevolent one, to be given, for that reason, the greatest possible scope. It has been claimed, for example, that a *jus cogens* norm can overcome a defect in jurisdiction before the ICJ, or may override State immunity, but such claims have not been found acceptable by the ICJ. The relevant case-law will be considered further.[10]

Another aspect of traditional international law in its character as *jus dispositivum* is that a State is in principle free to choose its partners in a treaty-relationship. Rights and obligations of this kind are owed by, and enforceable at the suit of, defined legal persons, either specific to the obligation concerned, or falling within a specific class. This is the relative effect of treaties (and, in domestic law, of contracts): only the parties to the treaty are bound

shelf off its shores. The extent of such rights may be—in fact has to be—determined by agreement with neighbouring States, and there seems no reason in principle why a State could not renounce all its continental shelf rights pertaining to a particular coastline in favour of a neighbouring State, presumably in return for concessions elsewhere or of another kind. Yet this would be a disposal of vested rights: it would not be possible, it is suggested, for two States to agree that a given coastline possessed no shelf or no rights over it. Cf. the observations, at an early stage of the development of the continental shelf doctrine, of Judges Padilla Nervo (*ICJ Reports 1969*, p. 97), Tanaka (p. 182), and Sørensen (p. 248) in the *North Sea Continental Shelf* case, all of whom use *jus cogens* to refer to the institution of the continental shelf (in connection with the question of reservations to the 1958 Continental Shelf Convention).

[7] Brownlie observed in 1988 that 'the vehicle does not often leave the garage' in Cassese et al. (eds), *Change and Stability in International Law-Making* (Berlin: Walter de Gruyter, 1988) p.110; and see Espaliu Berdud, 'El *jus cogens* - ¿Salió del Garaje?', 67 Rivista Española de Derecho Internacional (2015), 95–121, who concedes that the concept is more evident in treaties, international judicial decisions, and statements of international organizations than in direct State practice.

[8] *Application of the Genocide Convention (Bosnia v. Serbia)* [2007-I] ICJ Rep 43; *Application of the Genocide Convention (Croatia v. Serbia)* [2008] ICJ Rep 412 and [2016-I] ICJ Rep 3. 45–47.

[9] ILC, First, Second, and Third Report on *jus cogens* by Dire Tladi, Special Rapporteur, UN Doc. A/CN.4.693, 8 March 2016; UN Doc A/CN.4/706, 16 March 2017; UN Doc.A/CN.4/714, 12 February 2018 and see the 14 draft conclusions provisionally adopted by the Drafting Committee by the end of the ILC's 2018 session, annexed to the statement of the Chairperson of the Drafting Committee, 26 July 2018: http://legal.un.org/docs/?path=../ilc/documentation/english/statements/2018_dc_chairman_statement_jc_26july.pdf&lang=E

[10] See also generally the article of J. Vidmar, 'Rethinking *jus cogens* after *Germany v. Italy*: Back to Article 53?', 60 Netherlands ILR (2013), 2.

to perform its stipulations, and to require the other party or parties to do the same. But in international law the same is generally true of obligations deriving from other sources. In the field of State responsibility, an injury by one State to another State's sovereignty or legal rights would traditionally be regarded as entitling the latter State, and only that State, to seek a remedy (cessation and/or reparation); no other State or body would have, in principle, any concern with the matter. Modern international law has, however, come to recognize a category of obligations of such importance to the international community that they may potentially be enforced by that community; or, more precisely, in view of the absence of bodies truly representative of the community, by any member of the community. These are designated 'obligations *erga omnes*', that is 'obligations [owed] towards all'. Reference is often made to a wider class of 'rights and obligations *erga omnes*', but this must be regarded as a shorter way of saying 'obligations *erga omnes* and the corresponding rights', that is the rights to require performance of an obligation *erga omnes*, since a 'right *erga omnes*' would be a right that its possessor is entitled to assert against all other subjects of law; and the majority of rights, other than those derived from treaty, are of this nature.[11]

Given then that obligations *erga omnes*, and rules of *jus cogens*, exist—and there is thus general recognition, both by scholars and in statements made by or on behalf of States that they do[12]—the question arises of their source or sources. The idea that they might derive from a unique source, one not included in the classic Article 38 list, is implausible, but has been advanced, on the basis that they are a manifestation of the fundamental values of the international community, and as such exist independently of the will of States.[13] It is suggested that the question is rather, why or how does it come about that some of the norms generated by a recognized source have, or acquire, the special quality of *jus cogens* or *erga omnes*, while others—in fact the

---

[11] Nevertheless, in the case-law of the PCIJ and ICJ, the term was first used as attached to *rights*: see S. Villalpando, 'Some Archaeological Explorations on the Birth of Obligations *erga omnes*', in M. Kamga and M. M. Mbengue (eds.), *Liber Amicorum Raymond Ranjeva* (Paris: Pedone, 2013), 625–6.

[12] There is less unanimity of opinion on the question of the relationship between the two concepts. A valuable study is that of C. Tams, *Enforcing Obligations* Erga Omnes *in International Law*, Cambridge Studies in International and Comparative Law (Cambridge: Cambridge University Press, 2005), 139ff. For our purposes the only relevant aspect of the relationship is whether the establishment of the existence of a customary obligation of the one category by appropriate State practice entails acceptance of that same obligation as one of the other category. For example, if State practice shows that the obligation not to cause irreparable damage to the environment is regarded as one of *jus cogens*, does it necessarily follow that it is also an obligation *erga omnes*? The same question might theoretically arise for an obligation established by treaty, but would probably be answered by the terms of the relevant treaty.

[13] ILC Fragmentation Report (n. 44), para. 361.

majority—do not. Is there something in the operation of the source in relation to a norm that stamps it with either of those qualities from the outset; or if the quality is acquired subsequently, is this due to a fresh intervention of one of the sources?

Principally this involves an enquiry into customary law; while the concepts of *jus cogens* norms, and of obligations *erga omnes*, are not normally invoked under those names in the field of treaty-law, they would, however, seem to be present, and this aspect will also be examined. The possibility that norms of *jus cogens* might derive directly from the 'general principles of law' of Article 38, paragraph 1(*c*) of the ICJ Statute does not seem to have attracted support;[14] the question seems to have become merged with the question whether they may derive from an autonomous source, discussed further in this chapter.

Whether all obligations *erga omnes* are also matters of *jus cogens*, or whether all norms of *jus cogens* necessarily impose obligations *erga omnes* is not a matter that need be determined here; what is clear is that the two concepts are related, and neither can be discussed in complete isolation from the other. For the purpose of our enquiry into sources, we shall, however, endeavour to deal with them successively.

1(a) The source or sources of obligations *erga omnes*

The existence of obligations owed by a State to 'the international community of States as a whole' of this kind was recognized by the International Law Commission in the preparation of the Articles on State Responsibility. These first recognize the general situation in which the responsibility of a State for an unlawful act is invoked primarily by the State or States that have been injured by that act; Article 48, paragraph 1, of the Articles, however, provides further:

Any State other than an injured State is entitled to invoke the responsibility of another State ... if:

  ...

  (b) the obligation breached is owed to the international community as a whole.

This provision was avowedly based on the classic judicial text on the subject of obligations *erga omnes*, which, however, in fact amounts to an *obiter dictum*,

---

[14] Though this is one reading of such statements as that 'the acknowledgement of the existence of obligations *erga omnes* breaks away from the traditional synallagmatic structure of international legal obligations, and presupposes a set of values that are more important than others to the international community', A. Bianchi, *International Law Theories* (OUP, 2016), 49.

being marginal (at most) to the decision. In the case concerning the *Barcelona Traction, Light and Power Company, Limited*, the ICJ was examining a claim by Belgium against Spain for injury to the Belgian shareholders in a Canadian company operating in Spain, alleged to have been unlawfully wound up there for the benefit of Spanish financial interests. The ICJ noted the existence of obligations on the part of States that admit foreign investments or foreign nationals to its territory, and continued:

[A]n essential distinction should be drawn between the obligations of a State towards the international community as a whole, and those arising vis-à-vis another State in the field of diplomatic protection. By their very nature the former are the concern of all States. In view of the importance of the rights involved, all States can be held to have a legal interest in their protection; they are obligations *erga omnes*.[15]

The Court then gave a number of examples;[16] and the whole passage has become one of the most quoted in the jurisprudence of the Court. Since it was clear that Belgium's claim was in the field of diplomatic protection, the dictum served little or no purpose in the judgment; but that has not prevented its being enormously influential. The term 'obligations *erga omnes*' is generally used in this connection, but was avoided by the ILC, as being less informative than the formula quoted, and also capable of being confused with obligations owed by a party to a multilateral treaty to all the other parties.[17]

If an international obligation is claimed to exist under customary law as one owed *erga omnes*, the practice invoked to support the custom would have to consist of more than the fact that States do not generally infringe that obligation, and that those that do are exposed to claims for reparation by any State whose citizens, or whose interests, have allegedly suffered from its commission. As basis for an obligation under general customary law to have the characteristic of being owed *erga omnes*, there would have to be a practice whereby allegedly unlawful acts exposed the State responsible to successful claims also by States having no direct connection, normally through their citizens, with the acts in question. These are heavy demands, and it is doubtful whether much supporting practice, of either kind, has been demonstrated up to now.[18] More generally, it has been shrewdly observed by Simma

---

[15] [1970] ICJ Rep 32, para. 33.

[16] Norms outlawing aggression and genocide, some human rights principles, such as those prohibiting slavery and racial discrimination: [1970] ICJ Rep 32, para. 34.

[17] J. Crawford, *The International Law Commission's Articles on State Responsibility* (Cambridge: Cambridge University Press, 2002), 278, para. 9.

[18] The problem is even more marked in the case of peremptory norms (*jus cogens*): see this chapter, text and nn. 34, 35, and 36.

and Alston, in a passage that in terms deals with *jus cogens*, but fits the case of obligations *erga omnes* also, that

Settled practices of States as regards *jus cogens* are elusive to grasp because most, if not all, rules of *jus cogens* are prohibitive in substance; they are rules of abstention. How does one marshal conclusive evidence of abstentions? Abstentions *per se* mean nothing; they become meaningful only when considered in the light of the intention underlying them.[19]

Similarly, an interesting contention put forward by Judge Cançado Trindade in his opinion in the *Obligation to Prosecute or Extradite* case was that obligations which are of *jus cogens* are thereby *ipso facto* obligations of result, and not obligations of conduct.[20]

An extensive study by Christian Tams,[21] on the other hand, contains a very full account and analysis of State practice advanced as showing the existence of obligations *erga omnes*, in the form of 'actions, statements, and other forms of conduct that might help to assess whether the *erga omnes* concept has actually influenced the rules governing countermeasures'.[22] Tams devotes a section of his study to 'The question of sources', which includes an examination of the issue whether the concept of obligations *erga omnes* overlaps with that of *jus cogens*;[23] and the 'practice' referred to in that context is principally the comments supplied by States to the ILC during its work on State responsibility, and some scattered decisions of municipal courts. Much attention is paid to countermeasures, taken or threatened: as the author points out, a right to take counter-measures in reliance on an *erga omnes* obligation would be of fundamental importance: such a right 'would not be subject to jurisdictional constraints; it could be exercised by all States, and, more importantly, *against* all States'.[24] A considerable

---

[19] B. Simma and P. Alston, 'The Sources of Human Rights Law', 12 Australian YIL (1988–9), 82 at 103–4, citing the International Law Association report, p. 16. In the same sense, M. E. O'Connell, '*Jus cogens*: International Law's Higher Ethical Norms', in D. E. Childress III (ed.), *The Role of Ethics in International Law* (Cambridge: Cambridge University Press, 2012), 80. Similarly, Glennon, faced with the argument, in response to the positivist objection to the possible existence of *jus cogens*, that States have accepted its existence, enquires pertinently where exactly are the supporting precedents to be found, evidencing that acceptance: M. J. Glennon, 'De l'absurdité du droit imperatif (*jus cogens*)', RGDIP (2006), 529 at 532.

[20] Separate opinion, sect. V, paras. 44ff, [2012] ICJ Rep 505–6. Assuming that the distinction is meaningful in international law, this may well be so; but it is difficult to see how, as a matter of logic, the conclusion follows from the simple premise that these are obligations that may not be contractually waived; and a treaty can, of course, make provision for obligations of either category.

[21] Tams, *Enforcing Obligations* Erga Omnes (this chapter, n. 12).

[22] Tams, *Enforcing Obligations* Erga Omnes, 207.

[23] Tams, *Enforcing Obligations* Erga Omnes, 149.

[24] Tams, *Enforcing Obligations* Erga Omnes, 198.

quantity of material, dating from 1971 (the case of Uganda) to 2002/3 (Zimbabwe) is assembled, and the author's careful examination of it shows that it is often difficult to distinguish true counter-measures in reliance on general law from (in particular) sanctions justified on the basis of a particular treaty: for example, for some, measures directed against Argentina over the Falklands invasion could be based on the national security exemption in Article XXI of GATT.[25]

The ICJ in its *Barcelona Traction* dictum stated that some of the rights of protection corresponding to what it saw as obligations *erga omnes* had 'entered into the body of general international law', that is to say, customary law, but that 'others are conferred by international instruments of a universal or quasi-universal character'.[26] Turning then to the question of obligations *erga omnes* arising under such instruments, it is of course normal for each party to a multilateral treaty to be bound in relation to each other party. However, it is not merely a question of being bound: the essence of *erga omnes* obligations is that they are enforceable by any member of the relevant community (in this case, that of parties to the treaty), even if the breach of the obligation has caused that member no injury, and may or may not have caused injury to some other member. That too could no doubt be provided for in the treaty, though it is difficult to trace any examples of a specific and unambiguous provision in a multilateral convention to that effect. It has, however, been judicially established, notably by the case concerning the *Obligation to Prosecute or Extradite*, discussed further in this chapter, that an obligation under a multilateral convention may, in appropriate cases, be treated as enforceable at the suit of any other party to the convention, so that the obligation is *erga omnes partes*, though not *erga omnes* in the sense of any other subject of international law. This is, of course, a question of interpretation of the convention concerned.[27]

Where an obligation regarded as *erga omnes* in customary law is doubled by a treaty, as for example in the case of the Genocide Convention, probably the only element that the treaty will in effect add is a compromissory clause, for example conferring jurisdiction on the ICJ; but this is only valid for the parties to the treaty. The result is that a non-party to the Convention may be able to invoke customary law in order to react appropriately to an alleged breach on the part of another State (whether or not the latter State is party to

---

[25] Tams, *Enforcing Obligations* Erga Omnes, 215–16.

[26] [1970] ICJ Rep 32, para. 34.

[27] For the emphasis in the decision in this case in question on the 'common interest' of '[a]ll the other States parties', rather than an interpretation of the intentions of the States parties to the convention, or of those who drafted it, see the further discussion later in this chapter.

the Convention), but cannot enforce its claim through the ICJ unless there exists a separate basis of general jurisdiction.[28]

There is thus no difficulty in recognizing that a multilateral convention may prescribe obligations for the parties that are enforceable by any other party, and even are so enforceable even if the alleged breach of the obligation has no impact on the State party seeking enforcement: a conventional obligation *erga omnes partes*. If such an obligation is specifically provided for in the text, there is no more to be said. But if it is not, in what circumstances may a multilateral convention properly be interpreted as containing such an obligation? This was the reading of the United Nations Torture Convention adopted by the International Court in the case of the *Obligation to Prosecute or Extradite*, but the decision is not free from obscurities.

In that case, the relevant obligations were those imposed under the 1984 United Nations Convention against Torture. Belgium complained that Senegal had failed to perform its obligations (to prosecute or extradite persons suspected of having committed or authorized torture) under the Convention in relation to a M. Habré; Senegal observed that there was nothing to show that any of his alleged victims had been of Belgian nationality.[29] In reply to a question put by Judge Cançado Trindade, however, counsel for Senegal stated that in Senegal's view, 'The nature of the international obligation to prohibit torture has undergone a major change. From being a conventional obligation of relative effect, it has had an *erga omnes* effect attributed to it.'[30] Similarly, Belgium expressed the view that the rights set forth in the Torture Convention 'are ... opposable to *all* the States Parties to the Convention'.[31] By what process then could this change have come about? A treaty may provide for the rights that it creates to be opposable to all States parties, an obligation *erga omnes partes*, or it may not; and in the latter event, such rights can only be enforced by the party injured by a breach of the relevant provision of the treaty. For those rights subsequently to *become* so opposable involves a revision or amendment of the treaty, which presumably would in this case have to comply with Article 29 (the amendment clause) of the 1984 Convention, and with Article 40 of the Vienna Convention.[32] Alternatively (and one may

---

[28] e.g. an unconditional acceptance of ICJ jurisdiction under the 'optional clause'.

[29] See [2012] ICJ Rep 448, para. 64.

[30] Cited in the separate opinion of Judge Cançado Trindade [2012] ICJ Rep 529, para. 107. Senegal also put forward, in reply to a question by Judge Donoghue, a rather obscure argument that the obligation in question belonged to 'the category of divisible *erga omnes* obligations', which apparently means not *erga omnes* at all: see [2012] ICJ Rep 458, para. 103, and the answers to questions put by Members of the Court (available at <http://www.icj-cij.org/docket/files/144/17642.pdf>, accessed December 2013), p. 52.

[31] [2012] ICJ Rep 528, para. 106.

[32] Assuming that provision to correspond to customary law on the point.

suspect this is closer to the thinking reflected in Judge Cançado Trindade's question and the replies), the obligations not to employ torture stated in the 1984 Convention reflect a rule of customary law, by virtue of which the obligation is a true obligation *erga omnes*; in which case the status of party or non-party to the Convention, emphasized in Judge Cançado Trindade's question, would appear to be irrelevant.

While the Court did begin its analysis by citing the Preamble to the Convention (giving its object and purpose as 'to make more effective the struggle against torture ... throughout the world'), it does not appear to have viewed the question as one of treaty-interpretation, which would imply consideration of the intentions of those who drew up the Convention in 1948. Rather, it applied to the 1948 Convention what one may call the mindset expressed, more than twenty years earlier, by the Court in the *Barcelona Traction* judgment, so as to find that all the States parties have a 'common interest' in compliance by each other party with the obligations imposed by the Convention to enquire into and, where appropriate, prosecute alleged instances of torture, and continuing by defining those obligations as 'obligations *erga omnes partes* in the sense that each State party has an interest in compliance with them in any given case'.[33]

A distinction is perhaps here in point. Belgium, in its reply to the question, observed that 'all States Parties to the CAT Convention are entitled to seek ensuring compliance with the conventional obligations ... undertaken by each State Party in relation to all other States Parties ...'.[34] This, however, is the much attenuated form of an obligation *erga omnes* (if indeed the Latin designation is appropriate at all) that the ILC feared might be confused with the true obligations owed to the international community.[35] Put simply: States parties to the CAT Convention are bound not to torture each others' nationals, and are bound to take certain steps if a person allegedly guilty of torture is found on their territory. If State A tortures a national of State B, or fails to intercept the alleged torturer on its territory, State B may make a claim of responsibility, but State C may not. If the obligation is,

---

[33] The Court also quoted its 1951 opinion in the case of *Reservations to the Genocide Convention*: 'In such a convention the contracting States do not have any interests of their own; they merely have, one and all, a common interest, namely the accomplishment of those high purposes which are the *raison d'être* of the Convention': [1951] ICJ Rep 23. The emphasis here is less on the existence of a common interest than on the absence of an individual interest: if the 'common interest' discerned by the Court had been such as to generate an obligation *erga omnes*, or a right *omnium*, its further disquisition on reservations would have been inappropriate, or would at least have had to be greatly modified. While the quotation therefore looks as though it supports the argument of the Court in 2012, in fact it does not.

[34] As summarized in Judge Cançado Trindade's opinion: [2012] ICJ Rep 528, para. 106.

[35] See this Chapter, n. 12.

however, one owed *erga omnes*—'towards all'—then State C may also complain.[36] This may mean, inter alia, that State C may collaborate with State B in enforcing State A's obligations; but it does not mean that State C is *obliged* to collaborate with State B to that end, as was argued in the Belgium/Senegal case. What the parties (and Judge Cançado Trindade) were arguing for was not an obligation *erga omnes*, but an obligation *omnium*, an obligation shared by all.

The confusion is in fact visible in the judgment in the case. The Court enumerates the conventional obligations to pursue those guilty of torture, and continues:

All the other States parties have a common interest in compliance with these obligations by the State in whose territory the alleged offender is present. That common interest implies that the obligations in question are owed by any State party to all the other States parties to the Convention. All the States parties 'have a legal interest' in the protection of the rights involved (*Barcelona Traction, Light and Power Company, Limited, Judgment, I.C.J. Reports 1970*, p. 32, para. 33). These obligations may be defined as 'obligations *erga omnes partes*' in the sense that each State party has an interest in compliance with them in any given case.[37]

Thus the obligation is a *treaty-obligation* for the Court, owed only to parties to the convention. The Court might have welcomed the opportunity to declare the existence of a customary-law obligation *erga omnes* parallel to the conventional one, but this would have been an excess of jurisdiction.[38] But was that treaty-obligation always there, despite not being spelled out in the text? If not, how did it arise? As noted already, the Court cites the Preamble, which indicates that the object of the Convention was 'to make more effective the struggle against torture ... throughout the world', which suggests it was seeking a reading of the text as *already* containing an *erga omnes* obligation. One may recognize that all States have 'an interest' (though not necessarily a legal interest) in the suppression of torture, and of genocide, and similar crimes, whether or not they are parties to the relevant convention.[39] Nor

---

[36] This was Belgium's argument: '[u]nder the Convention, every State party, irrespective of the nationality of the victims, is entitled to claim performance of the obligation concerned, and, therefore, can invoke the responsibility resulting from the failure to perform'; quoted at [2012] ICJ Rep 449, para. 65.

[37] [2012] ICJ Rep 449, para. 68.

[38] Belgium did, in fact, present a claim based on customary law, invoking the parties' declarations under Art. 36 of the Statute accepting jurisdiction; the Court found that it had no jurisdiction in this respect, on the basis that, 'at the time of the filing of the Application, the dispute between the Parties did not relate to breaches of obligations under customary law', Belgium having invoked at that stage solely the duties of Senegal under the Convention: [2012] ICJ Rep 445, para. 55.

[39] Nor should it be overlooked that it is possible for a party to the Convention to denounce it under Art. 31, and thereafter to be free of its conventional obligations.

should it be overlooked that it is possible for a party to the Convention to denounce it,[40] and thereafter to be free of its conventional obligations; it will remain subject to any customary law obligation to similar effect, but this will apparently not necessarily be *erga omnes* and will not be backed by a jurisdictional provision.

The Court then continues:

> The common interest in compliance with the relevant obligations under the Convention against Torture implies the entitlement of each State party to the Convention to make a claim concerning the cessation of an alleged breach by another State party. If a special interest were required for that purpose, in many cases no State would be in the position to make such a claim. It follows that any State party to the Convention may invoke the responsibility of another State party with a view to ascertaining the alleged failure to comply with its obligations *erga omnes partes*, such as those under Article 6, paragraph 2, and Article 7, paragraph 1, of the Convention, and to bring that failure to an end.

This looks like an appeal to the doctrine of effective application of treaties. The Court does not indicate in what circumstances 'no State would be in a position' to demand compliance with the Convention, but it may well have had in mind the possibility that the national State of a victim of torture was not a party to the Convention, or indeed that the victim was stateless. The time at which the 'common interest' existed is left open. If, at the time that the Convention was prepared and signed, States had been asked whether the Convention signified that a party could be held to account by another party in the absence of any direct interest shown, it must be doubtful whether this would have been the general view of the effect of the Convention.

Enough has been said to show that the *erga omnes* quality of an obligation may be added to the obligation itself on the basis of the same source of law as constitutes the basis of that obligation: treaty-law or customary international law; and that in this respect no extension or modification of the classical doctrine of sources is called for.

1(b) The source or sources of norms of *jus cogens*

The concept of *jus cogens* was not originally based on any judicial statement analogous to that found in the *Barcelona Traction* judgment, quoted earlier; this indeed is relevant to the problem of the existence of such obligations, since only a court decision could authoritatively invalidate an agreement between

---

[40] Art. 13 of the Convention.

States as contrary to *jus cogens*, and thus demonstrate that the category of *jus cogens* exists.[41] The *potential* existence of peremptory norms had however some recognition in the judgment in the *South West Africa* case, when the Court rejected arguments based on humanitarian considerations, explaining that it could 'take account of moral principles only in so far as these are given a sufficient expression in legal form'.[42] The concept as observable today was in effect developed by the ILC in its work on the law of treaties, and thus, as noted already, it has the recognition of Articles 53 and 64 of the Vienna Convention on the Law of Treaties, to the extent that a treaty is void if it conflicts with a norm of *jus cogens*; but this implies a very limited field of operation, since if a norm clearly has such status, States will be very unlikely to conclude treaties contemplating breaches of such a norm;[43] and if two States *do* agree by treaty to misbehave in this way, neither party is likely to wish to denounce the treaty as void under the Vienna Convention. In themselves, these provisions of the Convention are simply treaty law, binding only on the parties to the Convention; but that of course is not the end of the story. More recently the concept and its operation have been examined and reported on by a Study Group of the ILC.[44]

It appears that the 'sufficient expression in legal form' has now, to a greater or lesser extent, been achieved by a number of norms. What sort of rules have in practice been claimed to rank as *jus cogens*? The ILC Fragmentation Study Group identified as the most commonly adduced candidates:

(a) The prohibition of aggressive use of force; (b) the right to self-defence; (c) the prohibition of genocide; (d) the prohibition of torture; (e) crimes against humanity; (f) the prohibition of slavery and the slave trade; (g) the prohibition of piracy; (h) the prohibition of racial discrimination and *apartheid*; and (i) the prohibition of hostilities directed at civilian populations ('basic rules of international humanitarian law').[45]

The ICJ, at least, has never been called upon to invalidate a treaty as contrary to *jus cogens*, either on the basis of Articles 65 (3) or 66 (a) of the UN Charter or otherwise, but has nevertheless recognized, or at least assumed,

---

[41] The States parties to a treaty might in theory later come to an agreement that their treaty had been contrary to *jus cogens*, and was void; but the scenario is unlikely, to say the least.

[42] *South West Africa, Second Phase* [1966] ICJ Rep 34, para. 49.

[43] In this sense J. Vidmar, 'Rethinking *jus cogens* after *Germany* v. *Italy*: Back to Article 53?', 60 Netherlands ILR (2013), 2.

[44] ILC Study Group on Fragmentation of International Law: Difficulties Arising from the Diversification and Expansion of International Law, Report, UN doc. A/CN.4/L/682, Section E (paras. 324–409), (hereinafter 'Fragmentation Report').

[45] ILC Fragmentation Report, para. 374.

the existence of, the concept in three successive cases,[46] which will be further considered in Section 1 (b).[47] In none of these, however, was it called upon to base its decision directly on a finding that a particular asserted norm was, or was not, one of *jus cogens*. In each, however, the existence and nature of the concept was relevant in the background to the decision, and was discussed unquestioningly by the parties and the Court as part of the fabric of international law. Rather as it had done in *Barcelona Traction*, the Court in effect established by its decision something which was not legally relevant to that decision actually given.[48] It is striking to what extent the judgment, when dealing with the arguments relating to the operation of *jus cogens*, treats that concept as an undisputed part of the legal landscape of the twenty first century.[49]

The most recent decision involving arguments over *jus cogens* is that of *Jurisdictional Immunities of the State*: claims had been made against Germany for compensation for acts committed during the Second World War, which it was asserted, had been in breach of rules of the law of armed conflict; these claims were met with reliance on the law of State immunity. It was argued that such immunity was excluded by the *jus cogens* nature of the rules allegedly violated, but the Court did not accept this, inasmuch as the two sets of rules (those of armed conflict and those of immunity) were not in conflict: they addressed different matters. 'The rules of State immunity are procedural in character' and 'do not bear upon the question whether or not the conduct in respect of which the proceedings are brought was lawful or unlawful'.[50] The Court's decision was thus limited to finding that there had been a violation of Germany's immunity, and it was not called upon to decide anything else. Specifically it did not, because it could not, decide whether Germany had committed the wartime acts complained of, whether they had been contrary to provisions of the law of armed conflict, and—most importantly for our purpose—whether those provisions fell in

---

[46] *Armed Activities on the Territory of the Congo (DRC v. Rwanda)* [2006] ICJ Rep 32; *Arrest Warrant of 11 April 2000 (DRC v. Belgium)* [2002] ICJ Rep 24, which did not in fact use the term '*jus cogens*'; and *Jurisdictional Immunities of the State (Germany v. Italy)* [2012-] ICJ Rep 140.

[47] For instances of questions of *Jus cogens* being raised in domestic courts, see ILC Fragmentation Report, paras. 370–3.

[48] The separate and dissenting opinions of Members of the Court, on the other hand, feature much discussion of *jus cogens*: the index to the Court's *Reports 2016*, for example, lists 22 page references (some to multiple pages) to opinions, and not one to a decision.

[49] For example, [2012-I] ICJ Rep pp. 141–2, paras. 95–7.

[50] [2012-I] ICJ Rep 140, para. 93.

a category known as *jus cogens*, or even whether that category was part of international law.[51]

Since rules of *jus cogens* thus principally exist outside the domain of treaty provisions, must they not come into existence in the same way as any other rule, through the operation of one of the other recognized sources? The most recent and far-reaching study of peremptory norms is the book on the subject by Daniel Cottesloe:[52] unfortunately—for our purposes—he leaves this question open, as it is the consequences of the existence and operation of such norms that is the subject of his enquiry.[53] The question was however studied extensively by Alexander Orakhelashvili in his treatise on *Peremptory Norms in International Law*.[54] He examined both the possibility that *jus cogens* might be an autonomous source of law, and the way in which such norms might derive from each of the classical sources: treaties, custom, and the general principles of law.[55] Can the question be side-stepped, however, by claiming, for example, that *jus cogens* rules evolve from the common values of all nations, and that therefore '[t]o establish them is therefore less a constitutive than a declaratory

---

[51] The Court also relied on its own earlier decision in *Armed Activities on the Territory of the Congo (DRC v. Rwanda)* [2006] ICJ Rep 32; also *Arrest Warrant of 11 April 2000 (DRC v. Belgium)* [2002] ICJ Rep 24, which did not in fact use the term '*jus cogens*'.

[52] D. Cottesloe, *Legal Consequences of Peremptory Norms in International Law* (Cambridge University Press, 2017).

[53] He observes that '[o]n the whole this long-standing debate has not led to much common ground', and that scholarly agreement on the source 'is no necessary condition for the application of these norms and their legal consequences': Cottesloe (previous note) p.2.

[54] Oxford University Press, 2006. This is of course not the last word on the subject, but a useful reference point. For subsequent writings, see for example E. Canizzaro (ed.) *The Present and Future of Jus Cogens* (Rome: Sapienza Università Editrice, 2015); R. Kolb, *Peremptory International Law – Jus cogens – A General Inventory* (Hart Publishing, 2015); T. Weatherall, Jus Cogens: *International Law and Social Contract* (CUP, 2015); E. de Wet, 'The Place of Peremptory Norms and Article 103 of the UN Charter within the Sources of International Law', in Besson and d'Aspremont (eds.) *The Oxford Handbook on the Sources of International Law* (Oxford University Press, 2017); T. Weatherall, Jus Cogens: *International Law and Social Contract*, (Cambridge University Press, 2015); and the review of some of these by T. Kleinlein, 28 EJIL (2018) 295–315.

[55] As Orakhelashvili observes, 'many peremptory norms would conceivably fail to satisfy the State practice requirements of the custom-generation process': A. Orakhelashvili, *Peremptory Norms in International Law* (Oxford: Oxford University Press, 2006), 113; but in his view they do not have to satisfy those requirements (see here, sect. 1(*b*)). Cassese, a major exponent of the doctrine of *jus cogens*, has offered examples of practice in support ('For an Enhanced Role of *Jus Cogens*', in A. Cassese (ed.), *Realizing Utopia: The Future of International Law* (Oxford: Oxford University Press, 2012), 158–71 at 160–2). However, none of the examples are of State to State recognition of the invalidity of an attempt to contract out of a rule found to be of *jus cogens*; they include some passing remarks of judges in the *North Sea Continental Shelf* cases (already noted, this chapter, n. 6), and the case of *Application of the Convention on Genocide*, two decisions of the Swiss Federal Tribunal, and Opinion No. 3 of 4 July 1992 of the Arbitration Commission on Yugoslavia. This last does indeed apply the 'well-established principle of international law that the alteration of existing boundaries or frontiers by force is not capable of producing any legal effect', but cites a number of texts in support.

process'?[56] There is all the greater temptation to do so, inasmuch as the values to be sanctioned or protected by norms of this kind are, *ex hypothesi*, eminently such as to require to be so sanctioned or protected. The ILC Fragmentation Study Group, which did not pose the source question directly, however pointed out a 'disturbing circularity' in an approach of this kind: 'If the point of *jus cogens* is to limit what may be lawfully agreed by States, can its content simultaneously be made dependent on what is agreed by States?'[57] There is also, of course, a danger that the acceptance 'by the international community as a whole' may have an existence in the mind of the observer rather than in the hard facts of international relations. There is no real distinction between such a position and the bolder assertion that peremptory norms constitute 'an autonomous body of superior rules, independent of any source of international law'.[58]

There are a number of problems attaching to this thesis. One that seems often to be overlooked is so simple as perhaps to appear trivial the International Court has recognized the concept of *jus cogens*, and has declared and applied certain precepts as falling within that category. If these do not fall within the scope of Article 38, paragraph 1, of the ICJ Statute, on what basis may the Court apply them, without acting *ultra vires*? The Court has never itself specified what is the formal source (if any) of *jus cogens* norms that it has recognized; but it does not normally need to specify the source of a rule it is applying, unless this is necessary to identify the parties bound by it (e.g. parties to a treaty as distinct from those subject to a general customary rule).

Furthermore, the concept of peremptory norms implies a hierarchy of norms: a rule of *jus cogens* by definition prevails over a contrary treaty-provision.[59] This suggests that the source of such a rule must be not merely an autonomous source on a par with the other recognized sources (a sort of extra sub-paragraph of paragraph 1 of Article 38 of the ICJ Statute), but be on a higher level than the sources in sub-paragraphs (*a*) to (*d*), or, in other words, rest outside the body of norms derived from recognized sources, being of a higher rank.[60]

---

[56] C. Tomuschat, 'Obligations Arising for States without or against their Will', 241 Recueil des cours (1993), 307. Similarly, Simma regards the question of the formal source of peremptory norms as more or less irrelevant, once the rule has been recognized as such by the international community as a whole: B. Simma, 'From Bilateralism to Community Interest', 250 Recueil des cours (1994-VI), 292. Cf. also G. I. Hernandez, 'A Reluctant Guardian: the International Court of Justice and the Concept of "International Community"', 83 BYIL (2013) at 38–9.

[57] Fragmentation Report, para. 375.   [58] Orakhelashvili, *Peremptory Norms*, 105.

[59] And indeed, according to the Vienna Convention on the Law of Treaties, renders the whole treaty void: see Art. 53.

[60] This view is, however, rejected by Kolb, who considers that the problem is not one of production of norms, but one of collision of norms: R. Kolb, 'Formal Source of *Jus Cogens* in Public International Law', 53 Zeitschrift für öffentliches Recht (1998), 76; see further in this section.

Do peremptory norms then form part of general customary international law?[61] If so, they must result, like any other norm deriving from that source, from the combination of appropriate State practice and the psychological element of *opinio juris*.[62] It is however the role of these factors together not merely to point to the existence of a customary law on a given subject, but also to define its characteristics. To support a customary rule not merely forbidding genocide, but also providing that the obligation not to commit it is a matter of *jus cogens*, the practice invoked would have to consist of, or include, one or more failed attempts to contract out of its application, by treaty or informal agreement —'failed' in the sense that it was accepted, or authoritatively declared, that the norm over-rode the agreement. Examples of such State practice are not easy to find, and most commentators appear to concentrate on what States say rather than what they do, or to treat dicta of the ICJ as (in effect) norm-creating.[63]

If such rules exist at all as customary law, therefore, either they must come into existence by some process other than the traditional one of practice plus *opinio juris*, or there must be some additional element, some extra ingredient in the mix, that distinguishes a developing rule of customary law that is subject to contracting out from one that is not. The problem has been tackled directly by Cassese:

> for the purpose of establishing whether a *jus cogens* rule or principle has evolved, should we resort to the habitual method for establishing whether a customary rule of international law has emerged, namely determine whether *usus* and *opinio juris* show that such a rule has taken root in the world community? Or should we resort to a different method?[64]

His conclusion is that in this respect 'the two elements of *usus* and *opinio juris* are not required'.[65] The basis for this is apparently that it suffices if, in the

---

[61] As is asserted by e.g. I. Brownlie, *Principles of Public International Law*, 7th edn. (Oxford: Oxford University Press, 2008), 510; see also L. Hannikainen, *Peremptory Norms (Jus Cogens) in International Law* (Helsinki: Finnish Lawyers' Publishing Company, 1988), 226–42.

[62] When provision was made for *jus cogens* in the Vienna Convention on the Law of Treaties, the ILC did not give any indication how such norms might come into existence. Cf. G. Danilenko, 'International *jus cogens*: Issues of Law-Making', 2 EJIL (1991) 42, 43.

[63] See e.g. the study by Christian Tams already referred to at n. 12 and discussed in connection with *erga omnes* obligations.

[64] Cassese, 'For an Enhanced Role of *jus cogens*', 164.

[65] Cassese, 'For an Enhanced Role of *jus cogens*', 165. *Contra*, C. Focarelli, 'I limiti dello *jus cogens* nella giurisprudenza più recente', in *Studi in onore Vincenzo Starace* (Naples: Editoriale Scientifica, 2008), 269, who also considers that failed attempts to invoke *jus cogens* (as in e.g. the *Armed Activities* case [2006] ICJ Rep 52, para. 125), may constitute the *opinio juris*, and, *semble*, the practice contributing to a new norm to the effect asserted, but if and when that norm comes into existence, it will be a normal rule of *jus dispositivum*.

terms of Article 53 of the Vienna Convention on the Law of Treaties, a norm is 'accepted and recognized [as non-derogable] by the international community of States as a whole'. This approach of course leaves to be settled precisely how, other than by practice and *opinio*, such acceptance and recognition is to be seen to have occurred; but it is also open to the comment that it is strange to seek the source for a method of *customary* lawmaking in the provisions of a treaty, however widely ratified.

This view seems, however, to be broadly supported by, for example, Orakhelashvili, on the basis of the decision of the International Court in the *Nicaragua* case.[66] In that case, the Court found the existence of a principle of *jus cogens* concerning the non-use of force, embodied in non-binding General Assembly resolutions, and in an ILC report,[67] the attitude of States towards which supplied the *opinio juris*. The finding of *jus cogens* was not in itself required for the decision, since there was no suggestion that the parties had attempted to contract out of it; it was simply a step to finding that the rule existed as a binding general rule, and apparently the only recognized category it could fit into was that of custom, with (in the present writer's view) all the requirements that that category entails.[68] Orakhelashvili, however, considers that 'what the Court's judgment affirms is that once a norm is part of *jus cogens*, its customary status can be proved by criteria different from those applicable to other norms and the consent by individual States as opposed to the community acceptance is not crucially relevant'.[69] This is a possible interpretation, but not one spelled out in the judgment, and it is one that invites the application of Ockham's razor. If *jus cogens* norms exist without the custom-generative process being followed, then why class them as custom at all: why not recognize them as something different?

Also significant may be the nature of a *jus cogens* norm as seen by the ICJ in more recent jurisprudence. In one such case the ICJ seems to have recognized both that *jus cogens* norms arise from, or as a form of, customary law, according to the usual processes. In its judgment in the *Obligation to Extradite or Prosecute* case, it indicated specifically that '[i]n the Court's opinion, the prohibition of torture is part of customary international law and it has become a peremptory norm *(jus cogens)*'.[70] It found that 'That prohibition is grounded in a widespread international practice and on the *opinio juris* of States'. In this connection it

---

[66] *Military and Paramilitary Activities in and against Nicaragua* [1986] ICJ Rep 14.

[67] [1986] ICJ Rep 100–1, para. 190; cf. separate opinion of President Nagendra Singh [1986] ICJ Rep 153. It also noted that the United States (party to the case) had quoted the principle as having that status.

[68] See H. Thirlway, *The Law and Procedure of the International Court of Justice: Fifty Years of Jurisprudence* (Oxford: Oxford University Press, 2013), i. 229–31.

[69] *Peremptory Norms*, 119.   [70] [2012] ICJ Rep 457, para. 99.

cited numerous international instruments of universal application, and the fact that 'it has been introduced into the domestic law of almost all States; finally, acts of torture are regularly denounced within national and international fora'.[71] The Court did not indicate any more precisely how these elements supported the view that not only was there here a rule of customary law, but one having the character of *jus cogens*. The only practice capable of establishing unambiguously the *jus cogens* nature of the norm forbidding torture would be for an inter-State agreement that in some way permitted or recognized the possibility of torture, as between the contracting States, to be treated as void by some appropriate authority or body, or successfully denounced as invalid by one of the parties to it. Such an agreement would however, in the nature of things, be kept secret, so that the situation is and has been unlikely to arise. One possible analysis would be to suppose that, in the case of these norms a reasonable amount of evidence of the existence of an *opinio* to the effect that they *are* matters of *jus cogens* (or involve obligations *erga omnes*), should suffice even in the absence of actual practice supporting or demonstrating such *opinio*.

As may be observed in the ICJ jurisprudence already cited, there is a tendency, not encouraged by the Court, to regard norms of *jus cogens* as super-norms to such an extent that they do not merely override any agreement between States to set them aside, but also prevail over any norm, of any source or kind, that would impede their operation. In the case of *Armed Activities on the Territory of the Congo (DRC v. Rwanda)*, it was sought to overcome the lack of a jurisdictional basis for the claim by appealing to the *erga omnes* nature of the rules and principles, breach of which was being alleged. Similarly, in the case of *Jurisdictional Immunities of the State (Germany v. Italy, Greece intervening)*, it was contended that the normal rules of sovereign immunity were not applicable to a claim before a municipal court made against a foreign State, and alleging acts that were clearly contrary to norms of *jus cogens*. In the earlier case, the Court held it 'necessary' to recall that 'the mere fact that rights and obligations *erga omnes* or peremptory norms of general international law *(jus cogens)* are at issue in a dispute cannot in itself constitute an exception to the principle that its jurisdiction always depends on the consent of the parties'.[72] In the *Jurisdictional Immunities* case, the ICJ noted that the argument 'depends upon the existence of a conflict between a rule, or rules, of *jus cogens*, and

---

[71] [2012] ICJ Rep 457, para. 99. Note that in Judge Abraham's view (which, it is submitted, is correct) this finding is, in the context of the decision, no more than an *obiter dictum*: see separate opinion of Judge Abraham [2012] ICJ Rep 477, para. 27.

[72] [2006] ICJ Rep 52, para. 125.

the rule of customary law which requires one State to accord immunity to another', and continued:

In the opinion of the Court, however, no such conflict exists. Assuming for this purpose that the rules [allegedly breached] ... are rules of *jus cogens*, there is no conflict between those rules and the rules on State immunity. The two sets of rules address different matters. The rules of State immunity are procedural in character and are confined to determining whether or not the courts of one State may exercise jurisdiction in respect of another State. They do not bear upon the question whether or not the conduct in respect of which the proceedings are brought was lawful or unlawful.[73]

What these two decisions suggest is that, in the Court's thinking, the only feature unique to a norm of *jus cogens* is that it is *jus cogens*, that it has the status to prevail inasmuch as it cannot be excluded by agreement. In other respects, it fits (with however much analytical difficulty) into the regular pattern of derivation of international legal norms from the generally recognized sources, and does not bypass them by virtue of its 'supernorm' status.

Another aspect of traditional thinking on customary law that needs to be considered in relation to rules that are claimed to be of *jus cogens* is this: the position of the State that has always and consistently objected to the application to itself of a new developing rule of customary law, the 'persistent objector'.[74] If the possibility of achieving and retaining this status exists in relation even to a rule which is or becomes one of *jus cogens*, there is some conceptual inconsistency, as well as some possible practical difficulty in application.[75] If, however, a rule of *jus cogens* and the status of persistent objector are incompatible, how does this come about? In his opinion in the *North Sea Continental Shelf* case, Judge Lachs discussed the formation of a customary rule through practice plus *opinio juris*, commenting on, and recognizing the validity of, the position of the 'persistent objector'; but he reserved the question of *jus cogens*.[76] His view appears to have been that if a rule of *jus cogens* develops, no one may claim to have been a persistent objector; this is consistent, but it raises the question: how does one distinguish a *jus cogens* rule *in*

---

[73] [2012] ICJ Rep 140, para. 93. For a critical view of the decision in this case, see C. Talmon, '*Jus cogens* after *Germany* v. *Italy*: Substantive and Procedural Rules Distinguished', 25 Leiden JIL (2012), 979.

[74] See Ch. III sect. 5 (a).

[75] This may be more than a *hypothèse d'école*: the position of the Islamic States in relation to some provisions of human rights texts would seem to be defensible on grounds, if no other, of their status as persistent objectors. See further Ch. VIII sect. 2(*c*).

[76] 'Nor can a general rule which is not of the nature of *jus cogens* prevent some States from adopting an attitude apart. They may have opposed the rule from its inception and may, unilaterally, or in agreement with others, decide upon different solutions of the problem involved' [1969] ICJ Rep 229.

statu nascendi from a normal rule? Must the *opinio* and practice be explicable only on the basis that it is seen as such from the start? The persistent objector does not block the emergence of a normal rule; but he is not bound by it. If the status of persistent objector is inimical to a budding *jus cogens* rule, does universality require that status to be excluded; or does the existence of a persistent objector so contradict the universality of the presumed desire of States for the rule that it prevents, not the emergence of the rule, but the emergence of the rule as *jus cogens*?

In face of these problems, or as a matter of principle, it has been suggested that norms of *jus cogens* require a separate source from those of general international law, and that such a source must therefore exist. As long ago as 1983, Monaco argued for the hierarchical equivalence of treaty-law and customary law, neither being capable of prevailing over the other, and deduced from this that norms of *jus cogens*, since they do *ex hypothesi* override treaty provisions, must derive from some source other than international custom.[77] Against this, Kolb has observed that the necessary hierarchy is not between sources, but between norms; that customary or conventional norms 'would be superior to ordinary rules flowing from the same sources exclusively by their character of peremptory norms rather than by their formal source'.[78] Another approach was to derive norms of *jus cogens* from an international consensus, which presumably would not be the same as, and thus would not be subject to the same requirements as, customary law.[79] The general popularity of, or at least lip-service paid to, the concept of *jus cogens* in modern times lends some verisimilitude to this thesis. However, there is the general problem of the source of the source: if consensus can now operate in this way, how does it relate to the closed category of Article 38 sources?[80] It has also been suggested that *jus cogens* norms may draw their special character from natural law; to paraphrase again the excellent argument of Kolb, natural law may found the content of the norm (as being one essentially just or humanitarian) but does not suffice to found its overriding nature. This is indeed confirmed by the historical development of the concept: genocide was just as repugnant before it became accepted that the norm forbidding it is one of *jus cogens*. Nevertheless, some scholars hold that norms of *jus cogens* may, and do, derive directly from ethical considerations.

---

[77] R. Monaco, 'Observations sur la hiérarchie des normes de droit international', in *Festschrift für Hermann Mosler* (Berlin: Springer, 1983), 106ff.

[78] 'The Formal Source of *Ius Cogens*', 76.

[79] N. V. Onuf and R. K. Birney, 'Peremptory Norms of International Law: Their Source, Their Function and Future', 4 Denver JIL and Policy (1974), 193ff.

[80] And, as Kolb, 'The Formal Source of *Ius Cogens*', 77, points out, if *jus cogens* can be created by consensus, why by consensus *only*, and not by custom or treaty? (n. 42).

Norms of *jus cogens* are essentially a feature of general customary law, since one of their distinguishing features is their universal application; and the impossibility of contracting out of them by agreement, that is by treaty. Is there, however, a sense in which a norm derived solely from a treaty source, and thus only applicable as such to the parties to that treaty, might have a *cogens* quality within that context? If the norm is also one of customary law, the question may appear meaningless; whether or not an agreement between two parties to the treaty to set aside such a norm would be a breach of the treaty, it would be unlawful as conflicting with the parallel customary norm.[81]

A multilateral treaty may, however, contain provisions that are regarded as essential components of the treaty system, and these are often signalled by a clause excluding the making of reservations to these provisions; or the possibility of making reservations at all to the treaty may be expressly excluded, as in the case of Article 309 of the United Nations Convention on the Law of the Sea. Does such a clause confer on the provisions contemplated a sort of *jus cogens* quality? In the *North Sea Continental Shelf* case the ICJ had occasion to consider a clause (Art. 12) in the Geneva Convention on the Continental Shelf excluding reservations to certain key articles of the Convention. The importance of this clause for the Court was that it signified that those Articles were regarded 'reflecting, or as crystallizing, received or at least emergent rules of customary international law'.[82] This deduction was based on the consideration that the 'faculty of making unilateral reservations' could not be admitted 'in the case of general or customary law rules and obligations which, by their very nature, must have equal force for all members of the international community, and cannot therefore be the subject of any right of unilateral exclusion exercisable at will by any one of them in its own favour'.[83] Yet this dictum must be read against the background of the limited effect of reservations to multilateral conventions established in the case of *Reservations to the Genocide*

---

[81] This does not render the question entirely academic, however; if the treaty contained a compromissory clause, for example giving the ICJ jurisdiction for disputes concerning the interpretation or application of the treaty, this would confer jurisdiction over a dispute as to whether the treaty had been infringed by the agreement, but not over a dispute as to whether the agreement was in breach of the customary rule. Cf. the cases of *Application of the Genocide Convention* brought by Bosnia and Herzegovina, and by Croatia, against the FRY, on the basis of Art. IX of the Genocide Convention.

[82] [1969] ICJ Rep 39, para. 63.

[83] [1969] ICJ Rep 38, para. 63. There is here a slight ambiguity, but it seems clear that the Court had in mind not all 'general or customary law rules and obligations' but only those that 'by their very nature, must have equal force for all members of the international community'; the mere generality of a rule does not necessarily imply that it cannot be departed from by agreement. The word order in the French text of the judgment, and the use of 'qui par nature ... ' rather than 'lesquels par nature ... ', makes it unambiguous in this sense.

Convention, whereby such reservations in any event operate only between the reserving State and such other States parties to the relevant convention as accept the reservation. The effect, or the intended effect, of such texts as Article 12 of the Geneva Convention must be that if a multilateral treaty bars reservations (or excludes them as regards certain articles), then a reservation that is nonetheless made is not to be regarded as valid even in relation to States that do not object to such reservation, and however many of such 'consenting' States there may be. To this extent, the articles excluded from the faculty of making reservations have something of a *cogens* nature. Furthermore, even in the absence of reservations, States parties to a convention containing a clause of this kind are presumably also barred from making agreements between themselves in contradiction with the *quasi-cogens* provisions—or rather, such agreements are to be treated as ineffective.

There is, however, an evident difference between the concept of *jus cogens* and the idea of rules which 'by their very nature must have equal force for all members of the international community'. As noted, the idea of *jus cogens* contains an ineradicable moral element: it excludes actions which no State *ought* to do, or ought to be permitted to do, even with the consent of any other State or States affected. The articles of the Geneva Continental Shelf Convention to which no reservation might be made were Article 1, defining the continental shelf, Article 2, defining the rights which could be exercised over the shelf, and Article 3, reserving the question of the legal status of the superjacent waters and airspace. No element of morality enters into the question:[84] but the essential characteristics of the legal regime being established had, for purely practical reasons, to be the same for all States involved.

It follows that a treaty, or the articles of a treaty, to which it is provided that no reservations may be made do not necessarily constitute matters of *jus cogens*. Contrariwise, a convention declaring matters of *jus cogens* need not necessarily specifically provide for the exclusion of reservations (the Genocide Convention, for example, does not do so). The question of the effect of reservations to treaty provisions that reflect or represent norms of *jus cogens* is the subject of Draft Conclusion 13 of the ILC's texts on the subject, whereby such a reservation 'does not affect the binding quality of that norm, which shall continue to apply as such', and 'cannot exclude or modify the legal effect of a treaty in a manner contrary to a peremptory norm of general international law (*jus cogens*)'.[85]

---

[84] See this chapter, n. 6.

[85] UN Doc A/CN4/714. See also paragraph 3.1.5.4. of the ILC Guide to Practice on Reservations to Treaties, ILC Report on its 63rd session, A/66/10, para. 75; and note the Joint Separate opinion of Judges Higgins, Kooijmans, Elaraby, Owada, and Simma in the case of *Armed Activities on the Territory of the Congo (New Application: 2002), DRC v. Rwanda* [2006] ICJ Rep 72, paras. 27–9.

It appears doubtful whether a treaty can be creative of rules of *jus cogens*: it may state such rules as already exist with that quality, or it may constitute one element of State practice, or one element of evidence of *opinio juris*, supporting the existence of a rule of *jus cogens* or contributing to bringing it into existence; but no more.

As noted, Article 309 of the UN Convention on the Law of the Sea excludes reservations altogether; but in addition, Article 293 provides that courts and tribunals having jurisdiction under Part XV, Section 2, of the Convention are to apply 'this Convention and other rules of international law not incompatible with this Convention'. Does this make the Convention to that extent, and for those courts and tribunals, *jus cogens*? In a case before such a tribunal, can the parties agree to apply some general rule *not* compatible with the Convention? Can States be restrained from conducting their bilateral relations on a basis that departs from the Convention?[86] In practice, provided the problem was foreseen by the parties, they could arrange to have their dispute decided by a tribunal *not* set up under Part XV of the Convention.

Of the sources named in Article 38 of the ICJ Statute, there remain, of course, the general principles of law. If appeal is made to this source in order to explain the generally admitted presence of *jus cogens* norms in present-day international law, what follows? Such an approach would entail recognizing that the general principles contemplated by Article 38 of the ICJ Statute go beyond the logical principles, grounded in the very philosophy of legal thinking, that were discussed in Chapter IV. To take an extreme example, while genocide is repugnant to virtually every thinking person at the present day, for reasons that may be based on a principle of respect for the human person and on the right to life, historic examples show that such principles were not always regarded as axiomatic to this degree. In any event that is not the real point. A system of international law that did *not* contain a prohibition of genocide would be perfectly thinkable and workable: indeed, it existed until comparatively recent times.[87] If such a prohibition has now been

---

[86] Wolfrum comments on this that such courts and tribunals are not free 'to apply international law in its totality, *at least theoretically*' ('Sources of International Law', in R. Wolfrum ed.), *Max Planck Encyclopedia of International Law* (Oxford: Oxford University Press, 2012), ix. 299–313 at 301, para. 8, emphasis added).

[87] There are numerous ancient historical examples of conquerors of a country endeavouring to eradicate the defeated possessors: e.g. the Mongols in China. Cf. also the separate opinion of Judge Cançado Trindade in the case of the *Obligation to Prosecute or Extradite* case, where he recognizes that the prohibition of torture 'is a definitive achievement of civilization, one that admits no regression' (para. 84). In much of the discussion in this opinion, as in quite a lot of areas where *jus cogens* is invoked, the term is used as though it meant 'very important'.

introduced, it is due to a development, a more humanitarian approach to international law; and this in itself suggests that it does not rest on a general principle *of law*, but has been chosen by the international community and introduced into the law. The appropriate process—source—for this operation is custom, not general principles.

A question of some relevance to that of the source of peremptory norms is this: it is the nature of those norms to over-ride other rules or obligations; but which other rule or which obligations? Essentially, peremptory norms mark the legal limits of the powers of agreement; may they also invalidate something that is not an agreement: a unilateral declaration, or a Security Council resolution for example?[88] For this, Article 53 and its customary-law *doppelgänger* would seem not necessarily to be adequate. The ILC has declared that '[a] unilateral declaration which is in conflict with a peremptory norm of international law is void', explaining that thus 'derives from the analogous rule contained in Article 53' VCLT: 'derives from' is disconcertingly imprecise. The position in regard to Security Council resolutions is more obscure, and to examine it further here would take us too far afield.[89]

2. Soft law

It seems to be accepted that, for better or for worse, on the international legal landscape, alongside 'hard' law, that is to say law of which the binding quality is generally recognized, there exists at least a conceptual category of 'soft law'; for most writers, that signifies that in 'soft law' that binding quality is somehow missing or attenuated.[90] It has been convincingly argued that in a rapidly changing and developing world order, soft law is a vital intermediate stage towards a more rigorously binding system, permitting experiment and

---

[88] Such effect is studied in detail by Cottesloe, *Legal Consequences of Peremptory Norms in International Law*, Chapters 4 and 5, but as explained (text and n.53), without enquiring into the source or sources of this possibility.

[89] The detailed examination in Cottesloe, n. 53 above, Chapter 4, is recommended. He draws attention to, inter alia, the observation of the ICTY Appeals Chamber in *Tadić* that 'neither the text nor the spirit of the Charter conceives of the Security Council as *legibus solutus* (unbound by law)': Decision on Defence Motion for Interlocutory Appeal on Jurisdiction, 465, para. 28.

[90] An exceptional use of the term is that of D. Kennedy, 'The Sources of International Law', University Journal of International Law and Policy (1987) 1, 21–2: 'In sources argument, one characteristically seeks to convince someone that a state which does not currently believe it to be in its interests to follow a given norm should do so anyway. Sources rhetoric provides two rhetorical or persuasive styles which we might call "hard" and "soft." A "hard" argument will seek to ground compliance in the "consent" of the state to be bound. A "soft" argument relies upon some extraconsensual notion of the good or the just.' This is of course a real and a useful distinction, but Kennedy's terminology is idiosyncratic and thus confusing; it will not be employed here.

rapid modification.[91] Unfortunately, however, there is great disagreement as to what exactly is covered by the term, whether what the term denotes has a real existence, or whether it ought to be permitted to have a real existence.[92]

When introducing a debate on 'soft law' in the columns of the *Leiden Journal of International Law* in 2012, the editors noted that the concept had become 'the object of severe criticism, resulting in a chasm in the international legal scholarship'.

On the one hand, there are the advocates of the notion for whom the binary nature of law is incapable of explaining the complexity of the international exercise of public authority in a pluralized world or who see soft law as an instrument of [programming of] the development of hard law. These apostles of the notion of soft law are opposed by those who see the notion as redundant because it turns into either hard law or not law at all, it is self-serving for the profession, or it is a weakening of the general authority of law.[93]

It is thus a hazardous enterprise to venture on to this battlefield, but one corner of the terrain does require our attention: assuming that there is such a thing as soft law, does it come into existence through one or other of the recognized sources, as enumerated in Article 38, paragraph 1, of the ICJ Statute; or must it be admitted that, at least so far as such law does exist, and is a form of international law, it derives from a separate and novel source; and if so what is the nature of that source?

We may leave aside one use of the term: it is sometimes employed to refer to potential law, that is to say, rules or norms that are not recognized as such in international relations, but that enjoy sufficient support, and sufficient reflection

---

[91] See e.g. M. E. O'Connell, 'The Role of Soft law in a Global Order', in D. Shelton (ed.), *Commitment and Compliance: The Role of Non-Binding Norms in the International Legal System* (Oxford: Oxford University Press, 2000), 100. Another essay in this collection suggests that 'issues of social justice are deemed by States as inherently soft, or perhaps too intrusive into domestic jurisdiction to be the subject of binding obligation': C. Chinkin, 'Normative Development in the International Legal System', in Shelton, *Commitment and Compliance*, 21 at 28.

[92] It has even been suggested that the whole concept has been invented by scholars to provide themselves with extra raw material to work with, and therefore reduce the number of scholars focusing on the same object of study': J. d'Aspremont, 'Softness in International Law: A Self-Serving quest for New Legal Materials', 5 EJIL (2008), 1090. Another view is that the idea is traceable to the efforts of Third World Countries to use their numerical majority in the UN General Assembly to effect changes in the law through instruments that do not in themselves have binding effects (resolutions, declarations etc.) but still constitute law—soft law, but law nonetheless: see A. Bianchi, *International Law Theories* (OUP, 2016), Ch. 10, 214.

[93] J. d'Aspremont and T. Aalberts, 'Which Future for the Scholarly Concept of Soft Law? Editors' Introductory Remarks', Symposium on Soft Law, 25 Leiden JIL (2012), 309. The principal authors here cited as hostile to soft law are J. Klabbers ('The Redundancy of Soft Law', 65 Netherlands JIL (1996), 173), and J. d'Aspremont ('Softness in International Law: A Self-serving Quest for New Legal Materials', 19 EJIL (2008), 10075).

in practice, for it to be possible that they will become recognized binding rules or norms in the course of time—perhaps quite a short time.[94] This category is more generally classified as that of *lex ferenda*, but the latter term may carry an implication that the rule *ought* for some reason to be adopted,[95] which is not necessarily the case for all potential norms of the kind here considered. In this case the question of a source does not arise, since it is not asserted that these norms have yet entered international law. At all events, *lex ferenda* is not yet law, and the source by which it may become so may evidently be by treaty or convention, or through custom; thus far there is no controversy.

The existence and precise meaning of soft law, in its strict sense, is thus controversial, but for present purposes we may take it that it does exist, with the attributes generally allotted to it, and must derive from somewhere, that is it must have a source. It may itself constitute a *material* source, in the sense that a non-binding instrument (e.g. a General Assembly declaration) may prescribe something that thereafter becomes a rule of customary law through the usual processes.[96] In this sense, however, as just observed, it is virtually synonymous with *lex ferenda*; and needs no more discussion here. A source of soft law could either be one of the traditionally recognized sources, but operating in a different gear, so to speak; or it could be contended that soft law is created in a radically different way, that is that it has its own source or system of sources; or even that soft law might 'constitute a source in its own right in addition to the traditional sources of international law'.[97]

A suggested working definition of 'soft law', purely for the purposes of this chapter, would be that it is a system of international commitments or

---

[94] See e.g. Besson, 'Theorizing the Sources of International Law', 170. This seems to be also what is meant by Goldmann, when itemizing the possible functions of soft law, who suggests that it 'may evidence the formation of customary law': see n. 108. A specialized field in which reference is frequently made to norms or rules to be regarded as 'soft law', signifiying that this is, or may be, an intermediate stage in their passage to true law, is that of outer space: see for example F. G. von der Dunk, 'Customary International Law and Outer Space', in Lepard (ed.), *Reexamining Customary International Law* (CUP, 2017) 346, and references cited.

[95] The Latin grammatical form of the gerundive carries this meaning, as in the famous obsession of Cato the Elder (234–149 BC) with the need to destroy Rome's great rival, Carthage: *delenda est Carthago*.

[96] In this sense A. Boyle and C. Chinkin, *The Making of International Law* (Oxford: Oxford University Press, 2007), 212.

[97] Proposition advanced by Daniel Thürer in *Max Planck Encyclopedia*, ix. 273, para. 18, and refuted, ix. 274, para. 24, apparently primarily on the ground that, while codification of international law is a slow and laborious process, international organizations 'provide a framework for harmonising legal opinions, and ... can work out legal projects in a relatively short time'. This seems to assume that all soft law is law *in statu nascendi*, that it is a preliminary stage in the development of 'real' law; but a lot of soft law works well as it is, and would not benefit from being codified or made rigid. Thürer, by observing that soft law 'can play a major role in the evolution' of international law, seems to recognize that is not always its function (ix. 276, para. 32).

obligations that are not regarded by those concerned as binding in the sense that can be enforced in the same way as those imposed by international law proper,[98] but yet are considered as something more than mere political gestures, so that there is an expectation of compliance even if there is no legal duty.[99] It should be emphasized that it is purely for convenience that the approach here has to take sides in the controversy mentioned, viewing soft law as incorporated into the international legal system, not as something apart from it.[100] Writing in 1996, Klabbers suggested that it was 'not at all obvious that States can conclude agreements yet at the same time deny that such agreements would amount to hard law'; that a 'treaty' is a legal concept with an unchangeable nature, and that 'whether or not something is a treaty (i.e. hard law) must be established following objective standards, and cannot solely depend on the intention of the author of the document'.[101] Whether or not such a systematically nominalist view was correct at the time, it may be that subsequent practice is only consistent with a more generous interpretation of the treaty-making powers of States.

Two kinds, or categories, of soft law can be distinguished,[102] to which d'Aspremont, following Abi-Saab,[103] gives the useful titles of a soft *negotium* or a soft *instrumentum*.[104] On the one hand, the means resorted to, the *instrumentum*, for the purpose of creating a commitment may be such that a fully binding obligation could have been established by those means (e.g. by a formal treaty), but those concerned have made it clear, probably by the language used, that something less, a mere soft-law commitment (the *negotium*), was intended.[105] This is perhaps the commonest kind of soft law, and the easiest to appreciate; it has been recognized (though not specifically

---

[98] As to which, note the working definition given at the beginning of Ch. I.

[99] Condorelli suggests that there is the additional element that to act in accordance with a soft-law precept is necessarily not an illicit act: see Condorelli, *La Pratique et le droit international*, Colloque de Genéve (Paris: Pedone, 2004), 292. But is this so?—presumably always subject to considerations of *jus cogens*.

[100] *Contra* e.g. P. F. Diehl and C. Ku, *The Dynamics of International Law* (Cambridge: Cambridge University Press, 2010), 52; J. L. Charney, 'Compliance with International Soft Law', in D. Shelton (ed.), *Commitment and Compliance: The Role of Non-Binding Norms in the International Legal System* (Oxford: Oxford University Press, 2000), 115.

[101] J. Klabbers, 'The Redundancy of Soft Law', 65 Nordic JIL (1996), 167 at 172.

[102] In this sense e.g. Condorelli, in *La Pratique et le droit international*, 291, though he does not use the expression 'soft law' to describe them.

[103] G. Abi-Saab, 'Éloge du "droit assourdi": Quelques reflexions sur le role du *soft law* en droit international', in *Nouveaux itinéraires en droit: Mélanges en hommage à François Rigaux* (Brussels: Bruylant, 1993), 61–2.

[104] J. d'Aspremont, 'Softness in International Law: A Self-Serving Quest for New Legal Materials', 19 EJIL (2008), 1081ff.

[105] The ILA Committee on the Formation of Customary Law referred in passing to '"soft law" provisions in a treaty', apparently with this possibility in mind: Report of the Committee, 53 n. 137.

as 'soft law'), in a number of ICJ decisions.[106] To expand on the definition of soft law already offered, an enumeration from an authoritative writer may be cited: examples of soft law include the resolutions of international organizations, programmes of action, the texts of treaties which are not yet in force or are not binding for a particular actor, interpretative declarations to international conventions, non-binding agreements and codes of conduct, recommendations, and reports adopted by international agencies or within international conferences as well as similar instruments and arrangements used in international relations to express commitments which are more than just policy statements but less than law in its strict sense.[107]

To a large extent, these may be referred back ultimately to a treaty or convention as a source, even if this involves a lengthy line of descent. A treaty may create an organization, and powers may be conferred on a specified organ to take decisions binding on the parties to the treaty; this power is lawfully delegated to a sub-organ, or even to a sub-sub-organ, and so on; so far there exists 'hard law' of a convention-based nature. But the sub-organ may exceed its specific powers, and its action may yet be tolerated (not accepted: that would create conventional 'hard' law), but tolerated as soft law. Or, applying the distinction already made, the terms in which the decision is taken may be such that it does not purport to give more than guidance or non-binding direction, so that for that reason what is produced is soft law. As a recent commentator observes,

It is a well-known fact that international organizations, formal ones like the United Nations as much as informal ones like the G8, more and more frequently adopt rules which their drafters do not consider to be 'legally binding', although they otherwise have all the textual characteristics of binding international treaties or binding resolutions of international organizations.[108]

It seems, at first sight, that even a judicial decision may itself, according to its terms, amount to law of a certain degree of softness. In the *Gabčíkovo/*

---

[106] e.g. the *Oil Platforms* case, where Iran relied on the compromissory clause (Art. XXI) of a 1955 Treaty with the USA, to the effect that '[t]here shall be firm and enduring peace and sincere friendship between the United States ... and Iran' (cited at [1996-II] ICJ Rep 812, para. 24.) The Court held that this 'must be regarded as fixing an objective, in the light of which the other Treaty provisions are to be interpreted and applied', and not as a provision laying down a binding obligation that would be breached as soon as some action inimical to peace and friendship were committed. In itself, the Article was thus a form of soft law. The Court did, however, find that it could take account of Art. I when construing other provisions of the Treaty: see [1996-II] ICJ Rep 820, para. 52; whether this 'hardens' Art. I is perhaps merely a question of terminology.

[107] Thürer, 'Soft Law', *Max Planck Encyclopedia*, ix. 270, para. 2.

[108] M. Goldman, 'We Need to Cut Off the Head of the King: Past, Present and Future Approaches to International Soft Law', Symposium on Soft Law, 25 Leiden JIL (2012), 335.

Nagymaros case, the Court directed the parties to pursue negotiations, to which they had committed themselves by the Special Agreement seizing the Court, and indicated that they were 'under a legal obligation ... to consider, within the context of the 1977 Treaty, in what way the multiple objectives of the Treaty can best be served, keeping in mind that all of them should be fulfilled'.[109] It is difficult to see how it could be determined whether a party had failed to comply with this directive, save in the case of a complete refusal to take account of one of those objectives (and there would not necessarily be agreement as to what they were).[110] The softness was, however, in the treaty-provision interpreted by the judgment rather than in the judgment itself.

On the other hand, a commitment may be entered into or created that according to its terms may be read as definite and definitive, but of which the manner of creation was such that it could not, or was clearly chosen as not intended to, produce a binding result. This category would include a very important class of soft law, regarded by some as the archetypal forms: legislative action by bodies lacking the authority, under international 'hard' law to impose binding obligations. These categories may of course overlap. A resolution of an international body that does not have constitutional (i.e. treaty-based) power to bind may be expressed in the most specific and compulsory terms, but it remains—as such—merely soft law. (It may of course express a principle or rule of customary law which *is* binding, but the two bases of normativity need to be kept separate.) In contrast to soft law of the category already discussed, the 'softness' may in these cases not have been intentional. If the choice is made to use non-binding language in a text which could of its nature embody a binding commitment, that is because those responsible for the text did not intend it to be binding—they knowingly created soft law. In the case, however, of a General Assembly resolution, for example, it may have been the ardent wish of the drafters and those voting in favour that it should create hard law, that it should establish a binding obligation, but the

---

[109] [1997] ICJ Rep 77, para. 139.

[110] It has also been suggested that the first decision of the International Court in the *Qatar/Bahrain* case is significant in this connection as showing that a commitment of which the 'exact modalities' were left 'rather indeterminate'; that it did not therefore have to be treated as 'soft law', but that it showed 'the way in which law, without losing its binding character, is able to do justice to politics: see J. Klabbers, 'The Redundancy of Soft Law', 65 Nordic JIL (1996), 167 at 131. In that case, however, the view advanced by Bahrain as to the non-binding quality of the Doha Minutes was a perfectly possible scenario, one that could equally well have been the parties' intention, even though the Court found otherwise. The Court's ruling that '[h]aving signed such a text, the Foreign Minister of Bahrain is not in a position subsequently to say that he intended to subscribe to a "statement recording a political understanding" and not to an international agreement' ([1994] ICJ Rep 122, para. 27) simply teaches that if an instrument is intended to create soft law only, the intention to do so must be made clear.

instrumentum is not capable of bearing that burden, and the result, in principle is soft law at most. Hence the ingenuity devoted to finding legal bases for a much 'harder' status for texts of this kind.

In these cases, the genealogy of the 'soft law' commitments is clearly traceable to a recognized source: a treaty.[111] If or in so far as there may be decisions of this kind of which the authority cannot be so traced back to a treaty source, or if there is soft law that is otherwise not referable to a treaty basis, then a more difficult question arises. This is whether, assuming the applicability of the classic list of sources, soft law may arise otherwise than through 'treaties and conventions'. That it should arise through the application of 'general principles of law' seems excluded by its nature; can a general principle be soft in its operation?[112] The problem is therefore essentially whether soft law may come into existence through 'international custom, as evidence of a general practice accepted as [soft] law'. In one sense, there is a clearly established example: what the International Court, in the *North Sea Continental Shelf* cases, referred to as 'many international acts, e.g., in the field of ceremonial and protocol, which are performed almost invariably, but which are motivated only by considerations of courtesy, convenience or tradition, and not by any sense of legal duty'.[113] This is not normally treated as soft law, but it is submitted that it falls conveniently within the definition. It has also been suggested that 'such unwritten principles as comity and good faith' may be included in the category of soft law: and the same writer points out that failure to observe comity 'may lead to acts of retorsion'.[114] This intriguing suggestion amounts to arguing that a failure to observe a soft-law obligation may lead to a soft-law retaliation, thus showing that there is something of 'law' about the whole exchange.

It is enlightening in this context to take note of a distinction well known to continental lawyers, but comparatively unnoticed by Anglo-American lawyers, or indeed English-speaking lawyers generally. This is the distinction between the *legal act* (*acte juridique*) and the *legal fact* (*fait juridique*). These have in common that each is an act producing legal consequences, but the difference

---

[111] In the case of the *Gabčíkovo/Nagymaros* decision, while the terms of that decision were 'soft' the ultimate source of the commitment, and thus of the softness, was the Special Agreement, a treaty.

[112] There seems to be some suggestion that they can operate to produce soft law in the field of international investment law: see S. W. Schill, 'General Principles of Law and International Investment Law', in T. Gazzini and E. de Brabandere (eds.), *International Investment Law: The Sources of Rights and Obligations* (The Hague: Nijhoff, 2012).

[113] [1969] ICJ Rep 44, para. 72. This example of a soft *negotium* has already been mentioned in Ch. I: see text and n.22.

[114] C. Chinkin, 'Normative Developments in the International Legal System' in Shelton (ed.), *Commitment and Compliance*, 25.

is that in the case of the *acte juridique* these consequences are the direct result of the will of the actor, whereas in the case of the *fait juridique* they result from the operation of the law, which is merely set in motion, triggered, by the deliberate act of the actor.[115] The importance of the distinction in this context relates, as explained by d'Aspremont, to the question whether soft law can truly be said to be law, but it may also be read as excluding the creation of soft law through customary processes. d'Aspremont points out that

> [I]t can solidly be argued from a positivist standpoint that the claim of the softness of international law does not pertain to those behaviours which create legal effects irrespective of the will of the State (*fait juridique*). There is no such thing as a *soft international legal fact*. In a positivist logic ... softness can be envisaged only in connection with legal acts in the strict sense, as it is necessarily the outcome of the intention of the subjects, not the result of a pre-existing rule of the international legal system.[116]

In other words, the duties that are imposed on States by customary international law simply as a result of the State taking a step to which international law attaches automatic consequences (whether or not these are intended by the State), are always matters of 'hard' law.[117] The conclusion may seem surprising, but is logical: soft law obligations require the consent of both sides, not merely to the content of the obligation, but also to its 'soft' character, and a rule of law imposing an automatic obligation must assume the will of the beneficiary of the rule that it have a binding character.

The opposite view is however taken by Lepard who sees customary law as comprising not merely binding norms but also 'persuasive norms', on the basis that 'states themselves believe that there can be legally authoritative norms that are persuasive rather than binding', and he argues that norms of this kind 'can play a uniquely beneficial role in solving certain types of problem'.[118]

---

[115] For a lucid explanation in English of the distinction, d'Aspremont, 'Softness in International Law', 1078–80.

[116] d'Aspremont, 'Softness in International Law', 1080. Note that the author is here explaining a view that is not his own, and which he proceeds, further on in his paper, to subject to critical examination.

[117] A similar view is taken by Jonathan Charney, 'in theory at least': '[A] norm is either international law or it is not. If a "soft" norm meets the requirements of the doctrine of sources of international law, it is "hard law". If it does not, it is not law; the choice is binary.' However, '[n]on-binding [international] agreements are not within the realm of international law and might be classified as "soft" norms': 'Compliance with International Soft Law', in Shelton (ed.), *Commitment and Compliance*, 115.

[118] B. D. Lepard, *Customary International Law: A New Theory with Practical Applications* (Cambridge: Cambridge University Press, 2010), 372. Similarly, in his essay 'Towards a New Theory of Customary International Human Rights Law', he contemplates legal effect for a view by States that a prospective customary rule might impose no more than a 'persuasive' obligation: in B. D. Lepard (ed.) *Reexamining Customary International Law*, (Cambridge University Press, 2017), 233 at 263,

An example that he offers is the right, or freedom, to change one's religion or belief, on the basis that there is 'compelling evidence' that 'states generally believe that the norms in the [1981] Declaration [on religious discrimination], like those in the Universal Declaration before it, should have at least persuasive legal authority and that states must give the freedoms it enshrines great weight in their decision making'.[119] This, however, is a right conferred on individuals, not on a State as a subject of international law; and what is less clear, as in relation to much soft law, is the consequence of failure to comply with a persuasive norm of this kind.[120]

To sum up, on the basis that soft law does exist and is correctly classified as a form of 'law', its manifestations seem to be fully explicable on the basis of the operation of traditionally recognized sources—custom and treaty—and not to require any new or additional source to be postulated.

---

[119] Lepard, *Customary International Law*, 361.

[120] It would also usually be difficult to establish that a State had failed 'to give great weight' to such considerations, since by definition the fact that they had not, ultimately, accorded religious freedom would not automatically constitute an infringement of the norm. This may be a paradigm for many, if not most, soft law obligations.

VIII

Subsystems of International Law

1. 'Self-contained regimes' and their limits

As a starting-point for discussion of sources, it has been assumed (Ch. I) that international law is in this respect a homogenous system, and specialized fields of international law draw upon the same sources for their content.[1] This is certainly so for such major areas as the law of the sea and air law, each of which is dominated by international conventions (UNCLOS, and the Chicago Convention and its two annexes), supplemented by international custom. It is however now convenient to consider the possibility that one or more of the other specialized fields constitute 'self-contained regimes'.

This term forms part of the semantic armoury of the international lawyer, as referring to a subsystem within the system of general international law, with distinguishing characteristics; but its precise definition is not easy to pin down, and one authority has gone so far as to say that 'no international law sub-system qualifies for a self-contained regime, at least at present'.[2] In the case of the *United States Diplomatic and Consular Staff in Tehran*, the International Court referred to 'the rules of diplomatic law' as a 'self-contained regime';[3] what it apparently meant by this was that a receiving State is entitled to deal with breaches of diplomatic law by a sending State by the means foreseen by diplomatic law itself for that purpose, up to and including breaking off relations, *and by those means only*. An earlier paragraph of the decision indicates that the illegalities attributed to US staff could not be invoked by Iran as

---

[1] Ch. I sect. 3; even if in some of these fields, as compared with general law, 'on ne respire pas tout à fait le même air ici et là': P. Weil, 'Le Droit international économique', in *Aspects de droit international économique: Élaboration, contrôle, sanction*, Colloque SFDI, Orléans (Paris: Pedone, 1972), 3. A fundamentally different approach is that of legal pluralism, the essence of which is perhaps that two or more distinct legal regimes may exist and operate within one society; whether in such case there are two sets of sources is a point that does not seem to have attracted attention. On the concept generally, see Bianchi, *International Law Theories* (OUP, 2016), Chapter 11.

[2] E. Klein, 'Self-Contained Regime', in R. Wolfrum (ed.), *Max Planck Encyclopedia of Public International Law* (Oxford: Oxford University Press, 2012), ix. 97.

[3] [1980] ICJ Rep 40, para. 86.

defence to the claim by the US for seizure of its Embassy, because 'diplomatic law itself provides the necessary means of defence against, and sanction for, illicit activities by members of diplomatic or consular missions'.[4] The decision has been severely criticized, as has the whole concept: the ILC study group on the fragmentation of international law recognized the existence of special regimes, but emphasized that '[t]he application of the special law does not normally extinguish the relevant general law',[5] so that it appears that there is in any event no such thing as a self-contained regime that is fully detached from general international law.[6]

There are, however, a number of subsystems of international law that are sometimes claimed to be, at least in some sense, self-contained regimes.[7] The key aspect seems to have been whether special remedies for non-compliance with the rules of the sub-system are provided for within the system, especially if they are asserted to be exclusive of the remedies provided by general international law. For our purpose the sole question is, however: may the law applicable within the framework of the regime in question be derived from some source peculiar to that regime, not being one of those recognized in Article 38 of the ICJ Statute?[8] With this purpose, some brief examination is indicated of human rights law, humanitarian law, international criminal law, and international trade law, with special reference to the practice of the settlement systems of the World Trade Organization (WTO) and of the International Centre for the Settlement of Investment Disputes (ICSID).

These specialized subsystems will here be approached on the basis announced at the outset,[9] namely that, unless the contrary conclusion is unavoidable, it

---

[4] [1980] ICJ Rep 38, para. 81. *Quaere* whether this argument would be valid in response to a claim by Iran for international responsibility of the US for the alleged illicit activities.

[5] *Conclusions of the Work of the Study Group on the Fragmentation of International Law: Difficulties Arising from the Diversification and Expansion of International Law* (2006), para. (9): see UN doc. A/61/10. A more recent multi-author study concludes, broadly, that the current tendency is, if anything, rather in the direction of convergence than in that of fragmentation: see M. Andernas and E. Bjorge (eds.), *A Farewell to Fragmentation: Reassertion and Convergence in International Law*, (Cambridge: Cambridge University Press, 2015), particularly Part 2, on Sources of Law.

[6] The Study Group reported that 'To this extent, the notion of a "self-contained regime" is simply misleading': A/CN.4/L.682, 82, para. (5).

[7] Not dealt with here are unconventional uses of the term whereby soft law (see Ch. VI) might be deemed in itself a self-contained regime (H. Hillgenberg, 'A Fresh Look at Soft Law', 10 EJIL (1999), 499), or individual categories of 'instruments for the exercise of international public authority' as proposed by Goldmann (this volume, Ch. VIII): 'The Exercise of International Public Authority' 9 German LJ (2008), 1877.

[8] The ICJ has recently declined to conclude from rulings in arbitral awards in a specialized field (international investment law) that a principle parallel to that applied there exists in 'general international law', which might appear to suggest that those rulings were based on a non-general source; but in fact they were based on the application of treaty-clauses: see *Obligation to Negotiate Access to the Pacific Ocean (Bolivia v. Chile)*, 1 October 2018, para. 162.

[9] Ch. I sect. 4.

is to be presumed that, as they are branches of international law, their provisions and prescriptions derive from the same sources as any other branch.[10] As regards custom as a source, the International Law Commission, while not commenting directly on the point, found no need, in its recent Report on the identification of customary law, to single out any particular field of international law as one in which the normal rules and processes did not, or not fully, apply.[11] The need not to lose sight of international law as an integrated whole may be illustrated by an example indicated in a report of the special rapporteur appointed by the UN Human Rights Council to look into the illicit movement and dumping of dangerous products and wastes. He found States reluctant to 'engage in constructive dialogue', taking the view that the matter was one for environmental rather than human rights institutions.[12] Is this short-sighted on the States' part; or was the decision of the UNHR, to overlap with another legal 'area', an unwise one?

As regards human rights law and humanitarian law, these will also be treated as two separate disciplines: for much of the period of their development, they were clearly distinct, humanitarian law being in essence an aspect of the law of war, and human rights law operating in an internal political, generally peaceful environment. Something of a merger has subsequently taken place;[13] but for the study of sources it will still be convenient to treat them separately.

2. Human rights law

In view of the greatly increased role in international legal relations played, over the last sixty years, by consideration of human rights, it has been suggested that for many observers, human rights law is no longer seen as a separate branch that is nonetheless governed in principle by general international law; rather it is a philosophy of 'human rightism' that has increasingly taken over general international law. What may be observed is a specific legal technique which seeks to accommodate human rights norms, or considerations of the protection of individuals more broadly, either expressly through the inclusion in legal texts of positive rules or more subtly through the reinterpretation or

---

[10] As regards human rights law, note the criticism of I. Brownlie, *Principles of Public International Law*, 7th edn. (Oxford: Oxford University Press, 2008), 554 of the idea of 'International Human Rights Law' as 'a separate body of norms'.

[11] See UN document A/73/10.

[12] See the report in UN Doc. A/HRC/9/22, 13 August 2008, quoted in A. Boyle, 'Human Rights and the Environment: Where Next?', 21 EJIL (2012), 613 at 619.

[13] For a lucid explanation of the process, see R. Kolb, 'Human Rights and Humanitarian Law', in Wolfrum (ed.), *Max Planck Encyclopedia*, iv. 1043–5, paras. 16–25.

reorientation of existing international law norms to accord with overarching human rights protection imperatives.[14]

In consequence, the same writer argues, it is 'increasingly possible to speak of general international law as "sources" of human rights obligations'.[15] However, on examination, this contention reveals itself as an interpretation of the way in which human rights considerations interlock with other, more general, rules of international law; it is not suggested that any 'source', additional to those of Article 38 of the ICJ Statute, operates in this field.

2(a) Human rights law under treaty and as custom

Much of human rights law is essentially treaty-law in origin, and to that extent its binding character on States depends in principle on acceptance by the relevant State of the appropriate treaty. From an academic standpoint, it might have been expected that the principles of treaty law—essentially the basic principle that treaties are binding on the parties to them, and not binding on non-parties—would apply in exactly the same way in the field of human rights as they do in other areas of law. The acceptance and implementation by States, and even the drafting, of such treaties tends, however, to be inspired by a certain grudging approach attributable to the remarkable interference thus made in the relations between a State and its own nationals, formerly immune from scrutiny.[16] Tribunals and international supervisory bodies, on the other hand, show an opposite interventionist trend;[17] the two phenomena suggest at the least a certain idiosyncrasy of general treaty-law in this field.

In the field of treaties, first and foremost are of course Articles 55 and 56 of the United Nations Charter; secondly there are multilateral conventions such as the Genocide Convention. There are also, of course, numerous and extensive declarations and resolutions, the most important being the Universal Declaration of Human Rights; these are not treaties, and the nature of their authority will be considered further.[18] One line of approach is, of course, to treat them as codifications or embodiments of customary law, which raises the question whether human rights law, which is concerned with the relations

[14] A. N. Pronto, '"Human-Rightism" and the Development of General International Law', in T. Skouteris et al. (eds.), *The Protection of the Individual in International Law: Essays in Honour of John Dugard*, LJIL Special Issue (Cambridge: Cambridge University Press, 2007), 27.

[15] Pronto, in Skouteris et al. (eds.), *The Protection of the Individual*, 31.

[16] In this sense, Simma and Alston, 'The Sources of Human Rights Law: Custom, *Jus Cogens* and General Principles', 12 Australian YIL (1988–9), 82, 83–4.

[17] See e.g. the decisions in the *Loizidou* and *Bellilos* cases discussed at Ch. II, text and n. 38, 39.

[18] This chapter, text and n. 31.

between States and non-State actors (individuals and groups), can grow out of custom, and if so in what way.

This is not entirely a straightforward matter. At first sight, there is a problem with basing international human rights law on custom. Some forty years ago, the present writer could confidently assert that 'the relationship of a State with its own subjects ... has been generally immune from the impact of developing customary law', the reason being that

Custom derives from the *de facto* adjustment of conflicting claims and interests of the subjects of international law, and it has always been—and probably still is—one of the most fundamental tenets of international law that individuals and private corporations are not subjects of international law.[19]

This is no longer the case; the ICJ has stated unambiguously that 'the prohibition of torture' (including the torture by a State of one of its own nationals) is not only 'a part of customary international law', but has become a peremptory norm (*jus cogens*).'[20] Indeed some scholars would even say that the contrary view could with difficulty be regarded as tenable since the adoption of the United Nations Charter;[21] but some teasing intellectual problems remain. First and foremost, how did the change come about? The Charter was broad in its expression, and could not of itself transform the requirements for the creation of a rule of customary law. So long as individuals remained outside the category of subjects of international law for purposes of custom-creating practice, no treatment of an individual by his national State could constitute even the beginning of such practice. Similarly, even if the State treated its own national in a way that corresponded to what human rights doctrine would demand, it did so—at the time we are speaking of—because it freely chose to do so (or in the conviction that it could freely choose), and not out of a sense of obligation equivalent to *opinio juris*.[22]

---

[19] H. Thirlway, *International Customary Law and Codification* (Leiden: Sijthoff, 1972), 7. Similarly, it was argued that even consistent practice by States in the treatment of their own nationals was, as practice, 'of no value in the creation of custom, because no obligation of which international law can take cognizance can come into existence between a State and persons who are not subjects of international law' (p. 78).

[20] *Questions Relating to the Obligation to Extradite or Prosecute* [2012] ICJ Rep 457, para. 99.

[21] Though as authoritative a specialist as Buergenthal does not accept the idea that 'as soon as the UN Charter had entered into force, all human rights issues were no longer matters essentially within the domestic jurisdiction of States': 'Human Rights', in Wolfrum (ed.), *Max Planck Encyclopedia*, iv. 1021 at 1023, para. 8.

[22] This is possibly the reason why, as late as 2003, I. Brownlie could state that 'The literature of human rights tends to neglect the role, or potential role, of customary law'I. Brownlie, *Principles of Public International Law*, 6th edn. (Oxford: Oxford University Press) 538. This passage was not reproduced in the subsequent (2008) edition.

The problem of developing the customary law of human rights was very well explained by Meron as long ago as 1989:

States parties to human rights instruments and supporters of declarations and resolutions promulgating human rights naturally seek to promote the universality of human rights by attempting to assure concordant behaviour by non-parties to the instruments concerned and by states which have not supported the adoption of the declarations and resolutions. But this approach generates tension between important human rights values advocated by states parties to human rights instruments and the sovereignty of non-parties. The credibility of international human rights therefore requires that attempts to extend their universality utilize irreproachable legal methods.[23]

He might have added that the nature of the question is such that to express a sceptical view as to the universal *legal* validity of human rights can be portrayed as an unfeeling opposition to the human rights themselves; many have come to be considered as having a sacred quality.

Even if the treatment by a State of its nationals is no longer confined to the 'reserved domain', the 'inter-State' element of custom creation remains a practical if not a legal obstacle. The essence of custom, in the traditional view, is that its provisions have been hammered out in the resolution of conflicts of interests, or disputes, between States in their day-to-day relations. A comment in an important paper by Simma and Alston, already noted, is here in point:

[A]n element of interaction—in a broad sense—is intrinsic to, and essential to, the kind of State practice leading to the formation of customary international law ... [T]he processes of customary international law can only be triggered, and continue working, in situations in which States interact, where they apportion or delimit in some tangible way. But, at least in most cases, this is not what happens when a consensus about substantive human rights obligations, to be performed domestically, grows into international law.[24]

Similarly, attention has been drawn to 'the striking differences between the settings in which customary law traditionally arose and the issues on which it spoke, on the one hand, and the contemporary settings in which advocates of customary international law'—particularly, one might add, in the human rights field—'seek to employ customary norms, on the other'.[25] In respect of the issues historically settled by custom, worked out by interactions among

---

[23] T. Meron, *Humanitarian Norms as Customary Law* (Oxford: Clarendon, 1989), 81.

[24] B. Simma and P. Alston, 'The Sources of Human Rights Law: Custom, *Jus Cogens* and General Principles', 12 Australian YIL (1988–9), 82 at 99; see also Ch. III, n. 48.

[25] E. Kadens and E. Young, 'How Customary is Customary International Law?', 54 William & Mary LR 885–920 (2013), at 914.

the participants, 'in most cases, it was more important that the relevant principles be settled than that they be settled *right*'.[26] This does not suggest itself as a suitable paradigm in the human rights field.

One possible line of argument is that in the field of human rights, custom is created by a process different from that generally applicable. Thus in 1991 Schachter based human rights law on such elements as provisions in national laws, UN and other international resolutions, and some national court decisions, and also invoked the *Barcelona Traction* ruling on obligations *erga omnes*. He continued, however: 'None of the foregoing items of "evidence" of custom conform to the traditional criteria'.[27] He also accepted, however, that State practice in international fora could, on a case-by-case basis, supply 'practice' and *opinio juris*.[28] In order to show that international human rights law rests on a customary foundation, it appears to be necessary to renounce the requirement of practice in the form of State-to-State contact, involving the resolution of a clash of contentions, and be contented with, on the one hand, announcements on the international stage, and on the other such internal elements as domestic legislation and court decisions.[29]

Another approach has been to see the ultimate authority for human rights law in Articles 55 and 56 of the United Nations Charter, a view ardently put forward by Sohn. The Universal Declaration of Human Rights constitutes, according to this view, an authoritative interpretation of those provisions, so as to make them universally applicable, or at least applicable to all parties to the Charter. On this basis, '[t]he Declaration, as an authoritative listing of human rights, has become a basic component of customary law, binding on all States, not only on members of the United Nations.'[30] This is certainly a reasonable intellectual basis for almost universal application on the basis of *treaty-law*; but it does not seem to follow that because a norm derives its authority from the Charter, which is an instrument of quasi-universal

---

[26] Kadens and Young, 'How Customary is Customary International Law?' 917. To avoid natural law creeping in, it might be better to say '... than that they be settled in the most ideal way'.

[27] O. Schachter, *International Law in Theory and Practice* (Dordrecht: Martinus Nijhoff, 1991), 137.

[28] Schachter, *International Law*, 138.

[29] The ILA Committee on the Formation of Customary (General) International Law, after drawing attention to the role of international resolutions etc., particularly in the field of human rights, concluded, 'This is not to say that the fundamentals of customary law creation have been entirely overturned: but it is desirable to be aware of the changes and to take them into account as appropriate' (Report, 3, para. 3).

[30] Sohn, 'The New International Law: Protection of the Rights of Individuals Rather Than States', 32 Am. ULR (1992), 17.

acceptance, that it therefore ranks as *customary* law.[31] The end result may be (almost) the same in terms of binding effect; but the process of law-creation is wholly different.

In order to have a clear picture of the various possibilities, let us pose the question: why does a State incur responsibility if its organs commit a breach of a recognized human right (reserving the question of what is a 'recognized' right for this purpose)? To whom is that responsibility owed, and how may it be enforced? The simplest answer is furnished by the case in which the State has bound itself by bilateral treaty to another State; probably only the nationals of that other State will be protected, and the responsibility is incurred towards that other State. Secondly, the peccant State may have become a party to one of the multilateral lawmaking conventions in this field; in this case, and its responsibility, and the enforcement mechanism, will be as determined by the convention. In the case of *Application of the Genocide Convention* between Bosnia and Serbia, and between Croatia and Serbia, the responsibility was inter-State, any compensation for injury was due to the claimant State, not to the individual nationals harmed, and it was enforced through the compromissory clause (Art. IX of the Convention), giving jurisdiction to the ICJ. However, under other conventions, particularly regional conventions, responsibility is incurred by the State[32] directly to the individual injured, compensation is due to him or her, and enforcement is through a regional organization, for example the European Court of Human Rights. So far the source of the international rule is uncontroversial: it is the treaty-obligation accepted by the State concerned (Art. 38, para. 1(*a*), of the ICJ Statute).

A whole new theory of the customary international law relating to human rights has recently been offered by Brian Lepard.[33] it is however closely related to his theory as to customary international law in general, commented on in Chapter IX, Section 2 (*a*), of the previous edition of this book. For reasons explained in the corresponding chapter of the present work (see p. 234), it

---

[31] For Meron, this method of analysis is 'perfectly legitimate', even though he sees difficulties in harmonizing some of the existing human instruments with the Charter provisions: *Human Rights and Humanitarian Norms*, 84.

[32] An additional development is the possibility that has been recognized in some cases of a responsibility of an individual to an individual being declared by this means, the so-called *Drittwirkung*; but consideration of this would take us too far afield: see e.g. the judgment of the European Court of Human Rights in *Pla and Puncernau* v. *Andorra*, and A. Clapham, *Human Rights Obligations of Non-State Actors* (Oxford: Oxford University Press, 2006).

[33] B. D. Lepard, 'Towards a New Theory of Customary International Human Rights Law' in Lepard (ed.), *Reexamining Customary International Law*, (Cambridge University Press, 2017), 233–65.

will be dealt with in less detail, but will receive some consideration in its human rights context in the later chapter.

2(b)　Human rights as deriving from general principles

An alternative assessment of the line of thinking exemplified in these cases and in the UN Committee's approach is the suggestion that human rights law, in so far as it rests on something other than treaty-law, derives its status from the general principles of law; this of course keeps the discussion firmly within the framework of Article 38 of the ICJ Statute. It is the view taken notably by Bruno Simma and Philip Alston,[34] who draw attention to the limited and patchy operation of conventions in this field, and the unsatisfactory nature of the attempts to wrest customary law out of shape to accommodate enforcement of human rights norms.

One objection might be that the principles in question have traditionally been regarded as limited to those that may be derived from an examination and comparison of municipal legal systems. This point has already been considered in Chapter IV, and need not be re-examined here. For Simma and Alston, this approach 'was simply caused by the necessity to validate general principles in a reliable way'; in their view 'it cannot be read as closing the door to alternative means of objective validation'.[35] Their reliance on general principles in this domain was not grounded on a natural-law approach,[36] but rather on a consensualist conception. Evidence of general acceptance and recognition of, for example, human rights norms is to be sought not as constituting customary law, but for establishing those norms as general principles. The relevant material is 'not equated with State practice but is rather seen in a variety of ways in which moral and humanitarian considerations find a more direct and spontaneous "expression in legal form"'.[37]

There is much to be said for this approach, particularly as contrasted with the alternative of attributing the force of human rights law to international custom, which (as already noted) entails the virtual abandonment of any element corresponding to the practice traditionally required. However, any support for the general principles approach in the conduct of State relations and in international jurisprudence seems to be negative in nature. Simma

---

[34] Simma and Alston, 'The Sources of Human Rights Law', 82.

[35] Simma and Alston, 'The Sources of Human Rights Law', 102.

[36] Exemplified by e.g. A. Verdross, 'Les Principles généraux de droit dans la jurisprudence internationale', 52 Recueil des cours (1935-II), 204–6, and the dissenting opinion of Judge Tanaka in the *South West Africa* case [1966] ICJ Rep 298.

[37] Simma and Alston, 'The Sources of Human Rights Law', 105; the phrase quoted is from the *South West Africa* judgment [1966] ICJ Rep 34.

and Alston argue that the International Court 'has unambiguously accepted that the obligation to respect fundamental human rights is an obligation under general international law', but consider it significant also that in none of the relevant cases 'does the Court speak of customary international law in this regard'.[38] As for the material indicating a 'direct and spontaneous expression in legal form', none is enumerated; and the same difficulty seems to exist as the authors point out in relation to *jus cogens* in customary law, in a passage already quoted:[39] like obligations of that nature, many obligations relating to human rights are prohibitive, are rules of abstention; and 'How does one marshal conclusive evidence of abstention? Abstentions per se mean nothing; they become meaningful only when considered in the light of the intention motivating them.'[40] The authors, however, insist that the material they have in mind 'is not equated with State practice'; this presumably enables them to rely on the innumerable resolutions, declarations, and other per se non-binding instruments, which certainly 'give expression' to human rights norms; but the words 'in legal form' prove to be somewhat question-begging—legal in formulation, but in effect also? The case for human rights law as derived from general principles must, it seems, be regarded as unproved.

2(c) Human rights and Islam

It was indicated in Chapter I that this question would be examined in relation to international human rights law, even though the issues involved are potentially wider.[41] As a general issue, the asserted status of the *Shari'ah* in relation to international law is clearly indicated in the 2012 Report of the International Law Association Committee on Islamic Law and International Law:

In terms of how any conflicting norms or legal orders should be resolved through an Islamic paradigm, the position appears to be that Islamic *Shari'ah* advocates its own primacy, and, due to the divine and quasi-divine nature of its sources, cannot permit any man-made law (which by implication includes international law) to have priority over its principles and rules in the event of any issues of conflict or incompatibility.

---

[38] Simma and Alston, 'The Sources of Human Rights Law', 105–6, citing *Corfu Channel* [1949] ICJ Rep 22; *Reservations to the Genocide Convention* [1951] ICJ Rep 23; *United States Diplomatic and Consular Staff in Tehran* [1980] ICJ Rep 42.

[39] See Ch. VII n. 14.

[40] Simma and Alston, 'The Sources of Human Rights Law', 103–4.

[41] The subject is very thoroughly surveyed in the collection of essays edited by M. Frick and A. Th. Müller, *Islam and International Law, Engaging Selfcentrism from a Plurality of Perspectives* (Brill, 2013).

Presumably, this would even include its supremacy over an international peremptory norm if a conflict were to arise.[42]

So long as international law concerned itself with relations between States, leaving the relationships between individual States and their citizens out of its purview, there was no reason for Islamic law to conflict with general international law. As the ILA Committee observed in its 2010 Report, Islamic law did contain 'provisions regarding international relations, treaties and diplomacy, law of war and peace, humanitarian law, law of the sea, [and] international economic relations'; but these were for the most part in harmony with more widely held ideas. Difficulties have arisen, in the words of the Report, inasmuch as while 'international law continues to deal with issues that pertain exclusively or more closely to the coexistence and cooperation among States', in modern times 'it has been increasingly regulating fields that were traditionally thought to be within the exclusive regulatory competence of domestic law. Islamic Law contains rules that relate to all aspects of life, including, for example, relationships between private persons, which are regulated by domestic law, and international relations of the Islamic State or nation'.[43]

With the growth of international human rights law, the consequent difficulties faced by Islamic States in reconciling such law with the *Shari'ah* are well known and have already been touched on in Chapter I. The values inspiring attitudes on both sides deserve full respect, and no suggestion is made here that Western ideas of human rights are in some way the only authentic ones, and that the Islamic States are 'out of step'.[44] The fact remains that the world of human rights is easily pictured as one in which the Western approach is the rule and the Islamic one the exception; this is due not so much to the fact that Islamic States are in a minority among the States of the world, as to the fact that the major international instruments in this field have been drafted from a Western perspective, and the customary law has tended to be modelled on the texts.

The question with which we are here concerned is whether, in relying on *Shari'ah* law to explain or justify their position in relation to what we may

[42] International Law Association, Sofia Conference (2012), First Report of the Committee on Islamic Law and International Law, pp. 15–16.

[43] International Law Association, The Hague Conference (2010), Draft Report of the Committee on Islamic Law and International Law Report, p. 6.

[44] The existence of international human rights instruments devised by and for the Islamic States should not be overlooked: see the Cairo Declaration on Human Rights in Islam, 1990, and the Arab Charter on Human Rights, 22 May 2004, in force since 15 March 2008: ratified by Qatar, Saudi Arabia, and Yemen: <http://www1.umn.edu/humanrts/instree/loas2005.html?msource=UNWDE C19001&tr=y&auid=3337655> (accessed November 2013).

perhaps legitimately call 'general human rights law', the Islamic States are asserting something that can, in the light of its intended operation, only be classified as an alternative or additional source of law. This would seem consistent with the general statement in the ILA study, quoted earlier, as to the relationship between the two systems. In some cases, the action taken by Islamic States is fully in accordance with the operation of recognized sources: for example, to accede to a multilateral human rights convention while entering reservations to such of its provisions as are unacceptable to Muslims is a perfectly normal and proper step—provided, of course, that such reservations are authorized by the convention.[45] Acceptance by Islamic States of the Convention on the Elimination of all Forms of Discrimination against Women has been accompanied by reservations, sometimes in such forms as to limit 'Article X, in order to ensure its implementation within the bounds of the provisions of the Islamic sharia' or to exclude 'Article Y, insofar as it is incompatible with the provisions of the Islamic sharia'.[46] Some of these reservations are regarded by the UN Committee on the Elimination of Discrimination against Women as unacceptable on the ground that they are incompatible with the object and purpose of the Convention;[47] this controversy is outside the scope of our study, as the States concerned are doing no more than rely, correctly or incorrectly, on their normal rights under treaty-law.

One issue on which some conflict might have been expected is that of the freedom of religion itself, and specifically the freedom to change one's religion. This aspect has been thoroughly examined by Lepard in his recent work on customary international law.[48] Lepard observes that there has been surprisingly little overt opposition by Islamic States to the international human rights texts proclaiming specifically freedom to change one's religion as such a right.[49] 'Freedom of religion' is asserted in Article 56 the UN Charter; Article 18 of the Universal Declaration of

---

[45] A reservation may, of course, also be regarded as 'incompatible with the object and purpose' of the convention (Vienna Convention on the Law of Treaties, Art. 19(*c*)), but this will result in the exclusion of the reserving State, not the invalidity of the reservation (see however the cases discussed in Chap. II, text and n. 38, 39).

[46] Taken from the reservations of Bahrain, CEDAW/SP/2006/2, p. 9 (Arts. 2 and 16).

[47] See <http://www.un.org/womenwatch/daw/cedaw/>, accessed November 2013.

[48] B. D. Lepard, *Customary International Law: A New Theory with Practical Applications* (Cambridge: Cambridge University Press, 2010), ch. 24, 346ff. See also Lepard, 'Toward A New Theory of International Human Rights Law', in Lepard (ed.)_ *Reexamining Customary International Law* (CUP, 2017), 233 at 257–8.

[49] It is, however, understood that there is in fact more determined—and more effective— opposition than meets the eye.

Human Rights, specifically naming 'freedom to change' religion or belief was adopted with Islamic States abstaining, but with no negative votes.[50] As Baderin explains, while Islam asserts that apostasy will be severely punished in the hereafter, Muslim scholarly views generally consider that it is only in case of its manifestation in a manner threatening public safety, morals, or the freedom of others that the State should intervene;[51] and this is in harmony with the qualification in paragraph 3 of Article 18 of the Universal Declaration.[52]

More difficult are questions as to the status of women, and in particular that of polygamy, which has clear Koranic authority, but is regarded by Western scholars, and by the Human Rights Commission,[53] as contrary to the principle of equal rights in marriage, since it is only the husband who may take more than one spouse, not the wife. Nor, it appears, could the situation be redressed by authorizing polyandry (assuming that that would meet the Western objection), since consensual polyandry is also contrary to Koranic teachings.[54] Baderin suggests an ingenious 'way round';[55] but his conclusion is significant: if his suggestion were adopted, 'The focus of international human rights law would be seen to be specifically on human rights and not on questioning the basis of religious teachings per se, and thus promote a complementary approach to solving human rights problems.'[56] This is a wholly admirable position; but it does perhaps reveal that there is a real conflict between modern human rights law and Islamic teachings; and if such accommodations cannot be reached, the logical position of the Islamicists cannot be other than an assertion of religion as a source of law which is not only separate but overriding. That stage may never be reached; but intellectually it cannot be evaded.

[50] Whether the right is now a matter of customary law, and even a norm of *jus cogens*, as suggested by Lepard, is another matter; in this connection he examines, and rejects, the possibility that the Islamic States could claim to be 'persistent objectors' as regards a customary norm endorsing religious freedom: *Customary International Law*, 364–5.

[51] M. A. Baderin, *International Human Rights and Islamic Law* (Oxford: Oxford University Press, 2003), 123–35.

[52] Another potential source of conflict which should not be overlooked is the relationship of the right of freedom of speech to Islamic conceptions (and legal prohibition and punishment) of blasphemy. For reasons which need not be gone into here, in a number of Muslim countries anything seen as criticism of Islam or of the Prophet has been subjected to violent, often physical, attack.

[53] General Comment no. 28, 29 March 2000, CCPR/C/21/Rev.1/Add.10.

[54] Baderin, *International Human Rights*, 142.

[55] He suggests that women in Islamic countries should be formally told of their rights under Islamic law to stipulate at the time of marriage that subsequent taking of a second wife by the husband would be grounds for ending the marriage: Baderin, *International Human Rights*, 142–4.

[56] Baderin, *International Human Rights*, 144.

3. Humanitarian law

3(a) Treaties and conventions

The role of international treaties and conventions in this field of law is too evident to require demonstration, at least as regards their direct operation. However, this is also a field in which other instruments exist which are not themselves of a treaty nature, not having been directly concluded between States, but that are made in exercise of a power to decide or to recommend created by a treaty instrument. While these may therefore appear to constitute a legal act or legal source of a novel kind, in terms of sources of law, they are thus equally conventional instruments. The question has been discussed more fully in connection with treaties and conventions as a source, in Chapter II and in Chapter VI section 2.

There is nonetheless an important role for law not deriving directly from a specific treaty source; unless there is any source special to international humanitarian law, this can only be customary law.[57] Apart from the fact that not all the international conventions in this field enjoy universal acceptance and ratification, there is the growing problem of non-international conflicts, to which the majority of the conventional rules do not specifically apply.[58] In this context, no suggestion appears to have been made that any separate source would operate; the gap may be and is being filled by State practice generative of customary rules parallel to the treaty rules for international conflicts.[59] Yet there have been in the past suggestions of an additional or special source for humanitarian law.

3(b) Customary law or an independent source of law?

At a fairly early stage after the Second World War, the view could be expressed that 'considerations of humanity' could be regarded as an independent source of law, the decision of the ICJ in the *Corfu Channel* case, already referred to, being prayed in aid.[60] This case is, however, often referred to as an almost

---

[57] It was for this reason that the ICRC commissioned a report on the subject, published in 2005: J. -M. Henckaerts and L. Doswald-Beck (eds.), *Customary International Humanitarian Law* (Cambridge: ICRC/Cambridge University Press, 2005).

[58] See e.g. Yves Sandoz, Foreword to Henckaerts and Beck, *Customary International Humanitarian Law*, i. p. xxii.

[59] See e.g. commentary to Rule 151 (Individual criminal responsibility), Henckaerts and Beck, *Customary International Humanitarian Law*, i. 553.

[60] See G. G. Fitzmaurice, 'The Law and Procedure of the International Court of Justice', 27 BYIL (1950), 17; reproduced in G. G. Fitzmaurice, *The Law and Procedure of the International*

unique example of the International Court invoking general principles of law as basis for part of its decision: the legal obligation of the Albanian authorities to warn the British warships that they were approaching a minefield was specifically based

not on the Hague Convention of 1907, no. VIII, which is applicable in time of war, but on certain general and well-recognized principles, namely, elementary considerations of humanity ...; the principle of the freedom of maritime communication; and every State's obligation not to allow knowingly its territory to be used for acts contrary to the rights of other States.[61]

However, the decision of the Court in the *South West Africa* case emphatically expressed the view that no novel and additional source existed in this respect; and rejected the idea that 'humanitarian considerations are sufficient in themselves to generate legal rights and obligations'.[62] In the later case of *Military and Paramilitary Activities in and against Nicaragua*, the Court veered towards an independent role for humanitarian considerations in connection with the mines laid off Nicaraguan ports, but finally ruled that what the United States had breached was 'customary international law'.[63] In connection with the 1949 Geneva Conventions, however, the ICJ was ready to see the Conventions as 'in some respects a development, and in other respects no more than the expression' of the 'fundamental principles of humanitarian law'.[64] More complex was its handling of an allegation that the United States had 'encouraged the commission' by the Contras in Nicaragua of 'acts contrary to general principles of humanitarian law'.[65]

The advisory opinion on the *Legality of the Threat or Use of Nuclear Weapons* is clearer on this issue. The ICJ began its examination of 'the principles and rules of international humanitarian law' by noting that 'A large number of customary rules have [*sic*] been developed by the practice of States and are an

---

Court of Justice (Cambridge: Grotius, 1986), i. 17. Sir Gerald later came to revise this view, attributing the force of humanitarian considerations in this respect to 'a received rule of customary international law': 'Judicial Innovation: Its Uses and Perils', in *Cambridge Essays in Honour of Lord McNair* (Dobbsferry, NY: Oceana, 1965), 24.

[61] [1949] ICJ Rep 4 at 22, quoted in Lepard, *Customary International Law*, 146.

[62] [1966] ICJ Rep 34, para. 49. The Court recognized that '[h]umanitarian considerations may constitute the inspirational basis for rules of law', adding the striking example of 'the preambular parts of the United Nations Charter' as 'moral and political basis for the specific legal provisions thereafter set out' (para. 50). This judgment was very ill-received internationally, but for reasons not directly related to this finding, which, it is suggested, was perfectly correct at the time.

[63] [1986] ICJ Rep 112, para. 215; 147–8, para. 292(8).

[64] [1986] ICJ Rep 113–14, para. 218.

[65] [1986] ICJ Rep 148, para. 292(9). See the discussion of the case in H. Thirlway, 'The Law and Procedure of the International Court of Justice', 62 BYIL (1990) 9–13; reproduced in Thirlway, *The Law and Procedure of the International Court of Justice*, i. 144–7.

integral part of the international law relevant to the question posed' by the General Assembly.[66] It referred to codification by international convention, and new specific prohibitions effected by multilateral treaty.

It then enumerated what it termed 'the cardinal principles contained in the texts'; only thereafter did the Court quote the phrase 'elementary considerations of humanity' from the *Corfu Channel* decision.[67] It did so in order to suggest that it was because 'a great many rules of humanitarian law applicable in armed conflict are so fundamental to the respect of the human person', and so fundamental to those considerations, that 'the Hague and Geneva Conventions have enjoyed a broad accession'.[68]

The ICJ therefore did not base any rules or principles of international law upon humanitarian considerations alone: it found that they were solidly based in custom and in conventional law. This is clear, not only from the wording of the advisory opinion, but also from the dissenting opinion of Judge Weeramantry and (in particular) that of Judge Shahabuddeen. Judge Weeramantry based humanitarian norms on the 'general principles of law' of Article 38, paragraph 1 (*c*), of the ICJ Statute.[69] Judge Shahabuddeen argued that the celebrated 'de Martens clause' in the Preamble to the 1899 Hague Convention was normative in itself, and not merely as a declaration of existing customary law,[70] as 'indicating the state of the public conscience', and saw no need for an enquiry to determine the existence or otherwise of an *opinio juris*,[71] since for him the source of the legal obligations in question was not customary law. He did not comment on the question of the application of Article 38 of the Statute, which does not empower the Court to employ considerations of humanity, as such, as a source; it may be that, like Judge Weeramantry, he envisaged their inclusion as an aspect of the general principles of law under paragraph 1(*c*).

The ICJ chose also to consider the question whether the principles and rules of humanitarian law that had come into existence before nuclear weapons were invented applied also to those weapons, in particular since 'there is a qualitative as well as quantitative difference between nuclear weapons and all conventional arms'.[72] A conclusion that those principles and rules did not so apply, it declared, 'would be incompatible with the intrinsically humanitarian character of the legal principles in question which permeates the entire law of

---

[66] [1996-I] ICJ Rep 256, paras. 74–5.
[67] [1949] ICJ Rep, quoted in [1996-I] ICJ Rep 257, para. 79.
[68] [1996-I] ICJ Rep 257, para. 79.　　　[69] [1996-I] ICJ Rep 259, 493–4.
[70] For a fuller discussion of the case, and of Judge Shahabuddeen's opinion, see H. Thirlway, 'The Law and Procedure of the International Court of Justice', 76 BYIL (2006) 78–80.
[71] [1996-I] ICJ Rep 409–10.　　　[72] [1996-I] ICJ Rep 86.

armed conflict and applies to all forms of warfare and to all kinds of weapons, those of the past, those of the present, and those of the future'.[73]

So far as conventional prohibitions were concerned, strictly speaking the question is one of interpretation of the relevant texts: were they intended to cover not merely the weapons existing at the time, but also 'those of the future'? The Court reasoned on the basis that they were so intended, and found it unnecessary to go into the detail of such interpretations. As to customary law, there is no difficulty in considering that the rules and principles were from the outset sufficiently broad in scope to embrace the use of novel weapons.[74] The conclusion is that the reference to the 'intrinsically humanitarian character of the legal principles in question' does not add, and was not intended to add, anything as regards the bases of humanitarian law in the sources of international law.[75]

In its opinion on *Legal Consequences of the Construction of a Wall on the Occupied Palestinian Territory*, the Court adopted a similar classical approach to the question of sources:

The Court will now determine the rules and principles of international law which are relevant in assessing the legality of the measures taken by Israel. Such rules and principles can be found in the United Nations Charter and certain other treaties, in customary international law and in the relevant resolutions adopted pursuant to the Charter by the General Assembly and the Security Council.[76]

The inclusion of General Assembly and Security Council resolutions is justified by recourse to them later in the opinion, but they are not advanced as a source of international law in themselves.[77] In any event, it is clear that the Court saw no need, or considered it incorrect, to refer to 'considerations of

---

[73] [1996-I] ICJ Rep 86.

[74] It may be significant that the Court regarded as relevant the fact that no State before it had argued that the established rules did *not* apply to nuclear weapons—indeed it quoted the statements made by several States to the opposite effect: [1996-I] ICJ Rep 259–60, para. 86. This could be a finding indicative of the existence of *opinio juris*.

[75] Meron concludes that the Martens clause, in its accepted interpretation, may be a statement of the obvious, but 'does serve a humanitarian purpose and is therefore not redundant'; yet he goes on: 'Except in extreme cases, its references to the principles of humanity and dictates of public conscience cannot, alone, delegitimize weapons and methods of war …': T. Meron, 'The Martens Clause: Principles of Humanity and Dictates of Public Conscience', 94 AJIL (2000) 79.

[76] [2004] ICJ Rep 171, para. 86.

[77] '[Security] Council resolutions need not challenge the traditional doctrine of sources if we see them as simply the output of a body authorized by a treaty, the UN Charter': S. R. Ratner, 'War Crimes and the Limits of the Doctrine of Sources' in S. Besson and J. d'Aspremont (eds.) *The Oxford Handbook on the Sources of International Law*, (Oxford University Press, 2017), 917. However, the author continues: 'Yet, for situation-specific resolutions, their normative effect extends far beyond that they are meant to influence', and some '(e.g. Resolution 1373) resemble a form of instant global legislation that is harder to fit within the idea of mere delegation from a treaty'.

humanity' in general as justifying its findings concerning the obligations of Israel.

The operation of general principles in this domain could take one of two forms: they could be regarded as a direct source, under paragraph 1(*c*) of Article 38 of the ICJ Statute; or it might, it has been suggested, be possible for a customary rule to develop directly from certain principles, specifically principles of humanitarian law, without the normal criteria of the existence of practice and *opinio juris* being satisfied. One commentator who appears to take this view is Lepard, in his 2010 work *Customary International Law: A New Theory with Practical Applications* Lepard contends that application of ethical (humanitarian) principles in the establishment of a customary rule can be traced in certain PCIJ and ICJ decisions. For example, he mentions the *Lotus* case before the Permanent Court,[78] and suggests that it was the 'fundamental ethical principle of securing punishment of criminals' which led the Court to find that, as a matter of customary law, in a case of collision between two ships, the national States of each of them had jurisdiction over the matter; but it is equally possible to regard this simply as a matter of jurisdictional convenience. The Court did indeed refer to 'the requirements of justice', but also to the need 'effectively to protect the interests of the two States'.

Similarly, the case of *Reservations to the Genocide Convention* is sometimes invoked in this context (though Lepard more correctly regards it as revealing no more than 'a background role for ethical principles'[79]). The Court observed, for example, that one of the objects of the convention was 'to confirm and endorse the most elementary principles of morality'; but the fact this was the object of a convention says nothing about the relevance of such principles to customary law: indeed, if customary law had been, or were likely to be, influenced by those principles, one might have questioned the need for a convention.

As for the *Corfu Channel* case, Lepard reads the decision as emphasizing 'that many norms articulated in treaties involving international humanitarian law now form part of customary law'. There is no indication of this in the judgment; what it derives from the principle is not a customary rule imposing an obligation, but simply and directly an obligation.

That humanitarian law forms part of international customary law is indisputable. It is also indisputable that it became so under the influence of 'the

---

[78] (1927) PCIJ Series A, No. 10, at pp. 30–1, discussed in Lepard, *Customary International Law*, 142–3. He also attaches importance to the views expressed in a dissenting opinion by Judge Altamira on a slightly different point, which chime with the views expressed by Lepard, but were in 1927 not recognizable as generally accepted customary law.

[79] Lepard, *Customary International Law*, 144.

principles of humanity and ... the dictates of public conscience', to quote the de Martens clause[80] (which, of course, mentions these along with 'established custom' rather than as the inspiration for it). What does not appear established is that this field of law affords an example of a transition directly from high principles to customary law, without the mediating, not to say creative, input of practice guided by *opinio juris*. Still less does it support the view that this process, if it occurred, is capable of generalization: that where the need is felt (for whatever reasons, ethical, practical, or other) for a customary rule that the traditional mechanism has not, or not yet, supplied, then the need itself affords the lawmaking basis.

4. WTO, ICSID: trade and investment law dispute settlement

If there is still an institution that may be regarded as embodying a self-contained regime on the lines here contemplated, it is the World Trade Organization with its system for the settlement of disputes. An active discussion remains open on the question whether expert panels set up under this system, and the appeals organ, the Appellate Body, may or may not apply rules and principles of general international law, falling outside the strict ambit of the system set up under the treaties establishing the WTO and the Dispute Settlement Body.[81] The source of the law applicable, however, remains, for the partisans of both views, primarily or exclusively 'WTO law', that is to say essentially treaty-based;[82] and it does not appear to be suggested that any law relied on alongside WTO law may be derived from any source other than those offered by general international law, that is those enumerated in Article 38 of the ICJ Statute. Accordingly, no problem of sources theory would appear to be raised.

---

[80] See Art. 1 para. 2 of Additional Protocol I (1977) to the Hague Conventions, cited in [1996-I] ICJ Rep 257.

[81] See e.g. J. Pauwelyn, 'The Role of Public International Law in the WTO: How Far Can We Go?', 95 AJIL (2001), 535 (for a restrictive view), and J. Trachtman, 'Conflict of Norms in Public International Law: How WTO Law Relates to Other Rules of International Law', 98 AJIL (2004), 855 (for a more liberal view).

[82] Or 'treaty based and Member-driven', in the terms recently suggested by J. Pauwelyn: 'Mantras and Controversies at the World Trade Organization', in Besson and d'Aspremont (eds.) *The Oxford Handbook on the Sources of International Law*. For a specific reference to customary international law, by the WTO Appellate Body, see however the *Hormones* case (WTO Report of the Appellate Body: Australia—Measures Affecting Importation of Salmon, 6 November 1998, WT/DS18/AB/R. para. 123; discussed in D. Pulkowski, 'Universal International Law's Grammar', in Fastenrath et al. (eds.), *From Bilateralism to Community Interest, Essays in Honour of Judge Bruno Simma*, (Oxford: Oxford University Press, 2011) 144–5.

One suggested departure or variation from general law may, however, be noted. Mention has been made already of the role of the decisions of international courts and tribunals as a subsidiary source of international law, as contemplated by Article 38, paragraph 1(*c*), of the ICJ Statute, and of the view that in modern law such decisions, or certain decisions in certain fields, have come to be a primary rather than a subsidiary source.[83]

A particularly strong case can be made for this development having occurred in the context of WTO law, by reference to the decisions of the panels and the Appellate Body set up under the Disputes Settlement Understanding. Essentially the contention is that these judicial bodies have come to apply the governing texts according to judicially discovered interpretations rather than according to the letter of the texts; and that States engaged in disputes have come to accept such interpretations as applicable in cases involving parties and facts different from those before the judicial body in the cases where the interpretations have been laid down.[84]

Accepting that in this context (and indeed in others), judicial decisions are in fact treated as precedents, to be relied on, argued over, or 'distinguished', this does not, it is suggested, confer on them any higher status than that of 'subsidiary sources' as contemplated by Article 38. The reason for this has already been stated:[85] they do not purport to be any more than the vehicle of law that already exists, and owes its existence to a non-subsidiary source (in the case of the WTO decisions, the governing treaty provisions). The fact that the judicial 'interpretation' of such texts may appear to have reached a point of utter detachment from, or inconsistency with these provisions does not affect the principle of the subsidiarity of the judicial decision as a source. Nevertheless, questions of applicable sources of law have come to give rise to considerable controversy within the organization; examination of the details would take us too far afield; the curious reader is referred to the article by Joost Pauwelyn, already mentioned, in the *Oxford Handbook on the Sources of International Law*[86]

---

[83] See Ch. V, sect. 2(*a*).

[84] Reference is here made to the work of I. Venzke, 'Making General Exceptions: The Spell of Precedents in Developing Article XX into Standards for Domestic Regulatory Policy', 12 German LJ (2011), 1111; I. Venzke, *How Interpretation Makes International Law: On Semantic Change and Normative Twists* (Oxford: Oxford University Press, 2012). The WTO Appellate Body itself has endorsed the force of *stare decisis* in this field, declaring that 'absent cogent reasons, an adjudicatory body [of the Organization] will resolve the same legal question in the same way in a subsequent case': *US – Stainless Steel (Mexico)* Appellate Body Report, 30 April 2008.

[85] Ch. I sect. 2; Ch. V, sect. 1.

[86] See note 78. The author identifies three problems: the role of jurisprudence as a source alongside the treaties; the relevance of treaties outside the category of 'covered agreements' and the relevance of non-binding instruments.

In the special field of international investment law, the role of treaties is evident, but much use has also been made by arbitral bodies, particularly tribunals established under the auspices of the International Centre for the Settlement of Investment Disputes (ICSID), of general principles of law, as is perhaps to be expected in a newly developed, and developing, field. These do not however constitute the only traditional sources to have been prayed in aid in this domain: customary law has (though not without complications) also had a role to play.[87] If there is any doubt as to the identity of sources in this domain with those of general international law, it is in a different area. Mention was made earlier[88] of the legal status of unilateral undertakings in the field of international investment law, and of a suggestion by Professor Mbengue that this practice, if not revealing a possible novel source, is at least 'challenging for the theory of sources of international investment law'.[89] It was suggested earlier (Ch. I, sect 6(a) and Ch. II sect. 4) that unilateral undertakings by States, notwithstanding the effect attributed to them in the *Nuclear Tests* decisions, amount to inchoate treaties, since they normally remain ineffective unless and until there is express or tacit acceptance by the State addressed. Mbengue suggests that the ICJ's position 'should be rethought'; contrary to the Court's express statement that 'not all unilateral acts imply obligation',[90] he adopts an absolutist position that '[e]ither an act of a state is a unilateral act or it is not' and '[i]f it is a unilateral act of a state, then it has a legally generative force and is binding upon the state under international law'.[91] Such a position, it is suggested, might bring more certainty to international legal relations; but it is not clear that the matter is more than one of definition. Was the off-the-cuff remark of the Malian Head of State in the *Frontier Dispute*[92] a unilateral act without legally generative force, or not a unilateral act at all?

Essentially, the problem as Mbengue sees it is this: the ILC report, already mentioned,[93] identified certain criteria as the marks of an international unilateral act; but municipal investment laws do not match those criteria.

---

[87] See the very thorough essay by d'Aspremont, 'International Customary Investment Law: Story of A Paradox', in Gazzini and de Brabandere (eds.), *International Investment Law: The Sources of Rights and Obligations*, (Nijhoff, 2012), and the book by P. Dumberry, *The Formation and Identification of Rules of Customary International Law in International Investment Law*, (Cambridge: Cambridge University Press, 2016).

[88] Ch. II sect. 4, n. 73.

[89] M. M. Mbengue, 'National Legislation and Unilateral Acts of States', in Gazzini and de Brabandere, *International Investment Law*, 183 at 185 (fn. omitted).

[90] [1974] ICJ Rep 267, para. 44; 472, para. 47.

[91] Mbengue, 'National Legislation and Unilateral Acts of States', 190 n. 37.

[92] [1986] ICJ Rep 573–4, paras. 39–40, cited here at Ch. II sect. 4, text and n. 69.

[93] Ch. II sect. 4.

First, [these laws] are not addressed to third states and do not intend to 'create a new legal relationship with a third state' ... Secondly, the ILC's interpretation of the autonomy of a unilateral act does not correspond to the rationale that governs foreign investment statutes ... [which are] first and foremost, rooted in the domestic legal order of the state ...[94]

To consider that strictly unilateral acts solely derive from the exercise by a State of its 'free will and power of auto-limitation *conferred on it by international law*' leads to a subversive result: excluding municipal investment laws from the realm of (strictly) unilateral acts under international law.[95]

It is apparently on the basis of reasoning on these lines that international arbitrators have shown themselves uncertain whether or not to attribute to foreign investment laws the status of unilateral acts.

For our purposes, the question is whether, for these laws to have effect internationally, they must be given a status outside the recognized system of sources. If, as suggested in Chapter II, unilateral acts are treated as inchoate treaties, the legal effect of which derives from their 'completion' by express or implied acceptance, the problem perhaps takes on a different dimension. If one considers the legal situation when a dispute has arisen relating to municipal legislation of this kind, rather than the categorization of the legislation at the time of its enactment, it becomes easier to trace a legal relationship at the least analogous to a claim for breach of treaty. Nor is the problem as novel as might appear; Mbengue himself draws attention to the view, expressed as long ago as 1970 by Judge Morelli in his separate opinion in the *Barcelona Traction* case, that the existence of international obligations towards foreign investors 'depends on a *state of affairs created in municipal law*'.[96] His deduction is that if a State commits itself unilaterally, in the context of municipal law, with respect to foreign investment protection, 'the instrument at stake acquires *prima facie* the legal nature of an autonomous unilateral act under international law',[97] but for the reasons just mentioned, he moves away from this provisional conclusion.

The view expressed by Morelli, however, it is submitted, remains pertinent. One of the situations discussed in his opinion appears to present a highly relevant analogy:

---

[94] Mbengue, 'National Legislation and Unilateral Acts of States', 196.

[95] Mbengue, 'National Legislation and Unilateral Acts of States', 197. The passage quoted and italicized is taken from the ILC Report, para. 141.

[96] [1970] ICJ Rep 234, para. 4, italics added by Mbengue.

[97] Mbengue, 'National Legislation and Unilateral Acts of States', 187.

The conduct which international law renders incumbent upon a State with regard to the rights which the same State confers on foreign nationals within its own municipal order consists, in the first place, in the judicial protection of those rights. Any State which, having attributed certain rights to foreign nationals, prevents them from gaining access to the courts for the purpose of asserting those rights is guilty, in international law, of a denial of justice. In addition, international law lays upon a State, within certain limits and on certain conditions, the obligation to respect, in the conduct of its administrative or even legislative organs, the rights which the municipal legal order of the same State confers on foreign nationals. This is what is known as respecting the acquired rights of foreigners.[98]

Similarly, Mbengue observes that national investment legislation 'embodies, *inter alia*, substantive standards of investment treatment', and that these serve 'as matrices of legal commitments in favour of foreign investors and/or investments'.[99]

It is, in short, suggested that the reasons, outlined in the passage quoted, why Mbengue does not consider that national investment legislation meets the requirements (at least as identified by the ILC) to qualify as an international unilateral act are only applicable to the legislation at the time of enactment; and that the acceptance by foreign States or their nationals adds to the act in question the necessary international flavour, and brings it into the category of inchoate—or indeed, completed and bilateral—treaties. There is of course much more to Mbengue's thesis as to the treatment of municipal investment protection legislation, but it does not, in the present writer's view, take further the question of possible 'challenge' to the classical theory of sources of international law.

Particularly since the turn of the century, international investment treaties have referred questions of compensation to the standard of 'fair and equitable treatment', and questions have inevitably arisen as to what this means, by what law it is to be assessed, and the source or sources of that law.[100] Since the term is originally derived from a series of investment treaties, in one sense this is more a matter of treaty interpretation than of general law; but the discussion has covered also the possibility that customary law, or all the recognized sources, might be invoked,[101] including the good faith principle; but in 2004 it was considered too early to establish a definitive interpretation of the FET standard.[102]

---

[98] [1970] ICJ Rep 233, para. 3. [99] [1970] ICJ Rep 185–6.

[100] See the very substantial OECD study *Fair and Equitable Treatment in International Investment Law* (September 20014).

[101] See n. 100 Section II. [102] See n. 100 Final paragraph.

5. International environmental issues

Over the last fifty years, there has been built up a formidable body of international instruments directed to the protection of the environment,[103] to the extent that international environmental law has come to be regarded as, if not a special regime, at least a subject of specialization. The obligations involved are, once again, essentially conventional in nature; their peculiarity depends on the systems established to achieve the aims of the conventions. In view, in particular, of the fact that the interests affected by any failure to implement the agreed norms are likely to be multilateral, or even universal, the enforcement systems rest not so much on bilateral claims for breach of contractual obligations as on 'providing assistance and facilitating cooperation in order to enable States to comply with their international obligations'.[104] These systems do, however, characteristically involve the intervention of a body with decision-making powers, generally of a political rather than judicial nature.[105]

As in the case of the WTO system, the law applied is, however, essentially the convention under which the compliance body is acting. Therefore, while the general body of law in this field is complex and highly institutionalized, so as to bear little resemblance to the classical pattern of international organization contemplated by Article 38 of the ICJ Statute, it does not seem to involve the invocation of any source or purported source not foreseen in that instrument.[106]

Environmental issues were at the heart of the ICJ case of *Pulp Mills on the River Uruguay*, but the case was eventually decided essentially on the basis of interpretation and application of the treaty-instruments concluded between the parties, without invoking general principles or principles of customary

---

[103] It has been suggested that this is not a separate domain, but rather an aspect of international economic law: see P. M. Dupuy, 'Où en est le droit international de l'environnement à la fin du siècle?', 101 Revue générale (1997), 899. For a list of international instruments, compiled from the point of view of compliance procedures, see the appendix to K. N. Scott, 'Non-Compliance Procedures and Dispute Resolution Mechanisms under International Environmental Agreements', in D. French et al. (eds.), *International Law and Dispute Settlement: New Problems and Techniques* (Oxford: Hart, 2012), 259–61.

[104] Scott, 'Non-Compliance Procedures and Dispute Resolution Mechanisms', 225 at 226.

[105] e.g. The Implementation Committee established under the 1979 Convention on Long-Range Transboundary Air Pollution (LRTAP); the Compliance Committee established under the 1997 Kyoto Protocol; etc.

[106] For an example of a concept, related to environmental law, lacking roots in any of the recognized sources, see the modern idea of 'sustainable development'.

law. As already mentioned in Chapter IV, Judge Cançado Trindade noted that the parties had referred to such principles 'in a general way', but had not invoked them in support of their respective arguments; he considered that the Court should nevertheless have 'elaborate[d] on the General Principles of International Environmental Law', as 'this is what is generally expected of it'.[107] His opinion therefore contains an extensive discussion of the principle of prevention, the precautionary principle, and their operation in conjunction, as well as that of 'intergenerational equity'.[108]

It cannot be denied that scientific research in respect of climate change, and the extent to which this is the result of human activity, suggests that it is becoming more and more desirable, if not essential, that certain activities which are beneficial to the State conducting them, but which are, in this context, proven to be, or strongly suspected of being, harmful to humanity, be subject to legal control. An enforceable and generally accepted international convention on the subject could achieve this result, but looks unattainable. It would be reassuring to think that customary law, basing itself, if not on sheer necessity, on numerous non-binding instruments, could fill the gap; but the nature of custom, as analysed here, is such that it cannot operate in that way.[109] What is encouraging, however, is the extent to which combinations of conventions, non-binding resolutions and declarations are leading to the establishment in new law in this area where it is sorely needed. This is not the place for a detailed examination of these processes, but attention should be drawn to the following indications, by a leading author, of four features to be highlighted:

The first is the relative importance of treaty regimes for the articulation of primary and secondary (subsidiary) norms of IEL [International Environmental Law]. The second is that this norm generation process is pluralized and decentralized, with a particularly distinctive role for institutions and non-State actors. The third is the relative importance of informal normative sources – non-legally binding instruments or soft law – in the environmental context. Finally IEL is a clear illustration of the permeability of categories of source: treaties may codify or generate custom, fit within the Article 38 (1) (*c*) category of general principles, or be found in soft law.[110]

---

[107] Separate opinion [2010] ICJ Rep 156–7, para. 54.

[108] [2010] ICJ Rep 177–182. Since this concept does not yet, *pace* Judge Cançado Trindade, appear to exist in general international law, it need not be further explained here.

[109] Cf. Tesón, 'Fake Custom' in Lepard (ed.), *Reeexamining Customary International Law*, 86, 93, criticizing in this respect Kiss and Shelton, *International Environmental Law* (Transnational Publishers Inc., 2004), 206–12.

[110] C. Redgwell, 'Sources of International Environmental Law' in Besson and d'Aspremont (eds.), *The Oxford Handbook on the Sources of International Law*, 939, 943.

6. International criminal law

Controversial questions as to the operation of international criminal law may be seen as rooted in uncertainty as to the sources of the law in this field. The criminal law here referred to is, of course, supranational criminal law, which establishes individual criminal responsibility directly under international law.[111] Essentially this field of law is treaty-based,[112] the key texts being the constitutive Statutes of the various international criminal tribunals: the International Criminal Court,[113] the only permanent tribunal of this nature; the International Criminal Tribunal for the Former Yugoslavia and the International Criminal Tribunal for Rwanda;[114] to which may be added the major pertinent international conventions such as the Genocide Convention. At the time that the first tribunal, the ICTY, was being established, the possibility of creating it directly by treaty was examined, and rejected because of the lack of certainty that ratification by the key States concerned would be obtained.[115] The method adopted—a decision of the Security Council adopting a Statute, under Chapter VII of the Charter, nevertheless remains a treaty-based technique, in terms of sources of law, owing its effectiveness ultimately to the commitments accepted by UN Members as parties to the

---

[111] It is thus to be distinguished from international criminal law in the sense of (*a*) national laws governing the territorial scope of municipal criminal law, (*b*) the law of international co-operation in criminal matters, and (*c*) transnational criminal law; see Kreß in Wolfrum (ed.), *Max Planck Encyclopedia* v. 717–21, s.v. 'International Criminal Law'. There is less ambiguity in other languages, both *Völkerstrafrecht* and *droit international penal* (with that word-order) being specific to this subject: see Kreß, 720, para. 14.

[112] A special case, with deep historical roots, is that of piracy: the universal jurisdiction of every State to deal with pirates undoubtedly derives from customary law (in a somewhat negative manner, as the customary rule forbade the interference by one State with vessels flying the flag of another, and pirates sailed under no national flag). Piracy is now dealt with in Articles 100–7 of the United Nations Convention on the Law of the Sea, with a definition in Art. 101, but this is probably purely codificatory, and corresponds to current customary law. Though the skull-and-crossbones flag is probably no longer to be encountered on the high seas, piracy has of course by no means disappeared, but has taken on a modern form off the coast of Africa. For an excellent survey of the problem, and its link with that of 'failed States', see R.-J. Dupuy and C. Hoss, 'La Chasse aux pirates par la communauté international: le cas de la Somalie', in M. Kamga and M. M. Mbengue (eds.), *Liber Amicorum Raymond Ranjeva* (Paris: Pedone, 2013), 135.

[113] Rome Statute of the ICC, 17 July 1998.

[114] ICTY: Statute approved by Security Council resolution 803 (1993), 25 May 1993; ICTR: Security Council resolution 955 (1994) of 8 November 1994. Both, having completed their mandates, have been replaced by the Mechanism for International Criminal Tribunals (MICT): Security Council resolution 1966 (22 December 2010).

[115] UNSC, Report of the Secretary-General pursuant to para. 2 of Security Council resolution 808 (1993), UN doc. S/25704, para. 20.

Charter.[116] At the time that the ICTY was established, however, the relevant Report of the UN Secretary-General indicated that the tribunal was to apply international humanitarian law, and noted that 'while there is international customary law which is not laid down in conventions, some of the major conventional humanitarian law has become part of international customary law', and that 'the international tribunal should apply rules of international humanitarian law which are beyond doubt part of customary law, so that the problem of adherence of some but not all States to specific conventions does not arise'.[117]

However, international conventions are binding on the States parties to them (setting aside for the present the possible companion obligations in customary law mentioned by the Secretary-General's report), whereas international criminal responsibility is that of individuals. There is, of course, no reason why States should not agree by treaty that their nationals should be subjected to criminal prosecution at the international level, or in each others' territories, for certain defined offences; by so agreeing they are waiving their sovereign rights, which it is in their power to do. The criminal law so applied is, in terms of sources, firmly based on 'treaties and conventions in force'; it may be created by the agreement itself, or that agreement may incorporate by reference the provisions of international conventions such as the Genocide Convention.[118] This is probably the position of the International Criminal Court.[119] However, more controversial is the decision of the ICTY in the *Tadić* case that individual responsibility for war crimes can be derived from an international treaty on humanitarian law provided that that treaty provision is binding on the parties to the conflict.[120] The tribunal explained that

the only reason behind the stated purpose of the drafters [of the ICTY Statute] that the International Tribunal should apply customary international law was to avoid violating the principle of *nullum crimen sine lege* in the event that a party to the conflict did not adhere to a specific treaty ... It follows that the International Tribunal is

---

[116] The legal position was exhaustively analysed by the Appeals Chamber in *Prosecutor* v. *Tadić*, Decision on the Defence Motion for Interlocutory Appeal on Jurisdiction, paras. 28–48.

[117] UNSC, Report of the Secretary-General pursuant to para. 2 of Security Council resolution 808 (1993), UN doc. S/25704, paras. 33, 34. The conventional provisions that the Secretary-General regarded as having this status were enumerated in the following paragraph of the Report.

[118] This would seem to be possible whether or not the States concerned are also parties to the relevant convention, which here serves merely as formal source of law.

[119] The Rome Statute of the ICC is unusual in that it contains, in Arts. 6, 7, and 8, detailed lists of the crimes subject to the Court's jurisdiction; it then provides in Art. 9 for the 'Elements of Crimes', which are to serve as a means to assist the Court in its interpretation and application of the previous three articles.

[120] *Prosecutor* v. *Tadić*, Decision on the Defence Motion for Interlocutory Appeal on Jurisdiction, para. 143.

authorised to apply, in addition to customary international law, any treaty which: (i) was unquestionably binding on the parties at the time of the alleged offence; and (ii) was not in conflict with or derogating from peremptory norms of international law, as are most customary rules of international humanitarian law.[121]

The confusion here is essentially in relation to sources-theory: the humanitarian law that the tribunal wished to apply might, in its own right, as it were, be treaty-based or custom-based, or both. The law to be applied by the tribunal was, however, defined by its Statute, which specified certain conventions, and customary law; conventions not so mentioned simply fall outside this definition, whether or not they are binding on the *States* parties to the conflict.[122] As regards customary law, the various international criminal tribunals have found themselves faced with a difficulty in establishing the required State practice from what States actually do, and have actually done; they have therefore tended to fall back on 'State declarations, including national legislation and case-law, codes of conduct, military manuals' and 'resolutions of international organizations'.[123]

The sources of international criminal law are not in fact identical with the case sources of international humanitarian law as applicable at the level of States, in the sense that any principle or rule of the latter is necessarily applicable at the level of individual criminal responsibility. International criminal law is treaty-based, though customary international law may also be invoked, not of itself, but by a sort of conventional *renvoi*.

The Rome Statute of the ICC lays down specifically, in Articles 5 to 8, the crimes as to which the Court 'has jurisdiction'. Is this text then the sole source of the international criminal law to be applied by the Court? The crimes mentioned in the Statute were not just plucked out of the air: they already existed, under international conventions and under international customary law, and the intention of the Statute was codifying rather than creative; the relation between the text and pre-existing law is therefore not entirely clear. However, as in the case of the ICTY, it is the Statute that applies the inter-State law as a matter of criminal responsibility of the individual; and in that sense there is no problem in terms of sources of law.[124]

---

[121] *Prosecutor* v. *Tadić*, Decision on the Defence Motion, para. 143.

[122] See Kreß in Wolfrum (ed.), Max Planck Encyclopedia, v. 720, para. 12.

[123] R. van Sternberghe, in S. Besson and J. d'Aspremont (eds.), *The Oxford Handbook on the Sources of International Law*, 896, citing (inter alia) the *Tadić* case, and decisions of the Extraordinary Chambers of the Courts of Cambodia.

[124] Difficulties have arisen in the context of *procedural* rules, involving the hierarchical or other relationship between sources internal to the ICC; these are exhaustively examined by G. Bitti, 'The ICC and its Applicable Law: Article 21 and the Hierarchy of Sources of Law before the ICC', in C. Stahn (ed.), *The Law and Practice of the International Criminal Court* (Oxford: Oxford University Press, 2015).

IX

Some Alternative Approaches

In the previous edition of this book, this chapter was divided into two sections, devoted respectively to 'Alternatives to the traditional doctrine of sources as a whole' and 'New approaches to customary law'. Since it has always been customary law that provoked the most controversy, the distinction was by no means sharp, not perhaps really helpful, and capable of being misleading; it has therefore not been maintained in that form in this edition. The structure of the chapter also involved the selection of a number of specific published theories, and submitting each to critical examination. These were taken as being, at the time, broadly representative of theories in the field that did not adopt, or start from, the broadly positivist approach taken in previous chapters.

In the light of (inter alia) comments received from other internationalists, the writer now feels that this was not the most helpful approach for the general reader, and a different treatment seems preferable. This is: to note and analyse some of the lines of thought and approach underlying criticism of the positivist analysis, shared in differing degrees by a number of writers who have, in recent years (both before and since publication of the earlier edition) presented alternative theories or approaches. The standpoint here adopted is, generally speaking, not so much that these theories are erroneous, as that they are superfluous: that the positivist viewpoint explains what needs to be explained, and harmonizes with the observable conduct of States; and that that is how that viewpoint came to obtain wide acceptance in the first place.

There are, of course, or have been in the past a number of ways of 'thinking about international law', and these are presented, in detail and with great skill, by Andrea Bianchi in a recently published work entitled 'International Law Theories: An Enquiry into Different Ways of Thinking'.[1] Professor Bianchi's canvas is however much broader than that of the present work: as well as, for example, critical legal studies, the New Haven school, and Third World approaches, she examines the ways in which international law is seen

---

[1] Oxford University Press, 2016.

by exponents of Marxism, Feminism, Social Idealism, and many more. One chapter among fourteen is devoted to 'Traditional Approaches'. What is here attempted lies within the purview of that chapter; its purpose, in contrast, is to look at some theses recently or currently presented that, while seeking to offer some new insights, remain within the general orbit of the traditional approach.

In the meantime, international life goes on. There used to be a popular belief that 'science had proved' that, according to aeronautical principles, the bumblebee could not possibly fly; but that the insect, being happily unaware of this, went ahead and flew anyway.[2] Something of a parallel may be traced in the relationship between international State practice and the attitudes of scholars to the traditional doctrine of sources, and in particular to the traditional view of the formation of customary international law. Sources doctrine has widely been regarded as outdated and inadequate: in particular, many writers have rejoiced in pointing out the incoherences and inconsistencies of the classical theory of law-creation through custom. Yet in this particular field the ILC has, without any great struggle, adopted clear Conclusions, at the close of a lengthy process involving the participation of States, who in their daily interaction operate customary law in practice, and thereby develop it.

In 2000 a very experienced government legal adviser could say that '[f]or the most part, the day-to-day affairs of international intercourse run smoothly, and international law—which underpins them—plays its essential role without fanfare. The world goes on with its life in the (unstated) assumption that order exists in the international community. No doubt 95 per cent, perhaps more, of international life is like that'.[3] One of that writer's successors as legal adviser, who also acted as ILC Special Rapporteur responsible for the Conclusions on customary law already mentioned, recently expressed the view that 'customary international law has probably never been in better shape'.[4] Similarly, one of the most insightful recent writers on the subject has pointed out that, for those engaged in the practice of international law, apart from some borderline cases, and ambiguities, 'international law may seem to

---

[2] This 'observation' used to be attributed to the aviation pioneer Igor Sikorsky (1889–1972), but there seems little real authority for such attribution.

[3] Sir A. Watts, 'The Importance of International Law', in M. Byers (ed.), *The Role of Law in International Politics: Essays in International Relations and International Law* (Oxford: Oxford University Press, 2000), 5 at 9. Even better known is the observation of Louis Henkin in 1979, that 'it is probably the case that almost all nations observe almost all principles of international law and almost all of their obligations all of the time': L. Henkin, *How Nations Behave* (New York: Columbia University Press, 1979), 47.

[4] M. Wood and O. Sender, 'Custom's Bright Future', in C. A. Bradley (ed.) *Custom's Future: International Law in a Changing World* (New York: Cambridge University Press, 2016) 360.

work properly, and an invitation for a return to greater formalism' (or, one might add, even a complete rethinking) '[to] be a purely academic whim'. The same author continues: 'It is true that, by contrast to the determination of the content of law, the ascertainment of international legal rules is not a continuous and recurring controversy in practice.'[5]

Furthermore, no single coherent alternative has received widespread, let alone universal, acceptance among scholars,[6] so that for that reason, if no other, parties and courts cling to the positivist system of sources. As already noted, Article 38 of the ICJ Statute, while applicable in terms only to the International Court, and not necessarily even to other tribunals, let alone to the relations between States, casts a long shadow; it is well-known, its meaning is tolerably clear (in the light of years of application), and it is easily cited.

A difficulty that thus confronts the proponent of any alternative system directed to addressing the problem met, in traditional legal thinking, by the theory of sources of law, is that that theory is firmly established in the practice of States and of international tribunals.[7] There is good reason to suppose that States, including their human representatives and decision-makers, make use—without particular *arrière-pensées*—of the structure of legal argument based upon the traditional theory, even though they are not blind to some of the logical difficulties and inconsistencies to which scholars have drawn attention.

Accordingly, the authors or devisers of a new system that, as a more logical and efficient analysis, should in their contention take the place of the old, have to contemplate a modification of legal thinking that, logically, can only take effect through the medium of the existing system.[8] To take a simple example:[9] let it be contended that a new source of law has come into being beside the old categories—how can this have happened? It is difficult to see that the proposition can lift itself by its own bootstraps, as it were; if, however, it had become customary to attribute the status of an independent source of international law to, shall we say, certain acts of international organizations, they might attain that status (though such a principle would then have to

---

[5] J. d'Aspremont, *Formalism and the Sources of International Law* (Oxford: Oxford University Press, 2011), 8: hereinafter 'd'Aspremont'.

[6] d'Aspremont, 34, on the 'cacophony' or 'Tower of Babel' of current scholarly debate.

[7] It is also to be noted that the preamble to the UN Charter refers to 'respect for the obligations arising from treaties *and other sources of international law*', thus embodying the idea of sources in the UN system.

[8] A similar point is made by d'Aspremont, 34–5: 'Besides preserving the environment where a critique of law can take place ... formal law-ascertainment of international legal rules is ... a necessary condition for that critique itself.'

[9] One that the writer first employed many years ago: see H. Thirlway, *International Customary Law and Codification*, (Sijthoff: Leiden, 1972), 39–40.

be regarded as continuing as a matter of custom, and therefore not an independent source).

In answer to the question, 'Why is this a binding rule of law?',[10] the traditional doctrine gives the answer, 'Because it came into existence as such through one of the recognized sources', that is by looking to see where the rule came from, how it got there. If this approach is not to be followed, by what other route is the question to be answered? For some scholars, the validity of the rule is to be determined by looking at the *quality* of the rule: 'this is a binding rule of law because it ought to be', thus bringing in either an ethical/moral dimension, or simply an argument based on the supposed greater efficiency of a non-source-based structure.[11] Such a qualitative approach was alien to the traditional doctrine of sources, and to international law as source-based: note the ICJ dictum in the *South West Africa* case that '[r]ights cannot be presumed to exist merely because it might seem desirable that they should.'[12] That this may now be too sweeping a statement clear from the development of, in particular, the law of human rights.[13]

It is also possible to adopt a legal-sociological approach, and consider, not what rules have been followed in the past, and thereby acquired an 'established' status, nor what individual rules would recommend themselves as just or ethical, nor by what ideal rules the necessarily conflicting interests of States can most effectively be harmonized; but simply how States perceive and follow their own interests. Approaches of this kind draw on such insights as the well-known 'prisoner's dilemma',[14] and the sociological techniques

[10] d'Aspremont has argued that the precepts that are derived from the sources of law are not properly to be called 'rules' at all, but rather 'communitarian constraints' but in a lengthy article he does not make entirely clear the nature of the distinction, or its advantages: see J. d'Aspremont, 'The Idea of "Rules" in the Sources of International Law', 84 BYIL (2014) 103.

[11] The first alternative has been touched on in Ch. 1, text and n. 24. d'Aspremont distinguishes between source-based law and impact-based, or effect-based, or process-based theories (*Formalism and the Sources of International Law*, p. 4 n. 14; pp. 29, 122ff., 127ff.).

[12] [1966] ICJ Rep 48, para. 91; the unpopularity at the time of this decision should not blind the reader to the force of its general arguments.

[13] See Chapter VIII.

[14] This is one of the 'games', representing, in this context, State relations, 'in which the parties can maximise their joint payoff through mutual cooperation, but each player does better by defecting' (A. T. Guzman, *How International Law Works: A Rational Choice Theory* (Oxford: Oxford University Press, 2008), 30). It takes its name from the situation in which two prisoners are suspected of joint commission of a major crime, and there is evidence to convict each on a minor one. In order to induce a confession, they are interrogated separately, and denied communication with each other; each is told that if one admits the major crime, incriminating the other, he will receive a mild punishment, and the other a severe one; if both prisoners admit the major crime, each will receive a moderate punishment; if there is no admission, each will be given a mild punishment for the minor crime. More complex is the 'dilemma of common aversion'; it does not seem necessary here to explain more of this than that the actors have a common interest in *avoiding* a particular outcome, rather than (as in the prisoner's dilemma) in *achieving* a particular outcome. (This description

developed to get over such obstacles. These too, however valuable in theory, cannot operate effectively in international society on the basis of desirability, but have to be adopted by the subjects of international law; these arrangements too 'cannot be presumed to exist merely because it might seem desirable that they should'.

Another possibility is to address the matter on a pragmatic basis, by asking whether a suggested rule is in fact accepted in inter-State relations, or assessing the degree of compliance with it; this is what the author already quoted calls 'effect-based' or 'impact-based' conceptions of international law-ascertainment.[15] The emphasis here is less on the content of the legal rules (and still less on the formal ways in which they come into existence) than on the sanctions that the system provides to encourage compliance and discourage breach. (It might be said that the traditional doctrine does exactly that, and asks in addition *why* certain norms are so accepted; the answer given being, of course, because they emerge from recognized sources.) The 'added value' of such a theory, of institutionalism, though, is of course that it can account, if necessary, for the force of law being attributed, by international actors, to certain norms that have *not* emerged from the traditional source-process.

At its base, institutionalism is a behavioural school of thought, asking how international institutions change patterns of conduct ... [L]egal scholars have in recent years borrowed the insights from institutionalist theory to explain why international legal institutions look as they do and when we can expect international law to generate compliance and change state behaviour.[16]

This approach has the merit of making it much less difficult to accommodate within the system phenomena such as soft law, since State behaviour can be influenced (towards change or for stability) by sanctions falling short of penalties or responsibility for breach.

Some modern theories will now be briefly mentioned, on the basis of a rough classification; but it should be emphasized, first that the primary aim of this book is to convey an understanding of the traditional positivist approach,

---

is based on B. D. Lepard, *Customary International Law: A New Theory with Practical Applications* (Cambridge: Cambridge University Press, 2010).

[15] d'Aspremont, 122ff. The severance of 'is' from 'ought' tends, however, to be incomplete, since, as the author notes, 'it is uncontested that the fairness or justness of a rule encourages compliance by those subjected to it—a contention also at the heart of modern natural law theories ...' (126, citing T. Franck, *The Power of Legitimacy among Nations* (Oxford: Oxford University Press, 1990), 25).

[16] T. L. Meyer, 'Towards a Communicative Theory of International Law', University of Georgia School of Law, Research Paper No. 2013-05 (February 2013), available at <http://digitacommons.law.uga.edu/fac_artchop/905>, accessed November 2013.

and secondly that all that is here offered is a *selection* of the rival ideas currently or recently mooted, sketched in outline only: no more than a few sips of the Pierian spring![17] This is not the place for detailed or far-reaching criticisms, let alone refutation (if such were thought possible). For those who wish to pursue study of any of these proposals, the references given, here and elsewhere in the footnotes to this book, may be found useful.

There is no lack of material to choose from. Reference has already been made (Ch. V, sect. 3) to the modern plethora of scholarly writing, and analogy drawn with the situation in the field of scientific research. The analogy is suggestive, but may however be inappropriate. In the scientific world, there is almost infinite scope for new discoveries about the world around us, and thus innumerable fruitful (or possibly fruitful) subjects of enquiry: in law (including international law), setting aside historical research, for example, what the scholar may hope to offer is not newly discovered facts, but newly-minted theories, and of these, or at least of useful or convincing ones, there is a limited supply. Often a new theory or view of, or new approach to a legal subject may involve no more than word-spinning; this is (in the present writer's view) particularly so in the case of theories concerning customary law, where there already exists a long-established approach which has, as we have noted, received widespread endorsement.

Mention has been made already of the distinction between those scholars who call for a change in thinking as regards, for example, sources of law, and those scholars who prefer to present a system in the context of a whole philosophy of law that, according to its supporters, represents a more realistic, or more correct, representation of legal reality. The danger of such conceptions is, however, that this vision would only be accessible to the illuminati, the world of legal scholarship (even of partisan legal scholarship); in the workaday world, States and statesmen would consider that they were still operating under the traditional system, while in fact conforming to the greater reality of the new philosophy; speaking prose without realizing it.[18]

To present a new or different approach to international law, concerning specifically, or including, the sources of international law, implies a conviction in the author that there is something lacking, or something unsatisfactory about international law in its present condition, and as it is currently taught and practised. The change in thinking about international law that is urged or recommended is therefore presented as definitive, because it

---

[17] Cf. the famous lines from Alexander Pope's *Essay on Criticism* (1711).

[18] Cf. Molière, *Le Bourgeois Gentilhomme*, act II, scene 4: 'Par ma foi! il y a plus de quarante ans que je dis de la prose sans que j'en susse rien, et je vous suis le plus obligée du monde de m'avoir appris cela.'

is justified. Something of an oddity, to be noticed in passing, is therefore Professor d'Amato's study entitled *International Law as a Belief System*. This work appears to offer a rival way of thinking to the classic doctrine of sources, though it seems to be framed as a thought-experiment rather than presented as a more 'correct' or appropriate way of looking at the operation of international law. Professor d'Amato invites international lawyers to see international law as a 'belief system', and then 'to temporarily suspend' that system, 'and unlearn some of the knowledge and sensibilities about the fundamental doctrines they have been trained to reproduce and respond to'.[19] The word 'temporarily' is significant: if lawyers are therefore expected, or permitted, to suspend the suspension and resume their old ways, those ways must surely have continuing merit? Apparently what is proposed is a learning exercise: they will see those old ways in a new light. The presentation of the analysis as a 'reduction' of international law to a belief system is, it is indicated, a response to the current vision of law put in place by the 'liberal paradigm', namely its reduction to a 'legal-technical instead of ethico-political matter, whereby rules are formally, objectively, and content-independently ascertainable and distinct from a programme of governance or a catalogue of moral values'.[20] Once again, space is lacking to examine in detail this contention (and its combination or compatibility with d'Aspremont's views on formalism, mentioned below).

Most, if not all, of the exercises of reforming zeal here to be noted derive from one or other, or a combination, of the following points of departure:

First, that the creation (or discovery) of international law can no longer be regarded as a process of generation from one or other of a list of recognized sources; or that that list is incomplete or insufficient, that there are other materials that are in practice treated as sources, but not acknowledged as such,

Secondly, that international law, as generated by the recognized sources, fails to take sufficient account of ethical or moral requirements; these involve, almost *ex definitione*, interests of individual human beings, as distinct from those of States. As has been conceded in the discussion in Chapter VIII, the way in which international law has developed, at least until the existence of human rights found its way into international law, has been such that this was inevitable.

---

[19] J. d'Aspremont, *International Law as a Belief System*, (Cambridge University Press, 2017), 1.

[20] *International Law as a Belief System*, p.11. Such a distinction would seem to be the basis of the generally accepted ideal of the 'separation of powers' in a structure of governance, and therefore not lightly to be suspended,

Thirdly, that specifically as regards the major source of law that is customary international law, the long-established 'two-element' theory is inadequate, unrealistic, or otherwise unsatisfactory.

1. Inadequacy or irrelevance of recognized sources

One criticism, already noted, that may with some justification be addressed to the classical system of sources is that it does not easily comprehend the multifarious instruments affecting the rights and interests of States (and indeed of other actors on both the international and national level) that come into existence in the complex framework of bodies operating at these levels, other than direct State-to-State relations, or State-to-public-international-organization relations.[21] This is particularly to be observed in specialized fields of international law that have come into existence comparatively recently, for example, international trade law, international human rights law, and international criminal law. In many, if not most, cases, these can be situated in a hierarchy of bodies or instruments that relate ultimately back to a treaty or convention, and can thus be said to be grounded upon that as a traditional source; but in some circumstances this process has an air of unreality.[22] The logical solution offered is of course the recognition that such instruments are just as much sources as the traditional three.

The same issue may be seen, as it were, from the other side: can the existing sources 'take over', as it were, the orphan almost-sources? For example, if the matters to which these apply are increasingly the subject of judicial settlement, at many levels, are not those decisions themselves sources on the classical model, recognized by Article 38? This is a view that emerges (among other thought-provoking theses) from the extensive coverage of international judicial settlement by Professor K. J. Alter in her book entitled *The New Terrain of International Law*.[23] In a wider frame of reference, it is the contention of Professor d'Aspremont that scholarly approaches to the phenomenon of increasingly wide and varied techniques of producing international law (or

---

[21] Cf. Decaux, 'Déclarations et conventions en droit international', Cahiers du conseil constitutionel 21 (January 2007), 1–2, who observes that 'La société international juxtapose désormais un "droit relationnel" fondé sur les rapports juridiques entre les sujets primaires du droit international qui sont les États, à un "droit institutionnel" caractérisé par: apparition de nouveaux sujets secondaires, les organisations internationales'.

[22] M. Goldman, 'International institutions exercise considerable public authority that is only remotely related to State consent': 'Inside Relative Normativity: From Sources to Standard Instruments for the Exercise of International Public Authority', 11 German LJ (2008) 1865–908 at 1874.

[23] Princeton, 2104 (*sic*), presumably 2014.

what looks very much like it) have sought to bring these techniques under the auspices of the traditional conception of sources, with as a consequence an unnecessary 'de-formalization of law-ascertainment' being permitted to be entailed by a 'deformalization of norm-making processes', which itself results from 'pluralization of international norm-making'.[24] Nevertheless, he makes clear that his recommended approach, involving a return to a new and more satisfactory formalist approach, is 'alien to any endeavour to rehabilitate or defend mainstream theory of the sources of international law',[25] the inadequacies of which require a 'rejuvenated' formalism preserving the distinction between law-and non-law—indeed, formalism is 'championed ... for its virtues in distinguishing law from non-law and ascertaining legal rules'.[26] A key issue appears to be the respective roles of the law-creating instrument, as the element of form, and of intent—the intent of the parties concerned—in the act of creation.

The mainstream position as to the decisive criterion for the determination of the nature of the written instrument [i.e, intent of the parties] significantly changes the nature of the ascertainment of legal acts.... [N]othing could be more at loggerheads with formal law-identification than the intent-based law-ascertainment criterion that does not require intent to materialize in a linguistic or a material sign'.[27]

Against this, d'Aspremont invokes what he terms the 'social thesis' as developed by Hart, whereby all 'secondary legal rules are derived as grounded in the social practice of the law-applying authorities'.[28] For our purposes, this sketch of how d'Aspremont's views diverge from those set out in the present work will, for reasons of space and balance, have to suffice.

It has also been maintained that a realistic look at inter-State relations may lead the observer to marginalize the recognized sources, as less relevant than the behaviour that States exhibit, and in particular the fact, mentioned already, that they do (most of the time) comply with international law. This is in particular the 'rational choice' theory of Professor Andrew Guzman.[29] This is a theory that, in one form or another, has in recent years frequently been invoked for the analysis of international law. Drawing on such classic thought experiments as the 'prisoner's dilemma',[30] this theory lays the emphasis on the

---

[24] *Formalism and the Sources of International Law*, in particular p. 22. [25] See n. 24.

[26] See n. 24, p. 5. [27] See n. 24, pp. 179–80.

[28] See n. 24, Ch. 3, specifically p. 53.

[29] A. Guzman, 'A Compliance-Based Theory of International Law', 90 California Law Review (2002); A. Guzman, *How International Law Works* (Oxford University Press, 2008). The latter work lives up to its title inasmuch as it is presented as a different way of seeing international law in operation at the present time, rather than a proposal for its reform or renovation.

[30] See Ch. 3, n. 37, and for a suggested solution, in the context of customary law as imported into US law, J. D. Ohlin, *The Assault om International Law* (Oxford University Press, 2015), Chapter 4.

role of international law, not so much as ensuring compliance with its rules, as changing the behaviour of States (needless to say, in the direction regarded by the observer—and, one hopes, by the States concerned—as beneficial).[31] Such a theory is, of course, less useful to the decision-maker, particularly the international judge, or participant in an international dispute, than the traditional approach: it is less 'how international law works' than 'how international law should work'.

As broadly in the same category we may consider the concept of global government developed by Professor Joel Trachtmann.[32] While Guzman concentrates on the choices offered to, and exercised by, States in the context of the global structures and organization in which they are situate, Trachtmann places the emphasis rather on that context itself, as created by States and serving then as the field in which they operate. As he observes, 'international law will not grow to replace the state but will grow to supplement the state as a form of government in a federal or divided power sense'.[33] It is not so much a matter of devising new law to meet new situations, as that the vast changes to be expected through increased globalization will themselves dictate new international law. '[W]e can expect increasing density of international law', the demand for which 'will arise organically, through the demands of individuals on their states for better government addressing the issues that cross borders. The demand for more international law in particular areas will give rise to greater capacity to legislate international law. The border between national politics and international law will grow increasingly indistinct'.[34] What Professor Trachtman offers is less a nostrum than a prophecy, and therefore does not fall to be compared with the various proposals for a new international law mentioned here on the same terms.

2. The role of ethical principles

There is a temptation when examining the state of international law to move, either unconsciously or deliberately, from contemplation of what the law *is* to exposition of what it ought to be. There is obviously merit in such work—provided that the one process is not confused with the other—since no internationalist Pangloss would assert that the system we have is the best possible.

---

[31] An example of this approach, specifically in the context of human rights in customary international law, is that of Lepard (see sect. 2(*a*)).

[32] J. Trachtmann, *The Future of International Law: Global Government* (Cambridge University Press, 2013).

[33] See n. 32, p. 41.   [34] See n. 32, p. 288.

Most rules of international law exist, and are thus recognizable as law, independently of the moral commendability of their content—in the sense that whether a rule *is* a rule does not depend on (for example) whether it serves to advance an ethical principle or a humanitarian goal. We should however also note that this feature does not necessarily mean that ethical principles had no role to play in its creation as a rule. The obligations imposed by the Genocide Convention are obligations of the parties because they are parties to the Convention, not because they are ethical dictates, but that does not deprive them of their widely accepted status as expressing ethical values. This is a path that is, however, barred to the international judge, and has indeed been avoided in the decisions of the International Court, though not in many of the increasingly far-reaching separate and dissenting opinions filed in recent years.[35] There is thus a danger of a fissure developing between judicial law and law as embodied in daily practice.

It is also the case that, in the context here considered, rules of law criticized for inadequacy in the ethical dimension are usually, if not always, rules of customary international law. Ethical considerations nowadays are usually only relevant in relation to customary law; treaty law does not take into account such considerations in relation to the validity of effect of a treaty, except to the extent that a treaty may not conflict with *jus cogens*.[36] The content of that concept is notoriously ill-defined; '[t]here is general agreement that it relates to norms of high moral fibre' (including genocide)[37], but there is up to the present no example of a treaty being alleged to be invalid as contradicting an ethical norm. (It is only fair to note that such treaties, if they exist, are likely also to take the form of confidential understandings, invisible to the outside observer or to the scholar.) As for the general principles of law, these are commendable by definition, in so far as their generality permits of a value-judgment of this kind.

It is in this category that most proposals currently ranking as *lex ferenda* will fall, since that category, as already noted, means more than 'something that is not yet law' but 'something that *should be* law but isn't yet': the reason

---

[35] In the day-to-day relations between one State and another, what is likely to matter to the respective legal advisers in doubtful cases is less 'what the law ought to be' than 'what the law would be to suit my client'. This approach may be tempered, possibly in the ways contemplated by 'game theory'; cf. text and n. 14 above.

[36] Contrast the comment of Wheaton on the eighteenth century partitions of Poland, effected by treaty, as being 'the most flagrant violation of *natural justice* and international law': (H. Wheaton, *History of the Law of Nations in Europe and America* (New York: Gould, Banks & Co. 1845) 269, italics added. In the twentieth century, cf. the article by A. Verdross, 'Forbidden Treaties in International Law', 31 AJIL (1937) 575–7.

[37] J. Klabbers, 'The Validity and Invalidity of Treaties' in D. B. Hollis (ed.), *Treaties* (Oxford University Press, 2012), 551 at 571. See also the work of the ILC on *jus cogens*, 2015–8.

why it 'should' may be on the lines of 'because that would make for a more coherent or workable system', but is more likely to be in the ethical domain.

It is in the context of custom that a carefully thought-out incorporation of ethical considerations into international law is presented by Professor Brian Lepard, who diverges from the centrist ILC approach in recognizing ethical considerations as material in determining the existence of a customary rule. When the possible existence of *opinio juris* in favour of a given norm is being considered, '[i]f the norm objectively has a direct and significant impact on fundamental ethical principles, either positive or negative, this impact is a reason to presume that states either favour or disfavour implementation of the rule'.[38] He identifies what he regards as a 'fundamental ethical principle', from which the other ethical principles that he identifies 'logically flow':[39] this is the principle of 'unity in diversity', which is not itself part of customary international law, but 'follows from a vision of dynamic and reciprocal communities of states and individuals'. 'It maintains that all individuals are ethically members of one human family which morally ought to be united', while recognizing 'that differences of race, nationality, culture, religion and even opinion are to be cherished and valued'.[40]

This approach is clearly highly relevant to the law of human rights, and Professor Lepard has recently explored this aspect, in a chapter of *Reexamining Customary International Law* entitled 'Toward a New Theory of Customary International Human Rights Law'.[41] First, he points out that 'the reality is that very often there appears to be a consistent State practice of *violating* many rights, not respecting them'.[42] The implied question is, how then is the requirement of 'consistent State practice' satisfied? Secondly, 'the omnipresence of human rights violations also casts doubt on the existence of *opinio juris* as traditionally defined. States often seem to believe not that they are already bound to observe certain human rights norms, but that the norms are still in process of formation and that they may therefore comply with them, or fail to do so, at their pleasure ....'[43] Unless everything that has been asserted or suggested as a human right automatically earns protection, the belief must sometimes be well-founded; but the point is nevertheless valid.

It is by invoking the 'fundamental ethical principles' which already feature in his general recasting of customary international law in general that Lepard responds to this dual problem.[44] There is clearly force in this approach: if

---

[38] Lepard, *Customary International Law: A New Theory with Practical Applications*, ASIL Studies in International Legal Theory, (Cambridge University Press, 2010), 140.

[39] Lepard, n. 38, p. 140.   [40] Lepard, n. 38, p. 78.

[41] Lepard (ed.) *Reexamining Customary International Law*, ASIL Studies in International Legal Theory, (Cambridge University Press, 2017), 233–65.

[42] See n. 41, p. 249.   [43] See n. 41, pp. 249–50.   [44] See n. 41, pp. 255–6.

the background to the development of general custom is the give-and-take between sovereign States adjusting the competition between their respective interests, as suggested in Chapter III,[45] the picture is different when respect for the interests of the individual (whether or not a national of the State) would impede the advancement of the interests of the State. The ethical principle, it may be supposed, was always there, but States were free to override it in this context: the recognition that human rights have entered customary law means this is no longer so.

3. The insufficiencies of the theory of international customary law

Scholars who have examined and criticized the workings of customary international law have not always specified the precise object in view, or have done so only in somewhat esoteric terminology. It appears probable, to say the least, that the aim in view is in fact to devise a theory of customary international law that is so ordered and complete that two competent observers of the same set of circumstances will be able to agree, in all cases, whether a custom exists, and if so, what it prescribes or authorizes. There is much emphasis on the incoherence of the classic theory, and the contrasting coherence of the system proposed.

This prompts the question whether such an end is really achievable. May it not be the case that, human affairs being what they are, and with the added circumstance of differences of approach by the various international actors whose conduct is under examination, such 'tidiness' is simply not possible? Except in the rare cases in which an international tribunal would have to declare a *non liquet*,[46] there will be an answer that could be given by a court seised of a dispute over an alleged custom; but this would almost always be the product of a process of weighing-up peculiar to that tribunal. A different tribunal, in face of the same materials, might well come to a different conclusion; and disagreement among scholars can practically be guaranteed. This may not be an entirely satisfactory state of affairs; but it is doubtful whether any systematization of custom could lead to any greater degree of unanimity of response. This observation does not, of course, amount to denying any value to such academic studies; but it does suggest that the order they seek to display may be chimerical, and that the criticisms of the existing theory or theories of the formation of custom—and

---

[45] See Chapter III.   [46] See the discussion in Ch. IV, sect. 3.

indeed of the classic theory of sources—may have the less justification, inasmuch as untidiness is built into the system.[47] Furthermore, in face of some of the subtle and intricate (to use only positive adjectives) arguments underpinning some modern theories, one may wonder how useful they will be to the perplexed Legal Adviser dealing with an international dispute. Without viewing the world of international law through rose-tinted spectacles, one may wonder whether the present system may not prove to be the best achievable: a conclusion supported by the recent achievement of the International Law Commission.

Nevertheless, much attention has been devoted to ways in which the classic mechanism of creation (or discovery) of customary law might or should be improved. One writer who has specialized in this field, and written prolifically on the subject, is Professor Brian Lepard.[48] One of the recurrent problems of application of the accepted theory of custom is the tension between the two requirements, of *opinio juris* and State practice, and there has always been a temptation to try to get rid of one of them, and allow the other (haunted by the ghost of its companion) to do the heavy work. This may happen in specific cases, even in judicial decisions;[49] but it is also offered here as a recommended new theory.[50] Lepard proposes:

- that *opinio juris* be interpreted as a requirement that *states generally believe that it is desirable now or in the near future to have an authoritative legal principle or rule prescribing, permitting or prohibiting certain State conduct* ...

---

[47] This does not, however, in the present writer's view, signify that customary law is too subject to conflicting and idiosyncratic interpretations to be useful, that it is simply 'a matter of taste' (in this sense, J. Patrick Kelly, 'The Twilight of Customary International Law', 40 Virginia JIL (2000), 449 at 451).

[48] See in particular B. D. Lepard, *Customary International Law: A New Theory with Practical Applications*, ASIL Studies in International Legal Theory, (Cambridge University Press, 2010); B. D. Lepard, *Customary International Law as a Dynamic Process*, in C. Bradley (ed.) *Custom's Future*, (Cambridge University Press, 2016); and contributions to Lepard (ed.), *Reexamining Customary International Law*, ASIL Studies in International Legal Theory, (Cambridge University Press, 2017).

[49] See the Judgment in the *Military and Paramilitary Activities* case, where the ICJ, dealing with the prohibition of the use of force, while paying decorous lip-service to the two-element theory and citing much by way of *opinio juris*, passes rather rapidly over the question of the existence of State practice in support of its findings: [1986] ICJ Rep 100–3, paras. 189–92; there are other examples. The ICJ has in fact been accused of basing its decisions on a sort of custom-'light', hardly recognizable as meeting the traditional requirements re-iterated by the ILC: see for example F. R. Tesón, 'Fake Custom' in Lepard (ed.) *Reexamining Customary International Law* (Cambridge University Press, 2017), 86, 96–7.

[50] Other scholars have of course suggested similar approaches: see e.g. M. Mendelson, 'The Formation of Customary International Law', 272 Recueil des cours (1998), 292; A. T. Guzman, 'Saving Customary International Law', 27 Michigan JIL (2005), 115; N. Petersen, 'Customary Law without Custom?—Rules, Principles, and the Role of State Practice in International Norm Creation', 23 AmULR (2008), 275.

- that the state practice requirement should be viewed [only] as requiring appropriate *evidence* that states believe that a particular authoritative principle is desirable now or in the near future, such evidence not necessarily being 'practice' in the traditional sense.[51]

This is to be contrasted with the traditional view, as now expressed in Conclusion 9 of the ILC's work on Identification of Customary International Law, that *opinio juris* signifies 'that the practice in question must be undertaken with a sense of legal right or obligation', that is to say, an *existing* legal right or obligation, not merely a 'desirable' one. In face of the ILC's continued assertion of the traditional approach, Professor Lepard has maintained his own view as recently as 2016 and 2017;[52] elements of the critique offered here in the first edition of this work may therefore be maintained.

Another writer to have made a notable contribution to the discussion of what she refers to as 'modern' custom is Professor Anthea Roberts.[53] Professor Roberts defines traditional custom, in a brief but orthodox manner, by reference to its creation: it 'results from general and consistent practice followed by states from a sense of legal obligation'.[54] In her view, however, 'modern' custom 'is derived by a *deductive* process that begins with general statements of rules rather than particular instances of practice'.[55] These deductions are made 'from multilateral treaties and declarations by international fora such as the General Assembly, which can declare existing customs, crystallise emerging customs, and generate new customs'. However, 'Whether these texts become custom depends on factors such as whether they are phrased in declaratory terms, supported by a widespread and representative body of states, and confirmed by state practice.'[56] Similarly, the role of international courts may be (unavowedly) to take the initiative of announcing a customary rule, rather than waiting for, and looking for, evidence of State practice: '[c]ustom is often identified by international courts and tribunals, and, if States and other actors do not protest, it often becomes accepted, particularly if other entities cite it with approval'.[57]

---

[51] *Customary International Law*, 97–8; italics original.

[52] See the references in footnote 49 above.

[53] See A. Roberts 'Traditional and Modern Approaches to Customary International Law: A Reconciliation', 95 AJIL (2001) 757, supplemented by a chapter on 'The Theory and Reality of the Sources of International Law' in Evans (ed.), *International Law* (5th edn., 2018), written by Professor Roberts and Sandesh Sivakumaran (already cited in Ch. I, n. 24). The latter article is wider in scope, dealing with sources in general, but it will be convenient to discuss it in conjunction with the earlier piece on custom.

[54] Roberts AJIL, 758.   [55] Roberts AJIL, 758 (italics original).

[56] Roberts AJIL, 758.   [57] Roberts in Evans, *International Law*, 112.

X

A Brief Note in Conclusion

In this book I have tried to give a picture of the long-established theory of the creation of international law that attributes each norm, directly or ultimately, to one of the sources identified in Article 38 of the ICJ Statute. To some extent, in this context to describe is to defend; I have referred to and attempted to refute some criticisms of sources theory. I have also endeavoured to give a glimpse of how some modern scholars approach in individual ways the problem of the existence of law on the international level. However, a picture of the operation of international law that suggested the existence of a perfectly integrated and coherent system would be misleading. There are intellectual puzzles, such as the development of custom, which has to exist, in order to be believed to exist, in order to exist. Integration of the operation of law in all the separate categories discussed in Chapter VIII is far from perfect (though this is not, I suggest, something to be remedied by identifying some new source, or new method of law-creation).

All current writing on international law, or on international relations, emphasizes the rapid and accelerating pace of change; is the doctrine of sources to be exempt? So long as Article 38 of the ICJ Statute is not amended (an event that is politically highly unlikely), the principal judicial body of the world will be bound to identify and apply law in essentially the same way as was contemplated in 1920. Respect for that text has been shown, by the work of the Court, not to prevent development of the law, but merely to limit—or rather, perhaps, to guide—the way in which such development is to be looked for, and looked at. It is striking, and has been emphasized in Chapter III above, that the International Law Commission, having devoted six years to the study of the identification of customary international law—of the traditional, Article 38 ICJ Statute, sources perhaps the most controversial in application—and enjoying the benefit of the most authoritative scholarly opinion and of the views expressed by States themselves as the work progressed, has set out in its Conclusions essentially what has been 'mainstream' legal thinking since the Statute was drafted. More and more aspects of the operation of international law are becoming subjects of study by the ILC, and its Reports—which go beyond merely recording what is there—have earned wide respect. While it remains true, as noted earlier,[1] that the Commission, as a non-State actor has not acquired a law-creating status, it is undeniable that the international legal landscape has been altered by its operation, in the direction of a higher degree of orderliness. International customary law, it appears, needed no reforming hand, no drastic re-arrangement, merely an orderly re-statement.

Article 38 may be regarded by some as a survival, a solitary pillar of rock around which much of surrounding landscape has eroded away—or perhaps a better image is of the rock not yet undermined or swept away by the crashing waves of international developments; but it remains geologically and structurally solid.

It has been suggested here that any rethinking of international law may have to occur consistently with Article 38 itself; but that is not the only reason why it is submitted that sources theory is still a sound approach to law-ascertainment. Even in a globalized or institutionalized world, international law is ultimately what those subject to it—essentially, States—will it to be. They would have to be convinced that the current system is not merely less intellectually tidy than is desirable (or than other schemes devised by jurists might be) but is an actual impediment to efficient international relations. That surely is not the case. An undeniable merit of the system based on traditional sources theory is that it is there, and it works.

[1] Ch. II, sect. 5.

Index

.